Law Relating to Banking Services

David Palfreman BA FCIB

Senior Lecturer
London Guildhall University

Fourth edition

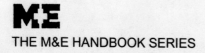

THE M&E HANDBOOK SERIES

Pitman Publishing
128 Long Acre, London WC2E 9AN

A Division of Longman Group UK Limited

First published in 1993

A CIP catalogue record for this book can be obtained from the British
Library.

ISBN 0 7121 1194 8

Typeset by ROM-Data Corporation Ltd, Falmouth, Cornwall
Printed and bound in Singapore

To Hellen, Chris and Rula

Contents

Preface

This book was originally conceived as a new edition of *The Law Relating to Banking* with a few additional chapters to cover the evolution of the Chartered Institute of Bankers' Associateship examination in banking law into the 'Law Relating to Banking services'. So much for the theory! This is substantially a new book. Apart from completely new chapters on Consumer Credit Act lending, financial services regulation and electronic payment systems, the chapters on the banker–customer relationship and cheques have been rewritten and all the remaining chapters have been substantially reworked. I hope the result is an explanation of the law relating to banking services which is both comprehensive and accessible.

At the start of the rewriting process I decided to retain most of the general information about agency, partnerships and companies in the relevant chapters from *The Law Relating to Banking* and as such the relevant chapters go beyond the express requirements of the syllabus. My reasoning was simple. In my experience very few students studying 'Law Relating to Banking Services' have previously studied this and yet the CIB syllabus impliedly assumes such knowledge. To a lesser extent the same applies to the chapter on land as security. However, those aspects of the law related directly to banking take precedence for examination purposes.

Those of you who are studying law for the first time, may consider that you would benefit from an introductory text that explains the wider legal system into which banking law fits. I recommend to you *Banking: The Legal Environment* – also published by Pitman – that I wrote for the Banking Certificate subject of the same name and which covers the sources of law, contract law and the court system from a banking perspective, as well providing an introduction to most of the Associateship syllabus.

In the discussion of cases, I have used the following standard abbreviations: (HL) for House of Lords, (PC) for Privy Council and (CA) for Court of Appeal.

Finally, a 'thank you' to my friends and colleagues Vaumini Amin, Peter Eales and Barry Toseland for reading through my drafts and making such helpful comments.

David Palfreman
November, 1992

Tables of cases

Tables of statutes

1
The banker–customer relationship

Definitions

1. Banker

(a) *By statute.* A variety of statutes define a bank or a banker for particular purposes without actually explaining the term itself. For example, the Bills of Exchange Act 1882, s.2 states that a banker is 'someone who carries on the business of banking'. This is, to say the least, not very helpful. The same is also largely true of the Banking Act 1987, which talks in terms of 'authorised institutions' and not 'banks' as such. The Act's purpose is the regulation of deposit-taking and so it only deals specifically with 'banks' in so far as the use of the name 'bank' is restricted by the Bank of England to larger authorised institutions. Even then, overseas banks are exempt from this restriction. The Act tells us very little about the role and characteristics of a bank and it does not directly regulate the way in which banks carry out their business.

(b) *At common law.* The common law has considered the activities inherent in the *business of banking* as being the criteria for determining who is and who is not a banker. In *United Dominions Trust* v *Kirkwood* (1966), where it had to be decided whether UDT were moneylenders within the meaning of the Moneylenders Act 1900 or, as they maintained, bankers and therefore exempt from registration under the Act, the Court of Appeal identified three activities as being the definitive characteristics of bankers. They:

(i) Accept money from and collect cheques for their customers and place them to their credit.

(ii) Honour cheques or orders drawn on them by their customers when presented for payment and debit their customers' accounts accordingly.

(iii) Keep current accounts in which the credits and debits are entered.

In addition, the Court of Appeal stressed that the definition was not static and would always depend on current practice. Indeed, the majority of the Court accepted a secondary test of the reputation of the organisation in question with other bankers as a means of determining whether the organisation could be regarded at law as a bank. (On the facts, UDT were bankers: although they did not satisfy the primary test, they were considered to be bankers by other bankers and therefore satisfied the secondary test.)

2. Customer

Again the definition is to be found in judicial statements and not in statute law.

A customer of a bank is *a person who has entered into a contract with the bank for the opening of an account in his or her name.*

Strictly speaking, the account must be a current account, but it is submitted that a contract to open a deposit account or a credit card account should also make a person a customer as the same or very similar activities are performed for the 'customer'. There is no modern authority on this point.

NOTE: In defining 'customer' in this way we are using the term in a strict legal sense. In the more usual sense, a customer is anyone who makes a contract for any of a bank's services (such as foreign currency or travel insurance) even though they may not have an account with the bank. This is the approach taken in the Code of Banking Practice (*see* 1:**21**).

It is *not* essential for a course of dealings to be maintained over a period of time, the relationship is contractual and therefore arises immediately the customer's offer to open the account is accepted by the bank: *Barclays Bank Ltd* v *Okenarhe* (1966). The existence of an account or a contractual agreement to open one *is* essential however. No matter how many transactions have taken place between a bank and an individual, that person will not be a customer unless, and until, their application to open an account has been made and accepted, i.e. a contractual relationship has been established: *Great Western Railway Co Ltd* v *London and County Banking Co Ltd* (1901) (HL) where cashing uncrossed cheques payable to a person who had no account with the bank did not make that person a customer of the bank.

To cite authority, in *Ladbroke & Co* v *Todd* (1914), it was stated that 'a person becomes a customer of a bank when he goes to the bank with money or a cheque and asks to have an account opened in his name, and the bank accepts the money or cheque and is prepared to open an account in the name of that person'; and in *Commissioners of Taxation* v *English, Scottish & Australian Bank* (1920) (PC) 'the word "customer" signifies a relationship in which duration is not of the essence'.

NOTE: A bank may owe duties to another person before an account is opened, and even if an account is never opened. In *Woods* v *Martins Bank Ltd* (1959), a bank that negligently gave bad investment advice to a person lacking any business experience who intended to become a customer, and who did so shortly afterwards, was held to owe a customer the same contractual duty of care as it would have done if the person had already been a customer. Today, the action would probably have been brought under the *Hedley Byrne* principle (*see* 1:**18**).

If a person opens an account under a false name, a valid banker–customer contract arises, but it can be avoided by the bank if it was opened to fraudulently deceive the bank. The same situation arises if a person opens an account fraudulently representing themselves to be another person. If a person opens an account for another without authority, no banker–customer contract arises with either the actual applicant or the purported customer. Should the bank suffer loss, the applicant will be liable for breach of warranty of authority (*see* 3:**11**).

3. The importance of the definitions

The definitions are of far more than academic interest, although they are rarely called into question.

In *United Dominions Trust* v *Kirkwood* (1966), the definition was central to the case, but the best illustrations are found in the rights and duties owed under the banker–customer contract, particularly the bank's duty of confidentiality to its customers (*see* 1:**13**) and in the statutory protection afforded to banks when they collect and pay cheques.

Under the Cheques Act 1957, s.4, a collecting bank is protected against an action for conversion by the cheque's true owner if it collects a cheque on behalf of a *customer* and the Bills of Exchange Act 1882 s.60, protects a *bank* if it pays a cheque bearing a forged or unauthorised endorsement (*see* 9:**24** and **34**). An account may be opened with a stolen cheque, for example, and if a course of business was necessary to establish a person as a 'customer', collection of this first cheque would not be protected under s.4.

Nature of the relationship

4. A debtor–creditor contractual relationship

The relationship between a bank and its customer is contractual and is primarily that of debtor (the bank) and creditor (the customer), with the roles being reversed when the customer is indebted to the bank: *Foley* v *Hill* (1848) (HL).

The decision also established that, contrary to the usual debtor–creditor relationship, where the debtor is obliged to seek out their creditor to make repayment, the customer (the creditor) must come to the debtor for repayment. If it were otherwise, a bank would have to try to persuade customers to withdraw their balances every time they visited the bank! The customer must demand repayment from the bank.

> NOTE: The fact that a bank becomes its customer's debtor when money is paid in means that the money immediately becomes the property of the bank and the bank can use it in its own business – primarily lending to other customers – until such time as its customer asks for the debt to be repaid. This principle applies even to trust funds held and administered by a bank: *Space Investments Ltd* v *Canadian Imperial Bank of Commerce Trust Co (Bahamas) Ltd* (1986) (PC) (but also *see Barclays Bank Ltd* v *Quistclose Investments Ltd* (1970), 1:7). The debtor–creditor nature of the relationship is therefore fundamental to commercial banking.

Various categories of rules govern the workings of the relationship.

5.   General rules of contract law

(a) *Introduction. Joachimson* v *Swiss Bank Corporation* (1921) (CA) emphasised the single, indivisible nature of the banker–customer contract but recognised that there might be separate additional contracts entered into for specific purposes, such as a contract of loan. Banking was, of course, a far simpler business in those days and these additional contracts have become more numerous and more important over the years. The whole area of electronic banking is perhaps the prime example of this. In terms of describing the contract(s) between a bank and its customer it is evident that the contract to open an account (the 'initial' contract) is rather different in its form to these additional contracts.

Compared to many other contracts, the initial banker–customer contract lacks formality, there is no document headed, say, 'Contract for Banking Services' that the customer is asked to sign. Unusually in business these days it is also based on *implied* rather than *express* terms, that is terms imposed by statute or established by case law on the basis of commercial custom (as in the case of the banker–customer contract), which the courts recognise as being included in the contract although at the time it was made there was no mention of them. This lack of formality means that the contract is made by oral rather than by written agreement, completion of largely administrative forms, the sending of brief letters and on the basis of banking custom and practice.

However, the position is arguably changing. At least one major bank has produced customer leaflets explaining in everyday language the main terms of the banker–customer contract. This trend is, in fact, nothing more than a reflection of a general trend towards standard form contracts that has been apparent in business for many years. It is certainly in the interests of a supplier of goods or services and, often, also in the interests of the purchaser to have their respective rights and duties codified in an undisputable (hopefully) document.

The Code of Banking Practice, published in 1992 (*see* 1:**21**), is likely to accelerate this trend. While not seeking to regulate the relationship between banks and their customers, the Code does require that customers have clear information about their relationship with their bank. Where banks (and building societies) express the terms and conditions of a banking service in writing, they must do so in plain language with the aim of providing a fair and balanced view of the banker–customer relationship (s.3). More specifically, they must explain how any variation of the terms and conditions will be notified and they must give customers reasonable notice before any variation takes effect. This latter provision is, however, merely a confirmation of the common law position.

Under the Code, banks are also required to provide customers with details of charges payable in connection with the normal operation of their accounts and the basis of interest payments on borrowing. Customers must also be given information on the bank's complaints procedure.

In contrast, the 'additional contracts' are far more formal. Credit card agreements detail the terms of issue and the responsibilities of the cardholder and the increasing use of electronic banking is likely to continue this trend, particularly in relation to a customer's obligations with respect to the use and care of automated teller machine (ATM)/debit cards or credit cards and any associated personal identification number (PIN). The same is true of security contracts; nothing is left to chance, the written contracts precisely state the rights of the bank.

One problem is, perhaps, that it is debatable *where* the initial contract stops and the additional contracts start. For example, it could be argued that providing a cheque/ATM/debit card is today as basic as providing a cheque book and therefore that this is incorporated in the initial contract. If this is so, then an important part of the initial contract is found in a formal written contract containing comprehensive express terms. The truth is probably that, while the fundamental terms governing the contractual relationship of a bank with its customer are implied, many practical aspects of the relationship are governed by more formal agreements. Examples include account mandates, facility letters, standing order instructions and direct debit agreements, currency instructions and safe custody arrangements. In practice, of course, providing that the terms do form part of the contract and do not infringe rules of law, e.g. the provisions of the Unfair Contract Terms Act 1977 (*see* below), the position of the parties is the same whether the contract consists of express terms, implied terms or combination of both.

(b) *The implied contract.* Over the years, the customs and practices of banking have become 'codified' by case law into what is referred to as the *implied contract* between banker and customer. While *Foley* v *Hill* (1848) (HL) established the true basis of the relationship as debtor–creditor, *Joachimson* v *Swiss Bank Corporation* (1921) (CA) laid down the basic implied terms in the contract.

Among other implied terms recognised in *Joachimson* are that a bank undertakes:

(i) To receive money and collect cheques for its customer's account.

(ii) To comply with its customer's written orders, e.g. cheques, addressed to the customer's branch to repay any part of the funds deposited.

(iii) To give its customer reasonable notice before closing the account if it is in credit.

The case also established:

(iv) That the bank is not obliged to pay the customer the full amount of their balance until the customer makes a formal demand for the balance to the branch at which the current account is kept; and

(v) That the customer must exercise reasonable care in drawing cheques and writing other orders so as not to mislead the bank or facilitate forgery.

NOTE: The legal rights and duties of a bank are, in large part, derived from the 'codification' of judicially implied terms in *Joachimson*.

In *Tai Hing Cotton Mill Ltd* v *Liu Chong Hing Bank* (1985), the Privy Council reviewed some of the more important aspects of this implied contract.

The case concerned an extensive fraud in which L, the accounts clerk of TH, had forged its Managing Director's signature on some 300 cheques, totalling $HK5.5m over a period of 5 years. The cheques were payable to companies for whom L opened bank accounts and thereby obtained payment. On the facts, TH's accounting system was extremely poor: L had not been effectively supervised and only L had examined the statements for the period of the fraud. It was held that the bank was liable to repay to the company the amount of the cheques; it had no mandate to pay them.

The Privy Council reaffirmed the customer's duties:

(*i*) To draw cheques with reasonable care in order to prevent fraud (*see London Joint Stock Bank* v *Macmillan & Arthur* (1918) (HL)), but held that there is no wider duty to take reasonable precautions in managing their affairs so as to prevent cheques being forged (for example by being careful where they keep their cheque book).

(*ii*) To inform their bank of any forged cheque drawn on their account of which they were aware (*see Greenwood* v *Martins Bank* (1933) (HL)), but held that there is no duty to check bank statements for unauthorised debit items.

The Privy Council also rejected the bank's argument that customers are under a duty in the tort of negligence to take care to prevent forgeries and check their statements for incorrect entries.

NOTE: One specific and particularly important rule established by case law is the *Rule in Clayton's Case* (1816) (*see* 1:**15**).

(c) *Express terms.* The banker–customer contract consists mainly of implied terms, although at least two important aspects of it will be covered by express terms: the mandate covering signing instructions on the account and the assumption of joint and several liability on joint accounts. However, it is open to any bank and, at least in theory, any customer to include other express terms in the contract to protect their position (overriding) perhaps established implied terms. Of course, a bank would only accept an express term from its customer if it did not prejudice its own position, e.g. that the bank should not reply to status enquiries on the customer.

The enforceability of an express term is subject to two general limitations.

(*i*) Any term that attempts to limit or exclude the liability of one of the parties is subject to the Unfair Contract Terms Act 1977 and will only be enforceable if the court considers that the term is reasonable.

(ii) The courts are very unwilling to accept and enforce express terms that vary from established practice unless there is the clearest evidence that the other party was made aware of them, understood them and accepted them. (This is particularly so if the effect of them is to take away rights the other party would otherwise have enjoyed.)

Example

In *Tai Hing* (1985) the bank had included express terms in the contract imposing a duty on TH to examine its monthly bank statements and preventing the statements being challenged after a specified period.

It was held that, on the facts, the bank had not brought home to TH the importance and effect of the terms and they, therefore, could not be relied upon.

6. Rules of agency

(a) *Introduction.* In important respects, a bank acts as its customer's agent, e.g. in collecting and paying cheques for its customer or in, say, buying and selling shares. As such, a bank is subject to the general rules of agency (*see* Chapter 3).

> NOTE: Traditionally agency has not been the main basis of the banker–customer relationship; it certainly has never been the basis of the banker–customer *contract*. If it had been, a bank would have to account for the use of its customer's (its principal's) money and pay to its customer any profits made unless it had its customer's authority to keep them. Commercial banking would be impossible. Today, however, what in law is a bank acting as an agent is increasingly important to its commercial operations. Banks sell financial services, many on behalf of third-party providers, although these providers may well be part of the same bank group. Commission income is vital, particularly as disintermediation (the withdrawal of funds from interest-bearing deposit accounts when competing financial instruments offer the investor a better return) is surely here to stay. This being the case, it can be argued that, while the debtor–creditor relationship (albeit modified in *Foley* v *Hill* (1848)) is central to the banker–customer *contract*, agency is today central to, if not the main basis of, the wider banker–customer *relationship*.

(b) *Duty of care.* Where a bank acts as an agent, it owes a duty of care to its principal – its customer. This duty is most relevant in relation to cheques.

A bank is liable to its customer if it pays a forged or altered cheque (*see* 9:**30**), but it can also be liable if it pays a cheque that is unaltered and drawn exactly in accordance with its customer's mandate. Such a cheque must *not* be paid if a reasonable and honest banker who was aware of the relevant facts would have considered that there was a serious and real possibility of the account being operated fraudulently: *Lipkin Gorman* v *Karpnale Ltd and Lloyds Bank PLC* (1989) (CA). Two recent cases where banks have sued for breach of this duty have been decided in the banks' favour on the facts.

Example 1

In *Lipkin Gorman* v *Karpnale Ltd and Lloyds Bank PLC* (1989) (CA), LG, a firm of solicitors, maintained its client account with Lloyds Bank and the mandate allowed any one partner to operate the account. C, a partner in the firm, withdrew over £200 000 from the account by drawing cheques to cash and sending a clerk to cash them. C then gambled the money away in the Playboy Club, which was owned by K. C had his personal account at the same branch of Lloyds Bank and the branch manager knew that C was a compulsive gambler because of his heavy drawings for gambling on his personal account.

It was held that LG's action against K for conversion succeeded, but its action against the bank as constructive trustee of the money (*see* 1:7 below) and for breach of the mandate failed. The basic obligation of a bank is to pay its customer's cheques in accordance with the mandate and therefore only when the circumstances are such that any reasonable cashier would hesitate to pay a cheque at once should a cheque not be paid immediately on presentation. On the facts, the drawing of the cheques was not sufficiently unusual to warrant them not being paid. Although the branch manager knew of C's gambling and could have prevented the fraud by informing LG, his knowledge was based solely on C's conduct of his personal account and so informing LG would have broken the bank's duty of confidentiality to C.

Example 2

In *Barclays Bank PLC* v *Quincecare Ltd* (1988), the bank advanced £400 000 to Q, which was controlled by S, to purchase chemist shops. The loan was guaranteed by US instructed the bank to transfer a large sum from Q's account to that of a firm of solicitors who, he informed the bank, were acting in connection with the purchase. S then instructed the solicitors to transfer the money to the USA from where it was not recovered. The bank sued Q for the debt and U on its guarantee and they, in turn, alleged breach by the bank of its duty of care, even though it had acted in accordance with its mandate.

It was held that the bank's claims succeeded. On the facts, there was no reason for the bank to have suspected S's fraudulent intention and it, therefore, had not broken its duty of care.

7. Trust principles

A trust arises where title to property is vested in one person (the trustee) and that person is under an equitable obligation to use the property for the benefit of a third person or persons (the beneficiary(ies)). (Trustees and trust accounts are considered at 2:**11–12**.)

(a) *Express trusts.* A bank may expressly act as a trustee for its customers through, for example, its trust department or subsidiaries. Where it does, the law of trusts imposes on it duties and liabilities with respect to the care and use of the trust property. Indeed, if a bank holds itself out as having particular expertise as a trustee – which will presumably always be the case – it owes a greater duty of care than an ordinary individual who assumes a role as trustee, e.g. under a will or a family property settlement: *Bartlett* v *Barclays Bank Co Ltd* (1980).

> NOTE: However, a bank does *not* hold its customer's deposits on trust for the customer. If this were the case, the bank would be unable to use the funds (the trust property) for its own commercial purposes. (For the same reason a bank does not act as its customer's agent in relation to the customer's deposits.)

(b) *Constructive trusts.* A bank can also incur liability in relation to *constructive trusts*, that is situations where a person becomes involved in the affairs of a trust, and therefore incurs duties in relation to the trust property, without being appointed as a trustee.

In *Barnes* v *Addy* (1874) (CA), it was held that a bank may be liable as a constructive trustee where it either:

(i) Received trust funds in such a way as to become accountable for them, that is it had actual or constructive notice that they were trust funds and that the transfer of the funds was a breach of the trust; or

(ii) Knowingly participated in a dishonest and fraudulent purpose of the trustees.

In *Lipkin Gorman* v *Karpnale Ltd and Lloyds Bank PLC* (1989) (CA), where LG failed in their action against the bank for breach of trust, it was held that 'knowingly' allowing trust funds to be misappropriated as in *(ii)* above required:

(i) Actual knowledge; or

(ii) Wilfully shutting your eyes to the obvious; or

(iii) Wilfully and recklessly failing to make such enquiries as an honest and reasonable person would make.

Alternatively, in *Re Montagu's Settlement Trusts* (1987), it was held that

(iv) Acting with a 'want of probity' (integrity) is required – a question of fact in each case.

Example _____

In *Lipkin Gorman* v *Karpnale Ltd and Lloyds Bank PLC* (1989) (CA) (see 6), it was held on the facts that the bank neither knew that C was misappropriating clients' funds nor was reckless in paying the cheques. Nor had it acted with a 'want of probity'.

_____

(c) *'Quistclose' trusts.* Such a trust arises where money is paid to a bank for a specific purpose and the bank is aware of this purpose. The bank then owes a duty to ensure that the money is used for this purpose.

Example _____

In *Barclays Bank Ltd* v *Quistclose Investments Ltd* (1970), R's account with the bank was overdrawn and Q lent R money expressly to pay a dividend R had declared. The money was paid into a separate account in R's name with the bank, which was aware of the purpose of the loan. R went into liquidation before the dividend was paid and the bank set off the money lent to R by Q against R's overdraft. Q sought to recover the money.

It was held that Q was able to do so. As the bank was aware of the loan's purpose, it held the money on trust to pay the dividend but if that purpose failed, as it did, it held it for the benefit of Q (under a 'resulting trust').

_____

(d) *Liability as constructive trustee and as agent.* The liabilities are not co-extensive. A 'want of probity' is required for liability as a constructive trustee and this would also constitute a breach of contract: *Lipkin Gorman* v *Karpnale Ltd and Lloyds Bank PLC* (1989) (CA). However, negligence that would give rise to an action for breach of contract would be insufficient to give rise to liability as a constructive trustee. Negligence is not 'knowingly' acting, nor is it acting with a 'want of probity'. Thus, liability for breach of contract is more extensive than liability as a constructive trustee. It follows that the issue of whether a bank is liable as a constructive trustee is likely to be of academic interest only in future, all such claims being dealt with on the simpler basis of breach of contract.

8. Rules of bailment

A bailment arises where one person (the *bailor*) deposits goods with another (the *bailee*) for a specific purpose on terms that the goods will ultimately be redelivered to the bailor or otherwise dealt with according to the bailor's instructions. (Possession is transferred to the bailee but ownership remains with the bailor.)

The use of a bank's safe custody/deposit facilities by its customer gives rise to a bailment agreement. (Safe custody and bailment are dealt with in 1:**19**.)

9. Special relationship

The law recognises a number of *fiduciary relationships* where one party is presumed to be in a position of dominance over the other and that render voidable any contract made between them where the stronger party exerts their dominance to the detriment of the weaker party. The relationships between solicitor and client and between parent and child are examples of this.

The banker–customer relationship is *not* one of these specific relationships but a very similar *special relationship* can arise that imposes on the bank a duty very similar to that owed under a fiduciary relationship: *Lloyds Bank Ltd* v *Bundy* (1975) (CA). In *Bundy*, such a duty arose because B had come to rely on the bank for advice and the bank knew this (*see* 11:20).

The point to note is that if such a special relationship is proved to exist, the bank's position is no longer governed merely by the terms of the original contract. The bank will owe its customer a separate and strict duty of good faith, particularly where the possibility of a conflict of interests arises, and the concept of undue influence assumes greater importance.

10. Termination of the banker–customer contract

The contract can be terminated by the customer, by the bank and by operation of law.

(a) *By the customer.* By demanding full repayment of their credit balance: *Joachimson* v *Swiss Bank Corporation* (1921) (CA). An overdraft, together with any associated charges, must first be repaid before an account can be closed.

(b) *By the bank.* By giving reasonable notice if the account is in credit and immediately if the account is overdrawn (*see* 2:5).

(c) *By operation of law.* Following the customer's:

    (i) death;

    (ii) mental incapacity;

    (iii) insolvency.

NOTE: Aspects of the relationship can continue even though the contract has been terminated, e.g. the bank's common law qualified duty of confidentiality.

A bank's legal rights and duties

11. Rights

(a) To *make reasonable charges* for services rendered to customers and to *charge interest* on loans made to them. A bank also has the implied right under the Supply of Goods and Services 1882 s.15 to make a reasonable charge for its services where charges have not been expressly agreed.

Section 4 of the Code of Banking Practice provides that banks will publish tariffs covering basic account services that will be given or sent to customers when the account is opened, at any time on request and before changes are made. They will also tell customers the interest rates applicable to their accounts, the basis on which interest is calculated and when it will be charged to their accounts and explain the basis on which they may vary interest rates.

(b) To *repayment on demand* from its customers of any overdrawn balance that has been permitted on a current account.

> NOTE: In *Williams and Glyn's Bank* v *Barnes* (1980), however, it was held that a reasonable period of notice must be given where the terms and circumstances of the contract of lending clearly *imply* such notice.

The Limitation Act 1980 prevents legal action on a contract six years after the cause of action arises. In the case of a bank overdraft the six-year period begins to run under the Act from the date a demand for repayment is made, not from the date the overdraft was agreed.

(c) To be *indemnified* by its customers for expenses and liabilities incurred while acting for them.

Example

Indemnifying the bank for liability in conversion when collecting a cheque to which its customer had no title and where the Cheques Act 1957 s.4 could not be relied upon (*see* 9:**24**).

(d) To *exercise a lien* over any of its customers' securities that are in its possession, other than those deposited for safe custody, for any money owing to it (*see* 1:**17**).

(e) To *dispose of its customers' money as it pleases* provided it honours its customers' valid cheques. This right derives from the decision in *Foley* v *Hill* (1848) (HL).

(f) To *combine* or set-off accounts (*see* 1:**16**).

The final two legal rights of a bank are probably better termed *duties of the customer*, that is the duty incurred by the customer is a right enjoyed by the bank.

(g) A customer is under a duty *to exercise due care in drawing cheques* in order not to facilitate fraud: *London Joint Stock Bank Ltd* v *Macmillan and Arthur* (1918) (HL).

Example

In *London Joint Stock Bank Ltd* v *Macmillan and Arthur* (1918) (HL), a partner in MA signed a cheque payable to the payee or to bearer made out by a clerk for the sum of £2. The amount payable was shown in figures only. The clerk fraudulently altered the figures to read £120, wrote this amount on the cheque and obtained payment from the plaintiff, the firm's bank.

It was held that the bank was entitled to debit the firm's account with the value of the cheque as altered because the firm had broken its duty as a customer.

NOTE: The *Rule* in *Macmillan and Arthur*, by analogy, also applies to standing orders.

(h) A customer is under a duty to *inform their bank of any known forgeries on the account*: *Greenwood* v *Martins Bank Ltd* (1932) (HL).

Example

In *Greenwood* v *Martins Bank Ltd* (1932) (HL), G's wife held the cheque book for G's account and, over a period of time, drew a number of cheques by forging G's signature. G eventually discovered the forgeries but did not inform the bank. His wife committed suicide some eight months later and G then sought to recover the amount of the forged cheques.

It was held that he was unable to do so. The bank was entitled to debit G's account with the value of the cheques because G was estopped (prevented) from denying the genuineness of the signatures by his failure to inform the bank of the forgeries after he had discovered them. (A forgery of the drawer's signature is 'wholly inoperative', that is has no legal effect (Bills of Exchange Act 1882 s.24) and, therefore, does not normally entitle a bank to debit the account.)

NOTE: The duties imposed by *Macmillian and Arthur* and *Greenwood* were confirmed in *Tai Hing* (1986) by the Privy Council (*see* 1:**5**).

12. Duties

(a) To *abide by any express mandate from its customer*, for example the number of signatures required on a cheque. The mandate not only covers cheques but also standing orders and direct debits. A bank has no mandate to pay a cheque on which its customer's signature is forged.

(b) To *honour its customer's cheques*. This duty is subject to a number of provisos, for example (but *see* 9:**29** for a detailed discussion):

    (i) The cheque must be properly drawn, e.g. the amount in words and figures should agree (although the Bills of Exchange Act 1882 s 9 allows the bank to pay the amount in words) and not be stale.

    (ii) A sufficient credit balance or an agreed overdraft facility must exist – a bank can refuse to pay against uncleared effects unless it has agreed to do so.

    (iii) There must be no legal bar to payment, such as a garnishee order or an injunction.

    (iv) The customer must not have countermanded payment.

    (v) The bank must have had no notice that its customer has died, become mentally incapable of managing their affairs or have had an insolvency petition presented against them.

    (vi) There must not have been an insolvency order made against them.

By analogy this duty also applies to the payment of standing orders.

(c) *Not to disclose information about its customer's affairs*: *Tournier* v *National Provincial and Union Bank of England* (1924) (CA). (This duty of confidentiality is discussed in 1:**13**.)

(d) To *render statements of account* to its customer periodically or upon request.

> NOTE: Customers do not owe a duty to check their statements: *Tai Hing* (1986) (PC).

(e) To *collect cheques and other normal banking instruments* for its customer and to credit the amounts collected to their account.

(f) *To exercise proper care and skill* in carrying out any business it has agreed to transact for its customer.

By a term implied in contracts of service under the Supply of Goods and Services Act 1982 s.13, any person who supplies a service in the course of business must carry out the service with reasonable care and skill. Banking operations are therefore covered by this section. Furthermore, any purported exclusion of this implied term is subject to the 'reasonableness test' imposed by the Unfair Contract Terms Act 1977. Even without this statutory provision, a similar duty arises at common law when a bank acts as agent for its customer.

This duty of care and skill is evident in relation to any activity or transaction carried out or entered into on behalf of a customer, including safe deposit facilities, but it is of most practical importance in relation to the collection and payment of cheques.

NOTE: In *Barclays Bank PLC* v *Quincecare Ltd* (1988), it was held that a bank is under a duty to refrain from executing an order to transfer funds from a company's current account if it has reasonable grounds for believing that the order is an attempt to misappropriate the funds of the company. The test for breach of this duty is the perception of the ordinary prudent banker (*see* further 1:**6**.)

(g) To *inform its customer* if, and as soon as, it becomes aware that *forged cheques* are being presented for payment: *Greenwood* v *Martins Bank Ltd* (1932) (HL). (The bank would, of course, have no mandate to pay the cheques whether or not it knows of the forgery. Thus, this duty is rather academic.)

(h) To *give reasonable notice before closing a credit account.*

Specific aspects of the relationship

13. The common law duty of confidentiality

In *Tournier* v *National Provincial and Union Bank of England* (1924) (CA), it was held that a bank owed a *qualified* duty of confidentiality to its customer.

In the case, T had defaulted on a written agreement to repay his overdraft with the defendant bank by weekly instalments. The branch manager telephoned T's employer to find out his private address and, during the ensuing conversation, disclosed that the account was overdrawn and that an agreement for repayment was not being honoured. He also expressed the opinion that the plaintiff was betting heavily, having traced a cheque drawn by T to a bookmaker. As a result of the disclosure, T lost his job and successfully sued the bank for breach of an implied term in the contract that the bank would not disclose to third persons the state of his account or any transactions relating to it.

The Court of Appeal held that a bank's disclosure of its customer's affairs is only justified in *four* instances: where the bank is compelled by law to do so; where the bank has a duty to the public to do so; where the bank's own interests require disclosure; and where the bank has the express or implied consent of its customer to do so:

(a) *Where the bank is compelled by law to do so*:
(i) *By court order*. The more important examples in this category are orders made under the:
(1) *Bankers' Books Evidence Act 1879*, to provide evidence for a civil or criminal trial;

(2) *Police and Criminal Evidence Act 1984*, to assist the police in the investigation of a criminal offence;

NOTE: In *Barclays Bank PLC v Taylor and Another* (1989) (CA), it was held that where a bank receives notice of applications by the police for orders authorising their inspection of a customer's account under the Police and Criminal Evidence Act 1984, it owes no duty to either oppose the application or inform the customer of them.

(3) *Drug Trafficking Offences Act 1986*, to assist the police in investigating possible drug trafficking offences;

(4) *Witness orders*, to compel a bank employee to give evidence in a trial; and

(5) *Discovery orders*, made to assist a person seeking a *Mareva* injunction.

(ii) Following a valid request by an official to do so. The more important examples in this category are requests made under the:

(1) *Taxes Management Act 1970* and the *Income and Corporation Taxes Act 1988*, by the Inland Revenue;

(2) *Companies Act 1985*, by officials of the Department of Trade and Industry for information about a company;

(3) *Financial Services Act 1986*, by inspectors investigating possible 'insider dealing';

(4) *Criminal Justice Act 1987*, by the Director of the Serious Fraud Office in connection with an investigation.

(iii) Where, although there is no legal compulsion to disclose information, failure to do so may constitute a criminal offence by the bank and disclosure has statutory protection. The more important examples in this category are disclosures made under the:

(1) *Drug Trafficking Offences Act 1986*, disclosure to the police of a suspicion or belief about funds generated by illegal drug trafficking;

(2) *Criminal Justice Act 1988*, disclosure to the police of a suspicion or belief that property has been obtained as a result of an indictable offence (a serious offence triable by judge and jury in the Crown Court), for example robbery; (Non-disclosure under this Act is not itself an offence.)

(3) *Prevention of Terrorism (Temporary Provisions) Act 1989*, disclosure to the police on suspicion or belief of the location of funds or other property that might be used in connection with offences under the Act.

NOTE: To gain statutory protection under the three Acts above, the bank must be able to show that it had sufficient suspicion or belief to justify the disclosure.

(b) *Where the bank has a duty to the public to do so.* The extent of this exception is uncertain and certainly seldom invoked, most possible situations are now covered by specific statutes. It would probably apply in wartime if the bank disclosed that one of its customers was trading with the enemy.

(c) *Where the bank's own interests require disclosure.* This exception would apply where legal proceedings are required to enforce repayment of an overdraft or where a guarantor asks to be told the extent to which their guarantee is being relied upon by the bank. It would seem, however, that the exception can also apply in rather less well-defined situations.

Example
_____

In *Sunderland* v *Barclays Bank* (1938), the Bank dishonoured S's cheque to her dressmaker for insufficient funds, but it was also concerned about her gambling and it did not want her account to become overdrawn. She complained to the bank by telephone about the dishonour and, during the conversation, her husband interrupted to make his own protest. The bank then told him that his wife had previously drawn a number of cheques payable to bookmakers. S took action against the Bank.

It was held that the bank was justified in making the disclosure because it was in the bank's own interests – it was entitled to protect its reputation – and within the *Tournier* exception. (On the facts, the wife had also impliedly consented to the disclosure.)
_____

> NOTE: The Code of Banking Practice s.6, expressly reiterates the *Tournier* duty and states that banks and building societies will not use this exception to justify disclosure for marketing purposes of details of customers' accounts or their names and addresses to any third party, including other companies within the same group.

(d) *Where the bank has the express or implied consent of its customer to do so*, e.g. where it supplies a reference for its customer or where it replies to a status enquiry about its customer from another bank (but see 1:**18**).

> NOTE: The duty covers information gained about its customer from all sources and continues after the banker–customer contract has ended: *Tournier* v *National Provincial and Union Bank of England* (1924).
>
> To be awarded more than nominal damages in an action for breach of the duty, a plaintiff must establish actual monetary loss. This is merely an application of general contract law principles and, in practice, limits a bank's liability for breach of the *Tournier* duty.

14. The Data Protection Act 1984

(a) This Act imposes a separate *statutory* duty of confidentiality on all persons who hold information about *individuals* on computers. It does not apply to *paper-based information* and information on *corporate bodies*. Thus, in relation to banks, the Act only applies to information held on *personal customers* and, as much of this information, perhaps most of it, is paper-based, a significant part is therefore outside the Act. Customers do not, therefore, have a statutory right of access to it.

Information held on microfilm or microfiche is *not* covered by the Act if sorted, extracted and set up for viewing manually but *is* covered when these processes are controlled by computer.

A *data user* is defined by the Act as an organisation or individual that controls the contents and use of a collection of personal data processed automatically (by computer). A *computer bureau* is an organisation or individual that processes personal data for data users or allows data users to process personal data on their equipment. A *data subject* is an individual about whom personal data is held. The Data Protection Registrar is responsible for ensuring compliance with the Act.

(b) *Registration.* Any person who holds or processes data must register with the Registrar and must only hold, use and disclose information in accordance with their registration. Banks will register as data users and, possibly, as computer bureaux. The register, which is open to public inspection, must show four main things:

(*i*) Description of the personal data to be held.

(*ii*) The source of the information.

(*iii*) The purpose for which it is obtained.

(*iv*) The persons to whom it may be disclosed.

The register will also show the country or countries to which data may be transferred and the address to which people can write for information held about them.

(c) *The data protection principles.* All eight principles apply to data users, only the eighth applies to computer bureaux. Banks will be most concerned with the first two principles:

NOTE: The Code of Banking Practice s.6 states that banks and building societies will at all times comply with the Act when obtaining and processing customers' data.

(*i*) *The information to be contained in personal data shall be obtained, and personal data shall be processed fairly, and lawfully.*

The data subject must not be misled or deceived as to the purposes for which the information is held, used or disclosed. It follows that if information obtained on opening an account is actually intended to assist the bank in selling other financial products and this fact is not disclosed, this principle would be infringed.

(ii) Personal data shall be held only for one or more specified and lawful purposes. These purposes must be registered by the data user. It follows that banks must register *all* the possible purposes for which they wish to use information on personal customers to avoid infringing this principle. An example would be to use the information for marketing insurance services without the marketing of insurance being a registered purpose under the Act.

NOTE: A bank is entitled to use personal data for a registered purpose if it would be reasonable for the data subject to expect that the bank to use it for that purpose. For example, information obtained on opening a current account could be used to inform the customer of the bank's other types of accounts.

(iii) Personal data held for any purpose or purposes shall not be disclosed in any manner incompatible with that purpose or those purposes.

(iv) Personal data held for any purpose or purposes shall be adequate, relevant and not excessive in relation to that purpose or those purposes.

(v) Personal data shall be accurate and, where necessary, kept up to date.

(vi) Personal data held for any purpose or purposes shall not be kept for longer than is necessary for that purpose or those purposes.

(vii) An individual is entitled (a) at reasonable intervals and without undue delay or expense to be informed by a data user whether any personal data is held on them and to have access to it; and (b) where appropriate to have such data corrected or erased.

(viii) Appropriate security measures shall be taken against unauthorised access to, or alteration, disclosure or destruction of, personal data and against accidental loss or destruction of personal data. The level of security depends on the nature of the data and the damage likely to be caused by breach of this principle.

NOTE: Breach of any of the principles is a statutory offence.

(d) The rights of data subjects are:

(i) Access to personal data. A data subject is entitled to a copy of the data in an intelligible form within 40 days of the request. The data user may insist on a written request, checking the identity of the person making the request and payment of a fee of up to £10.

NOTE: Under the Code of Banking Practice, s.6 banks and building societies must explain to their customers that they have this right of access.

(ii) Compensation for inaccuracy. Two defences are available: (1) that reasonable care was taken to ensure the accuracy of the data; (2) the data is marked as having been received in the form in which it is held or that the data subject regards the information as inaccurate. The data subject can apply to the court for the erasure or rectification of inaccurate data held.

(iii) Compensation for loss or unauthorised disclosure of information. It is a defence to show that reasonable care was taken to prevent the loss or unauthorised disclosure. Disclosure may lawfully be made to (1) the data subject or their agent; (2) with the data subject's consent; (3) to relevant employees; (4) in an emergency to prevent injury to health; (5) where required by law.

(e) The Registrar's powers are:

(i) Enforcement notice – to observe the data protection principles. Failure to do so is an offence.

(ii) Transfer prohibition notice – to another country not a signatory to the European Convention on data protection or that does not have adequate data protection legislation. Failure to obey the notice is an offence.

(iii) De-registration notice – to remove some or all of the particulars of an entry where an enforcement notice is ineffective. Removal of an entry from the Register prevents a person from carrying out further automatic processing related to that entry without committing an offence.

(f) *Comparison with the Tournier duty.* The common law *Tournier* duty applies to all forms of information, however held, and is not restricted to personal customers – contrast which Act that applies only to personal customers and information held on computer. However, while *Tournier* applies only to disclosure to third parties, the Act also applies to the *obtaining* of information and the use of it *within* the bank.

NOTE: If a bank uses a credit reference agency when deciding whether to open an account for or advance funds to a customer, the customer must be informed of this. Under the Consumer Credit Act 1974, the customer then has the right to be told the name and address of the agency, to obtain a copy of the information about them and to have it changed or erased if it is incorrect.

15. Appropriation of payments

(a) *Introduction* Customers often have more than one account. Where this is so, customers have the right to appropriate funds deposited into whichever account they wish unless there was a contrary agreement in the original mandate. This rule applies even where one account is in credit and another in debit. In addition, customers have the right to appropriate within an account, that is they can specify that the funds paid in should meet a particular cheque (withdrawal) that has or will be drawn.

If the customer does not appropriate, the bank can appropriate the funds as it wishes. Such appropriations are, however, unusual although, by definition, an appropriation must be made because the credit has to be entered somewhere.

In most situations, the rules of appropriation are academic because where there are two or more accounts, the right to combine accounts (*see* 1:**16**) means that the only relevant issue is the combined balance. In a single account its balance is usually the only issue, which credits relate to which debits is immaterial.

However, where there are two or more accounts, one of which is a wages account – an overdrawn balance on which is a preferential debt – a bank would wish to appropriate funds paid in to a general account. Assuming adequate security is not held, on the customer's insolvency the bank would be an unsecured creditor for an overdrawn balance on a general account, which means that appropriation to such an account would reduce the unsecured claim while leaving the preferential claim unaffected.

(b) The rules of appropriation:

(i) Unless otherwise agreed, the customer can specify to which account, or to which debit item within an account, funds paid in are to be appropriated. For example, on an overdrawn account, the customer can specify that the funds are to be used to meet a cheque that has not yet been paid rather than to be used in reduction of the overdraft.

(ii) If the customer does not appropriate, the bank can.

(iii) Once the account is credited, the appropriation is final, although the right to combine accounts and the statutory right of set-off still apply (*see* 1:**16**).

(iv) If neither customer nor bank specifically appropriates, the default *Rule* in *Clayton's Case* applies.

(c) *The Rule in Clayton's Case* (1816) (*Devaynes* v *Noble*). The *Rule* states that in a current account, payments in are appropriated to payments out in the order in which the items occur unless the customer or the bank, if the customer does not, takes steps to appropriate particular credits against particular debits. Thus, in a *credit* account, the first sum paid in is the first sum to be paid out and in an *overdrawn* account, payments in are appropriated to undischarged debit item in date order.

Consider the account of XYZ below.

Date	Debits	Credits	Balance
1 June			c/f 5000 Dr
3 June		2000	3000 Dr
5 June		2000	1000 Dr
7 June	4000		5000 Dr
9 June	2000		7000 Dr
11 June		1000	6000 Dr

X, Y and Z were in partnership. At the date of X's retirement on 1 June – which determines X's liability – the firm's overdraft was £5000. The account is continued unbroken. The credit of £2000 on 3 June reduces the debit balance and X's liability for it to £3000 and the credit on 5 June further reduces both to £1000. The debit on 7 June increases the overdraft to £5000 but X's liability remains at £1000, as it does on 9 June when a debit increases the overdraft to £7000. The credit on 11 June then reduces the overdraft to £6000 but, through the operation of the *Rule*, also cancels X's remaining liability on the account. This is so even though the overdraft has actually increased and only Y and Z are now liable on it. (For this reason, banks will invariably take steps to avoid the *Rule* operating to their disadvantage wherever possible, most commonly by simply breaking the account when certain events happen.)

The rule is merely a presumption that can be rebutted by an *express* contrary intention; an implied intention is insufficient.

Example

In *Deeley* v *Lloyds Bank Ltd* (1912), the bank held a second mortgage over business premises to secure a customer's overdraft. The customer executed a third mortgage to D. Notice of this mortgage was given to the bank, but it continued the account instead of breaking it. (A subsequent mortgage takes precedence over fresh advances on the account: *see* 12:**28**.) Within a short time, credits received exceeded the amount owing and secured by the bank's mortgage at the date of the notice. Subsequently the customer was made bankrupt and the bank sold the property for just sufficient to pay off the first mortgagee and the amount it was owed. D received nothing and sued the bank.

It was held (HL) that her action succeeded. Although it was reasonable to think that the bank wished to preserve its security and therefore that it intended to appropriate payments to new, unsecured borrowing, *Clayton's Case* applied because there was no express evidence – the account had not been broken – that it should not do so. Thus, the overdraft covered by the original mortgage had been repaid by the payments in and not the further advances.

The standard practice evidencing the required express contrary intention is to break the account and to pass all subsequent entries through a new account. This avoids the *Rule* operating to a bank's detriment in the first four examples of the *Rule's* application outlined below. However, a clause excluding the operation of *Clayton's Case* may be included in charge forms to the effect that the account is deemed to be ruled off when the 'relevant event' occurs, e.g. notice of a subsequent mortgage: *Westminster Bank Ltd v Cond* (1940). The usual 'continuing security' clause (*see* 11:25) affords no protection when a bank receives notice of a subsequent mortgage on property that secures an overdraft.

Examples of the *Rule's* application are:

(i) Death of a joint account holder.

(ii) Retirement of a partner.

(iii) Determination of a guarantee.

(iv) Notice of a subsequent mortgage – the subsequent mortgage takes priority over further advances.

In all four of these situations, the determination of the mandate by the relevant event means that any subsequent payment into the account will reduce the amount for which the account holder or guarantor is liable or the amount covered by the mortgage. There will be no liability for subsequent payments out. Thus, the bank's position must be prejudiced.

(v) Invalidation of a floating charge: Insolvency Act 1986 s.245 (the '12-month rule'). Under s.245, a floating charge is invalidated if the company creating it was insolvent at the time or became insolvent as a result of creating the floating charge and goes into liquidation within 12 months of its creation, except for money paid in consideration for the charge at the time it is taken or subsequently. If the charge is in favour of a person closely con-nected with the company, the period is two years and the charge may be invalid even if the company was solvent when the charge was created (*see* 6:10). This is not quite so complicated as it might first seem. It has a simple purpose. It prevents insolvent compa-nies creating floating charges to secure past debts to the prejudice of their other unsecured creditors.

This example is the one important situation where the *Rule* works in a bank's favour. If the company's account is continued unbroken, payments in will reduce the unsecured debt while subsequent ad-vances will be covered by the floating charge.

(vi) Borrowing by a minor on a current account. Debts incurred by a minor are unenforceable unless the minor ratifies them after

becoming 18: Minors' Contracts Act 1987. However, payments into the account *after* the minor has become 18 will progressively reduce the amount of the unenforceable debt and eventually result in the continuing overdraft constituting 'new' and enforceable borrowing. In this example, the *Rule* again works in the bank's favour.

Situations where the *Rule* does not apply:

(i) Trust monies. Where a trustee pays trust funds into their own private account there is a presumption that the trustee intends to withdraw their own money first: *Re Hallett's Estate* (1880). (This presumption protects both the beneficiary and the trustee, from a possible breach of trust.) If the *Rule* applied, the presumption that the first funds paid in are the first funds to be paid out could prejudice the beneficiaries.

(ii) To *separate accounts* at the bank. This applies even if the accounts are held at the same branch.

(iii) To a *stopped account*. In effect, the bank has taken steps to appropriate the payment and thereby excluded the *Rule*.

(iv) Where there is an *express agreement* to the contrary or the bank *reserves the right of appropriation* at the time of payment. For example, banks frequently include terms in guarantees allowing a bank to continue the account even after a demand is made; the demand would normally fix the surety's liability: *Westminster Bank Ltd* v *Cond* (1940).

(v) Accounts other than current accounts.

16. Combination of accounts

(a) *Introduction* Combination is the right of a bank to set one account (in debit) off against another (in credit) held by the same customer in order to determine the net figure of indebtedness between them. The right arises whether or not the accounts are maintained at the same branch: *Garnett* v *McKewan* (1872). Thus, a bank could refuse to pay a cheque drawn on an account in credit at branch X when an account at branch Y is overdrawn by an amount greater than the credit balance on the account at branch X.

The right of combination arises by operation of law at common law and not by agreement, but it can be excluded by agreement, either express or implied. This would normally be the case where one of the accounts is a loan account for a fixed period. The right typically arises when a bank receives notice of the death or mental incapacity of its customer or a garnishee order relating to a customer is served on the bank.

An agreement *not* to combine accounts is terminated by the customer's insolvency as this terminates the banker–customer contract and the non-excludable statutory right of set-off under the Insolvency Act 1986 arises (*see* below).

NOTE: A customer has no right to combine accounts held at different branches, e.g. by presenting a cheque on an account in debit expecting it to be paid from an account in credit at another branch. A possible right to combine exists where two current accounts are maintained at the same branch and the customer draws a cheque generally, that is without referring to a particular account, but this is unlikely to be encountered in practice.

(b) Limits to the bank's right of combination are:

(*i*) An *express agreement* not to combine accounts.

(*ii*) Where the debit balance is *not a due debt*. This applies to a loan account, because the debt is not due until some future time, and to a contingent liability, such as that of a guarantor, because the liability may or may not arise.

(*iii*) Where the debt on a *loan account* is due, without giving reasonable notice. This is because of the implied agreement to keep the accounts separate; a customer in this situation should be given reasonable warning before having cheques dishonoured for lack of funds. This implied agreement also covers a frozen overdrawn account.

(*iv*) Where the claims *do not arise in the same right*, there must be mutuality. For example, combination does not apply where one account is a trust account and the bank is aware of this, for example *Barclays Bank Ltd* v *Quistclose Investments Ltd* (1970) (*see* 1:7), nor where one account is a joint account.

NOTE: In *Re K* (1990), it was held that the right of combination can be exercised in the face of a restraint order made under the Drug Trafficking Offences Act 1986 without recourse to the court. In exercising its right to combine accounts, a bank is not asserting a claim over assets – which would conflict with the Crown's right under the Act – but merely carrying out an accounting exercise in order to determine the position between itself and the customer.

(c) *The equitable right of set-off.* This arises where an account is operated by a nominee, e.g. X operates an account for Y. However, a bank can only combine a credit balance on X's account with a debit balance on Y's account if there is *indisputable evidence* of the nomineeship: *Bhogal* v *Punjab National Bank* (1988) (CA) and *Uttamchandani* v *Central Bank of India* (1989) (CA). Thus, if the ownership of the funds were the subject of court action, for example, the bank would not be entitled to refuse its customer access to the funds pending the decision.

(d) *Set-off following insolvency.* If either the bank or its customer become insolvent, the following rules apply:

(i) Under the Insolvency Act 1986 s.323 (individuals) and the Insolvency Rules 1986 4.90 (companies), there is a statutory right of set-off that cannot be excluded by an agreement between the parties: *Halesowen Presswork and Assemblies Ltd* v *Westminster Bank Ltd* (1972) (HL).

(ii) Any agreement to extend the right of set-off becomes void; the Insolvency Act 1986 governs the distribution of assets.

(iii) There must be mutuality between the claims; they must arise in the same right (*see* above).

(iv) Where a bank has both preferential and non-preferential claims against its customer, a credit balance must be set-off pro rata against the preferential and non-preferential claims: *Re Unit Two Windows Ltd* (1985).

NOTE: The bank's right to appropriate payments into an account *when they are received* would appear to be unaffected by the above rule. Thus, for example, a bank could realise security held and appropriate the proceeds to non-preferential debts in an account containing both preferential and non-preferential debts: *Re William Hall (Contractors) Ltd* (1967). The appropriation is final, however, and the rule in *Re Unit Two Windows* would apply subsequently.

(v) The claims involved need not be of the same type. Thus, debts that were not due become due and payable and subject to statutory set-off, as are contingent liabilities, e.g. the possible liability of a bank under a performance bond. In this respect statutory set-off differs from the common law right of combination.

(vi) Debits to an account (1) after notice of a bankruptcy petition (individual) or a winding up petition or notice of a meeting of creditors (company); or (2) after the commencement of bankruptcy, that is the date of the bankruptcy order, cannot be set-off.

17. Banker's lien

(a) *Introduction* A lien is a creditor's right to *retain* possession of property belonging to the debtor until a debt is paid. It arises by *operation of law*, not by agreement, from certain situations, e.g. a garage would be entitled to a lien over its customer's car until a bill for repairs was paid.

A lien differs from a mortgage or a pledge (a pledge involves the deposit of goods, e.g. pawnbroking) in that mortgages and pledges are both the result of express agreements between borrowers and lenders.

NOTE: Taking possession of documents of title under a security arrangement gives rise to the right to retain them until repayment is made. This is sometimes referred to as *contractual lien*, but, because such a lien arises by agreement and not by operation of law, it is not a lien in the legal sense.

A lien may be either particular or general. A *particular lien* gives the right to retain possession only to secure payment of money owing in respect of the particular property over which the lien is exercised, while *general lien* gives the right to retain possession until any amount outstanding is repaid.

By mercantile custom, a *banker's lien* is a general lien that confers the right of sale and recoupment: *Brandao v Barnett* (1846) (HL). (At common law a lien only confers the right to retain possession of property, but a statutory power of sale exists under the Torts (Interference with Goods) Act 1977.)

(b) *Exercising a lien.* A bank can exercise a lien over any of its customer's paper securities in its possession *as banker* other than those deposited for safe custody.

Thus, a lien can be exercised over:

(i) Cheques paid in to be collected and credited to the customer's account if the account is overdrawn, although the lien is lost when they are presented for payment (*see* below).

(ii) Share certificates and government stock.

(iii) Life policies.

(iv) Eurobonds, commercial paper and certificates of deposits.

(v) shipping documents (as part of a documentary credit transaction); and possibly

(vi) Title deeds to land.

NOTE: Documents such as life policies and share certificates are likely to be held under a specific agreement – either for safe custody or as security – and a lien cannot therefore arise over them while they are so held. However, if a life policy, say, was originally held as security but the debt has been discharged by repayment without the customer asking for the return of the life policy, a lien could arise over the policy in respect of subsequent borrowing.

(c) *Restrictions on a bank's lien.* A lien does not arise in the following circumstances:

(i) Where there is an agreement between the bank and its customer to this affect.

(ii) To securities held in safe custody. Safe custody (*see* 1:**19**) gives rise to a bailment and this is wholly inconsistent with a lien.

NOTE: A safe custody agreement may provide that items so held may be retained until charges incurred have been paid, but this is not a true lien.

(iii) In practice it will not cover cheques (and other bills) paid in for collection to an overdrawn account because a bank is under a contractual duty to present them for payment and once possession is given up the lien is lost. However, when the proceeds are received, the right of combination will be available to the bank.

NOTE: Having a lien over a cheque may enable a bank to establish itself as a holder for value of the cheque and possibly as holder in due course (*see* 9:**26**).

(iv) Where the bank has actual or constructive knowledge that the securities are held by its customer as trustee.

(v) To an in-credit balance in the customer's name – the money is the bank's property. The bank has, however, the right to combine accounts.

18. Banker's reference

A banker's reference, or, status enquiry is an opinion given by a bank to another bank about a customer's ability to meet a financial commitment. The reference is intended for the use of a customer of the bank requesting the reference and not by the bank itself.

NOTE: Under the Code of Banking Practice s.7, banks and building societies will, on request, advise customers whether they provide bankers' references in reply to status enquiries and explain how the system of bankers' references works.

When giving such an opinion, the bank can incur liability to the ultimate recipient and, possibly, to its customer.

(a) *Liability to the ultimate recipient.* If the reference is inaccurate and the recipient suffers loss as a result of relying on it, liability can arise in the torts of deceit or negligence.

(i) Deceit (fraudulent misrepresentation). This requires the bank to have intentionally lied – presumably a very rare occurrence.

Liability under this head can easily be avoided by ensuring that the opinion is not signed on behalf of the bank; the Statute of Frauds Amendment Act 1828 provides that liability for fraudulent misrepresentation of a person's creditworthiness only arises if the statement is in writing and signed by the maker of the statement.

(ii) Negligence. Liability in the tort of negligence for negligent statements causing purely financial loss can arise in the absence of an express disclaimer where the circumstances show that the skill and judgment of the person making the statement is being relied upon by the person to whom the statement is made: *Hedley Byrne* v *Heller & Partners Ltd* (1963) (HL).

Example

In *Hedley Byrne* v *Heller & Partners Ltd* (1963) (HL), HB, a firm of advertising agents, asked their bank to enquire into the creditworthiness of a potential client (E) through the latter's bank, HP. Satisfactory replies were given to two such enquiries, on the strength of which HB incurred substantial expenses on E's behalf. The opinion contained the disclaimer 'For your private use and without responsibility on the part of the bank or its officials'. E subsequently went into liquidation and HB sought to recover the losses they had incurred from HP on the grounds that the replies had been made negligently.

It was held that the action failed because of the disclaimer but the House held unanimously that but for the disclaimer, the action would have succeeded.

The *Hedley Byrne* principle was reviewed and refined by the House of Lords in *Caparo Industries* v *Dickman* (1990), where it was held that auditors of a company's accounts did not owe a duty of care to shareholders or members of the public who purchased shares in reliance on the audited accounts. The purpose of the audit was to enable shareholders to make corporate decisions, not for individuals to make personal decisions about whether or not to deal in a company's shares. The House of Lords emphasised that the duty of care will only arise where sufficient *proximity* exists between the plaintiff and defendant, that is where:

(1) A special relationship exists between the maker of the statement and the person acting on it, the special relationship being based on the statement having been directed towards specific persons in the knowledge that it will be relied on;

(2) The person making the statement has expertise in the matter; and

(3) It is reasonable to impose a duty of care.

NOTE: The *Hedley Byrne* situation is now subject to the Unfair Contract Terms Act 1977. This provides, *inter alia*, that any attempt to exclude or limit liability for negligence, e.g. by a disclaimer in a banker's opinion, is subject to a judicial test of reasonableness. Thus, it does not necessarily follow that a standard pre-printed disclaimer will be an effective defence.

(b) *Possible liability to its customer.* Liability *could* arise on one of the following three grounds.

(i) In contract, on the basis of an implied term in the banker–customer contract that the bank will not give an incorrect opinion about its customer.

(ii) In contract, for breach of the *Tournier* duty of confidentiality (*see* 1:**13**). A customer must consent, expressly or impliedly, to the disclosure of information and it could be argued that consent is logically impossible if the customer is unaware that an opinion has been requested or even that the system of bankers' opinions exists. However, the system is well established and all customers could be regarded as impliedly consenting to bona fide disclosures for this purpose. In the absence of a judicial decision, the legal position must be regarded as debatable.

(iii) In tort for libel, if the unfavourable reference lowers the customer in the eyes of 'right-thinking members of society generally'. However, it is a defence to show that the statement was true and a bank can claim *qualified privilege* as a defence if it made the statement in good faith: *London Association for Protection of Trade* v *Greenlands Ltd* (1916) (HL).

NOTE: A bank is not a credit reference agency when it replies to status enquiries. Under the Consumer Credit Act 1974, a credit reference agency is any business that provides 'persons with information relevant to the financial standing of individuals, being information collected by the agency for that purpose'. The information given by banks in opinions is not collected specifically for the purpose.

19. Safe custody

Use of a *safe deposit* facility gives rise to a *bailment* agreement.

(a) *Bailment* A bailment arises where one person (the *bailor*) deposits goods with another (the *bailee*) for a specific purpose on terms that the goods should be ultimately redelivered to the bailor or otherwise dealt with according to the bailor's instructions.

Under such an agreement the bank (as bailee) incurs a duty of care and acquires a right to be paid, if a fee is to be charged, and a (contractual) 'lien' over the property if payment is not made.

NOTE: The 'lien' – in fact it is not a lien at all in the legal sense – only applies to unpaid safe custody charges; it does not apply to borrowing on any account. Property held in safe custody would typically include jewellery, deeds and other documents and, increasingly, computer discs.

(b) *Gratuitous and paid bailees.* The law draws a distinction between a gratuitous (unpaid) bailee and a bailee for reward (a paid bailee). Both may be liable in *tort* for loss or damage to the property bailed, but a gratuitous bailee is only expected to take the same care of the property as a reasonably careful person would take of similar property of their own. A paid bailee, however, owes an additional *contractual duty* to the bailor under which they are judged against the highest professional standards.

A bank is always a *paid* bailee whether or not a specific fee is charged because safe custody is considered as part of the wider banker–customer contract: *Port Swettenham Authority* v *T W Wu & Co.* (1978) (PC).

(c) *A bank's liability as bailee.*

(i) Breach of contract. A bank will be in breach of contract if, through its negligence, the property held is destroyed by fire or otherwise lost or stolen. Note that the Unfair Contract Terms Act 1977 subjects any term or notice excluding or limiting liability for negligence in relation to goods to a test of reasonableness.

(ii) Conversion. A bank is perhaps more likely to incur liability in relation to a safe custody deposit in the tort of *conversion.* Conversion can be committed in many ways but most commonly by wrongfully taking possession of goods, wrongfully damaging or destroying them, wrongfully disposing of them or by refusing to part with them when possession is demanded by someone entitled to possession.

The essence of the tort is that the defendant's conduct amounts to a denial of the plaintiff's *right to possession and control* of the property, usually by denying the plaintiff's title in some way. A bank would, for example, commit conversion by refusing to hand over the property held in safe custody when the depositor (bailor) demands it or by delivering the property to an unauthorised person.

Liability in conversion is *strict*, that is the breach of the legal duty resulting in the infringement of the individual's legal right is enough, neither proof of intention nor negligence is necessary. This means that a bank would still be liable in conversion, even if it wrongfully delivers property held in safe custody by pure mistake or against the most skilfully forged authority; in both instances it would still have infringed the bailor's rights in the property bailed.

(c) *Other points to note.*

(i) Merely being in possession without title is not conversion. There must be an intention to keep the property in defiance of the owner's rights. This situation would arise if the property held in safe custody did not belong to the bailor or where there is doubt as to the ownership of the property. In the event of the ownership being disputed in such a situation, the bank would have to make

it clear that it was prepared to deliver the property to whomever was proved to be its true owner.

(ii) If there are joint bailors, delivery of the property must only be made on joint authority. If the right of survivorship arises on the death of one of the joint bailors, the property can be delivered to the survivor. If it does not, the personal representative(s) of the deceased must give a receipt.

(iii) A mandate from joint bailors can specify that any one can give a receipt for safe custody items. This would avoid liability for conversion, but a bank would be liable as constructive trustee if it has actual or constructive knowledge that a breach of trust is being committed in relation to the property, that is a wider duty exists.

(iv) A bank is only liable for conversion when an employee steals safe custody items if the employee's normal work involved duties in relation to them. However, the fact that the theft takes place would probably indicate a breach of the contractual duty to take reasonable care of the property irrespective of possible liability in tort.

(v) Safe custody items are not subject to the banker's lien: *Brandao* v *Barnett* (1846) (HL).

20. Bank statements

A bank owes a duty to its customers to keep accurate records of transactions on their accounts. Customers have no obligation to check bank statements and inform the bank of an inaccuracy in them. Furthermore, if a customer does check the statements, the customer is not estopped (prevented) from subsequently challenging their accuracy: *Chatterton* v *London & County Bank* (1890), reaffirmed by the Privy Council in the *Tai Hing Case* (1985) (PC).

NOTE: It would be possible for a bank to include an express term in the contract with its customer imposing a duty on the customer to check the accuracy of bank statements (*see* 1:5).

(a) *Overcrediting the account.* If a bank overcredits a customer's account, the excess credit can usually, but not invariably, be recovered.
Example _____
In *Lloyds Bank Ltd* v *Brooks* (1951), the bank, over a period of time, credited to B's account dividends for more shares than she, in fact, owned. She used the money for her own purposes, having relied on statements of her account in good faith.

It was held that the bank was not entitled to recover the amounts wrongly credited to B's account.

However, to defeat a claim for repayment, the customer must fulfil three conditions, as illustrated in *United Overseas Bank* v *Jiwani* (1976):

(i) The state of the account must have been misrepresented to the customer by the bank;

(ii) The customer must have been misled by the misrepresentation; and

(iii) As a result of the reliance, the customer must have changed their position in a way that would make it inequitable (unfair) to require them to repay the money.

Example

In *United Overseas Bank* v *Jiwani* (1976), $11 000 was credited by telex to J's Swiss bank account, making a total balance in the account of $21 000. J issued a cheque for $20 000 in connection with the purchase of a hotel. Subsequently, written confirmation of the telex was received, but the bank mistakenly treated this as a second credit and advised J accordingly. J then issued a second cheque, for $11 000, towards the hotel purchase. The bank sought to recover this amount from him.

It was held that the bank's claim succeeded. On the facts, J had alternative funds that he would have used for the purchase, irrespective of the mistaken credit. Thus, while the first two conditions were satisfied on the facts, J failed to satisfy the third.

NOTE: In *Lipkin Gorman* v *Karpnale* (1991) (HL), the view was expressed *obiter* (that is it was not pertinent to the appeal) that a claim for repayment of funds incorrectly credited to an account could be brought as a claim for restitution of property, the customer having been unjustly enriched by the payment. The representation by the payee would not be an issue in a claim for restitution and it would enable the court to order partial repayment whereas a claim based on the estoppel principle illustrated by *Jiwani* allows only full or nil recovery. The customer would be able to defend the claim for restitution by establishing that they had so changed their position that it would be inequitable in all the circumstances to require them to make restitution in whole or in part. (The claim against the bank in *Lipkin Gorman* was not pursued further than the Court of Appeal, the House of Lords appeal concerned the claim by the firm against the operators of the casino: *see* 1:**6** and **7**.)

(b) *Incorrectly debiting the account.* Whatever the reason for the incorrect debit, a bank is obliged to refund the amount; it has no mandate for the debit.

If, as a result of incorrect debits, cheques are dishonoured for apparent lack of funds, a bank is liable for the wrongful dishonour of the cheques and must compensate the customer for the injury to the customer's credit and reputation. This may result in an action for libel. By analogy, the position is the same where there is an incorrect debit of a standing order. (*see* 9:32.)

21. Code of Banking Practice

(a) In March 1992, the Code of Banking Practice, entitled *Good Banking* and prepared jointly by the British Bankers' Association (BBA), the Building Societies Association (BSA) and the Association for Payment Clearing Services (APACS) and adopted by all major banks, building societies and card issuers came into effect.

The Code only applies to *personal customers*. The Code defines a private customer as 'A private individual who maintains an account (including a joint account with another private individual or an account held as an executor or trustee, but excluding the accounts of sole traders, clubs and societies) or who takes other services from a bank or building society'. (It is open to the Banking Ombudsman to apply the Code to a complaint brought before him by a business customer.)

NOTE: Apart from applying only to a private individual, the definition of a customer in the Code differs in two ways from the common law definition discussed in 1:2. First, it clearly requires that an account has been opened and appears to imply that the account should have existed for a period of time. In this respect it would seem a narrower definition than at common law. Second, it clearly covers a person who does not have an account but who uses other services provided by a bank. In this respect it is wider than the common law definition. The different approaches can probably best be explained in that the common law definition is designed to lay down a criterion for partially establishing when a bank should receive statutory protection, while the Code is designed to protect a specific category of consumers of banking services.

The governing principles of the Code are:
(*i*) To set out the standards of good banking practice that banks, building societies and card issuers will follow in their dealings with their customers.
(*ii*) That banks, building societies and card issuers will act fairly and reasonably in all their dealings with their customers.
(*iii*) That banks, building societies and card issuers will help customers to understand how their accounts operate and will seek to give them a good understanding of banking services.
(*iv*) To maintain confidence in the security and integrity of banking and card payment systems – banks, building societies and

card issuers recognise that their systems and technology need to be reliable to protect their customers and themselves.

You should read and become familiar with the Code and also with any publication of your own bank that explains the Code to customers.

NOTE: It is open to any bank to observe higher standards than those set out in the Code. For example, Lloyds Bank PLC have published that it will not reply to requests for bankers' references about its customers, although presumably it would if so instructed by a customer.

(b) *The role of the Code.* The Code of Banking Practice is not law, although in practice it will observed as though it had the force of law. Should a court cite part of the Code as accurately representing the law, however, that part will become incorporated in the common law. More generally, it will become the basis on which the courts will determine usual bank practice where this is the issue between the parties.

The Code will also gain legal enforceability (as opposed to being recognised as law) in so far as its provisions must surely become part of the customary rules of the industry and, therefore, be implied into the banker–customer contract.

The Code's most immediate importance is that it forms the basis on which the Banking Ombudsman will determine good practice in order to rule in disputes submitted to him. As a personal customer will probably prefer to take a dispute with a bank to the Banking Ombudsman – he can make a binding award of up to £100 000 against a bank subscribing to the Scheme – rather than bring it before the court, the Code is likely to be the basis on which disputes between banks and their private customers will be resolved. Given this, banks (and building societies) will probably regard complying with the Code to be of greater practical importance than always complying strictly with every aspect of the law, particularly where they feel it does not reflect the changes to practices brought about by technological change and commercial innovation. (*See* also 10:2 for a discussion of the Code in relation to cash and debit cards where the lack of directly relevant case law makes the Code particularly important.)

Progress test 1

1. State the three activities that determine status as a banker. **(1)**

2. Who is a customer of a bank? **(2)**

3. State two reasons why the definitions of banker and customer are of practical importance. **(3)**

4. How does the banker–customer relationship differ from other debtor–creditor relationships? **(4)**

5. What is meant by an implied term in a contract? **(5)**

6. Explain the importance of the *Tai Hing Case* (1985). **(5)**

7. In what ways is a bank restricted in the express terms it can include in its contract with its customers? **(5)**

8. In what ways does a bank act as an agent for its customer? **(6)**

9. Explain the circumstances in which a bank can be liable to its customer even though it pays a cheque strictly in accordance with its mandate. **(6)**

10. Who is a constructive trustee? **(7)**

11. In what two general ways can a bank incur liability as a constructive trustee? **(7)**

12. What is a 'Quistclose' trust? **(7)**

13. When does a bailment arise? **(8)**

14. Explain the basis of the 'special relationship' held to exist in *Lloyds Bank v Bundy* (1975). **(9)**

15. In what circumstances does the banker–customer relationship terminate by operation of law? **(10)**

16. State a bank's legal rights. **(11)**

17. Explain the decisions in *London Joint Stock Bank Ltd v Macmillan and Arthur* (1918) and *Greenwood v Martins Bank Ltd* (1932). **(11)**

18. State a bank's legal duties. **(12)**

19. List the four exceptions to the bank's common law duty of confidentiality established in *Tournier v National Provincial and Union Bank of England* (1924). **(13)**

20. Give two examples in each of the three categories of banks being compelled by law to provide information about their customers. **(13)**

21. To what sort of information does the Data Protection Act 1984 apply? **(14)**

22. State the first two data protection principles in the Act. **(14)**

23. What are the rights of a data subject under the Act? **(14)**

24. Compare the duty of confidentiality under the Data Protection Act 1984 with the *Tournier* duty. **(14)**

25. State the rules governing the appropriation of payments. **(15)**

26. State the Rules in *Clayton's Case* (1816). **(15)**

27. State six specific situations in which the *Rule* applies. **(15)**

28. State the situations in which the *Rule* does not apply. **(15)**

29. In the context of the *Rule*, explain the importance of *Deeley* v *Lloyds Bank Ltd* (1912); *Westminster Bank Ltd* v *Cond* (1940); and Re Hallett's Estate (1800). **(15)**

30. What is meant by the bank's right of combination? **(16)**

31. List the limits to this right. **(16)**

32. State the rules of statutory set-off following insolvency. **(16)**

33. Define a lien. **(17)**

34. In the context of a lien, what is the importance of *Brandao* v *Barnett* (1846)? **(17)**

35. List the restrictions on a bank's ability to exercise its lien. **(17)**

36. What is the basis of liability under the *Hedley Byrne* principle? **(18)**

37. Explain a bank's possible liability to its customer in the context of a bankers reference. **(18)**

38. Explain a bank's possible liability in connection with property held in safe custody. **(19)**

39. If a bank overcredits a customer's account, what conditions must the customer satisfy in order possibly to defeat the bank's claim for repayment? **(20)**

40. Explain the relevance of the Code of Banking Practice to the contract between banker and customer. **(21)**

2

Individual and joint accounts

Individuals' accounts

1. Opening the account

Before opening an account, a bank must be satisfied as to the identity and character of the applicant and know their employer's name and nature of the employment. This information has traditionally been obtained by either:

(a) *A personal introduction* from an existing customer or another branch or bank; or

(b) *Taking references*, usually two, one of which should be from the applicant's employer.

In the latter case, if the referee is unknown to the bank, the authenticity of the reference should be checked, for example, through the referee's own bank.

Taking references should avoid opening what may become an unsatisfactory account and usually secures the protection of the Cheques Act 1957 s.4 when the bank collects cheques for its customer. However, although banks may insist on references in higher risk situations, the trend has been for few references to be taken and fewer to be checked. Accounts are usually opened as a result of simply producing satisfactory identification, for example a driving licence or passport. Certainly identification is the single most important thing to check, plus either a satisfactory enquiry through a credit reference agency or satisfactory internal credit scoring. (This aspect of opening an account is discussed more fully in 9:**25**.)

2. Opening formalities

Banks differ as to the exact procedures and formalities involved in opening an account. However, the following are the standard opening formalities:

(a) Specimen *signatures* of all parties to the account must be obtained.

(b) A *mandate* covering all operations on the account must be obtained if it is other than a sole account.

(c) A *cheque book* should only be issued when a satisfactory introduction or references have been obtained and checked and any cheque opening the account cleared.

(d) A *cheque card* should only be issued after the bank has established that the account will apparently be run in a regular and responsible manner or where there is no doubt about the person's integrity and responsibility as an account holder.

(e) If possible, *commission and interest charges* should be agreed when the account is opened in order to avoid having to rely on a banker's implied right to recover reasonable charges and commission. Most banks do, in fact, have standard tariffs for charges and commission.

> NOTE: The Code of Banking Practice section 4.1 provides that banks (and building societies) will provide customers with details of the basis of charges, if any, payable in connection with the operation of their accounts. These will be in the form of published tariffs for basic account services and will be sent or given to customers when accounts are opened, at any time on request and before changes are made. The tariffs will also be available in branches.

3. Operating the account

(a) *Mandate.* The account must be operated strictly in accordance with the mandate. Failure to do so is a breach of the banker–customer contract and, if a bank wrongly dishonours a cheque, an action against the bank by the drawer for damaging their credit and, in extreme circumstances, for libel is possible: see Jayson v *Midland Bank Ltd* (1968), 9:**32**.

(b) *Operation of the account by an agent.* Agency is covered in Chapter 3, but note particularly 3:**4**, *Power of attorney*, and 3:**15–18**, Banking aspects of agency.

(c) *Termination of authority to pay cheques.* This is covered in outline in 1:**12** and in detail in 9:**29**.

(d) *Mental incapacity.* Mental incapacity is governed by the Mental Health Act 1983. If a person, at law, becomes mentally incompetent, a receiver will be appointed by the Court of Protection to look after the person's affairs.

Notice of its customer's incapacity terminates the bank's authority to pay cheques on the account and the mental incapacity itself terminates the banker–customer contract. When satisfied as to the receiver's authority, the bank must stop the patient's account entirely and open a new one in the name of the receiver. The receiver's authority to operate the account lasts until the death of the patient or their certified recovery.

An ordinary power of attorney is automatically revoked on the donor's mental incapacity, but an enduring power of attorney is not, although the attorney must register the power with the Court of Protection (*see* 3:**4**).

In the period between receiving reasonable notice of its customer's incapacity and a receiver being appointed or an enduring power being registered, a bank must ensure that withdrawals from the account are for necessities, e.g. household bills and food. Subrogation would enable the bank to debit the account with such payments. The account must not become overdrawn because interest payments are not 'necessaries' and therefore cannot be recovered.

(e) *Bankruptcy.*

   (i) *Bankruptcy petition.* When a bank receives *notice* of a bankruptcy petition, it must not pay cheques on the account. This is because payments and dispositions of property by the debtor in the period between the presentation of the petition and the making of the bankruptcy order are *void unless ratified by the court*: Insolvency Act 1986 s.284(1).

Payments into the account, however, may be accepted as long as the funds are not subsequently withdrawn. Payments into an overdrawn account are protected provided the bank acts in good faith and in ignorance of the petition (s.284(4)).

   (ii) *Bankruptcy order.* The *making* of the order vests title to the bankrupt's property in their trustee in bankruptcy and the bank is under a duty to deliver funds and securities held to the trustee: Insolvency Act 1986 s.323. No cheques must therefore be paid and any credit balance on an account must only be dealt with according to the trustee's instructions.

(f) *Death.* Reliable *notice* of its customer's death terminates the bank's authority to pay cheques on the account: Bills of Exchange Act 1882 s.75. The account will be stopped. The death itself terminates the banker–customer contrac, s.75 is a recognition of the practicalities involved in paying cheques.

The persons appointed to wind up and distribute the estate of the deceased are called *personal representatives*. If appointed by a will, they are known as *executors*; if appointed by the court, they are known as *administrators*, for example, where the deceased dies intestate (without leaving a will).

Before an executor can deal with the deceased's account and

securities, their appointment and authority must be confirmed by *probate*. This is a process under which the will is exhibited and proved in court, the original being deposited in the court registry and a copy, called the *probate copy*, made out under the court's seal and delivered to the executor, together with a certificate of it having been proved. *Letters of administration* is the official document from the court empowering the administrator to handle the deceased's estate.

The probate certificate or letters of administration must be presented to the bank and recorded before the balance on any credit account can be withdrawn. The same applies to securities and safe custody items deposited by the deceased. The personal representatives will be informed of the liability on any account and if securities are held for any borrowing, the personal representatives must decide whether to pay off the amount, and thereby obtain the release of the securities, or have them sold to realise and pay off the amount owed.

Any credits received after the death can be credited to the account or held in a suspense account until the personal representatives obtain authority to act, provided that the bank does not have notice that the payments have ceased to be due on the death. This would be the position, for example, with an annuity payable during life.

An *executor's account* can be opened immediately on the death of the testator (the person making the will), but often the account is not opened until the probate certificate is seen (*see* above). An *administrator's account* is not usually opened until letters of administration are produced. In either case, references should be sought if the individuals are unknown to the bank.

The *mandate* for the account will normally provide that any one representative can sign for and bind all in connection with estate affairs and that all admit *joint and several liability*. The latter gives a right to combine credit balances on the personal representative's personal accounts with a debit balance on the executor's / administrator's account. Any one representative can countermand a cheque drawn on the personal representative's account.

4. Accounts of sole traders

There are only two differences between the opening and operation of a sole trader's account and that of any other individual. First, the account will be a business account and subject to different charges. Second, a business name may be used and this will be regulated by the Business Names Act 1985 (see 4:3). There is no legal distinction drawn between the liabilities and assets of the individual and those of the business.

5. Closing an account

(a) *Account in credit*. A bank must give reasonable notice before closing it. What is 'reasonable' is a question of fact in the circumstances, but a business customer would almost certainly be entitled to a longer period than a private customer.

Example

In *Prosperity Ltd v Lloyds Bank Ltd* (1923), it was held that one month was insufficient notice for the company to make alternative banking arrangements.

The use of a cheque card poses a practical problem in relation to closing accounts as debits must be paid although the account may be closed.

(b) *Overdrawn account*. Because an overdraft is normally repayable on demand, a bank has no difficulty in closing an unsatisfactory *current account in debit* that has been operated beyond the agreed limit.

In the case of a *loan account*, there must be a breach of the loan agreement, e.g. failure to make repayments as prescribed, before the account can be closed. This is because the loan agreement will have been entered into for a fixed period – a loan is not repayable on demand.

Minors

6. **Contractual capacity**

At common law, a minor has limited contractual capacity. In particular:

(i) Only contracts for 'necessaries' and contracts of employment that are substantially for the minor's benefit are enforceable; and

(ii) Contracts of loan made with a minor are unenforceable, although, after reaching their majority (18), minors can *ratify* loans. A cheque, or other bill of exchange, is also unenforceable against a minor in any capacity – drawer, acceptor (of a bill of exchange) or endorser – but the cheque, or other bill, can be enforced against other parties to it (see 9:2).

The term 'necessaries' definitely includes food, clothing and lodging but other things can be necessaries in the particular circumstances, e.g. a motor bike or a car could be considered a necessary for a minor who has to travel a considerable distance to college or work and for whom public transport is unavailable. A bank account for a minor aged, say, 15-17 would almost certainly be considered a necessary although, providing the account was maintained in credit, the bank would only ever need to sue for its charges.

NOTE: A trading contract, no matter of what kind and no matter how commercially advantageous, is never binding on a minor.

7. Minors' bank accounts

(a) *Operating the account.* Up to the age of seven, a minor's credit account will normally be treated as a *trust* account, the parent(s) being the trustee. After that age, the minor is usually allowed to operate the account personally. If 'unusually' frequent or large withdrawals are made, a bank would probably inform the parent(s) although technically, at least, this would constitute a breach of the bank's duty of secrecy.

(b) *Overdrawn accounts.* A minor should generally not be permitted to overdraw an account or be granted a loan because the debt created is not enforceable against the minor, although the minor can ratify the debt on attaining majority. This remains so *even if* the advance was intended to be used to buy necessaries.

Should part or all of an advance be spent on necessaries, however, that sum can be recovered from the minor on the basis of *subrogation*, that is the bank assumes the rights of the supplier of the necessaries against the minor: *Liggett (Liverpool) Ltd v Barclays Bank Ltd* (1928). For the same reason, a cheque representing the loan drawn in payment for necessaries can be debited to the minor's account.

NOTE: Neither of these rights alters the fact that the loan itself is *unenforceable*, recovery from the minor being based on a different legal principle.

Furthermore, under the Minors' Contracts Act 1987 s.3, the court can order the minor to repay any money lent or hand over any property bought with it if the court considers it just and equitable to do so. The former is far less likely to be possible than the latter because the funds advanced are likely to have been mixed with other funds, for example in an account, and are therefore not identifiable.

(c) *Guaranteeing a loan or overdraft.* The Minors' Contracts Act 1987 s.2 provides that a guarantee of a loan to a minor is enforceable even though the loan itself is not.

Joint accounts

8. The mandate

The mandate, signed by all the parties to the account, must include the following:

(a) A clear indication as to *who can make withdrawals* from the account, for example 'either to sign' or 'all to sign'. Without express authority to act on the signature of one party only, all cheques and other orders must be signed by all parties to the account.

The mandate will further provide that this authority will operate even though the account may become overdrawn or an existing overdraft be increased as a result.

> NOTE: If two or more signatures are required on a cheque and the bank pays a cheque on which one of the required signatures is a forgery, it is unable to debit the account: *Catlin* v *Cyprus Finance Corporation (London) Ltd* (1983), *see* 9:**30**.

If a bank pays a cheque contrary to the mandate, for example on the signature of one account holder only or, as above, on a forged signature, but this cheque discharges a debt for which both or all account holders were liable, the principle of subrogation enables the bank to debit the account: *B Liggett Ltd* v *Barclays Bank* (1928).

(b) A clause authorising the bank to *countermand* payment of a cheque or other payment order on the instructions of *one* of the account holders.

(c) A clause specifying whether the making of an *advance on the account*, with or without security, requires the authority of one or all account holders.

(d) Admission of *joint and several liability* for any overdraft (*see* below).

(e) A clause authorising the bank to deliver any securities, deeds or safe custody items on the instructions of *one or all* of the parties. This avoids the possible problem with the tort of conversion.

(f) The mandate will expressly provide that payments from the account can be made notwithstanding the *death* of one of the signatories on the account. But for this express term in the contract, at common law the death would cancel the mandate. Incorporating this term enables the account to be continued. Cheques drawn by the deceased must be returned unpaid marked 'Drawer deceased', unless they are validly backed by cheque card or their payment is authorised by the surviving account holder(s).

(g) A *survivorship clause*, that is a statement that the bank can pay the entire balance on the account to the survivor(s) on the death of one of the joint account holders.

> NOTE: The doctrine of 'survivorship' means that the surviving joint owners inherit the joint property. But for joint and several liability being accepted in a joint account mandate, they would also be solely responsible for any joint debt.

While the doctrine of 'survivorship' would probably apply to most joint accounts in any case, particularly if the mandate authorises the bank to continue the account on the death of one of the parties, without a survivorship clause the bank would have to obtain instructions on how to deal with the deceased's share of the funds from the deceased's personal representative to be absolutely sure of not incurring liability. The deceased account holder may, for example, have held as trustee for a third party.

9. Points to note

(a) The bankruptcy or mental incapacity of any one party *cancels the mandate.*

In the case of *bankruptcy*, any balance on the account and any items held in safe custody must only be released on the joint authority of the remaining account holder(s) and the trustee in bankruptcy – there is nothing analogous to the right of survivorship as with the death of a joint account holder. In the case of *mental incapacity* the account must be run according to the instructions of the receiver and the remaining account holder(s).

If the account is overdrawn, the account must be stopped to prevent the *Rule* in *Clayton's Case* (1816) operating to the bank's detriment (*see* 1:**15** and below).

(b) If an *agent* is to sign on the account, all the parties must sign the authority for the agent to do so.

(c) If one party opens an account in the joint names of themselves and another *without the latter's authority*, the authority of both parties is still necessary to authorise a release of funds.

(d) Under the Consumer Credit Act 1974, all parties to a joint account must receive a separate copy of each statement unless they sign a dispensing notice authorising the bank to send one statement.

(e) If the bank receives, formally or informally, notice of a dispute between the parties, e.g. a matrimonial dispute, the mandate can be considered to be cancelled and all parties to the account must authorise future payments from the account. If the parties dispute ownership of the funds or safe custody items, the bank must *not* attempt to decide the dispute. Ultimately, the court may have to decide between them and the bank must act according to its instructions. In the interim, the bank must indicate that its refusal to hand over funds or property is because it is waiting for such instructions. This is known as 'interpleading' and safeguards the bank from an action for conversion by one or more of the account holders.

10. Joint and joint and several liability
The distinction between these two forms of liability is important to a bank and a bank will always insist on joint and several liability being admitted on all joint accounts as well as on the accounts of partnerships and trustees.

(a) *Joint liability* is shared liability for a debt or other obligation. It gives a creditor a single joint right of action against all those liable on the contract. This can be exercised by suing one debtor, a combination of them or all of them, if need be in successive actions. (Originally, joint liability gave only *one* right of action, i.e. once judgment was obtained, the joint right of action was exhausted — no subsequent actions could be brought against any joint debtor not sued in the original action.)
(b) *Joint and several liability* is shared *and* individual liability. It there- fore gives a right of action against the debtors severally (individually and separately), that is each debtor is individually liable for the whole debt, in addition to a combined joint right of action against all parties liable. (This individual liability always meant that separate actions could be brought against the debtors until the debt was cumulatively satisfied.)

Given that the original main distinction between the two forms of liability is now part of legal history, joint and several liability is today imposed for three reasons:

(i) Joint and several liability gives a right of combination (*see* 1:**16**) between private accounts in credit and an overdrawn joint ac- count when the mandate on the joint account is determined or as otherwise agreed. This is because each party is separately liable for the joint debts. The right also means that security given to the bank to secure individual borrowing can be relied on to secure borrowing on the joint account. No such rights of combination exists where only joint liability is accepted.

The reverse, however, does not apply. A joint account in credit *cannot* be combined with an overdrawn sole account of one of the joint account holders, nor does any security taken to secure borrowing on the joint account cover borrowing on any sole account.

(ii) The death of one joint account holder releases the deceased's estate from liability for debts on the account if liability is joint; this is not so with joint and several liability.

(iii) Joint and several liability enables a bank to claim for money owing on the joint account against the estate of a bankrupt joint account holder while retaining its rights against the solvent parties. This is probably not so where only joint liability is admitted.

NOTE: While joint and several liability strengthens a bank's position where a joint account holder dies or becomes bankrupt, the account must be stopped and a new account opened to prevent the *Rule* in *Clayton's Case* (1816) operating to the bank's detriment. This is because breaking the account preserves the liability of the deceased or bankrupt joint account holder for any debit balance as at the date of death or bankruptcy. If the account is not broken, payments into the account will, under the *Rule*, steadily reduce the amount for which the deceased's or bankrupt's estate is liable, although the debit balance may remain the same or increase due to payments out of the account. (The mandate may expressly exclude the operation of the *Rule*: *Westminster Bank Ltd* v *Cond* (1946), in which case such action is not legally necessary, although a bank will almost invariably still stop the account.)

Trustees

11. Introduction
A trust arises where title to property is vested in one person (the trustee) and that person is under an equitable obligation to use the property for the benefit of a third person or persons (the beneficiaries). The beneficiaries, who may include the trustee, 'own' the property in equity and any one of them may enforce the trustee's obligation.

12. Trust accounts

(a) *What qualifies as a trust account*? A trust account is any account that, to the bank's actual or constructive knowledge, is being operated by trustees or persons acting in some other fiduciary capacity. It is not necessarily opened as such.

Sometimes the account may be opened as 'Trustee of ...', in which case the bank has actual notice that it is a trust account, and sometimes as, say, 'A N Other, Squash Club Account' or as a 'client account' by a firm of solicitors, in which case the bank has constructive notice. Whether or not a bank has sufficient knowledge to amount to constructive notice is a question of fact in each case. Alternatively the trust account may arise by operation of law. For example, where personal representatives become trustees under a trust created by the deceased's will.

Frequently, however, a trust will be created by a trust deed and the bank will need to examine this deed to establish how the account is to be run. Where a power of attorney is involved, the bank will also need to examine this.

(b) *Account mandate.* A mandate signed by all the trustees must be obtained. As trustees cannot normally delegate their authority among themselves, all trustees are required to sign on an account unless the trust instrument or law permits delegation. The Trustee Act 1925, as amended by the Powers of Attorney Act 1971, for example, allows a trustee to delegate their duties by power of attorney for a period of up to one year.

(c) *The duty of good faith.* A very strict duty of good faith is imposed on trustees. If they, even innocently, misapply trust property, they commit a breach of trust for which they are liable to the beneficiaries. Furthermore, the law also allows an action against any person that has actual or constructive notice of the trust and facilitates any such breach, e.g. a bank allowing a trustee to withdraw money from the account for their own purposes or otherwise in breach of the trust. It is immaterial whether or not the bank benefits from the breach of trust.

Whether or not a bank is liable when a breach of trust occurs is always a question of fact in the circumstances. A bank must have known or should have known of the breach. Thus, mere suspicion or an accusation by a beneficiary of trust funds being misapplied would not, of itself, justify dishonouring a trust cheque but allowing a trustee to draw a cheque on the trust account to reduce a personal overdraft, particularly if the bank had been pressing for repayment, would almost certainly mean that the bank had knowledge of the breach of trust and facilitated it.

NOTE: The decision in *Lipkin Gorman* v *Karpnale Ltd* (1989) seems to indicate that liability in contract law covers all situations where liability as constructive trustee could arise. If so, possible liability as constructive trustee becomes a non-issue.

(d) *Borrowing.* Trustees have no implied power to borrow or charge trust property as security. Power to borrow must be expressly given by the trust deed, by the beneficiaries (provided they are all over 18 years old) or as provided by the Trustee Act 1925.

If borrowing does take place, the trustees must accept joint and several liability because this enables the bank to combine a credit balance on a trustee's personal account with a debit balance on the trust account.

(e) *Mental incapacity or death of a trustee.* If there is more than one trustee, the account can be operated by the others. If there is only one trustee, in the former case their receiver will continue the account in accordance with the trust deed, unless the deed provides for the situation; in the latter, the personal representatives may act. Alternatively they or, ultimately, the court can appoint new trustees, again providing the deed does not contain specific provision.

(f) The *bankruptcy* of a trustee does not automatically prevent a person continuing to act as a trustee.

Progress test 2

1. What is the main legal reason for taking references or otherwise checking the identity and suitability of a prospective customer? **(1)**

2. Explain one situation in which a bank could libel a customer if it breaks its customer's mandate from that customer. **(3)**

3. What is the difference between an ordinary power of attorney and an enduring power of attorney? **(3)**

4. What are the legal consequences of the bank becoming aware of its customer's mental incapacity? **(3)**

5. Explain the effect of the Insolvency Act 1986 s.284 on the operation of an individual's account. **(3)**

6. What consequences does the making of a bankruptcy order against a customer have for a bank? **(3)**

7. Under the Bills of Exchange Act 1882 s.75, is it the death of the customer or notice of it that terminates a bank's authority to pay the deceased's cheques? **(3)**

8. When is a personal representative termed an administrator and when is the representative termed an executor. **(3)**

9. Why can an overdrawn account be closed immediately but not a loan account? **(5)**

10. Is a loan to a minor, which is used to purchase a necessary, enforceable? (6)

11. Explain 'subrogation' in relation to loans to minors. (7)

12. What does the Minors' Contracts Act 1987 s.2 provide? (7)

13. If one of two required signatures on a cheque drawn on a joint account is forged, can the bank debit the account? Name a case that illustrates the answer. (8)

14. What is meant by a 'survivorship' clause? (8)

15. Explain the difference between joint and joint and several liability. (10)

16. Explain why a bank insists on joint account holders accepting joint and several liability on the account mandate. (10)

17. Is joint and several liability a protection against the operation of the *Rule* in *Clayton's Case* (1816)? (10)

18. What is meant by a bank's constructive knowledge of a trust account? (12)

19. Explain how a bank can be held liable as constructive trustee for a breach of trust by its customer. (12)

20. Do trustees have implied power to borrow on a trust account? (12)

3

Agency and banking

The nature and creation of agency

1. The nature of agency

An *agent* is a person who acts on another's behalf, the other person being known as their *principal*. The essence of the relationship created is that the agent can alter their principal's legal position in relation to third parties by making contracts on their behalf.

As an agent contracts on their principal's behalf, it follows that:

(a) The agent generally incurs neither rights nor liabilities on the contract that he made.

(b) Lack of full contractual capacity does not affect a person's ability to act as an agent, e.g. a minor may be employed as an agent. The principal, however, must have contractual capacity to make the particular contract entered into by the agent.

2. Types of agent

(a) *Universal.* A universal agent is one appointed to handle all their principal's affairs. Such an agent must be appointed by deed and the agency is a form of *general power of attorney* (*see* 3:**4**).

(b) *General and special agents.* The distinction between a general and special agent lies in the extent of their authority.

   (*i*) A *general* agent has authority to act in all business of a certain kind, e.g. a director is a general agent of a company, while a partner is a general agent of a partnership.

A third party will not be affected by any limitation on a general agent's authority unless they are aware of it. This is because a general agent has *implied authority* to act in the ordinary course of their trade, business or profession (*see* 3:**3**). (The terms *usual* authority and *customary* authority are also used to describe this type of authority.)

Example

In *Watteau* v *Fenwick* (1893), the manager of a public house was forbidden to order tobaccos by his principal but did so.

It was held that the principal was liable to pay the seller because a manager of a public house would usually have authority to make orders of this kind. The seller could therefore rely on the agent's implied authority in the absence of express knowledge of the limitation imposed by the principal.

(ii) A *special* agent is appointed to effect a particular transaction that is not part of their normal business activities. As a special agent's authority is limited to the particular transaction, the principal is only bound by authorised acts.

(c) *Factors.* A factor is a 'mercantile agent', i.e. an agent who buys and sells goods for a commission.

By the Factors Act 1889 s.1, a factor 'has in the customary course of his business as such agent authority either to sell goods, or to consign goods for the purpose of sale, or to buy goods, or to raise money on the security of goods'.

A bona fide purchaser of goods from a factor that were in the factors possession with the owner's consent will obtain good title to them, even where the factor did not have their principal's actual authority to sell them.

A factor has possession of their principal's goods and a *lien* over them for any unpaid commission.

(d) *Brokers.* A broker is also a mercantile agent. While a broker is primarily the agent of the seller, their role is essentially that of a middleman between the buyer and seller. A broker has authority to act for both parties.

Brokers differ from factors in that they:

(i) Do not have possession of the goods that they sell.

(ii) Cannot act in their own name; and

(iii) Have no lien over goods that come into their possession.

3.   Creation of agency

The relationship of principal and agent can be created in four ways.

(a) *By express appointment.* Here the agent has *actual* authority to act for their principal. This actual authority may be *express*, that is it is given verbally or in writing, or *implied*, that is that the authority is presumed to exist by virtue of the circumstances although nothing is stated.

Partners, directors and other general agents possess implied authority in the ordinary course of their business. A special agent has implied authority to do things that are necessary for the completion of the task. For example an agent employed to sell land has implied authority to sign a written contract of sale and the banker–customer relationship gives a bank implied authority to collect cheques on behalf of its customer: *Joachimson* v *Swiss Bank Corporation* (1921) (CA).

(b) *By ratification.* Agency by ratification occurs where the principal confirms and adopts a contract entered into on their behalf by a person who had no authority to make the contract. The person so acting is probably an agent who exceeds their authority, but it could be a complete stranger.

Ratification is most likely to arise in a bank's dealings with its customers where:

*(i)*It pays a company cheque on an unauthorised signature – the company can ratify the cheque.

(ii) Money is lent to a 'company' before it is incorporated – here the company cannot ratify and a bank would be unwilling to lend without adequate indemnity.

Ratification is only possible under the following circumstances.

(i) The principal is fully aware of the material facts at the time of ratification or intends to ratify regardless of them.

(ii) The principal ratifies the entire contract.

(iii) The agent discloses the agency and names or otherwise sufficiently identifies the principal at the time of the contract. (An undisclosed principal cannot ratify.)

Example

In *Keighley Maxstead* v *Durant & Co* (1901) (HL), an agent, without disclosing his principal or his agency, purchased wheat at an unauthorised price. His principal purported to ratify the purchase, but subsequently refused to accept delivery and was sued for the price by the seller.

It was held that the principal could not ratify and was not, therefore, liable for the price. At the time of the sale, the seller had intended to sell to the agent personally.

(iv) Unless a fixed time within which ratification can take place was agreed between the agent and the third party, it *must* take place within a reasonable time after the transaction.

(v) The principal had legal existence and contractual capacity, both when the contract was made and when they ratified it. Thus, a company after incorporation cannot ratify a contract made by its agent before incorporation. Before incorporation, a company has no legal existence.

NOTE: The Companies Act 1985 s.36 provides that the person acting for the company in such a contract is personally liable upon it, unless otherwise agreed.

The same situation arises when a person acts on behalf of a minor, a mentally incapacitated person or, indeed, an enemy alien. Note, however, that the Minors' Contracts Act 1987 enables a minor to voluntarily ratify a contract made on their behalf (or made by them personally) during their minority after they reach the age of 18.

(vi) The act is capable of ratification. Thus, a contract that is void *ab initio*, for example for illegality or mistake, *cannot* be ratified – it is a legal nullity. On the other hand, a contract that is merely voidable, e.g. for fraud or misrepresentation, can be ratified *before* the party entitled to rescind does so.

NOTE: Ratification operates retrospectively, i.e. it dates back to the time when the contract was made by the agent. Thus, if after discovering the agent's lack of authority the third party attempted to rescind the contract, a prior ratification would prevent the third party from doing so: *Bolton Partners* v *Lambert* (1889).

(c) *By estoppel.* Such agency results from the principal's words or conduct, not from an agreement between the agent and the principal. It occurs where the principal allows a person to appear to be their agent to third parties. If a third party relies on this appearance and deals with that person as the principal's agent, the principal is estopped (prevented) from denying that person's authority. Agency by estoppel is also referred to as *ostensible* authority.

Agency by estoppel requires three specific things.

(i) An unambiguous representation by the person who it is sought to hold liable as principal. Ostensible authority does not arise if the third party relies on the 'agent's' own assertion of authority: *Armagas Ltd* v *Mundogas SA, The Ocean Frost* (1986)(HL);

(ii) A reliance on the representation by the person to whom the representation was made.

(iii) An alteration of their position to their detriment by that person because of the reliance.

Example

In *Panorama Development (Guildford) Ltd* v *Fidelis Furnishing Fabrics Ltd* (1971), the defendant company's secretary had entered into car hire contracts on the company's behalf.

It was held that the company was bound by the contracts. While a company secretary is not an agent of their company, the defendant company had held their secretary out as having authority to act on its behalf in a wide range of administrative matters. They were, therefore, estopped from denying his authority to enter into these contracts.

Two situations where a bank could maintain agency has been created by estoppel are where:

(*i*) A customer's clerk is regularly sent to collect a sealed envelope containing the customer's bank statements and on one occasion examines the statements, the customer subsequently claiming that the bank has broken its duty of confidentiality.

(*ii*) A customer becomes aware that their signature is being forged on cheques but does not immediately inform the bank: *Greenwood* v *Martins Bank Ltd* (1933) (*see* 9:30).

NOTE: Directors have ostensible authority to bind their company unless the third party knows of their lack of authority. This results from the abolition of the *ultra vires* rule (*see* 5:9).

(d) *By operation of law.* Such agency is the product of the law and arises neither from agreement nor from conduct. There are two types.

(*i*) *Agency of necessity.* This arises where the agent acts in excess of their authority in an emergency to save the principal's property. The classic example is that of a master of a ship acting to save the cargo or ship.

The person claiming agency of necessity must show:

(1) That it was impossible to obtain the principal's instructions: *Springer* v *G.W Railway* (1921);

(2) That there was a real commercial necessity for the action, e.g. perishable goods were endangered: *Prager* v *Blatspiel Stamp & Heacock Ltd* (1924);

(3) That the actions were taken in good faith and in the principal's interests.

(*ii*) *Agency from cohabitation.* A wife (or mistress) living with her husband is entitled to pledge his credit for necessaries (food, clothing and so on) that fall within her domestic responsibilities in the relationship.

NOTE: Both examples of agency created by operation of law are, perhaps, of historical rather than contemporary interest as neither are likely to be encountered today.

4. Power of attorney

(a) *Ordinary power of attorney.* A power of attorney must be given *by* *deed* and in the form prescribed by the Powers of Attorney Act 1971. If it is executed by someone other than the donor, for example, where a person of sound mind is, say, physically incapable of signing, the execution must be witnessed and attested by two witnesses. The Act provides that a photocopy of a power of attorney, certified by the donor or by a solicitor or stockbroker, and any copy of a photocopy likewise certified, is sufficient proof of the existence and contents of the power.

Power of attorney is necessary if an agent is to *execute deeds* (authority to do so must be given by deed) but it is also used for more general purposes, such as where a person is going abroad for a prolonged period.

The power may be *specific* (for a particular purpose) or *general* under s.10 of the 1971 Act. A bank can assume that a general power of attorney gives the attorney (the agent) the widest possible powers.

An ordinary power of attorney can be revoked by:

(i) The donor, without the consent of the attorney.

(ii) Automatically by the death, mental incapacity, bankruptcy or liquidation (in the case of a company) of the donor.

(iii) Automatically by the mental incapacity of the attorney.

(iv) By the attorney's renunciation.

It will also terminate at the end of the period for which it was given or when the objective expressed in the power has been achieved.

A power of attorney is irrevocable where it is expressed to be so and is given to secure either a *proprietary interest* of the attorney or the performance of an obligation owed to the attorney. It remains irrevocable for as long as the interest or obligation exists: Powers of Attorney Act 1971 s.4.

Example

A bank's equitable mortgage forms may give it an irrevocable power of attorney to transfer title to mortgaged property on the mortgagor's behalf, thereby enabling the bank to realise the security more easily if repayment of the advance is not made. The equitable mortgage gives the bank the necessary proprietary interest in the land.

(b) *Enduring power of attorney.* Under the Enduring Powers of Attorney Act 1985, a power of attorney can be created that is *not* automatically revoked when the donor becomes mentally incapable of looking after their affairs, indeed, it is intended to avoid the problems that this would create.

The power must be drafted precisely in accordance with the Act, executed by the donor (when mentally capable) and donee and witnessed.

Until the donor becomes mentally incapable, the enduring power operates as an ordinary power of attorney *except* that the attorney cannot renounce their agency without giving prior written notice to the donor.

When the donor becomes incapable of looking after their affairs, the attorney's powers are suspended and the attorney must register the power with the Court of Protection to regain them. Once the application is made, the attorney has limited powers to maintain the donor and, if necessary, themselves – the attorney may be the donor's spouse, for example. Payment of necessary bills would be an example of this limited power. Once the enduring power is registered by the Court, the attorney regains the original powers stated in the deed and they cannot be revoked later by the donor, even if the latter regains mental capability. An attorney wishing to renounce their power must give notice to the Court.

(c) *Banking considerations.* A bank must examine a power of attorney carefully to ascertain its exact nature and extent. It is usual for the donor's bank account to be specifically mentioned in a general power and authority given to the attorney to operate the account. However, specific clauses must be included if the attorney is to borrow money, charge the donor's property as security and withdraw safe custody items as a general power to operate a bank account does not usually include authority to do these things.

More generally, a bank must also ensure that:

(i) The attorney's identity is verified.

(ii) The power is still in force.

(iii) It is properly executed as a deed; and

(iv) The power is operated strictly according to its terms.

NOTE: Under the Law of Property (Miscellaneous Provisions) Act 1989, a deed must be executed as a deed, signed and witnessed.

The principal and agent relationship

5. Duties of the agent

(a) *Obediency.* An agent must obey the principal's lawful instructions.

(b) *Care and skill.* A paid agent is expected to exercise professional competence. An unpaid agent's actions are judged against the skill actually possessed.

NOTE: A gratuitous (unpaid) agent is liable to the principal only for *misfeasance* and not for *non-feasance*, that is the agent may be sued for negligence committed in the course of their agency, but they cannot be sued if they fail to perform their agency at all. No contract exists between a gratuitous agent and the principal on which to base an action for non-feasance.

(c) *Personal performance.* An agent must personally perform the task, the agent may not delegate it (*delegatus non potest delegare* – a delegate cannot delegate): *McCann* v *Pow* (1974). There are exceptions.

(i) Where the agent is expressly authorised to delegate: *De Bussche* v *Alt* (1878).

(ii) Where the agent has implied authority to do so in the circumstances, e.g. where a customer asks a bank to sell shares on their behalf, the bank has implied authority to employ a stockbroker to do so.

(iii) Where the task delegated does not require the exercise of skill and judgment, e.g. signing documents or sending notices.

Example

In *Allam & Co* v *Europa Poster Services* (1968), it was held that an agent who was told to revoke certain licences could delegate to their solicitor the task of actually sending the notices of revocation.

(iv) Where an unforeseen situation makes delegation necessary.

NOTE: Where delegation is allowed, the agent is liable to the principal for the sub-agent's acts.

(d) *Good faith.* An agent must not allow their own interests to conflict with those of their principal. This fiduciary duty applies whether or not the agent receives payment.

In particular, an agent must not disclose or misuse *confidential information* that is acquired in the course of the agency, nor must the agent make a *secret profit* over and above the agreed commission. If a secret profit is made and discovered, it may be claimed by the principal and the agent loses the right to commission.

Example

In *Turnbull* v *Garden* (1869), an agent was employed without payment to purchase clothes for his principal's son. He was allowed a trade discount on the transaction by the seller, but sought to charge his principal the full price.

It was held that he had to account to his principal for the discount that he had received.

Where a bank arranges to buy or sell shares for its customer, the contract note issued by the broker will state that the commission is shared between the broker and the bank, thereby avoiding any possibility of the customer claiming that the bank made a secret profit on the transaction.

The duty of good faith is very strict.

Example

In *Boardman* v *Phipps* (1967) (HL), a solicitor while acting as agent, acquired information relating to the value of certain shares. Acting in good faith, he used this information for his own benefit after the principal had declined to use it for his.

It was held that the agent was accountable to his principal for the profit made because the information that he had acquired and used for his own benefit belonged to his principal.

If an agent *takes a bribe*, the principal is entitled to the inducement or to damages against either the agent or the third party. The principal may summarily dismiss the agent. Both parties to the bribe are liable to prosecution.

(e) *To act for one principal.* An agent must avoid a conflict of interest between two principals and therefore an agent cannot become the agent of a second principal without the leave of the first: *North and South Trust Co* v *Berkeley* (1971). A solicitor, for example, will refuse to act for two clients whose interests conflict.

This presents a particular problem to banks because they frequently act in different capacities for different principals in relation to the same subject matter, e.g. advising a customer about investing in a company that itself is the bank's customer and about which the bank may have commercially sensitive information that would influence the investment decision. The problem is only partially solved by erecting administrative 'Chinese walls' between departments. In practice, the solution may be reliance on the integrity of the profession rather than elaborate procedures to avoid the conflict and/or to make customers fully aware of the (often complicated) relationships involved.

(f) *To account.* An agent must pay over to the principal all sums received on the principal's behalf.

6. Rights of the agent

(a) *Indemnity.* An agent is entitled to compensation from the principal for any loss or expense incurred by them in the performance of their agency: *Adamson* v *Jarvis* (1827).

An agent loses this right where they act negligently, in breach of duty or unlawfully.

NOTE: This right is available to a bank that incurs liability when it collects a cheque to which its customer had no title.

(b) *Remuneration.* The principal must pay the agent the agreed commission provided:

(i) The event has happened on which payment was made conditional.

(ii) The agent was the effective cause of that happening.

NOTE: No term will be *implied* in a contract of agency to restrain the principal from preventing the agent earning commission, e.g. by deciding not to proceed with a sale or purchase: *Luxor (Eastbourne) Ltd* v *Cooper* (1941) (HL).

(c) *Lien.* An agent has a lien on the principal's goods in their possession for commission owing.

The lien is lost when payment is made or offered by the principal, or where the agent gives up possession of the goods.

NOTE: Generally an agent's lien is a *particular* lien, i.e. it is limited to monies owed on the transaction under which the possession of the goods arose. Some agents, however, have a more extensive *general* lien arising from trade usage. This latter type of lien covers all monies owed by the principal to the agent and is not limited to monies owed on a particular transaction. Banks, factors and solicitors are entitled to general liens.

Relations with third parties

7.   Introduction
As an agent acts on behalf of a principal, an agent generally drops out of the transaction once they have made the contract. Privity of contract exists between the principal and the third party.

However, the exact legal position depends upon whether or not the agent disclosed their agency and/or the name of their principal.

8.   The agent discloses the agency and the principal
The contract made is the principal's contract, not that of the agent. Thus, the agent drops out immediately and generally incurs neither rights nor liabilities under the contract. To this there are a number of exceptions:

(a) Where the agent agrees to accept personal liability.

(b) Where the agent signs a deed the agent is personally liable on it.

The principal incurs no liability unless the agent was appointed by deed. Where this is so, the agent drops out and the principal alone is liable.

(c) Where the agent signs a bill of exchange in their own name without indicating that they are signing on behalf of the principal: Bills of Exchange Act 1882 s.26(1). It is insufficient for an agent to merely describe themselves as such, the agent must clearly indicate that they sign on behalf of a specified person, e.g. by using the words 'for and on behalf of X' or 'per pro X'. (*See* however, *Bondina Ltd v Rollaway Shower Blinds Ltd* (1986) in relation to company cheques.)

(d) Where trade custom makes the agent personally liable.

(e) Where the agent is, in fact, the principal, e.g. where the contracting party describes themselves as an agent but in truth makes the contract for themselves: *Schmalz v Avery* (1851). Alternatively, there may be no other person who can be responsible as principal, e.g. where the agent acts for a company that has yet to be incorporated: Companies Act 1985 s.36.

9. The agent discloses their agency but not their principal

Subject to the exceptions in **8** above, the agent drops out in the normal way and does not incur personal liability under the contract.

10. The agent does not disclose their agency

This is usually referred to as the *doctrine of the undisclosed principal*. The agent appears to be acting personally when entering into the contract. The agent discloses neither the identity nor the existence of their principal.

The third party may, consequently, enforce the contract against the agent. Alternatively, it may be enforced against the principal after discovering the principal's existence and identity. The third party may not, however, enforce it against both; an unequivocal election must be made.

Commencing proceedings against one of them is only prima-facie evidence of such an election, it is not conclusive: *Clarkson Booker v Andjel* (1964). Obtaining judgment against either principal or agent even if it is unsatisfied is, however, conclusive evidence of an election and bars subsequent action against the other.

Unless the agent acted without authority (an undisclosed principal cannot ratify) or the principal's identity is a material factor in the contract, the principal can enforce the contract against the third party.

Example

In *Said* v *Butt* (1920), the principal wished to buy a first-night ticket for a play, but the theatre's Managing Director, with whom he was on bad terms, would not sell him one. A friend therefore bought one for him, but he was refused admission on the night. In the ensuing action, his claim against the theatre failed. His identity was important to the theatre and he could not, therefore, enforce a contract made indirectly on his behalf when he would not have been able to make the contract directly.

The relevance of the principal's identity could arise in relation to a loan obtained by an agent that was apparently for their own use but was, in reality, for the use of their principal when the principal's own application for funds had been refused. Applying *Said* v *Butt* it would seem that the bank would not be bound to honour the loan agreement if it discovers that the funds were for the principal's use.

11. Breach of warranty of authority

By purporting to act as an agent, a person warrants, by implication, that they have the principal's authority to act. Lack of authority results in liability to the third party for any loss caused. However, the agent's liability is *not* under the contract made but for the breach of warranty of authority: *Collen* v *Wright* (1856).

The agent is still liable for exceeding their authority while acting in good faith, e.g. in ignorance that the authority has been terminated by the death or insanity of the principal or through the fraud of a third party.

Example

In *Starkey* v *Bank of England* (1903) (CA), a stockbroker, relying on a forged power of attorney that the stockbroker believed to be genuine, instructed the bank to transfer stock. This it did and the proceeds of the sale were applied by the forger of the power of attorney to his own use. The bank was obliged to transfer a like amount of stock to the true owner and its claim to be indemnified by the stockbroker succeeded because the stockbroker had given an implied warranty that he had authority to order the transfer.

The agent does not incur liability for exceeding the authority when acting in good faith following *ambiguous* instructions from the principal or where the third party is *aware* that the agent is exceeding the authority.

NOTE: If the agent *knows* that they lack authority to make the contract, the third party may bring an action against the agent for the *tort of deceit* for any loss caused.

12. Liability for an agent's torts

A principal is jointly and severally liable with the agent for any fraud or other tort committed by the agent in the course of the agency, provided the act was within the scope of the agent's authority.

This is so whether the agent acted for the principal's benefit or their own.

Example

In *Lloyd* v *Grace, Smith & Co* (1912) (HL), S, the managing clerk of the defendant solicitors, fraudulently induced a client to sign deeds transferring title to certain properties to him. S then mortgaged the properties and absconded with the money obtained.

It was held that his principals were liable because S was acting within the scope of his authority and it made no difference that he was intending to benefit himself and not his principals.

Termination of agency

13. By act of the parties

Agency can be terminated by:

(a) Mutual agreement.
(b) Revocation by the principal; or
(c) Renunciation by the agent.

If unjustified, however, revocation of renunciation will amount to a breach of contract.

To avoid the possible operation of estoppel, the principal should notify any revocation to persons who have previously dealt with the agent.

In certain circumstances agency is *irrevocable* (*see* generally 3:4).

14. By operation of law

Agency is automatically terminated in the following circumstances.

(a) By completion of the contract.
(b) By frustration of the contract, e.g. where the contract subsequently becomes impossible to perform or illegal.
(c) By the death or mental disorder of the principal or agent.
(d) By the bankruptcy or liquidation of the principal.

NOTE: The bankruptcy of the agent does not terminate the agency nor give the principal the right to revoke the agent's authority, unless the insolvency affects the agent's fitness or ability so to act.

(e) At the end of a specified period of time, where the agency was created to last for that period.

Banking aspects of agency

15. Agency and banking

For two reasons *agency* is a branch of commercial law particularly relevant to banking.

(a) A bank will often have to deal with people who are agents, e.g. directors of a company, partners in a firm and occasionally a person who has power of attorney. Thus, it is important for a banker to ascertain and understand the scope and extent of an agent's authority before dealing with them.

(b) An important aspect of the banker–customer relationship is a bank's role as its customer's agent in collecting cheques paid in by its customer for the credit of their account. In addition, a bank may act as an agent in dealing with securities on its customer's behalf and in connection with the numerous other services that a bank can provide or arrange.

16. The operation of an account by an agent

Where an agent is to operate an account for their principal or have authority to sign on it, a bank will normally insist upon a *written mandate* from its customer.

The agent is a *special agent* and the bank must ensure that this person does not exceed the authority. For example, an authority for an agent to draw cheques does not imply authority to negotiate new overdraft facilities or to give or withdraw security.

If there are two or more parties to the account, all must authorise the delegation. For example, where A and B operate a joint account, both must authorise C to sign cheques in place of B.

The agent must sign on the account in a way that avoids personal liability, e.g. by using the phrases 'per pro' or 'for and on behalf of' followed by the signature (*see* 3:8).

17. Borrowing by an agent

If an agent borrows money from a bank without authority, the debt cannot be enforced against the principal unless the principal (1) ratifies the loan or is (2) estopped from denying the agent's lack of authority.

NOTE: Unauthorised borrowing by an agent was previously a problem in relation to directors exceeding their authority under a company's Articles of Association. This problem was almost entirely removed by the abolition of the *ultra vires* doctrine by the Companies Act 1989 (*see* 5:9).

Should the principal not ratify the loan nor be estopped from denying the agent's authority, the bank has two possible remedies.

(a) Against the agent for *breach of warranty of authority*, although this assumes that the agent has the funds to pay.

(b) *Subrogation* – if the money is used to pay the principal's lawful existing debts, the bank is subrogated to (assumes the rights of) the creditor(s) repaid to the extent of the debt(s) paid off and may therefore sue for that amount.

18. Agency and cheques
A bank acts as an agent when it collects cheques for its customers. As such, it must ensure that it follows accepted banking practice when doing so (*see* 9:22).

Whenever an agent handles cheques for their principal, the possibility arises that the agent may be exceeding their authority. For example, the agent may, without authority, draw cheques on the principal's account payable to themselves or endorse cheques payable to their principal and pay them into their own account. Thus, a bank must always ensure that it does not lose its statutory protection under the Cheques Act 1957 s.4 when it collects cheques for known agents (*see* 9:24).

If a bank debits the principal's account with a cheque wrongly drawn by the agent but the cheque is used to pay the lawful existing debts of the principal, the bank is subrogated to the position of the creditor paid and can resist a claim to recredit the account to the extent that the debt is paid off: *Liggett (Liverpool) Ltd* v *Barclays Bank Ltd* (1928).

Progress test 3

1. Define an agent. What is the essential feature of the principal–agent relationship? **(1)**

2. Distinguish between general and special agents, and between factors and brokers. **(2)**

3. Explain the difference between actual and ostensible authority. **(3)**

4. What requirements must be fulfilled for agency to arise through ratification? (**3**)

5. Can a minor ratify an unauthorised act done on their behalf? (**3**)

6. What requirements must be met for agency by estoppel to arise? (**3**)

7. Give an example of ostensible authority relevant to banking. (**3**)

8. In what circumstances will a power of attorney be revoked? (**4**)

9. When is a power of attorney irrevocable? How does a bank make use of such a power? (**4**)

10. Explain how an enduring power of attorney differs from an ordinary power of attorney. (**4**)

11. List the duties of an agent. (**5**)

12. In what circumstances can an agent appoint a sub-agent? (**5**)

13. List the rights of an agent. (**6**)

14. List the circumstances where an agent incurs personal liability when they disclose both their agency and the principal's identity to the third party. (**8**)

15. Explain the position of a third party with whom an agent contracts on behalf of an undisclosed principal. (**10**)

16. In what circumstances might the decision in *Said* v *Butt* be relevant to banking? (**10**)

17. What is meant by breach of 'warranty of authority'? (**11**)

18. List the circumstances in which agency will be terminated by operation of law. (**14**)

19. What must an agent do to avoid personal liability on a cheque that they draw for the principal? (**16**)

20. Explain the possible value of subrogation where an agent borrows money from a bank without the principal's authority. (**17**)

4

Partnerships

The nature and formation of a partnership

1. Definition
'Partnership is the relation which subsists between persons carrying on a business in common with a view of profit.' Partnership Act 1890 s.1.

'Carrying on a business' includes any occupation or profession, not just commercial trading and a partnership exists from the very first common transaction, a course of common activity is not essential. The objective of 'profit' is essential for an association to be a partnership.

A partnership is, at law, a very different form of business organisation to that of a registered company. A registered company has a separate legal identity, a partnership *does not*. Thus, among other things, insolvency and tax law treats partnerships differently to the way it treats companies.

2. Possible tests for establishing a partnership
The Partnership Act 1890 does not lay down a specific test for establishing whether or not an organisation is a partnership. In particular, s.2 states that the following circumstances do not in themselves create a partnership between two or more persons.

(a) *Co-ownership of property*. This is so whether or not the co-owners share any profit derived from the use of the property.
(b) *Sharing gross returns*. This is so even if it is coupled with co-ownership of the property producing the return.
(c) *Sharing profits*. This is, however, prima-facie evidence of a partnership, but the facts may prove otherwise.

In particular, a person receiving a share of the profits is not a partner where the share is received:
(i) In repayment of a debt.
(ii) As payment by an employee or agent of the business.
(iii) As an annuity by a widow or child of a deceased partner.

(iv) As payment of interest (varying with profits) on money lent to the firm for business purposes.

(v) As payment for the goodwill of the business.

(d) *Sharing profits and losses.* Where two or more persons share both the profits and losses from the business, the evidence for the existence of a partnership is much stronger but still not conclusive. Ultimately it is a question of fact in each case.

Example
_____

In *Keith Spicer Ltd* v *Mansell* (1970) (CA), the formation of a company was planned. In preparation for this, goods were ordered, a bank account opened and a number of other acts undertaken. One of the two persons involved was made bankrupt and the other was sued on an outstanding contract on the grounds that before incorporation the two persons involved were trading in partnership.

It was held that the acts performed were not sufficient to establish a partnership, particularly as the objective was the formation of a company. Consequently, the solvent party was not liable for the bankrupt's business debts.

_____

3. Formation of a partnership

(a) *By contract.* A partnership is the result of an express or implied agreement. While the 1890 Act does not require the contract to be in a specific form, written *Articles of Partnership* or a *Deed of Partnership* are often drawn up as they enable the members to lay down rules relating to the firm's management, the sharing of the profits and losses and other rights and duties among them (*see* **4:10**). However, a partnership can be formed, at law, by the most informal of agreements and even simply by implication. All that is required is that the actual relationship satisfies s.1 of the 1890 Act.

If Articles of Partnership or other written agreement exist, these will govern the relationship between the parties. Where they do not, the Partnership Act 1890 applies and will regulate rights of management in the firm and the sharing of profits and losses and so on. With regard to a partnership's relationship with its bank, the mandate will expressly determine the position and take precedence over anything that might be stated in the Articles or the provisions of the Act, such as rights of partners to borrow on behalf of the firm and the partners' liability for the debts of the firm (joint and several and not joint).

(b) *Capacity.*

(i) Minors. A minor can enter into a partnership contract but can avoid it before reaching the age of 18 (majority) or within a

reasonable time thereafter. Thus, before repudiating the contract, the minor must share losses as well as profits and the minor's *capital contribution* is available to pay the debts of the firm. However, as they would not be for necessaries, a minor is not personally liable on the firm's contracts, even if the minor made the contract on behalf of the firm.

The debts of the firm incurred during a partner's minority are unenforceable against the minor, although the minor can ratify them after reaching majority.

(ii) Limited companies. A company can be a member of a partnership but the liability of its shareholders for the firm's debts is limited to the value of their share in the company.

(iii) Foreign nationals. EC law prohibits discrimination on the grounds of nationality and gives a national of any EC country the right to establish or join a partnership on the same terms and conditions as a British subject.

(iv) Mental patients. While rather unlikely to be encountered in practice, a mental patient can become a partner in a firm but can avoid the contract if they can show that they did not understand its nature and consequences of membership when they entered into it and that the other party was aware of this. More significantly, on the mental disorder of a partner, the court may order the firm's dissolution following an application by the 'patient' or other partner (*see* **4:14**).

(c) *Maximum numbers.* The Companies Act 1985 limits the number of partners in a firm to a maximum of 20 but allows certain professional partnerships, such as solicitors, to exceed 20 members.

NOTE: The Sex Discrimination Act 1986 makes it unlawful for any partnership to fail to offer membership to a person on the grounds of sex or to offer membership on different terms to other partners. The Race Relations Act 1976 forbids similar discrimination on the grounds of race in firms of six or more members.

(d) *The firm name.*

(i) Definition. The firm name is a partnership's *business name*. By the Business Names Act 1985 s.1, a business name is any name that does not consist solely of the surnames or corporate names of all the partners. The use of forenames and initials in addition is permitted, as is an indication that the present owners have succeeded to the business.

NOTE: The Act applies equally to sole traders and to registered companies.

Use of a business name confers no separate legal identity on a firm, but it may sue and be sued in this name and judgment made be exercised against the private property of both named and unnamed partners. This avoids having to take subsequent actions against previously unknown partners if the original judgment remains unsatisfied.

(ii) Disclosure of information. The *purpose* of the Business Names Act 1985 is to enable a person intending to do business with a partnership to discover who owns it where this is not made clear by the name it uses.

Section 4 requires any partnership using a business name to state legibly on all its business letters, written orders, invoices and receipts and written demands for payment the *names* of all its members. An *address* must be given at which documents relating to the business can be served and accepted.

In addition, the name and address of each partner must be displayed prominently in all premises where business is carried on and to which customers or suppliers have access.

An *exception* is made in the case of firms of more than 20 partners. Here the names can be all included *or* all omitted in these documents. If the latter option is chosen, the documents must give the address of the principal place of business and state that a full list of all the partners' names and addresses may be inspected there during normal business hours.

(iii) Compliance. Failure to comply with the Act is a criminal offence under s.7. It may also, at the court's discretion, prevent the partnership enforcing its contracts where the other party to the contract can show that failure to comply with the Act has caused them financial loss or prevented them pursuing an action against the partnership: s.5.

(e) *Illegality.* An association is illegal if:

(i) Its objects are illegal.

(ii) Its membership exceeds the statutory maximum numbers; or

(iii) It is an association forbidden by law, such as a professional partnership between a solicitor and an unqualified person.

The effects of illegality are that (1) rights and obligations among the partners are unenforceable; (2) contracts cannot be enforced against innocent third parties and; (3) the partners cannot raise the illegality of their association as a defence in any action brought against them by an innocent outsider.

4. Types of partners
There are five types.

(a) *A general partner.* A partner who takes an active part in the firm's management. A general partner is fully liable for the firm's debts.

(b) *A sleeping, or, dormant partner.* One who takes no part in the firm's management but who nevertheless contributes capital and shares profits and losses in the same way as a general partner.

(c) *A nominal partner.* A nominal partner is not actually a member of the firm but someone who has represented themselves or has knowingly allowed themselves to be represented as a partner. This is referred to as *holding out*. Under s.14(1) of the Partnership Act 1890, the person is liable as a partner to anyone who has, on the faith of any such representation, given credit to the firm. Liability is based on estoppel and extends only to persons who relied on the representation; no liability is incurred for other debts.

The most usual example of the operation of s.14(1) is where a partner who has retired from a firm fails to take reasonable steps to ensure that their name is removed from the firm's business stationery and notices as required by the Business Names Act 1985 (*see* **4:8**).

As a nominal partner is not a member of the firm, they obviously cannot take part in the firm's management or share in its profits.

(d) *A limited partner.* This type of partner is one whose liability for the firm's debts is limited to the amount of their capital contribution. Such a partner shares in the firm's profits but cannot participate in its management, is not an agent of the firm and their death, bankruptcy or mental disorder does not dissolve the firm.

A limited partner must be a member of a *limited partnership*, formed under the Limited Partnership Act 1907. Such a partnership is one that has one or more *general* partners, who assume personal liability for the firm's debts and manage the firm, and one or more *limited* partners, with liability limited as above. A limited partnership must be registered with the Registrar of Companies.

Limited partnerships are uncommon as corporate status as a private, limited company is usually a more attractive alternative where those concerned want limited liability.

(e) *A salaried partner.* Many large professional firms have a number of 'partners' who receive a predetermined and fixed salary instead of a share of the profits. The Act does not cover such members. They are perhaps best treated as a modern example of *holding out* under s.14. As such they are probably liable for the firm's debts. They enjoy whatever management rights the terms of their employment give them.

Relationships between partners and outsiders

5.   Partners as agents

Agency is the foundation of partnership law relating to a firm's dealings with outsiders.

Under the Partnership Act 1890 s.5, each partner is an agent of the firm and the other partners and has authority to bind the firm and the other partners when acting in the usual course of the firm's business, unless the third party either knew they had no authority (s. 8) or knew or believed that they were not a member of the firm. This is an example of *apparent,* or *ostensible, authority.* It follows that a person dealing with a partnership is not affected by any undisclosed limit on a particular partner's authority contained in the partnership agreement.

Examples
_____

In *Mercantile Credit Ltd* v *Garrod* (1962), A and B had entered into partnership to let garages and to repair motor cars. The partnership deed expressly excluded the buying and selling of cars. A, without B's knowledge, 'sold' a car, to which he had no title, to the plaintiff. The proceeds were paid into the partnership bank account.

It was held that B was accountable for the proceeds as the buying and selling of cars *appeared* to be within the firm's normal course of business. The limitation in the partnership deed was no defence.

In *Higgins* v *Beauchamp* (1914), however, it was held that it was not within the usual course of a firm's business for a partner to accept a 'bill of exchange' that lacked the drawer's name.

_____

6.   A partner's implied authority

Under the Partnership Act 1890 s.5, as applied by the courts, i.e. the Act is not specific, a partner in any type of partnership has implied authority to bind the firm by:

(a) *Buying and selling* goods in the course of the firm's business.

(b) *Receiving payment* of debts due to the firm and *giving receipts* for such payment.

(c) *Engaging* employees for the firm.

(d) *Drawing* cheques.

In a *trading partnership* (one whose business consists mainly of buying and selling) a partner's implied authority also includes:

(a) *Borrowing money* on the firm's credit (regardless of any applicable limitation of authority agreed among the partners unless the lender is aware of the limitation), this includes creating an overdraft on the firm's bank account.

(b) *Pledging* the firm's goods or *giving an equitable mortgage* over the firm's premises by deposit of title deeds or land certificate to secure such borrowing.
(c) *Signing of bills of exchange* on behalf of the firm.

No partner has implied authority to:

(a) Execute deeds on the firm's behalf – authority to execute a deed must be given by deed.
(b) Give a guarantee in the firm name. (Limitations (a) and (b) are both relevant to banking.)
(c) Submit disputes involving the firm to arbitration.
(d) Compromise a debt, e.g. by accepting a payment of 80p in the £1 in full satisfaction, or accept payment of the firm's debts in anything other than money, e.g. shares.
(e) Convey title to land or enter into a contract for the sale or purchase of land.

A partner who exceeds their authority is personally liable to an outsider for any loss caused to them by the breach of warranty of authority (*see* **2:11**).

NOTE: The implied authority of partners is of limited relevance to a bank because it will ensure that the authority of partners to draw cheques, charge partnership property as security and give guarantees is all covered by express written authority. This express written authority also prevents a bank relying on whatever apparent or ostensible authority the partners might otherwise have had (*see* **4:5**).

7. Liability of partners

All partners are *jointly liable* for the debts and other contractual obligations of the firm: Partnership Act 1890 s.9. Liability for wrongful acts (torts) by partners authorised by the firm or committed in the ordinary course of its business is *joint and several*: s.12. At common law, a firm is liable for the tortious acts of its employees committed within the scope of their employment. (Joint liability and joint and several liability is discussed generally at **2:10** and specifically in relation to partnership accounts at **4:18**).

8. Changes in membership

(a) *Retiring and incoming partners.*
   (i) *Existing debts and novation.* An *incoming partner* is not liable for partnership debts incurred before they joined the firm, but a *retiring partner* continues to be liable for debts

incurred before their retirement: Partnership Act 1890 s.17.

Both positions can be reversed by a contract of *novation*, an agreement between the retiring partner, the creditors and the firm as newly constituted to release the retiring partner from liability providing the remaining partners and the incoming partner assume it. In its simplest terms, novation means that the liability of the new firm is substituted for that of the old, that of the old being discharged. It cannot be forced upon a creditor, however, and is unlikely to be practicable where there are a large number of small creditors. Novation is normally the result of an express agreement, but can be gathered from the course of dealings between the creditor(s) and the firm as newly constituted.

(ii) Future debts and retirement. A partner who retires incurs no liability for debts incurred after retirement unless they allow creditors to believe that they are still a partner in the firm: s.36(1). An example of this, which amounts to *holding out* under s.14 (*see* 4:4), would be where a retired partner knowingly allows their name to continue to appear on the firm's business stationery.

NOTE: In *Tower Cabinet Co* v *Ingram* (1949), it was held that carelessness was insufficient to incur liability under the principle of holding out; a retiring partner must *knowingly* allow themselves to be held out as still being a partner in the firm. In this case the accidental use of old notepaper bearing the retired partner's name was insufficient to make him a partner by *holding out*.

Where a holding out situation exists, the principle in *Scarf* v *Jardine* (1882) (HL) applies, i.e. a creditor cannot take advantage of the situation by taking action against the firm both as it is *actually* constituted and as they *thought* it was. In other words, if X retires from partnership with Y and is replaced by Z, a previous client who deals with the firm not knowing of X's retirement may bring an action for debt against X and Y or Y and Z but not against X, Y *and* Z.

To avoid liability for later debts, a retiring partner must publish their retirement in the *London Gazette*. This acts as notice of retirement to anyone, whether they read it or not, who has not dealt with the firm before. *Actual notice* of retirement must be given to the firm's previous clients. No particular format is required for this notice. Although frequently made by circular, a letter on another matter written on the firm's new notepaper, which shows only the remaining partners, would suffice.

(b) *Death or bankruptcy.* The estate of a deceased or bankrupt partner remains liable for debts incurred before the death or bankruptcy but is not liable for debts incurred afterwards, whether or not notice of the event has been given: s.36(3). Except for defamation, a deceased partner's estate remains liable for the firm's torts committed while the deceased was a partner.

Relationships between partners

9. Introduction

Where formal articles or a deed of partnership exist, these will govern the relations between the partners. Where they do not, the Partnership Act 1890, ss.19–31, applies. Section 24, in particular, provides a code of rights and duties among partners.

NOTE: Any of the arrangements may be varied subsequently by an express agreement or course of dealing among the partners.

10. Rights and duties

(a) *Good faith.* The principle of *uberrima fides* is reflected in three specific duties owed by each partner:

(i) To render true accounts and full information on partnership matters to fellow partners: Partnership Act 1890 s.28.

(ii) To account for any benefit derived from the partnership business without the consent of the other partners, i.e. a 'secret profit' must not be made (*see* 3:**5**: Partnership Act 1890 s.29).

(iii) To account for any profit made by competing with the firm without the consent of the other partners: Partnership Act 1890 s.30.

(b) *Membership.* All partners must consent to the admission of a new member. Further, a partner can only be *expelled* from a firm if power to do so is contained in the Articles or Deed of Partnership. There is no implied power allowing one partner to be expelled by the others.

The *retirement* of partners is usually covered by express provisions in the Articles or Deed of Partnership, e.g. as to notice and the continuation of the firm after a retirement.

(c) *Management.* Every *general partner* is entitled to take part in the management of the firm. The right of 'junior' partners to do so, however, may be restricted by the partnership agreement.

Day-to-day decision making is by majority vote, but unanimity among the partners is required before any changes in the nature of the firm's business can take place.

Partnership books must be kept at the firm's principal place of business and every partner may inspect and copy them whenever they wish.

(d) *Equal shares.* Under the 1890 Act, partners are entitled to share equally in the firm's capital and profits and they must contribute equally to its losses.

NOTE: This provision is usually varied by the partnership agreement.

(e) *Interest on advances.* No partner is entitled to interest on their capital before profits have been determined. A partner is entitled to interest at 5 per cent on money (other than their agreed capital contribution) advanced for the use of the firm.

(f) *Remuneration.* Unless otherwise agreed, a partner is not entitled to any salary for services to the firm. In a partnership with one or more sleeping partners, however, it is common to find that the partnership agreement entitles the active or managing partner(s) to a salary in addition to a share of the profits.

(g) *Indemnity.* A partner is entitled to an indemnity from the firm for expenditure and liability incurred in the ordinary course of the firm's business and in preserving the business or property of the firm.

11. Assignment of a partner's share

A partner's share in the firm's business is that proportion of the proceeds of the notional sale of its assets to which they would be entitled after the firm's debts have been paid.

A partner may *assign* their share to another person either absolutely (by sale or gift) or by mortgage. The assignee does *not* become a partner in the firm and, unless the other partners agree, has no right to take an active part in management or to inspect the books. They are entitled, however, to the assignor's share of the profits and to their share of the assets in the event of the firm's dissolution.

The assignor remains liable for the firm's debts, although they can claim an indemnity from the assignee unless otherwise agreed.

NOTE: A bank may possibly accept an assignment of a partnership share as security for a loan to provide working capital. The bank would have to make its position as assignee as secure as possible by insisting that the other partners join in the agreement. In particular, the arrangement must prevent the remaining partners taking decisions that would reduce or prejudice the bank's share of the firm's profits, such as by a bona fide agreement between the partners to pay themselves salaries for their services to the firm: *Re Garwood's Trusts, Garwood v Paynter* (1903).

12. Partnership property
This includes:

(a) Property brought into the partnership stock: Partnership Act 1890 s.20(1).
(b) Property acquired for the firm in the course of the firm's business: s.20(1).
(c) Property purchased with the firm's money, unless otherwise agreed: s.21.

It is important to distinguish between partnership property and property owned by an individual partner, but used in the firm's business, for the following reasons.

(a) The firm takes the benefit of any increase in the value of partnership property.
(b) Partnership property must be used exclusively for partnership business.
(c) On the firm's dissolution, partnership property must be sold and the proceeds applied in satisfaction of the firm's debts and liabilities: s.39.
(d) In the event of the firm's insolvency, the claims of the partner's separate creditors against the partnership property are postponed to the claims of the firm's joint creditors (*see* 4:**19**).

> NOTE: Partnership land is treated among the partners as personal property and not as real property: Partnership Act 1890 s.22. It is usual to convey the land to the partners (or to four of them in a large firm) on *trust for sale*, thereby facilitating dealings in relation to it. Section 22 means that a partner's share of the partnership land is the specified portion of the proceeds that would be left after its notional sale, the firm's debts having been paid. It is not a specific piece of land or property.

Dissolution of a partnership

13. Introduction
In common with any other contract, a partnership agreement can be terminated by agreement between the parties to it. Similarly, contract law enables the agreement to be rescinded by the other partner(s) where it was entered into as a result of the fraud or misrepresentation of another partner.

14. Dissolution under the Partnership Act 1890

The Act provides that dissolution of a firm is automatic:

(a) When the partnership was entered into for a fixed term, by the ending of that term: s.32.

(b) If entered into for a single venture, by the completion of that venture: s.32.

(c) Where the partnership was entered into for an undefined time or where a fixed term of partnership has expired and the business is continued without an express agreement (a partnership at will), by any partner giving notice to the others: s.32.

(d) Unless otherwise agreed, by the death or bankruptcy of any partner: s.33(1) (dissolution operates from the date of death or the commencement of bankruptcy).

(e) At the option of the others, if a partner's share is charged by the court to secure payment of their judgment debts: s.33(2);

(f) Where an event occurs that makes the firm's business unlawful: s.34.

15. Dissolution by court order

Following an application by a partner, s.35 of the Partnership Act 1890 gives the courts power to dissolve a partnership on any of the following grounds.

(a) Where a partner has become mentally incapable of managing and administering their property and affairs (the Mental Health Act 1983 is now the relevant Act in this situation).

(b) Where any partner, other than the applicant, becomes permanently incapable of performing their duties within the firm.

(c) Where any partner, other than the applicant, is guilty of conduct prejudicial to the firm's business. (This may relate directly to the firm's business, such as a solicitor-partner misusing clients' money, or may indirectly affect the firm, e.g. conviction for a serious criminal offence. Each application must be judged on its own facts.)

(d) Where any partner, other than the applicant, wilfully or persistently breaks the partnership agreement or otherwise acts in a way that makes it impracticable for the other partners to continue the partnership, such as keeping erroneous accounts.

(e) Where the business can only be carried on at a loss.

(f) Where, in the court's opinion, it is just and equitable that the firm should be dissolved, e.g. where there is personal deadlock between the partners.

NOTE: Where a formal partnership agreement was drawn up, it is usual for it to include specific terms governing the dissolution/continuation of the firm, particularly on the death or retirement of a partner.

16. The effects of dissolution

(a) The partnership agreement is terminated.
(b) The authority of the partners to bind the firm and each other ceases, except for the purposes of winding up the business.

Example
In *Re Bourne* (1906) (CA), one partner died and, in order to secure the firm's overdraft while winding up the partnership business, the surviving partner gave the firm's bank an equitable mortgage over the partnership land by deposit of the title deeds.

It was held that the personal representatives of the deceased partner were bound by the equitable mortgage.

NOTE: In no circumstances is the firm bound by the acts of a partner who has been made bankrupt.

(c) Each partner is entitled to have the partnership property, including the firm's goodwill, sold and the proceeds applied in payment of the firm's debts and liabilities and for any surplus to be used in payment of what may be due to the partners.
(d) Where the firm is dissolved through fraud or misrepresentation, the innocent partner(s) who rescinds the partnership agreement has the following rights.

(i) A lien on the firm's assets, after its liabilities have been discharged, for their share of the partnership.
(ii) To be subrogated to the firm's creditors that they have discharged.
(iii) To be indemnified by the fraudulent partner against all the firm's liabilities.

17. Settling accounts

By the Partnership Act 1890 s.44(b), the firm must settle its liabilities in the following order.

(a) Repayment, rateably, to *creditors*.
(b) Repayment, rateably, of *loans to the firm* made by the partners.
(c) The *costs* of the dissolution.
(d) Repayment of each partner's *capital contribution*.

The ultimate residue, if any, is divided among the partners according to their respective rights to share in the firm's profits.

Should there be losses, including losses of capital, these must be met in the following order: Partnership Act 1890 s.44(a).

(a) From undrawn profits.
(b) From the partners' capital.
(c) By the partners individually in the proportions in which they were entitled to share profits.

Example
X, Y and Z contributed capital of £5000, £3000 and £1000 respectively, but shared profits and losses equally. Creditors are paid, resulting in a loss of capital of £6000. This must be shared equally by the partners and gives the following settlement.

	X	Y	Z	Total
Capital	£5000	3000	1000	9000
Loss of capital	£2000	2000	2000	6000
Balance	£3000	1000	(-1000)	3000

X is left with £3000 of his original £5000 capital and Y with £1000 of his original £3000. Z, however, must contribute £1000 to the dissolution.

NOTE: If one partner is insolvent and cannot contribute the amount required, the shortfall is made up by the solvent partners according to their rights to share capital, not profits: *Garner* v *Murray* (1904).

Partnership and banking

18.   The firm account

(a) *Opening of the account.* Rarely, if ever, will a bank have to verify the existence of the firm, but it must ensure that the names of all partners are known. A bank can rely on the requirements of the Business Names Act 1985 (*see* 4:**3**), unless there are circumstances that a reasonable banker would consider to warrant further investigation.

NOTE: Making such enquiries can be important where a collecting bank seeks to rely on its statutory protection under the Cheques Act 1957 s.4 (*see* 9:**24**).

References must be taken to ensure the firm's suitability as a customer, but may be waived where one or more of the partners is already known to the bank.

The account must be opened in the names of *all* the partners. One partner has no implied authority to open an account for the firm in their name only and, if they are allowed to do so, the firm is not bound by their action and so is not liable for any overdraft: *Alliance Bank* v *Kearsley* (1871). Express authority to open such an account is needed from the other partners.

NOTE: By opening an account in the firm name, the bank is able to take action against all partners, both known and unknown, should it need to (*see* 4:**3**).

A bank should not inspect the partnership agreement because if it did so it would be taken to know its contents and would have to operate the account and conduct any other business with the firm in strict accordance with them. Without an inspection, the bank should be able to rely on a partner's implied authority to bind the firm if the partner ever exceeded their express authority (*see* 4:**5–6**).

The bank's *mandate* form – showing how and by whom the account is to be operated – must be signed by all the partners. In it the partners will specifically assume *joint and several* liability for all their debts to the bank.

Joint and several liability is necessary for four reasons:

(*i*) A credit balance on a partner's private account may be combined with a debit balance on the firm account.

(*ii*) The bank will rank equally with the separate creditors should a partner die or become bankrupt. (Normally, separate estates pay separate creditors and joint estates joint creditors, any surplus on one going to augment the other estate.)

(*iii*) Should the partnership itself become bankrupt, the bank has a double right of proof, i.e. it may prove against both the joint estate of the firm and the separate estate of each partner.

NOTE: The practical effect of (a) and (c) is that the bank's chances of recovering an unsecured debt from the firm are considerably improved.

(*iv*) Security deposited by a partner for all personal liabilities may be appropriated by the bank against either their personal debt or the partnership debt.

NOTE: The separate estate of a deceased partner is severally (individually) liable for the partnership's debts, subject to the prior payment of the deceased's separate debts: Partnership Act 1890 s.9.

(b) *Operating the account.* While the mandate must be signed by *all* partners, it may be cancelled by any *one* partner. It is generally accepted that any one partner may countermand payment of a cheque, irrespective of whether they themselves signed it. Strictly speaking, however, this depends on the terms of the mandate, which should, therefore, expressly deal with it.

A bank would be put on enquiry if a partner paid into their personal account cheques payable to the partnership endorsed by that partner in their own favour or where cheques were drawn by the partnership payable to third parties and endorsed to the partner. (The collection of cheques is considered generally in 9:**22–27**.)

Under the Bills of Exchange Act 1882 s.23(2), the signature of the name of a firm is equivalent to the signature by the person so signing of the names of all persons liable as partners in that firm. Furthermore, a partner signing a cheque (in their own name) which bears the printed name of the partnership binds all the partners. In other words, a partner signing a cheque printed in this way is taken to have signed it in the name of the firm.

Example

In *Central Motors (Birmingham) Ltd* v *P A and S N Wadsworth* (1982) CA, one of two brothers in partnership signed a cheque as payment for a car in his name only and without his brother's authority; the mandate requiring both signatures. The cheque had the names of the brothers printed on it and below these the firm's name. The cheque was dishonoured and an action was brought against both brothers. The second brother unsuccessfully claimed that he was not liable for the cheque as he had not signed it.

A professional partnership, such as a firm of solicitors, must maintain a separate client account for its clients' monies. Such accounts are trust accounts and a bank must ensure that it does not become liable as constructive trustee for breach of trust by allowing a member of the firm to misuse the account, e.g. drawing cheques on the account for personal purposes: *Lipkin Gorman* v *Karpnale and Another* (1986).

(c) *Borrowing.* A partner in a *trading partnership* has implied authority to borrow money for use in the firm's business and to give security to cover such borrowing. However, the mandate usually contains the partners' express undertaking to be liable for any overdraft.

Express power must be given to a partner in a *non-trading partnership* to borrow money or to give securities on behalf of the firm (*see* **4:6**).

NOTE: Rather than rely on implied authority, it is usual for a bank to insist that the partners execute the necessary documents where the firm's property is pledged or mortgaged as security for an advance.

(d) *Events affecting the account* are as follows:

(i) Retirement. If a partner retires and the firm continues in business, new mandate forms must be signed by the remaining partners and any incoming partner. New security forms must also be completed, unless those held remain effective despite changes in the constitution of the firm.

If the firm's account is in *credit*, it may be continued unbroken, although cheques drawn by the retiring partner should be confirmed by the remaining partners.

A retiring partner remains liable for the firm's debts as at the date of retirement (Partnership Act 1890 s.17(2)), but the firm's account must be broken and future entries passed through a new account, in order to preserve their liability and to establish the bank's right over any security deposited by them to secure the account. This procedure results from the *Rule* in *Clayton's Case* (1816): *see* 1:**15**.

> NOTE: A clause nullifying *Clayton's Case* is often included in security forms (*see* 11:**26**) and, therefore, at law, breaking the account is unnecessary. Banks, however, prefer to be safe rather than sorry!

The doctrine of holding out would apply to a partner who retires without informing the firm's bank (*see* 4:**8**).

(ii) Death. If a firm is dissolved on a partner's death, the surviving partner(s) may continue the account in order to wind up the firm's business. For this purpose a mortgage may be granted to the firm's bank in order to secure the firm's overdraft: *Re Bourne* (1906) and see 4:**16**.

If the firm continues in business, new mandate forms must be signed. The completion of new security forms may also be necessary.

Should the firm's account be overdrawn, it must be broken and a new account opened in order to preserve the liability of the deceased partner for the overdrawn balance as at the date of death: *Clayton's Case* (1816).

Cheques previously drawn by the deceased partner and presented after death should be confirmed by the survivors.

(iii) Mental disorder. Cheques previously drawn by a partner who becomes mentally disordered should be confirmed by the others.

An overdrawn account must be broken to preserve the partner's liability for the overdraft: *Clayton's Case* (1816).

New mandate forms are necessary and new security forms may also have to be completed.

(iv) Bankruptcy of a partner. If the firm is continued, new mandate forms must be signed and new security forms may have to be completed.

Confirmation of cheques drawn by the partner before their bankruptcy *should* be sought, confirmation of cheques drawn by them afterwards *must* be sought, as bankruptcy terminates a partner's authority as an agent of the firm.

Should the bank wish to enter a proof against the estate, the firm's account must be broken to avoid the *Rule* in *Clayton's Case* (1816) operating to the bank's detriment.

(v) Insolvency of the firm. A bankruptcy petition can be presented against one, some or all the partners – the last being the most likely. Alternatively, a petition for the compulsory winding up of the partnership as an unregistered company can be made under the Insolvency Act 1986 s.221. The provisions of the Act relating to winding up of companies then apply, as does the Company Directors Disqualification Act 1986.

NOTE: If an insolvent partnership is wound up as an unregistered company, the personal assets of the members are not available to meet debts.

Whether in credit or overdrawn, the firm's account and the accounts of each partner must be stopped immediately. Any credit balances must be held available for the trustee or liquidator.

NOTE: The protection afforded by the Insolvency Act 1986 s.284(4) only applies to transactions entered into before the date of the bankruptcy order and without knowledge that a petition has been presented against the debtor. This is discussed fully in 6:4 and 41.

19. Distribution of assets on a firm's insolvency

The insolvency process is designed to ensure that the debtor's available assets are distributed fairly among the creditors.

(a) *General rights of proof.* By an order made under the Insolvent Partnerships Order 1986:

(i) The *joint estate* of the firm is used first to pay joint (the firm's) creditors.

(ii) The *separate estate* of each partner is used first to pay each partner's separate creditors.

(iii) A *surplus on any separate estate* is dealt with as joint estate.

(iv) Any *surplus on the joint estate* is divided among the separate estates of the partners in proportion to the right and interest of each partner in the partnership estate.

NOTE: As a partnership has no legal existence distinct from its members, no segregation of the joint and separate creditors on dissolution is necessary where the partners are *solvent*: all will be paid.

(b) *Exceptional rights of proof.* It follows from the general rule in the Insolvent Partnerships Order 1986 that the private creditors and the partnership creditors cannot prove in competition with each other, the private creditors cannot prove against the firm's estate and firm's creditors against each partner's separate estate. To this there are the following exceptions:

(i) Joint creditors may prove against the separate estates in competition with the separate creditors where there is *no joint estate*.

(ii) A joint creditor who submits a petition in the *separate bankruptcy* of one of the partners is allowed to prove for their joint debt in competition with the separate creditors.

(iii) A creditor may prove against both the joint and separate estates where they can establish *joint and several liability*. This could arise:

(1) Under the terms of a bank mandate (*see* 4:**18**).

(2) Where one or more partners defrauded the creditor (the creditor must, however, elect to prove against the firm or the partner(s) concerned).

(3) Where the creditor has separate rights of action against the firm and one or more partners individually, e.g. where a bill of exchange accepted by the firm was endorsed in a personal capacity by one or more of its members: *Re Jeffery, ex parte Honey* (1871).

(c) *The bank as a secured creditor.* A bank may take a charge over a partner's separate property as security when it makes a loan to the firm (or over the partnership property to secure a loan to an individual partner). Should the firm be made bankrupt, the security is *collateral* security as it need not be given up when a proof is entered against the joint estate. This is because the release of the charge over the separate property would not augment the joint estate.

Thus, a bank can enter a proof against the joint estate for the full amount owed and make up any deficiency from the security deposited.

Progress test 4

1. Define a partnership. (**1**)

2. What is the principle legal distinction between a partnership and a registered company? (**1**)

3. What is the best test by which to determine the existence of a partnership? (**3**)

4. What is the maximum number of members allowed to form a partnership? (**3**)

5. What information about the firm must be disclosed under the Business Names Act 1985? (**3**)

6. Explain the terms 'nominal partner' and 'limited partner'. (**4**)

7. What is meant by a partner's ostensible authority? (**5**)

8. How does the implied authority of a member of a trading firm differ from that of a member of a non-trading firm? (**6**)

9. To what extent is the implied authority of a partner relevant to a bank? (**6**)

10. What is meant by novation? (**8**)

11. In what circumstances is a retired partner liable for debts that the firm incurs after their retirement? (**8**)

12. Why is the assignee of a partner's share in a potentially vulnerable position? (**11**)

13. What is partnership property and why is it important to identify it? (**12**)

14. Explain briefly the circumstances in which a partnership may be dissolved. What is the effect of dissolution? (**14–16**)

15. On the dissolution of a partnership how, in the absence of a contrary agreement, should the accounts be settled? (**17**)

16. Why should a bank always open an account for a partnership in its firm name? (**18**)

17. Why is joint and several liability specifically assumed by the partners on a bank mandate form? (**18**)

18. Why should a bank not inspect the partnership articles or deed? (**18**)

19. Identify legal pitfalls when operating a partnership account. (**18**)

20. State and explain the importance of the *Rule* in *Clayton's Case* (1816). (**18**)

21. Why must cheques drawn by a partner after the commencement of their bankruptcy be confirmed by the other partners? (**18**)

22. How do insolvency proceedings against a partnership differ if it is treated as an unregistered company? **(18)**

23. State the general rights of proof on the bankruptcy of a firm. **(19)**

24. In what circumstances will a creditor be able to prove against both joint and separate estates? **(19)**

25. Why is a charge over a partner's separate property, which was taken as security for a loan to the firm, collateral security? **(19)**

5

Companies

The nature of a company

1. Definition

A company may be defined as an organisation of individuals who contribute finance to a common stock that is to be used for business activities and who share the profit or loss arising. The common stock is the company's *financial capital* and the contributories of it are its members, the *shareholders*.

A company is a *corporation*, that is an artificial legal person recognised by the law as having an existence, rights and duties quite separate and distinct from the individuals who are its members.

Example

In the leading case of *Salomon* v *Salomon & Co* (1897) (HL), Salomon had incorporated his business as a limited company in which he held 20 000 shares, his wife and 5 children 1 share each. Salomon made a loan to his company that it secured by a charge on its assets. The company went into liquidation with debts exceeding its assets.

It was held that Salomon and his company had quite separate legal identities and, as the only secured creditor, Salomon was entitled to the available assets in preference to the company's unsecured trade creditors.

As a separate legal entity a company can own property, enter into contracts, sue and be sued and be prosecuted.

2. Classifying registered companies

Two main classifications are possible: according to the limit, if any, of the shareholders' liability to contribute towards payment of the company's debts or according to whether the company is a public company or a private company.

(a) *Companies limited by shares, by guarantee and unlimited companies.*
   (i) Limited by shares. The liability of the shareholders to contribute towards payment of its debts is limited to their investment in the company, i.e. to the value of their shareholding. Most registered companies are limited by shares.

(ii) Limited by guarantee. The liability of its members is limited to the amount that they have undertaken to contribute should the company be wound up through insolvency.

Registered companies limited by guarantee are usually non-profit making organisations.

(iii) Unlimited companies. In the event of its insolvency there is no limit on the shareholders' liability to contribute towards the payment of its debts. Thus, their private property can be seized in order to pay the company's creditors.

Unlimited companies tend to provide services rather than trade. They are exempt from the duty to file annual accounts with the Registrar of Companies.

NOTE: An unlimited company can only be a private company: Companies Act 1985 s.1.

(b) *Public and private companies.*

(i) Public. A public company is a company limited by shares or guarantee, having a share capital, with a Memorandum which states that it is to be a public company and which has been registered or re-registered as a public company under the Companies Act 1985 s.1 or previous Acts. It has two or more members and can invite the general public to subscribe for its shares or debentures. It must have a minimum authorised and allotted share capital of (at present) £50 000.

NOTE: No *new* company limited by guarantee can have a share capital and therefore must be a private company: Companies Act 1985 s.1.

(ii) Private. A private company is any company that does not satisfy the requirements for a public company. In common with a public company, it has two or more members.

(iii) Distinctions. The main distinctions between a public and a private company are as follows.

(1) A public company can offer its shares or debentures to the public, a private company cannot. It is a criminal offence to invite the general public to subscribe for shares or debentures in a private company.

(2) A public company must have at least two directors. A private company need have only one but a sole director cannot also be the secretary.

(3) A public company must include the words 'public limited company' or 'PLC' in its registered name, a private company must only include the word 'limited' or 'Ltd'.

(4) Private companies are less regulated than public companies In many cases, private companies are able to dispense with calling formal company meetings requiring, for example, specific periods of notice They are instead able to pass unanimous written resolutions signed by all the company's members or, by the unanimous agreement of all its members entitled to vote, an 'elective resolution'. An elective resolution can, for example, dispense with the need to hold an annual general meeting.

(5) A public company requires a 'business certificate' before it can commence business.

NOTE: The Articles of Association of a private company will often contain restrictions on the number of shareholders and their ability to transfer shares. This, however, is not a legal requirement, merely a device to ensure that control of the company remains within a family or small group.

3. Registered companies and partnerships compared

(a) *Formation.* A partnership is formed by an express or implied agreement between its members. A registered company is formed by registration in accordance with the Companies Acts.

(b) *Legal status.* A company is a *corporation* and possesses a separate legal identity from its members. A partnership has no separate legal personality; at law it is merely a collection of individuals who find it an advantage to combine together to pursue their business ventures.

It follows that company property belongs to the company and not to its members as individuals, while partnership property is owned jointly by the partners.

(c) *Succession.* It follows from its corporate status that a company has perpetual legal existence until wound up under the Companies Act 1985 or the Insolvency Act 1986; a partnership has not.

(d) *Membership.* Both public and private companies must have at least two members but there is no upper limit. Private companies, however, will often limit their membership. A partnership must also have at least 2 members but, with certain exceptions, it must not exceed 20.

NOTE: The Twelfth Company Law Directive of the EC allows private limited companies to have only one member.

(e) *Transfer of shares.* Shares in a public company are freely transferable, but restriction on transfers are often imposed in a private company. A partner, however, may assign their share in the firm but may not transfer it without their fellow partners' consent.

(f) *Powers.* Statutory formalities and procedures apply to any alteration of a company's Memorandum or Articles, but the objects and internal organisation of a partnership, even if contained in a Deed or Articles of partnership, can be altered by simple agreement among the partners.

(g) *Publicity of affairs.* A company's *Memorandum of Association* and *Articles of Association* are public documents that, along with the various company registers, are open to public inspection. In contrast, partnership affairs are private and the contents of any Deed or Articles of Partnership may only be known to its members.

(h) *Agency.* Every partner is the firm's agent with power to bind the firm by contracts made in the usual course of its business. The members of a company – its shareholders – are not its agents unless expressly appointed as such, e.g. its directors.

(i) *Management.* Every general partner can take part in the management of the firm unless the partnership agreement states otherwise. Shareholders take no part in company management unless they are also directors.

(j) *Liability.* Except in a limited partnership, there is *no limit* on a partner's personal liability for the firm's debts and wrongs. However, legal action can only be taken against the company itself and the liability of the members to contribute to payment of its debts is *limited* to the amount of their investment or guarantees.

(k) *Raising loan capital.* Only a registered company can create a *floating charge* over its assets to secure a loan made to it. A partnership can only offer to mortgage partnership property or the separate property of the partners as security for a loan.

The formation of a registered company

4. Incorporation

Companies are incorporated (formed) by registration under the Companies Act 1985. (In theory a company can also be formed by Royal Charter or by special Act of Parliament.)

Its promoters obtain the necessary minimum number of members, register certain documents with the Registrar of Companies and pay certain fees and stamp duties. When satisfied that the statutory requirements have been met, the Registrar issues a *Certificate of Incorporation.* This brings the company into existence as a separate legal person (*see* 6:1).

NOTE: A private company may commence business as soon as its Certificate of Incorporation is granted. A public company, however, may not commence any activity until the registrar has issued it with a Certificate ('business certificate') under the Companies Act 1985 s.117 that it has complied with the requirements as to share capital. Alternatively, the company must re-register as a private company.

The formation, operation and winding up of a registered company is governed by the Companies Act 1985, as amended by the Companies Act 1989, and by the Insolvency Act 1986.

5.   Documents to be filed

(a) Memorandum of Association (*see* 5:6).
(b) Articles of Association (*see* 5:8).
(c) A statement of the names of the intended first director(s) and the first secretary, together with their written consents to act as such; the statement must also contain the intended address of the company's registered office.
(d) A statutory declaration of compliance with the Companies Act 1985 regarding registration.
(e) A statement of the company's capital, unless it is to have no share capital.

Of these documents, the Memorandum of Association and the Articles of Association are the most important.

6.   Memorandum of Association

This governs the external activities of a company, for example the contracts it makes and, as such, states both the objects and powers of the company (*see* below). The Memorandum is a public document and it can be inspected by any individual or organisation intending to deal with the company.

The Memorandum must be signed by the first members (subscribers) of the company and must contain the following.

(a) *Name.* If a private limited company, the name must end with the word 'limited' (or Ltd); if a public limited company, the words 'public limited company' (or PLC), or the Welsh equivalent for a company with its registered office in Wales, must be used.

General restrictions exist preventing a name being registered that suggests, for example, a Royal connection, or that might tend to mislead the public, e.g. a name that closely resembles that of an existing company.

A company can change its name by special resolution: Companies Act 1985 s.28. A private company can do this by a written resolution. Changing the name of companies bought 'off the peg' is fairly common.

A company trading under a name other than its registered name must comply with the disclosure and display requirements of the Business Names Act 1985.

(b) *Registered office.* The Memorandum does not state the actual address, only whether it is to be situated in England, Scotland or Wales. The actual address must, however, be filed with the Registrar on application for registration.

Under the Companies Act 1985 s.351, all business letters and order forms of a registered company must state its registered number and place of registration.

(c) *Objects clause.* The Memorandum must state the purposes for which the company was formed. Traditionally this meant that the objects clause listed a comprehensive range of activities covering every conceivable aspect of the company's operation. This was done because a company's activities were, until recently, subject to the *ultra vires* rule. In its extreme form, the rule meant that any transaction entered into by a company that was not authorised by its object clause or which was not reasonably incidental to its objects, was *ultra vires* (beyond the powers of) the company and void.

The *ultra vires* rule was virtually abolished by the Companies Act 1989, which substituted a new s.35 into the Companies Act 1985 (*see* further note below).

Section 3A of the 1985 Act (inserted by the 1989 Act) also provides that a company can state that it is a 'general commercial company' in its objects clause, a statement that permits the company to carry on any trade or business whatsoever and gives it power to do all things incidental or conducive to the carrying on of any trade or business by it.

NOTE: It is uncertain whether banks (and others) will rely on s.3A and it may not therefore be as significant an innovation as might otherwise have been the case. Banks have traditionally always ensured beyond doubt that a company has the power to enter into a specific transaction, such as borrowing or the giving of guarantees, rather than relying on the court's interpretation of what is 'incidental or conducive' to the company's activities. For example, would a guarantee of the overdraft of a supplier of the company be considered to be 'incidental or conducive' to the company's activities? This approach reflects the decision in *Charterbridge Corporation Ltd* v *Lloyds Bank Ltd* (1969) where it was held that, unless the directors exercise their powers for the benefit of the company, the transaction may not bind the company. Until there is a definitive ruling on whether s.3A negates the *Charterbridge* concern, banks may prefer to play safe.

A company may alter its objects clause by special resolution passed by a 75 per cent by number majority of shareholders at a general meeting: Companies Act 1985 s.4. However, 15 per cent by number of the shareholders may object to the change within 21 days of the resolution: Companies Act 1985 s.5. (This is designed to protect 'minority shareholders'.) The objection must be lodged with the court which can confirm, modify or alter the change to the objects clause: Companies Act 1985 s.6.

NOTE: The *ultra vires* rule still exists in relation to the *internal* affairs of a company. Thus, a shareholder can seek an injunction to stop the company acting *ultra vires* providing the act in question is not required to be done to fulfil a legal obligation arising from a previous act of the company: Companies Act 1985 s.35(2). An example would be completion of the purchase of land where the original contract was *ultra vires*.

(d) *Limitation of liability*. The Memorandum of Association must state that the liability of the members is limited.

(e) *The share capital*. The Memorandum of Association must state the amount of the company's authorised capital and its division into shares of a fixed amount.

7.   Articles of Association

These regulate the internal administration of the company, the relationship between the company and its members and the relationship between the members themselves. They also govern the issue and transfer of shares, the rights of shareholders, the conduct of meetings, the appointment and powers of directors and accounts. Many new companies adopt the model set of Articles, modified to their requirements, contained in Table A of the Companies Act 1985. Companies incorporated under earlier Companies Acts, however, are likely to use the standard Articles provided in those Acts, especially those in the Companies Act 1948.

The Articles must be printed and signed by each subscriber to the Memorandum of Association in the presence of a witness.

The Articles can be altered by special resolution at a general meeting. Any alteration must, however:

(a) Be consistent with the Memorandum of Association.

(b) Not amount to a fraud on a minority of members; and

(c) Not increase the liability of a member of the company in any way without their written consent.

8. Preliminary contracts

Should a person purport to make a contract on behalf of a company as its agent before its incorporation, the contract will not bind the company when it is formed and the agent will, subject to an agreement to the contrary when the contract is made, incur personal liability on it: Companies Act 1985 s.36. After incorporation, however, the company and the third party can make a new contract adopting the terms of the pre-incorporation contract.

> NOTE: In *OshKosh B'Gosh Inc* v *Dan Marbel Inc Ltd and Another* (1988) (CA), it was held that a director incurs no personal liability in respect of contracts entered into by a company under its new name when the company is awaiting a Certificate of Incorporation consequent on its change of name.

The operation of a company

9. Legal capacity

(a) *The company*. The validity of any act done by a company cannot be questioned on the grounds of *lack of capacity* irrespective of anything contained within the registered objects of the company: Companies Act 1985 s.35(1). Thus, in relation to the dealings of the company with third parties, a company has unlimited contractual capacity. Unless affected by other legal rules, e.g. lack of good faith under s.35A, a contract can be enforced against the company even though the company's objects clause does not sanction it. The company can also enforce such a contract against the third party.

> NOTE: Under s.35(3) an action by the directors that, but for s.35(1), would be beyond the company's capacity may be ratified by a special resolution of the company. (In practice this restricts a shareholder's right to challenge an *ultra vires* act and protects the directors.)

Section 130 of the Companies Act 1989 abolishes the requirement for a company to have a common seal, although many companies are likely to continue the practice of sealing important documents. Furthermore, the section provides that a document signed by two directors or by one director and the company secretary and expressed to be executed by the company has the same effect as if it had been executed under the company's common seal.

(b) *The directors.* A company acts through its directors; they are both its executive controllers and its principal agents. In addition, directors are regarded as *quasi-trustees* of their company's money and property and of the powers given to them. As such, they owe *fiduciary duties* to the company and they must exercise their powers in good faith and for the benefit of the company.

As agents they have actual and ostensible authority (*see* 3:3) to act for the company and they are subject to the general rules of agency (*see* especially 3:5) as amended by the Companies Act 1985. For example, they must not make a secret profit on any transaction they enter into for their company and they incur personal liability if they exceed their authority unless the company ratifies their action.

Of most importance, however, is that in favour of a person dealing with a company in *good faith*, the power of the board of directors to bind the company or authorise others to do so, shall be deemed to be *free of any limitation* under the company's constitution: Companies Act 1985 s.35A(1). Dealing with the company covers a transaction or other act – this would include a gift from the company – to which the company is a party.

A 'limitation' under s.35A(1) includes one derived from a resolution of the company in general meeting or from any agreement among the members as both these would be made under the company's constitution.

NOTE: Section 35A(1) applies only to the power of the *board of directors* and does not expressly cover decisions taken independently by individual directors, particularly those of a managing director. However, the general tenor of the section would suggest that, providing a third party acts in good faith, it can be assumed that the individual director's actions had been duly authorised by the board of directors. The director's ostensible authority could be relied on.

Of importance to banks is the phrase 'dealing with a company in *good faith*'. Section 35A(2) provides that a person does not deal in bad faith by reason *only* of knowledge that the act is beyond the powers of the board of directors under the company's constitution. Further, a person is *presumed to have acted in good faith* unless the contrary is proved.

It is not clear when a third party will deal with a company other than in 'good faith' – this will depend on judicial decisions – but the following hypothetical examples are relevant to banks. Note that in each case the bank has knowledge of what the documents contain, it is what the bank does or does not do having the knowledge that matters.

(i) A company banks with branch A, which has knowledge of the Memorandum and Articles of Association, but branch B, which does not, lends the company money for an *ultra vires* purpose. Although the bank is a single legal entity, branch B would presumably here be acting in good faith within the meaning of the Act and could enforce the loan. If branch A had lent the money, presumably it would have acted in bad faith and could not.

(ii) An individual could, presumably, be protected if they entered into an unauthorised transaction with the company with knowledge of the Memorandum and Articles of Association but failed to understand their implications. It is unlikely that a bank could argue that it failed to understand them.

(iii) If a bank is aware that a transaction with the bank had been sanctioned by an inquorate meeting of the board, it would seem not to have acted in good faith. (A quorum is the minimum number of directors that must be present at a meeting of the board to make the proceedings valid.) In particular this would apply where the company gives security to the bank in exchange for, say, the personal guarantees of one or more directors and the board meeting is inquorate because its Articles do not allow 'interested directors' to vote. The security would almost certainly be unenforceable. In such a situation, the bank may be caught by the proviso in s.711A(2) (*see* below).

NOTE: A third party is not protected where the act is (1) illegal, e.g. contrary to s.151; (2) the directors have acted in breach of their fiduciary duty to the company and the third party has received company property knowing of the breach and is therefore liable as a constructive trustee.

Where the third party dealing with the company is a director of the company or its holding company or is a person connected with the director or a company with which such a director is associated, s.35A cannot be relied on and the transaction is voidable by the company unless previously authorised: Companies Act 1985 s.322A.

A company is unable to rely on s.35A(1) to enforce a contract against a third party, the transaction must first be ratified by a special resolution of the company: s.35(3).

A company is not bound in the absence of ratification by those who purport to act for it without actual or ostensible authority. The company secretary's position is important in this respect. A secretary is the chief administrative officer of the company and may have authority to enter into contracts within the administrative side of the day-to-day running of the company's business. The extent of the authority will vary with the size of the company and the functions entrusted to the secretary.

Example

In *Panorama Developments (Guildford) Ltd* v *Fidelis Furnishing Fabrics Ltd* (1971), FFF was held liable to pay outstanding hire charges on cars that its secretary had hired, apparently on the company's business, but which he had fraudulently used for his own purposes.

(c) *Constructive notice.* A person dealing with a company owes no duty to find out the registered objects of the company or the powers of its directors: s.35B. Furthermore, s.711A(1) states that a person shall *not* be taken to have notice of such matters merely because they are contained in a company's registered documents or otherwise made available for inspection by the company. However, s.711A(2) contains a proviso that this does not affect the question of whether a person is affected by notice of any matter by reason of a failure to make such enquiries as *ought reasonably to be made.*

The proviso means that a bank and other commercially aware bodies are likely to be treated less favourably in relation to s.35A than other third parties. Thus, different banks have adopted different responses to s.35 in relation to requiring a copy or sight of a company's Memorandum and Articles of Association.

10. Borrowing by companies

It is established that borrowing by a company must only be for a purpose consistent with the company's objects. Borrowing is an ancillary power not an object in itself: *Introductions Ltd* v *National Provincial Bank* (1969) (CA).

Borrowing powers are usually vested in the directors but occasionally borrowing must be sanctioned by the company in general meeting. The Articles of Association will frequently limit the borrowing powers of the directors.

The virtual abolition of the *ultra vires* rule by the Companies Act 1989 means that, at law, (although not necessarily in practice) a bank need not concern itself with either the company's stated objects or the authority of the directors to enter into a loan or overdraft agreement, together with any associated security contract, *provided*, in the latter case, it acts in good faith (*see* 5:9). A bank clearly needs to exercise care when it has a copy of the company's Articles of Association on file or has had sight of them.

Should a bank lend to a company through the *ultra vires* act of its board of directors and not be able to rely on the Companies Act 1985 s.35A, that is repayment of the loan is not enforceable against the company, one or more of the following courses of action should enable the bank to recover some or all of the monies advanced:

(a) It can ask the company to *ratify* the transaction.

(b) It can ask the company to *alter its Articles* retrospectively to abolish or raise the limit on its directors' borrowing powers.

(c) It can sue the directors for *breach of warranty of authority*.

(d) It can seek an *injunction* to restrain the company from parting with the money.

(e) It is *subrogated* to the rights of the company's creditors who were paid off with the money advanced by the bank.

(f) It can seek a *tracing order* to recover any identifiable property purchased with the money.

NOTE: Any third party security, such as a personal guarantee given by a director, is unaffected by the unenforceability of the loan, provided the usual indemnity clause is included in the security document (*see* 15:9).

11. Making loans and giving guarantees

(a) *Loans to directors.* The Companies Act 1985 s.330(2) prohibits, with exceptions (ss.332–8), a company from making loans to its directors or to a director of its holding company and from giving guarantees or providing security for loans to directors from other persons.

To this there are a number of exceptions.

(i) Where the loan is by a subsidiary company and the director is its holding company.

(ii) Where the company's ordinary course of business includes lending money and giving guarantees and the arrangement made is within the ordinary course of its business. (A bank may, therefore, allow its directors ordinary overdrafts.)

(iii) Where the loan (up to £10 000) is made to provide a director with funds to meet expenses incurred by them for the company's purposes or to enable them to perform their duties properly.

(iv) Where the aggregate amount of the loan does not exceed £5000.

(b) *Financial assistance to purchase shares.* Section 151 of the Companies Act 1985 further prohibits, again with exceptions (s.153), a company from providing financial assistance to any person to purchase or subscribe for its own shares or the shares of its holding company. This would include a subsidiary company transferring assets to its new parent company at less than their true value and possibly a transfer at their true value if it could be shown that the transfer was not in the commercial interests of the subsidiary: *Belmont Finance Corporation Limited* v *William Furniture Ltd* (1979) (CA).

To this there are a number of exceptions.

(*i*) A loan by a company whose normal business includes the lending of money (thus, a bank may lend money to a customer so that the customer may purchase shares in the bank).

(*ii*) A loan made to a trust for the benefit of the company's employees, including a director holding a salaried employment or office in the company.

(*iii*) Financial assistance to enable employees, other than directors, to acquire fully paid shares in the company or its holding company.

(c) In favour of a private company, in order to provide a means by which its managers can obtain assistance from the company in acquiring its shares, thereby facilitating a smooth transfer of control, e.g. from retiring shareholders.

(d) *Bank involvement.* If a bank is involved in any such transaction and it knew or, more likely, *should have known* that the transaction was unlawful, it may find that it cannot enforce the guarantee or recover the loan or has to recredit the company's account. The bank, as well as the directors, would be liable as constructive trustees of the monies involved.

In the case of a company making loans to a director or guaranteeing their indebtedness, examples could include accepting a guarantee from a company to secure an advance by the bank to a director or, more likely, an advance to the company that then lends it to a director, or allowing a company to repay the overdraft of a director. In the case of a company providing assistance for the purchase of its shares, an example would be (wrongly) debiting the company's account with a cheque used to purchase the company's shares contrary to s.151. The 'reasonable banker' test in *Lipkin Gorman* v *Karpnale Ltd* (1989) would seem to apply in these situations (*see* 1:**6** and **7**).

The bank's position is secure if the transaction is within one of the exceptions listed under (a) or (b) above.

The capital of a company

12. Definitions of capital

The term capital is used in two senses:

(a) To describe *capital items*; or
(b) To describe *financial resources*. (In this latter sense a further distinction can be made between *invested finance* (share capital) and *loaned finance* (loan capital secured by debentures.)

A bank will be primarily concerned with capital used in the sense of a company's *financial resources*.

13. Types of capital

(a) *Authorised or nominal capital*. The total face value of shares that a company's Memorandum of Association authorises it to issue.
(b) *Issued capital*. The face value of the shares actually issued and may be only a part of the authorised capital.
(c) *Paid-up capital*. The amount of the issued capital that has been paid up by the shareholders.
(d) *Uncalled capital*. The remaining part of the issued capital that can be called up by the company from the shareholders at any time in accordance with the Articles of Association, i.e. their shares are only *partly paid up*.
(e) *Reserve capital*. That part of the uncalled capital which can only be called up for use in the event of the company's liquidation. As partly paid up shares are unusual, it follows that reserve capital is also rare.
(f) *Loan or debenture capital*. This is money *lent* to the company on the security of debentures. It is not true capital because it is a *debt*, not an asset.

14. Shares and debentures

Companies raise finance by issuing shares and debentures. While both produce money that the company can use to pursue its economic activities, there are three main differences between them.

(a) *Debentures* are loan capital that acknowledge and secure loans to the company while *shares* are evidence of part ownership of the company and investment in it. Thus, debenture holders are a company's creditors while shareholders are its members.
(b) Debentures normally provide for repayment and they are usually secured by a mortgage over the property of the company. A shareholder's investment is only completely repaid if and when the

company is wound up while solvent. Thus, shareholders take a much greater *risk* than debenture holders.

(c) Dividends on shares can only be paid out of profits and, therefore, presuppose a profitable year's trading, but the interest on debentures can be paid out of capital. Hence, debenture holders receive payment for the loans they make irrespective of whether the company makes a profit or a loss.

15. The issue of shares and debentures

A public company wishing to issue shares or debentures will invite the public to subscribe for them through a document known as a *prospectus*. This will set out the objectives and past performance of the company and give other information designed to prevent investors from being misled.

A copy of the prospectus must be delivered to the Registrar of Companies by the company or issuing house before the prospectus is issued.

16. Types of shares

(a) *Preference shares.* These have the following characteristics.

(*i*) Their holders have priority over all other shareholders in the payment of dividends.

(*ii*) The dividend paid is fixed. (Thus, the holders of preference shares receive a secure, if somewhat moderate, return on their investment.)

(*iii*) The shares are presumed to be cumulative, i.e. any deficiency in the payment of the fixed dividend is carried forward to the following year.

(*iv*) They normally carry very restricted voting rights.

(*v*) They carry no right to share in the surplus assets on winding up unless they are participating preference shares.

(b) *Ordinary shares.* Ordinary shareholders are entitled to:

(*i*) Attend and vote at meetings of the company.

(*ii*) Receive such dividends as the company decides to pay from time to time.

(*iii*) Share in the surplus assets after payment of all debts on winding up. (This right is called the *equity* of ordinary shareholders, hence the term *equity shares*.)

NOTE: The precise rights of ordinary shareholders vary widely from company to company according to their own Articles of Association. Ordinary shares are the *risk-bearing* shares because they have the greatest potential for either profit or loss.

(c) *Deferred shares*. These are rare but may be issued to the promoters or employees of a company. Their holders are only entitled to a dividend after full payment has been made to the preference and ordinary shareholders. However, they are then entitled to distribution of the whole available surplus as dividend. (Such shares are usually held to show confidence in the enterprise and to provide a personal interest in its success.)

(d) *Redeemable shares*. Redeemable shares may be issued provided the shares are issued fully paid, the Articles of Association allow this and there are also some irredeemable shares.

A public company can only redeem shares from profits or from the proceeds of a fresh share issue. A private company can also redeem the shares from capital by special resolution provided the directors issue a statement stating that the company will remain a going concern for the next 12 months, despite the redemption.

17. Stock and debenture stock

Fully paid-up shares may be converted into *stock*. There is, however, no advantage in doing this today and the holder's investment in the company remains the same, merely being expressed in different terms. For example, 1000 £1 shares can be converted into £1000's worth of stock.

The essential difference between stock and shares is that the former is expressed in terms of money and can be transferred in fractional amounts, for example £51.25's worth, although the Articles of the company usually provide that stock can only be transferred in round sums, while the latter are units, such as 10, 50 or 100 shares and can only be transferred as such.

Debenture or *loan stock* is borrowed finance consolidated into one debt in the same way that shares may be consolidated and converted into stock. It is usually issued for short periods and it avoids the expense and formality involved in a public issue. Debenture stock differs from debentures in the same way that stock differs from shares, i.e. it may be transferred in fractional amounts.

18. Alteration of share capital

A company may, if so authorised by its Articles, *increase* or *alter* (Companies Act 1985 s.121) or *reduce* (s.135) its share capital:

(a) *Increase*. This is done by issuing new shares and requires, according to the Articles, an ordinary or special resolution of the company in general meeting. Notice of the increase must be filed with the Registrar of Companies within 15 days of the resolution. When existing share-holders are given the right to apply for new shares in proportion to their existing shareholding, the issue is known as a *rights issue*.

(b) *Alteration.* This is achieved by:

(i) Consolidating shares, e.g. by converting every ten 10p shares into one £1 share.

(ii) Converting shares into stock.

(iii) Subdividing shares into shares of smaller amounts, e.g. by dividing one £1 share into five 20p shares.

(iv) Cancelling unissued shares.

Alteration of share capital requires an ordinary or special resolution of the company, depending on its Articles, and the alteration must be filed with the Registrar within one month of the resolution.

(c) *Reduction.* A company might reduce its share capital in order to relieve shareholders of their liability to pay any uncalled-up capital in respect of their shares, e.g. by reducing 50 000 £1 shares on which 50p per share has been paid to 50 000 50p shares fully paid; or to return paid-up capital in excess of its needs, such as where a company has issued 50 000 £1 shares fully paid-up and reduces its capital to 50 000 50p shares fully paid-up by repaying 50p per share.

A reduction in a company's share capital is only possible where:

(i) Authority to do so is contained in the company's Articles.

(ii) The reduction is approved by a special resolution of the company in a general meeting; and

(iii) The court sanctions the reduction.

The court's sanction is necessary because a reduction in share capital may adversely affect the company's creditors, i.e. they will be deprived of funds which would otherwise have been available to them in winding up. A bank that has made a loan on the security of a company's shares, would be particularly affected by a reduction in the company's share capital because its security would be automatically reduced.

The court must settle a list of the company's creditors and ensure that if they object to the reduction they will be paid off or given adequate security to protect their interests should their claim be disputed by the company.

In addition, the reduction must be fair and equitable between different classes of shareholders and it must not prejudice members of the public who may deal with or invest in the company.

Company bank accounts

19. Opening a company account

Before opening an account for a company, a banker must be certain of the following:

(a) That the company has been properly incorporated. Sight of the Certificate of Incorporation is required.

(b) In the case of a public company, that a Certificate under s.117 of the Companies Act 1985 has been issued by the Registrar.

> NOTE: A bank can open an account *solely* for the receipt of subscriptions from the public before a certificate has been issued.

(c) That it obtains or inspects a copy of the company's Memorandum and Articles of Association and makes sure that they are up to date, if need be by making a search at Companies House (but *see* 5:**6** and **9**).

(d) That it receives a certified copy of the resolution appointing the first directors, if they are not named in the Articles (and afterwards that it is notified when a director retires or a new director joins the board).

(e) That the bank's mandate form is signed by the chairman and secretary of the company after the resolutions that they contain have been passed by a meeting of the board of directors.

The mandate must cover all the banking operations relating to the account and incorporate the names, number and positions of persons authorised to:

(i) Draw, endorse and accept bills of exchange, promissory notes and cheques.

(ii) Deposit and withdraw security and safe custody items.

(iii) Overdraw the account.

Specimen signatures of the directors and all authorised signatories are required.

20. Operating a company account

(a) *Mandate*. A company bank account must be operated in strict accordance with the bank mandate form, e.g. each cheque must bear the required signature(s).

(b) *Company cheques*. A person signing a cheque incurs personal liability on it and, if a signatory wishes to avoid this liability, they must make it absolutely clear that they sign in a representative capacity. Traditionally, this is done by using words such as 'per pro', or 'for and on behalf of', followed by the full name of the company, the signature and the signatory's capacity within the company, e.g. director or secretary. However, in *Bondina Ltd* v *Rollaway Shower Blinds Ltd* (1986) (CA), it was held that, providing a cheque is printed with the company's name and account number, the company and *not* the person signing is liable on the cheque even if the representative nature of the signature is not stated. The reason is that it is clear that the drawer of the cheque is the company and not the person(s) signing it.

The exception above does not affect the rule that failure to state the company's name accurately and in full means that the person signing the cheque (or other bill of exchange) incurs personal liability if it is not paid by the company: Companies Act 1985 s.349. This provision is applied strictly.

Example

In *Hendon* v *Adelman* (1973), personal liability was incurred on a cheque printed 'L R Agencies' instead of 'L & R Agencies' and failure to include the word 'limited' in the name of a limited company was held to be sufficient to infringe s.349 in *British Airways Board* v *Parish* (1979).

An interesting situation would arise if the bank printed the company's name wrongly on the cheques. Under s.349, the signatories would incur personal liability if the cheque is dishonoured by the bank. However, they would probably be able to bring an action in negligence against the bank *if* the misprint is the bank's fault.

(The collection and payment of cheques generally is considered in Chapter 9).

(c) *Misuse of the account.* In operating a company's account a bank must always be aware of the possibility that one or more of its directors could be using the account for their own purposes. This is most likely to occur, perhaps innocently through ignorance of a director's duties and the requirements of company legislation, in the case of small and one–person operator companies in particular. If such misuse occurs and a reasonable banker should have realised that it was happening, a bank can be sued by the company for the loss incurred.

21. Wages accounts

(a) *Preferential debts.* Advances to cover wages and salaries are preferential debts in the insolvency of an individual or company: Insolvency Act 1986, Schedule 6. Under s.175 of the Act, preferential creditors have priority over unsecured creditors and creditors secured by a floating charge in insolvency (*see* **6:46**). This protected position explains the practice of opening wages accounts for company customers, especially if the company is in a weak financial position.

NOTE: Although wages accounts are discussed here in the context of companies, the principles apply equally to a sole trader or partnership that is an employer.

There is no legal requirement to operate a wages account to gain the protection of s.175: *Re Primrose (Builders) Ltd (1950)* – but in three ways it is to a bank's advantage to do so.

(*i*) It enables the bank more easily to keep the position under review, the exact amount of the preferential claim being known at any time.

(*ii*) It facilitates proving that the advance was made for the purpose of pay and salaries.

(*iii*) It prevents the operation of the *Rule* in *Clayton's Case* (1816) to the bank's detriment (*see* 1:**15**). Subsequent credits into a current account could easily cancel out the advances made for pay and salaries.

NOTE: Amounts debited to the wages account must be genuine advances. Thus, if the advances are only made after equivalent credits have been paid into another of the company's accounts, the bank will not be a preferential creditor: *Re E J Morel (1934) Ltd (1962)*.

A bank will usually still open a wages account when it holds a debenture from the company secured by the usual fixed and floating charges. This is because there may be other large preferential debts, e.g. unpaid PAYE income tax, and, as these will rank equally with its own preferential claim, no assets may be left on which its floating charge can crystallise.

(b) *Appropriation and combination.* A bank's rights of appropriation and combination are also relevant in the context of a wages account:

(*i*) *Appropriation.* If a bank realises security, it can appropriate the proceeds to an overdrawn general account, for which the bank has no preferential creditor status, still enabling it to rely on its preferential status in respect of the wages account: *Re William Hall (Contractors) Ltd (1967)*.

(*ii*) *Combination.* A bank may combine accounts as it chooses. Thus, if there are two general accounts, one in credit and one overdrawn, and an overdrawn wages account, it can combine the two general accounts leaving the debit balance on the wages account as a preferential debt.

NOTE: On the winding up of a company, a credit balance on one account has to be apportioned rateably between overdrawn accounts: *Re Unit Two Windows Ltd* (1985). For example, at the commencement of its winding up, a company's number 1 account has a credit balance of £6000, its number 2 account is overdrawn by £3000 and its wages account is overdrawn by £6000, the £6000 must be applied one third to two thirds between the number 2 account and the wages account, leaving the bank with an unsecured debt of £1000 and a preferential debt of £2000. Had the bank been able to combine the credit balance as it wished, it would have applied it first to the number 2 account and then applied the balance to the wages account, clearing the unsecured debt and leaving an outstanding preferential debt of £3000.

22. Closing a company account

The same principles apply to company accounts as to the accounts of individuals (*see* 2:**5**):

(a) *Account in credit.* If the account is in *credit*, the company must be given reasonable notice to close the account. Depending on the company and its affairs – they are likely to be far more complex than those of an individual – this period may be measured in months rather than weeks.

(b) *Account overdrawn.* If the account is overdrawn, the bank's position depends on the form the borrowing takes.

(*i*) An *overdraft* is repayable on demand and the account can therefore be closed 'immediately'.

(*ii*) Immediate repayment of a *loan* cannot be demanded unless the instalments are in arrears or the company has breached the terms of the loan agreement. Thus, provided the company does not break the agreement, the bank is unable to close the account until the contractual date for the loan to be fully repaid has been reached.

Winding up and dissolution of a company

23. Introduction

A registered company is an artificial legal person created by legal process. Its existence is similarly ended by legal process – *winding up* or *liquidation* (the terms are interchangeable) under the Insolvency Act 1986.

There are important similarities between the process of winding up companies and the process of bankruptcy of individuals and partnerships. For example, the rights of *preferential creditors* are the same and the concepts of *transactions at an undervalue* and *preferences* apply to both. However, in bankruptcy the debtor is always insolvent while the process of liquidation applies whether the company is solvent or insolvent.

The Insolvency Act 1986 provides two methods of winding up: (1) compulsorily by the court; (2) voluntarily.

24. Compulsory winding up by the court

(a) *Grounds for winding up.* A company can be wound up under the Insolvency Act 1986 s.122 by the court following a petition to it if one of the following situations arises.

(i) The company resolves by special resolution that it should be wound up by the court. (This is unusual because the company is in a position to wind up voluntarily and this is a cheaper and more convenient procedure.)

(ii) If a public company registered as such in its original incorporation has not been issued with a 'trading certificate' under the Companies Act 1985 s.117 and more than a year has expired since it was so registered.

(iii) The company has not commenced business within a year after its incorporation or suspends business for a whole year.

(iv) Its members fall below two.

(v) The company is unable to pay its debts. Winding-up petitions are most frequently presented on this ground. (Insolvency is covered in greater detail in Chapter 6.)

Under the Insolvency Act 1986 s.123, inability to pay its debts occurs where:

(1) A creditor to whom at least £750 is owed has made a proper demand for payment and the company, within three weeks, has neither paid, nor secured the sum or made a composition with and to the creditor's satisfaction.

(2) Execution issued on a judgment of the court in favour of a creditor is returned unsatisfied in whole or in part.

(3) The court is satisfied that the company is unable to pay its debts as they fall due.

NOTE: In *Re Capital Annuities Ltd* (1978), it was held that the mere fact that a company has insufficient *liquid assets* to pay its immediate debts does not necessarily satisfy (now) ss.122 and 123 of the 1986 Act. It might have, for example, other assets that could be readily realised in a few days to do so.

(4) The court is satisfied that the value of the company's assets is

less than the amount of its liabilities taking into account its contingent liabilities.

(vi) The court is of the opinion that it is just and equitable that the company should be wound up.

This residual power of the court is seldom invoked, but it could, for example, be used where personal deadlock exists between the only two directors of a company: *Re Yenidje Tobacco Co Ltd* (1916).

NOTE: In *Ebrahimi* v *Westbourne Galleries Ltd* (1973), the House of Lords recognised, for the purposes of winding up, the existence of the *incorporated partnership*, that is a business organisation to which, in practice, some important partnership principles apply although, at law, it is a registered company. In this case the plaintiff, one of the company's three directors, had been quite legally removed from office and prevented from participating in the management of the company by the other two directors. On the facts, however, the company had always been run along the lines of a partnership and this made their action inequitable. Consequently, the House found that it was just and equitable that the company be wound up on the plaintiff's petition.

(b) *Who may petition.* It is nearly always a *creditor* who petitions for a compulsory winding-up order.

A *contributory (see* 5:**26**) may petition under (d) above and in any other of the situations, provided the contributory has held shares for at least 6 months out of the 18 months preceding their petition. A petition by a contributory is unusual.

The *Department of Trade and Industry* has the power to present a petition against a company under the Companies Act 1985 s.440 if it appears to be in the public interest, after investigations by the Department's inspectors, that the company should be wound up.

The *Bank of England* is empowered by the Banking Act 1987 to present a petition for the winding up of an authorised institution and under the Companies Act 1985 if:

(i) The institution is unable to pay sums due and payable to its depositors or is able to pay such sums only by defaulting in its obligations to other creditors; or if

(ii) The value of the institution's assets is less than the amount of its liabilities.

(c) *Commencement of the winding up.* The effect of the winding-up order dates back to the commencement of the winding up. Under the Insolvency Act 1986, s.129 this occurs:

(a) At the time of the presentation of the petition to the court; or

(b) At the time of the passing of the resolution for voluntary winding up (*see* 5:**25**) where the company was in voluntary liquidation before the petition was presented.

(d) *Consequences of the winding-up order.* The main consequences are as follows.

(*i*) Any disposition of the company's property made after the commencement of the winding up is void unless sanctioned by the court: Insolvency Act 1986 s.127 – *see* 6:**21**.

(*ii*) Any action to enforce judgment against the effects of the company after the commencement of the winding up is void under s.128 and *no action* can be proceeded with or commenced against the company except by leave of the court: s.130.

(*iii*) Floating charges are void in certain circumstances: Insolvency Act 1986 ss.239 and 245 (*see* 16:**10**); and any lien or other right to retain possession of any books, papers or other records of the company is unenforceable against the liquidator: the Insolvency Act 1986, s.246.

NOTE: This does not apply to liens on documents that give title to property and are held as such. Thus, a bank's general lien over cheques, bills of exchange, promissory notes, share certificates and bills of lading or a particular lien over title deeds and insurance policies, is protected.

(*iv*) The liquidator assumes most of the powers of the directors.

(*v*) The employees are dismissed.

(*vi*) Under the Company Directors Disqualification Act 1986, the court can disqualify a person from being a director of a company for up to 15 years for fraud in the course of winding up a company (s. 4) or if they are or have been a director of a company that has, at any time, become insolvent and their conduct makes them unfit to be concerned in the management of a company (s.6).

NOTE: The winding-up order terminates the banker–customer relationship: *National Westminster Bank Ltd* v *Halesowen Presswork and Assemblies Ltd* (1972) (HL).

25. Voluntary winding up

The great majority of liquidations are voluntary.

(a) *How initiated.* Section 84 of the Insolvency Act 1986 provides that a company may be wound up voluntarily:

(*i*) By *ordinary resolution* at the end of the period, if any, fixed for its duration by the Articles or, if the Articles provide that the company is to be dissolved on the occurrence of a certain event, when that event occurs.

(ii) By *special resolution* (no particular reason is required).

(iii) By *extraordinary resolution* where, by reason of its liabilities, it cannot continue its business and it is therefore advisable to wind up.

Copies of the resolution must be filed within 15 days and advertised in the *London Gazette* within 14 days.

(b) *Commencement of the winding up.* A voluntary winding up commences from the passing of the resolution. Its effects are as follows.

(i) The company ceases business, except for business necessary to its beneficial winding up.

(ii) Transfers of shares are void unless made with the consent of the liquidator.

(iii) The powers of the directors cease on the appointment of the liquidator, unless sanctioned by the liquidator or by the company in a general meeting in a members' voluntary winding up (*see* below).

(iv) Floating charges made within the previous two years are void in certain circumstances (*see* 16:**10**).

(v) If the company is insolvent, its employees are dismissed.

Proceedings against the company are not stayed unless the court so orders.

(c) *Types of voluntary winding up.*

(i) A *members'* voluntary winding up. This can only take place when the company is solvent, e.g. where the directors and principal shareholders of a solvent company wish to retire but no buyer for the company can be found. The company's creditors are paid in full and therefore its members control the liquidation, appointing a liquidator of their choice.

A members' voluntary winding up requires that the directors file a *declaration of solvency* to the effect that, after having made a full enquiry into the company's affairs, they are of the opinion that the company will be able to pay its debts in full within a specified period not exceeding 12 months from the commencement of the winding up.

To be effective, the declaration must be made within the five weeks immediately preceding the date on which the resolution to wind up was passed and filed with the Registrar of Companies before that date. It must embody a statement of the company's assets as at the last practicable date before it is made.

(ii) A *creditors'* voluntary winding up. If no declaration of solvency can be made and filed, the creditors control a voluntary winding up and can appoint a liquidator of their choice.

A meeting of the creditors must be called and at least seven days' notice of the meeting must be sent by post to creditors and advertised in the *London Gazette* and in two local newspapers.

26. Contributories

A contributory is any person liable to contribute to the assets of the company in the event of its being wound up: Insolvency Act 1986, s.79. Both present and certain past members of the company are contributories.

(a) *Unlimited companies.* By definition, there is no limit on the members' liability to contribute.

(b) *Companies limited by guarantee.* Members are liable to contribute to the extent of their guarantees. Past members may be liable as 'B List' contributories (*see* below).

(c) *Companies limited by shares.* Members holding fully paid-up shares are under no further liability to contribute but members holding partly paid-up shares must (if called) contribute the amounts unpaid on their shares.

A two-part list of contributories is drawn up by the liquidator
(*i*) The 'A List', containing present members of the company.
(*ii*) The 'B List', which includes all persons who were members during the preceding 12 months.
In the case of shares that are not fully paid-up, the liquidator first makes calls on their holders on the 'A List'. If they cannot pay, the liquidator has recourse against the ex-holders of the shares on the 'B List', but only for contributions towards the debts and liabilities of the company contracted while they were members.

27. Dissolution of a company

On completion of a winding up, a company must be dissolved. An order to this effect may be made by the court on the liquidator's application following a *compulsory liquidation*. The company will be dissolved from the date of the order.

It is usual, however, for the liquidator to prefer to apply to have the company struck off the register by the Registrar under the Companies Act 1985 s.652 on the grounds that the company is defunct (*see* below).

Following a *voluntary liquidation*, the liquidator must submit accounts to a final general meeting of the company and also to a final meeting of the creditors if the company was insolvent and file a copy with the Registrar within one week. The company is automatically dissolved three months afterwards. The court may set aside the dissolution within two years on the application of the liquidator or any other interested party.

Under s.652, the Registrar may strike a company's name from the register, and thereby dissolve it, if the Registrar has reasonable cause to believe that the company is not carrying on business or otherwise not in operation, i.e. it is defunct. This does not affect the liability of any director or member or the power of the court to wind up the company. Any member or creditor may, within 20 years, apply to the court for the name to be restored to the register.

Progress test 5

1. Define a company. (1)

2. Define a corporation. (1)

3. Explain how companies can be classified. (2)

4. List the main distinctions between a public company and a private company. (2)

5. Explain the distinction between a company and a partnership. (3)

6. How is a company formed? (4)

7. List the contents of a Memorandum of Association. (6)

8. What significant change did the Companies Act 1989 introduce to the nature of a company's 'objects clause'? (6)

9. To what extent does the *ultra vires* rule still exist? (6)

10. What do the Articles of Association regulate? (7)

11. What does s.36 of the Companies Act 1985 provide? (8)

12. Explain the effect of the following sections of the Companies Act 1985: s.35(1); s.35A(1); s.35A(2); s.35B; s.130; s.711A. (9)

13. What limitation is there on a company's power to borrow? (10)

14. In what circumstances can a company make a loan to one of its directors? (11)

15. When can a company give financial assistance to a person to purchase its shares? (**11**)

16. How might a bank become involved in breaches of ss.151 and 320 of the Companies Act 1985? (**11**)

17. Distinguish between authorised and issued capital and between shares and debentures. (**13–4**)

18. List the characteristics of preference shares. (**16**)

19. How can a company reduce its share capital and how might this adversely affect a bank? (**18**)

20. Outline the procedure to be followed when opening a company account. (**19**)

21. To what extent are directors liable on company cheques that they sign? (**20**)

22. What is the purpose of operating a wages account? (**21**)

23. How is a bank's right to combine company accounts as it wishes affected by the winding up of the company? (**21**)

24. List the grounds on which a company can be compulsorily wound up by the court. (**24**)

25. When is a company deemed to be unable to pay its debts? (**24**)

26. What does s.127 of the Insolvency Act 1986 provide? (**24**)

27. List the consequences of a compulsory winding up order. (**24**)

28. Distinguish between a member's voluntary winding up and a creditors' voluntary winding up. (**25**)

29. Who is a contributory? (**26**)

30. How is a company dissolved? (**27**)

6

Insolvency

The Insolvency Act 1986

1. Introduction

(a) *The meaning of insolvency.* In simple terms, insolvency is where a debtor is unable to pay their debts: s.272 (in relation to individuals). Inability to pay debts is not, however, defined by the Act; instead the approach it adopts is to list the circumstances in which an insolvency petition can be presented against a debtor. This approach is more practical because it puts the onus on the debtor to show that they are *not* insolvent and avoids the accounting complications that could arise in distinguishing insolvency from cash flow problems.

More specific definitions of insolvency exist but they apply to particular situations and may still beg the question 'Yes, but what is ... ?' For example, s.247 states that insolvency in relation to a company includes the approval of a voluntary arrangement, the making of an administration order or the appointment of an administrative receiver. The Company Directors Disqualification Act 1986 s.6(2) states that a company becomes insolvent if, *inter alia*, it goes into liquidation at a time when its assets are insufficient for the payment of its debts and other liabilities and the expenses of winding up.

For our present purposes, the idea of inability to pay debts is sufficient.

(b) *The scope of the Act.* The Insolvency Act 1986 regulates both bankruptcy (individual insolvency) and the winding up of companies, whether solvent or insolvent. As an alternative to enforced insolvency, the Act provides voluntary procedures that are designed to offer debtors who recognise their financial problems sufficiently early the chance to come to some form of arrangement with their creditors, which may avoid insolvency altogether or be in the better interests of all concerned.

The Act also provides a way – the Administration Order – for the unsecured creditors of companies to protect their positions, and introduces a number of concepts common to bankruptcy and winding up, such as preferences and transactions at an undervalue, that, together with a specified order of priority among creditors, help to promote a fair distribution of assets to creditors.

The Act introduced the 'insolvency practitioner'. An insolvency practitioner is a person who acts:

(i) In relation to companies, as a liquidator, administrator, administrative receiver or as supervisor of a voluntary arrangement.

(ii) In relation to individuals or partnerships, as a trustee in bankruptcy or interim receiver, trustee under a deed of arrangement or the administrator of the insolvent estate of a deceased individual.

NOTE: The Official Receiver is not required to be an insolvency practitioner but can act in any of the capacities of an insolvency practitioner. (All the roles mentioned above are explained further elsewhere in this chapter.)

Under the Act, an insolvency practitioner must be *licensed* and it is a criminal offence to act in such a capacity *without* a licence. Authorisation is available from certain professional bodies, e.g. the leading accountancy bodies, or direct from the Secretary of State in the case of individuals experienced in insolvency practice who are not members of such professional bodies.

(c) *The structure of this chapter.* There are a variety of ways the contents of this chapter could have been ordered. Indeed, aspects of the winding up of companies not specifically involving insolvency are covered in Chapter 5 (*see* 5:**23–25**) and the statutory right of set-off under the Act in Chapter 1 (*see* 1:**16**). One particular issue is whether to consider bankruptcy and company insolvency quite separately, while another is whether to cover the aspects of insolvency affecting securities in a separate chapter. On balance, it was considered better to deal with insolvency as a single entity and to adopt the following order in this chapter.

(i) Individual insolvency: bankruptcy; the role of the trustee; assets; voluntary arrangements.

(ii) Company insolvency: a summary of the types of winding up; the consequences; voluntary arrangements; administration orders.

(iii) Common concepts: preferences; transactions at an undervalue; transactions defrauding creditors; extortionate credit transactions.

(iv) Creditors: proof of debts; types of creditors and their different priorities and rights.

(v) Insolvency and banking: largely a bringing together of aspects covered elsewhere.

NOTE: All references in this chapter are to the Insolvency Act 1986, unless otherwise stated.

The bankruptcy process

2. Introduction

(a) *Definitions.* Bankruptcy is the legal process by which the estate (property) of an insolvent person is taken into the control of a trustee who uses it to pay off the debts of that person. Bankruptcy does not apply to a company registered under one of the Companies Acts or to any other type of corporate body.

A *bankrupt* is a person against whom a *bankruptcy order* has been made by the court. Until the order is made they are referred to as a debtor.

(b) *The aims of the bankruptcy process.* The primary aim of the bankruptcy process is to secure a fair distribution of a debtor's assets among creditors, e.g. by ensuring some are not shown unfair preference.

The process also assists in freeing the honest and unfortunate debtor from a hopeless financial position and imposes penalties on the dishonest or reckless debtor, avoiding fraudulent transactions so that they may not subsequently enjoy any profits from such dishonest or reckless behaviour.

To a lesser extent, the process enquires into the reasons for a person's insolvency.

(c) *Capacity in bankruptcy.* Any person with contractual capacity can be made bankrupt but the following specific rules apply:

(i) Aliens must fulfil the general residence or business activity qualification (*see* 6:**3**).

(ii) Minors have only limited contractual capacity and they can only be made bankrupt in respect of debts incurred on contracts for necessaries (food, clothing, lodgings and so on) or on judgment debts arising from proceedings in tort or for liability created by statute, e.g. for taxes.

(iii) Persons of unsound mind can be made bankrupt, but the proceedings are subject to control by the court of protection.

(iv) Deceased persons cannot be made bankrupt but their estates may be administered in bankruptcy. The administration order operates in a similar way to a bankruptcy order and overrides a grant of probate or letters of administration.

(v) Partnerships can be made bankrupt and a bankruptcy order against a firm operates as a bankruptcy order against each named person who was a partner in the firm when the order was made (*see* 3:**19**).

NOTE: If an insolvent partnership is wound up as an unregistered company under the Act, this does not involve the insolvency of all the partners.

3. The petition
Bankruptcy proceedings begin with a petition for a bankruptcy order.

(a) *Who may petition?* Under s.264, a petition can be presented by:
(i) A creditor or two or more creditors jointly.
(ii) The debtor.
(iii) The supervisor or any other person bound by a voluntary scheme or composition made as part of a voluntary arrangement under the Act (*see* 6:**17**).
(iv) The Official Petitioner where a criminal bankruptcy order has been made against the debtor.

(b) *Conditions of a valid petition.*
(i) The *debtor* must:
(1) Be domiciled or personally present in England or Wales when the petition is presented; or
(2) Have, at any time during the previous three years, been ordinarily resident or had a place of residence or carried on business in England or Wales: s.265. (This last condition includes carrying on a business by means of an agent or manager or as a member of a partnership.)
(ii) The *debt or debts claimed* must be at least £750 and for a liquidated (certain) sum payable immediately or at some certain future time: s.267.
(iii) The *debt must be unsecured.*

NOTE: A secured creditor, such as a bank holding a charge over the debtor's property, can petition provided that the creditor's petition states that they are willing to give up the security or that it can be valued and the petition is based on the unsecured balance: s.269. This is a course of action a bank is most unlikely to pursue.

(c) *Creditor's petition.* The petition must allege that:
(i) The debtor appears *unable to pay* the debt(s) specified in the petition; and

(ii) There is *no outstanding application* to have a *statutory demand* set aside: s.267.

The petitioner can show apparent inability to pay by proving that they served on the debtor a *statutory demand* requiring the debtor to pay, compound for (come to an arrangement on) or secure the debt and that the debtor did not comply with this within three weeks. Alternatively, the petitioner can show that enforcement proceedings upon a judgment debt have been returned wholly or partly unsatisfied.

Once presented, a petition can only be withdrawn with the court's permission. The court *must* dismiss a petition if the statutory demand has been complied with. It *may* dismiss it if the debtor is able to pay all debts or if the petitioner has unreasonably refused to accept the debtor's offer to secure or compound for the debt following a statutory demand.

(d) *Petitions following a voluntary scheme.* A supervisor of, or other person bound by, a voluntary scheme (*see* 6:**18**) must allege that the debtor has *failed to comply* with the scheme or supplied *false or misleading information* to obtain the scheme or approval of it at any creditors' meeting.

(e) *Debtor's petition.* A debtor may present a petition only on the grounds of inability to pay their debts. The petition must be accompanied by a statement of affairs containing particulars of creditors, debts and other liabilities and assets.

4.   Consequences of the petition

(a) *Restrictions on dispositions of property.* Before a bankruptcy petition is presented, the debtor's affairs, including bank account(s), are unaffected by the Act, although payments and transactions may subsequently be avoided on a bankruptcy order being made as being *preferences* or *transactions at an undervalue* (*see* 6:**33** and **35**).

(i) Void transactions. Any disposition of property or payment of money made in the period between the petition being presented and the trustee in bankruptcy being appointed is *void* unless sanctioned by the court beforehand or subsequently ratified. Without the court's approval, the person to whom the property was transferred or the payment made, such as a bank receiving repayment of a loan or a charge over the debtor's property or the payee of a cheque, holds it as part of the debtor's estate: s.284(1).

(ii) Protected transactions: after the petition but before the bankruptcy. The effect of s.284(1) could easily be unfair, a person could receive

property or money from the debtor without the slightest idea that a bankruptcy petition has been presented – it does not have to be advertised in the *London Gazette*. The Act therefore offers partial protection in s.284(4). (A bankruptcy petition is not advertised in the *London Gazette* to guard against the possibility of malicious petitions and because an appeal may be made against it. A petition to wind up a company on the grounds of insolvency is *gazetted*.)

No action is possible against a person who *received* property or money from the debtor under a transaction entered into (1) in good faith, (2) for value and (3) *without notice* of the presentation of the petition in the period between the presentation of the petition and the making of the bankruptcy order: s.284(4).

Furthermore, any person acquiring that property or an interest in it from a protected person, such as a bank taking a charge over it, is similarly protected, (apparently) whether or not that person acts in good faith, for value and without notice of the presentation of the petition.

(iii) The position after the bankruptcy order. The protection of s.284(4) does not apply to dispositions of property or payments made *after* the commencement of the bankruptcy, i.e. the date of the bankruptcy order. Limited protection is however afforded by s.284(5) in the case of debts arising after the bankruptcy order but before the date of the trustee's appointment (*see* 6:8).

(b) *Proceedings against the debtor*. While bankruptcy proceedings are pending, the court can stay any legal action against the debtor or the debtor's property.

(c) *Interim receivers*. An interim receiver is appointed where it is necessary for the protection of the debtor's estate: s.286. The interim receiver has such powers as the court grants.

The Official Receiver will be the interim receiver unless the debtor presented the petition and an insolvency practitioner has been appointed to report on the debtor's affairs (*see* below). In this case, the insolvency practitioner may be appointed interim receiver.

(d) *Special managers*. The court can appoint a special manager with such powers as the court thinks fit where the appointment is required by the nature of the debtor's estate, property or business or by the interests of the creditors: s.370.

(e) *Voluntary arrangements and summary administrations*. As an alternative to making a bankruptcy order on a *debtor's petition*, the court can appoint an *insolvency practitioner* under s.273 to inquire into and report to the court on the debtor's affairs and willingness to propose a voluntary arrangement. This is done in an attempt to avoid the full effect of a bankruptcy.

This procedure can only be followed where (s. 273):

(i) Unsecured debts are below the *small bankruptcies level* (at present, £20 000).

(ii) The value of the assets is at least of a *minimum amount* (at present £2000).

(iii) The debtor has not been adjudged bankrupt nor made a composition or scheme with creditors within the five years before the presentation of the petition.

After receiving the report, the court may:

(i) Make an interim order to assist the making of a *voluntary arrangement* (*see* 6:**16**); or, where it thinks that this would be inappropriate because the debtor's assets are below the £2000 small bankruptcy minimum and therefore do not justify the cost of realising the estate or do not make a voluntary arrangement worth considering –

(ii) Make a *bankruptcy order* and issue a certificate for *summary administration*: s.275. This involves a much simplified form of administration by the Official Receiver.

5.   Bankruptcy order

Bankruptcy commences with the making of the bankruptcy order. This is published in the *London Gazette* and a local newspaper. The main consequences are as follows:

(a) The debtor becomes an *undischarged bankrupt*.

(b) Subject to exceptions (*see* 6:**14**), *title* to the bankrupt's property vests in the trustee in bankruptcy on the date of the latter's appointment: s.306.

(c) Unsecured creditors lose their *rights of action* against the debtor and they can only prove in the debtor's bankruptcy for the amounts owing to them.

(d) The undischarged bankrupt commits a criminal offence by obtaining credit of £250 or more without disclosing their status or engaging, directly or indirectly, in any business under a name different to the one in which they were made bankrupt without disclosing that name to all persons with whom business is transacted: s.360.

(e) The Company Directors Disqualification Act 1986 s.11 makes it a criminal offence for an undischarged bankrupt to act as a director or take part in the management of a registered company without the court's consent.

6. Proceedings following the bankruptcy order

(a) *Official Receiver.* Subject to the exceptions below, the Official Receiver becomes the receiver and manager of the bankrupt's estate pending the appointment of a trustee in bankruptcy: s.287. Exceptions to this are as follows.

(i) In criminal bankruptcy proceedings or summary administrations, the Official Receiver becomes trustee immediately the order is made.

(ii) If an insolvency practitioner was appointed following the debtor's own petition, that person can be appointed trustee at the time the bankruptcy order is made.

(iii) Where the order follows non-compliance with the terms of a scheme or composition, the supervisor of the scheme or composition may be appointed trustee at the time the order is made.

The Official Receiver must investigate the bankrupt's conduct and affairs, including matters that occurred before the bankruptcy order was made. The Official Receiver may make a report to the court and call a general meeting of the bankrupt's creditors and a meeting must be called if the court so directs.

(b) *Statement of affairs.* Unless the Official Receiver directs otherwise, the bankrupt has 21 days to prepare and submit to the Official Receiver a statement of affairs containing details of debts, liabilities and assets: s.288.

(c) *Public examination.* The Official Receiver may apply to the court for a public examination of the bankrupt. However, the court is only likely to order this where the sum involved is large or where the bankruptcy affects a considerable number of creditors or where it would be in the public interest.

(d) *Appointment of other officials.* A *special manager* can be appointed by the court on the Official Receiver's application (*see* 6:**4**). A *trustee in bankruptcy* must be appointed (*see* 6:**8**) and, unless the trustee is the Official Receiver, the creditors may appoint a *committee of creditors*.

7. Duration and discharge of bankruptcy

Bankruptcy *commences* with the day on which the bankruptcy order is made and *continues* until the bankrupt is discharged: s.278. *Discharge* occurs in:

(a) *Summary administrations*: two years from the making of the bankruptcy order.

(b) *Repeated bankruptcy*: if the bankrupt has been an undischarged bankrupt in the 15 years before the current bankruptcy commenced, the bankrupt can apply for discharge to the court when 5 years have elapsed since the making of the order (the court may allow, refuse, or suspend the discharge and/or make it conditional).

(c) *Other cases*: automatically after three years have elapsed since the making of the order.

> NOTE: The Official Receiver can defeat this automatic right by satisfying the court that the bankrupt failed to comply with the Act or committed one of a number of bankruptcy offences before their discharge. Examples of the latter include obtaining credit of more than £250 or engaging in business under another name without disclosing their bankruptcy (*see* 6:5), failure to disclose property or its disposal, failure to deliver up books and records and carrying on a business without proper accounts. A successful application stops time running: s.278.

8.   Conduct of an account

(a) *After the bankruptcy petition is presented*. Any disposition of property or payment of money made in the period between the petition being presented and the trustee being appointed is *void* unless sanctioned by the court beforehand or subsequently ratified: s.284(1):

(i) *Before notice of the petition*. Any property or money *received* from a transaction with the debtor entered into in good faith, for value and without notice of the petition is protected up until the making of the bankruptcy order: s.284(4). Thus, payments into an *overdrawn account* are protected *provided* the bank is without notice.

Payments from an *account in credit* would be void and the bank would have to repay the trustee unless the payment is sanctioned or ratified under s.284(1) by the court, although the debt created would be provable in the bankruptcy. Payments from an *overdrawn account* are dispositions of the bank's property, not that of the debtor's. They are therefore not void and the trustee cannot recover the payments from the bank. The debt incurred is provable in the bankruptcy.

(ii) *After notice of the petition*. Notice of the petition negates the protection of s.284(4).

If the account is in *credit*, payments from the account and delivery of securities and safe custody items may be made only to the debtor or to a person claiming by assignment from the debtor, e.g. the trustee named in a deed of arrangement. The account must be operated according to the instructions of the *interim receiver* or *special manager* if appointed by the court when the petition is presented, provided their authority covers the operation of the account. (Operation of the account by an interim receiver or special manager is unlikely to be encountered in practice.)

Cheques payable to *third* parties must *not* be paid without the court's sanction. They are void dispositions.

If the account is *overdrawn*, further payments from the account would still be dispositions of the *bank's* property and therefore not void under s.284(1) but notice of the petition would prevent the bank proving for the debt created.

Payments into the account, whether it is in credit or overdrawn, must be held in a *suspense account*.

NOTE: In *Re Gray's Inn Construction Company Ltd* (1980), the Court of Appeal held that both payments into an (overdrawn) account and payments out of a company's account in the period between the date of the presentation of the petition and the date the winding up order is made were dispositions within s.227 of the Companies Act 1948 (replaced by s.127 of the Insolvency Act 1986). By analogy this would also apply to a non-company customer.

(b) *After the bankruptcy order.* The account must be stopped entirely. No securities or safe custody items can be released. The protection afforded by s.284(4) does *not* apply after the making of the bankruptcy order because the order is *gazetted* and this is deemed to be notice to the world, i.e. it is irrelevant that the bank does not have actual knowledge of the order. Limited protection is, however, afforded by s.284(5).

Section 284(5) provides that where a bankrupt has incurred a debt to a bank or other person by virtue of a *payment* having been made that is void under s.284(1), this is deemed to be a debt incurred *before* the commencement of bankruptcy provided that (1) the bank or other person did not have notice of the bankruptcy before the debt was incurred; or that (2) it is not reasonably practicable for the payment to be recovered from the person to whom it was made. The effect is to render the debt *provable in the bankruptcy* when it would not otherwise have been.

The subsection would apply where a bank continues the debtor's account without notice of the bankruptcy order and paying third-party cheques increases an existing overdraft. It would appear not to apply to payments from an account in credit – ratification by the court of such payments would seem to be the only protection available for these.

NOTE: The protection of s.284(5) is very limited because *gazetting* of the order is deemed to be notice to the world. Thus, s.284(5) is only likely to apply where the publication of the order is delayed, e.g. pending an appeal against it or publication problems.

The balance, if any, of the account and any securities held are automatically transferred to the Official Receiver or the trustee, when appointed, on the making of the order. A bank is under a duty to make delivery of such funds and securities to the trustee: s.312.

NOTE: When a bank has already incurred obligations on its customer's behalf, it may debit its customer's account even after having received notice of a petition or a bankruptcy order, e.g. a payment following the purchase of shares on its customer's instructions. (The share certificate must be held for the trustee when it is received.)

The bankruptcy order terminates the banker–customer contract – the bank loses authority to pay its customer's cheques – and a non-excludable right of set-off arises (*see* 1:**16**).

Trustee in bankruptcy

9. Appointment

(a) *By the creditors* at a general meeting of creditors: s.292. Where the Official Receiver acts as receiver and manager after the bankruptcy order, they have 12 weeks in which to decide whether to call a meeting and notify creditors of it. A meeting must be called if one-quarter by value of the creditors demand it.

(b) *By the court*: s.297.

(i) In a *summary administration*, the court may appoint someone other than the Official Receiver on making the order.

(ii) On a *debtor's petition*, the insolvency practitioner who reported on the debtor's affairs can be appointed trustee by the court when the bankruptcy order is made.

(iii) Where the order results from the debtor not complying with a *scheme or composition* (*see* 6:**17**), the supervisor of the scheme may be appointed by the court when the bankruptcy order is made.

10. Duties

The trustee's task is to get in, realise and distribute the bankrupt's estate in accordance with the Act. The trustee's main specific duties are:

(a) To obtain possession and control over the debtor's property, e.g. by collecting debts due to the bankrupt.

NOTE: A bank holding property to the account of or for the bankrupt must pay or deliver this property to the trustee if it forms part of the bankrupt's estate unless it has the right to retain it as against the trustee or bankrupt. Thus, property that is the subject of a lien or a mortgage to the bank does not have to be delivered.

(b) To convert the bankrupt's assets into money as quickly and as effectively as possible.

(c) To make proper distribution of the proceeds among the creditors.

(d) To call a meeting of creditors when called upon to do so by one-tenth in value of them.

(e) To keep proper accounts.

(f) To act in the utmost good faith.

(g) To call a final meeting of creditors when the administration is complete.

11. Powers

(a) On their *own authority* under s.314, the trustee can:

(i) Sell all or any of the bankrupt's property.

(ii) Give receipts for money paid to the estate.

(iii) Exercise any powers reasonably incidental to their duties and execute any necessary document.

(b) With the *permission of the committee of creditors*, the trustee can (s.314):

(i) Carry on the bankrupt's business in order to achieve a winding up that is more to the creditors' benefit.

(ii) Bring or defend legal proceedings in respect of the bankrupt's property.

(iii) Mortgage or pledge assets in order to raise money for the estate.

(iv) Make a compromise or other arrangement on any claim by or against the bankrupt.

(v) Appoint the bankrupt to manage the business.

NOTE: Every bankruptcy is under the general control of the court. If the bankrupt, any creditor or any other person is dissatisfied with the trustee's decisions or intentions that person can apply to the court. The court can then make such an order as it thinks is appropriate.

Assets in bankruptcy

12. Introduction

(a) *Key dates*. The three dates that determine the position are:

(i) The date the *petition is presented*.

(ii) The date of the *bankruptcy order*.

(iii) The date the *trustee's appointment takes effect*, that is the date the bankrupt's estate vests in the trustee.

(b) *Key principles.*

(i) Under s.284, any *disposition of property or payment of money* made in the period between the petition being presented and the trustee in bankruptcy being appointed is *void* unless sanctioned by the court beforehand or subsequently ratified (*see* 6:**4**).

(ii) The bankrupt's estate, i.e. the *available assets*, consists of property belonging to or vested in the bankrupt at the commencement of the bankruptcy, i.e. when the bankruptcy order was made. However, the estate is subject to the rights of any person other than the bankrupt, e.g. those of a secured creditor: s.283. Thus, a bank is able to sell or otherwise deal with property that is the subject of a legal charge or a lien without reference to the trustee.

13. Trustee's title

(a) *Commencement.* The trustee's title commences on the day the bankruptcy order is made (s.278), but the bankrupt's property vests in the trustee (becomes under the trustee's control) on the day the appointment takes effect (s.306). These dates may be some weeks apart.

(b) *Property acquired after the trustee's appointment.* This may be claimed by the trustee by serving written notice on the bankrupt: s.307.

The trustee's title to such property *relates back* to the date it was acquired by the bankrupt *unless*:

(i) It is transferred to a bona fide purchaser for value without notice of the bankruptcy; or

(ii) A bank enters into a transaction concerning the property, e.g. taking a mortgage or making payments to the bankrupt's direction, without notice of the bankruptcy.

The trustee has no remedy in either case, nor against any person deriving title to the property from that person or bank: s.307.

(c) *Disclaimer of onerous property.* Under s.315, the trustee can disclaim the following onerous property:

(i) Unprofitable contracts.

(ii) Unsaleable or not readily saleable property.

(iii) Property that may give rise to a liability to pay money or perform any other onerous act.

The disclaimer determines all rights, liabilities and interests of the bankrupt in the property and discharges the trustee from any personal liability.

> NOTE: If a lease is disclaimed, a copy of the disclaimer must be served upon every person, e.g. a bank, claiming under the bankrupt as a mortgagee or underlessee. Within 14 days, such persons can apply to the court for an order making any person in whom the disclaimed property is vested subject to the same liabilities and obligations as those to which the bankrupt was subject under the lease on the day the bankruptcy petition was presented.

14. Unavailable assets

(a) *Trade and personal property.* Unavailable for distribution are such tools, books, vehicles and other items of equipment that are necessary to the bankrupt's employment, business or vocation and such clothing, bedding, furniture, household equipment and provisions as are necessary for satisfying the basic domestic needs of the bankrupt and their family: s.283.

Where the realisable value of any such asset appears to the trustee to exceed the cost of replacement, however, the trustee can claim it. This would apply where, say, the bankrupt has a house furnished with expensive antiques or an expensive car that is used for business purposes; even more so where the bankrupt was aware of the position before the bankruptcy and bought unnecessarily expensive household or business equipment in the hope that the trustee would not claim them. If the trustee *does* claim such property, the trustee is under an obligation to replace it, but with more utilitarian property!

(b) *Property held by the bankrupt as trustee.*

(c) *Personal income* necessary to support the bankrupt and their family. (The trustee can apply to the court for an income payments order to claim income over and above this on behalf of creditors.)

(d) *Rights of action* to recover damages for personal injuries or damage to reputation.

(e) *Family home.* Under the Matrimonial Homes Act 1983, a spouse who is not the legal owner of the matrimonial home has rights of occupation that can be registered as a charge on the home and can only be defeated by court order.

Should the other spouse be made bankrupt, the charge binds the trustee in bankruptcy. If the trustee wishes to realise the bankrupt's interest in the home, the trustee must apply to the court: s.336.

The court can make any order it thinks fit and just, having regard to the interests of the creditors, the conduct of the spouse or former spouse with regard to the bankruptcy, to the needs and financial resources of the spouse or former spouse, to the needs of any children and to all the circumstances of the case other than the needs of the bankrupt.

A trustee must also apply to the court to realise the bankrupt's share in a jointly owned matrimonial home and the same factors are considered.

Similarly, a bankrupt cannot be evicted without a court order from a dwelling house in which the bankrupt has children under 18 years of age living and in which the bankrupt has a beneficial interest: s.337.

(f) *Interests in property defeated by bankruptcy,* e.g. a lease containing an automatic revocation clause of the leaseholder is made bankrupt.

NOTE: A lending bank offered a lease as security must therefore inspect the lease for such a clause and thereby lend with full knowledge of this risk.

15. Recoverable property
The trustee has power to set aside certain transactions entered into by the bankrupt and possibly recover the property involved. These are:

(a) Preferences;
(b) Transactions at an undervalue;
(c) Transactions defrauding creditors;
(d) Extortionate credit transactions;
(e) An assignment of book debts, unless the assignment was registered under the Bills of Sale Act 1878 as though it was an absolute bill of sale. (This could affect a bank involved in factoring.)

(Transactions of the types (a)–(d) are discussed in 6:**34–39**.)

Voluntary arrangements: individual insolvency

16. Introduction
The aim of a voluntary arrangement is to avoid bankruptcy. Such an arrangement can be made under the Deeds of Arrangement 1914 (*see* 6:**19**) or under the Insolvency Act 1986, ss.252–263. The former is seldom used and sections 6:**17** and **18** deal with the 1986 Act.

The procedure under the 1986 Act can be used by an individual in financial difficulties in advance of bankruptcy proceeding. By applying for an *interim order*, a short period of protection from creditors' actions can be obtained in which a proposal for a *composition* of their debts or a *scheme of arrangement* of their affairs can be put forward.

> NOTE: A *scheme of arrangement* is a plan to rescue the individual (or company) from their financial difficulties. In the case of a company, this could be by creditors converting some of their debt into shares. A *composition* is an agreement with the creditors whereby they agree not to take action against the individual (company) in return for part payment of their debts or payment over a period of time.

17. Interim order

(a) *Application.* The application for an interim order is the first stage in the process. It may be made by the debtor or, if the debtor is an undischarged bankrupt, by the trustee in bankruptcy or the Official Receiver. No application may be made, however, if the debtor has already presented a bankruptcy petition and an insolvency practitioner has already been appointed by the court to prepare a report and supervise the implementation of the composition or scheme.

The court will make an interim order where the debtor intends to make a proposal to the creditors for a *composition* in satisfaction of their debts or a *scheme of arrangement* of their affairs and where it considers that it will assist its consideration and implementation. The proposal must provide for a *nominee* to act in relation to the composition or scheme.

(b) *Effect.* The interim order is effective for 14 days but the court may extend this period. While the interim order is in force:

(*i*) No bankruptcy petition relating to the debtor may be presented or proceeded with; and

(*ii*) No other proceedings and no execution or other legal process may be commenced or continued against the debtor or the debtor's property without the court's consent.

18. Subsequent procedure

(a) *Nominee's report.* The debtor must give the nominee details of the proposed scheme and a statement of affairs with details of creditors, debts, liabilities and assets. On the basis of this information, the nominee prepares and submits a report to the court. It must include a recommendation as to whether or not a creditors' meeting should be summoned to consider the proposals.

(b) *Creditors' meeting.* If a meeting is held, notice of it must be sent to all creditors. At the meeting the creditors can approve the scheme as it is or amend it. They may also replace the nominee with another insolvency practitioner.

The debtor must consent to any amendments.

Under s.258, the meeting cannot approve any proposal or amendment that:

> *(i)* Restricts the right of secured creditors to enforce their security, e.g. a bank holding a charge.
> *(ii)* Removes the priority of any preferential creditor.
> *(iii)* Would pay preferential creditors at unequal rates.

(c) *Approval of the proposal.* Where the meeting approves the proposal, it:

> *(ii)* Binds all creditors who had notice of the meeting, whether or not they attended and voted.
> *(ii)* Dismisses any pending bankruptcy petition; and
> *(iii)* If the debtor was an undischarged bankrupt, the court can annul any bankruptcy order and/or give directions as to the conduct of the bankruptcy and administration of the estate in order to facilitate the implementation of the approved composition or scheme.

(d) *Challenge of the meeting's decision.* The decision can be challenged within 28 days of the report of the meeting to the court on the grounds that it prejudices the interests of a creditor or that there was some material irregularity at or in relation to the meeting. The challenge can be made by the debtor, a creditor, the nominee or, if the debtor is an undischarged bankrupt, by the trustee in bankruptcy or the Official Receiver.

(e) *Supervision of the arrangement.* On its approval, the nominee becomes the *supervisor* of the scheme or composition. The supervisor can apply to the court for directions and, if dissatisfied with the supervisor's actions, the debtor or any creditor can apply to the court to confirm, reverse or modify any act or decision. The court can also replace the supervisor and appoint others to work with them: s.263.

NOTE: A voluntary procedure can be changed into a bankruptcy on the application of the supervisor or a creditor.

19. Deeds of arrangement

A deed of arrangement is an agreement embodied in a document (whether by deed or not) made for the benefit of creditors generally or by an insolvent debtor for the benefit of three or more creditors.

Alternatively, such an agreement may take the form of a *composition with creditors*.

Under the Deeds of Arrangement Act 1914, the agreement is *void* unless:

(a) It is registered at the Department of Trade and Industry within seven days of execution and is properly stamped.

(b) If made for the benefit of creditors generally, it is assented to by a majority in number and value within 21 days of registration.

NOTE: A deed of arrangement affecting unregistered land must also be registered at the Land Charges Registry in the Register of Pending Actions under the Land Charges Act 1925. If not registered, the assignment of property to the trustee will be void against a purchaser for value of the land.

The making of a deed of arrangement is a private arrangement outside the Insolvency Act 1986. It avoids the depletion of the bankrupt's assets through the high costs involved and the delay and publicity attendant on the bankruptcy process. However, the assets available for distribution will probably be less because the trustee is unable to set aside preferences, etc.

NOTE: Deeds of arrangement have been little used because they only bind the creditors who assented to them – other creditors being free to initiate bankruptcy proceedings. It is for this reason that the Insolvency Act 1986 provides for voluntary arrangements that bind *all* creditors who had notice of the creditors' meeting, whether or not they attended and voted.

The winding up of companies

20. Types of winding up

The winding up and dissolution of companies is dealt with in Chapter 5 (*see* 5:**23–27**). This is done to present all the relevant information in the most coherent and digestible way. For example, a company is not necessarily insolvent when it is wound up whereas a bankruptcy requires the debtor to be insolvent by definition. Thus, only a brief summary of the types of winding up is included here:

(a) *Compulsory winding up by the court*. Most frequently this occurs when a company is unable to pay its debts and a creditor to whom an unsecured debt of at least £750 is owed makes a proper demand for payment and the company, within three weeks, has neither paid nor secured the sum or made a composition with and to the creditor's satisfaction: s.123.

The winding up order takes effect from the commencement of the winding up, i.e. the date of the petition. The main consequences of the order are as follows.

(*i*) Any disposition of the company's property made after the commencement of the winding up is void unless sanctioned by the court: s.127 (*see* 6:**21**).

(*ii*) No legal action can be taken against the company.

(*iii*) Floating charges are void in certain circumstances.

(*iv*) The liquidator assumes most of the powers of the directors.

(*v*) The employees are dismissed.

(*vi*) Action may be taken against a director under the Company Directors Disqualification Act 1986.

(b) *Voluntary winding up.* This may be:

(*i*) A members' voluntary winding up when the company is solvent; or

(*ii*) A creditors' voluntary winding up when the company's directors are unable to file a declaration of solvency.

A voluntary winding up commences at the date of the passing of the resolution to do so. Its main consequences are that:

(*i*) The company ceases business.

(*ii*) Transfers of shares are void unless made with the consent of the liquidator.

(*iii*) The powers of the directors cease.

(*iv*) Floating charges are void in certain circumstances.

(*v*) The employees are dismissed if the company is insolvent.

Legal action against the company is not prevented unless the court so orders.

21. Dispositions of property after the commencement of winding up

Any disposition of the company's property made after the commencement of the winding up is void unless sanctioned by the court: s.127.

This poses a problem in a compulsory winding up but not in a voluntary winding up because in the latter the directors lose their actual authority to act for the company once the liquidator is appointed and their ostensible authority once the liquidation is advertised in the *London Gazette*. The liquidator is usually appointed on the same day as the resolution to wind up voluntarily is passed by the company. In a compulsory winding up there can be a substantial interval between the winding up petition is presented and the winding up order is made.

Example _____

In *Re Gray's Inn Construction Company Ltd* (1980), the Court of Appeal held that both payments into an (overdrawn) account and payments out of a company's account in the period between the date of the presentation of the petition and the date the winding up order is made were dispositions within s.227 of the Companies Act 1948 (replaced by s.127 of the Insolvency Act 1986).

Thus, as soon as a bank learns of the *petition* it should stop all accounts, return all company cheques unpaid and marked 'Winding up petition presented' and apply to the court for an order covering the accounts. The court will freeze an overdrawn account (the debt is provable in the liquidation) and, providing it considers that it would be in the interests of the creditors generally that the company should continue trading, allow a new account to be opened in the company's name.

NOTE: There is no statutory protection available to a person who deals with a company without notice of a petition for a compulsory winding up. This is because the petition is advertised in the *London Gazette* and *gazetting* is deemed to be notice to the world. Nevertheless, if a bank allows transactions to continue on the account before the petition is gazetted without actual notice of the petition and in good faith, the court will probably sanction the transactions retrospectively.

A bank must stop a company's accounts completely when a winding up order is made against the company. The liquidator will claim any credit balance and the bank can take steps to enforce any security that it holds from the company should the company be indebted to the bank.

On the making of the winding up order or the passing of the resolution to wind up voluntarily, the bank's statutory right of set-off arises: s.323 (*see* 1:**16**).

22. Official roles

(a) *The Official Receiver*. Where a company has been wound up compulsorily or a provisional liquidator has been appointed, the Official Receiver must investigate the company's failure and submit a report to the court. An application to the court for a public examination of any person who is or who has been an officer of the company can also be made.

By virtue of the office, the Official Receiver becomes the liquidator when a winding up order is made by the court and remains in office until replaced. They must decide whether or not to summons a *meeting of creditors* to choose another person to act as liquidator. This meeting can also appoint a *committee of inspection* to act with a liquidator other than the Official Receiver.

(b) *The liquidator.* The liquidator's main duties are to:

(i) Take the company's property into their custody.

(ii) Settle a list of contributories (*see* 5:**26**).

(iii) Collect the company's assets; and

(iv) Apply them in discharge of its liabilities.

(v) Distribute any surplus (where the company is solvent) among its members according to their rights.

NOTE: As with a trustee in bankruptcy, a liquidator can disclaim *onerous property* (*see* 6:**13**): s.178.

The liquidator must be a licensed insolvency practitioner.

(c) *Special manager.* In both a corporate and an individual insolvency, the liquidator or trustee can apply to the court for the appointment of a special manager of the debtor's affairs where such an appointment would be in the interests of the creditors or is required by the nature of the estate.

A special manager has whatever powers are given by the court.

23. Validity of charges

(a) A charge will be void against a liquidator, administrator and creditors if it was not registered in accordance with the Companies Act 1985 s.395 (*see* 16:**2**).

(b) A *floating charge* may be invalidated under s.245 (the '12-month rule': *see* 16:**10**) and *any charge* under s.239 (as a preference – *see* 6:**34**) or under s.238 (as a transaction at an undervalue: *see* 6:**36**).

(c) Any charge may be void if it amounts to a transaction defrauding creditors (*see* 6:**38**).

(d) Any charge associated with an extortionate credit transaction may be void (*see* 6:**39**).

(e) All charges will be affected by the appointment of an administrator, although the holder of a floating charge can prevent this by appointing an administrative receiver (*see* 16:**15**).

24. Liability of directors in insolvency

A basic consequence of a company's corporate status is that its debts are its own, not those of its members or managers (directors) –

a shareholder's liability is limited to the amount they have invested, or have agreed to invest, in the company. On a company's insolvency, the position of its directors is somewhat different, either because a director has entered into a legally enforceable undertaking to accept personal liability for the company's debts or because a rule of law imposes liability on directors, usually because of wrongdoing by them.

(a) *Liability as guarantor.* It is common when lending to small private companies controlled by one or two directors to take personal guarantees for the borrowing from the directors, supported by charges on their personal property. It is both correct in principal to require them to accept at least part of the risk involved in the venture and a good incentive for them to ensure that the company is able to and does make repayment. Directors' guarantees are less often taken when lending to large companies but are a useful security where one company is a director of another.

Very simply, if the company is unable to repay its debt to the bank when a demand for repayment is made, the bank will have a right of immediate recourse against the directors as guarantors. This is a course of action that may well be more attractive to the bank than a possibly protracted claim against the company in its liquidation. (The bank may be particularly prompted to pursue this course where it regards the directors as being 'at fault' regarding the insolvency.)

(b) *Liability on a cheque or other bill of exchange.* The Companies Act 1985, s.349 provides that any person signing a company cheque or other bill of exchange on which the company's name is not stated accurately and in full, incurs personal liability on it if it is not paid. If the company is *solvent*, s.349 is perhaps not important, but if the company is *insolvent* it assumes considerable importance, provided, of course, that the name is inaccurately or incompletely stated (*see* 5:**20**).

(c) *Liability for fraudulent trading.* Fraudulent trading is committed where, in the course of a liquidation of a company, its business has been carried on with the intention of defrauding its creditors or for any fraudulent purpose: s.213. It is a criminal offence.

The court may declare any person (not just a director) who is a party to the fraudulent trading to be personally responsible without limitation of liability for all or any of the company's debts and liabilities. A director guilty of fraudulent trading can be disqualified from acting as a director of another company for up to 15 years under the Company Directors Disqualification Act 1986.

(d) *Liability for wrongful trading.* Wrongful trading occurs where a company has gone into insolvent liquidation and at some time before this commenced a director knew or ought to have known that there was no reasonable prospect that this could be avoided and did not take the steps that ought to have been taken to minimise the potential loss to the company's creditors: s.214. Whether a director is liable for wrongful trading is a question of fact in each case but in *Re Produce Marketing Consortium Ltd* (1989) it was held that directors of public companies could be expected to demonstrate a higher level of skill, knowledge and experience than directors of small private companies.

On the application of the liquidator, the court may order the director to make whatever contribution it thinks proper to the company's assets. Proof of an intention to defraud a creditor is not necessary to incur this civil liability: s.214.

(e) *Liability of a bank as shadow director.* A shadow director is a person in accordance with whose directions and instructions the company is accustomed to act: s.251. Liability for wrongful trading under s.214 can be incurred by a shadow director, but does not extend to s.213 (fraudulent trading).

It is considered that a bank would not normally be liable as a shadow director because s.251 states that a shadow director is a person on whose instructions the company is 'accustomed to act' – a degree of continuity is clearly implied. If it does give directions or instructions to a company over a period of time, presumably it could be a shadow director.

A 'professional adviser' such as an accountant or a lawyer is *not* a shadow director within s.251, but it is unlikely that a bank manager would be classed as such for this purpose. However, a bank's business advisory service might well be within the scope of the 'professional adviser' defence if an action is brought against the bank under s.251, particularly if it receives specific payment for its services.

Nevertheless, to avoid the (probably remote) possibility of incurring civil liability as a shadow director for wrongful trading, banks must be careful not to give specific instructions to customers in financial difficulties. Advice only should be given. (The same position should also be taken in cases of a parent company giving instructions to a subsidiary.)

Voluntary arrangements: corporate insolvency

25. Introduction

These can be made under either the Companies Act 1985 or the Insolvency Act 1986. Neither involve the liquidation of the company.

26. Companies Act 1985 s.425

A compromise or arrangement with creditors under s.425 requires that the company ask the court to summons a meeting of creditors at which the compromise or arrangement must be agreed to by a majority in number, representing three quarters in value of those present and voting. It must be subsequently sanctioned by the court.

An arrangement under s.425 can also be used for the total reconstruction of a company, e.g. where the court orders dissolution and transfer of its undertaking to a new company, in which members and creditors shall have such rights as are agreed and sanctioned by the court.

> NOTE: A voluntary arrangement under s.425 is seldom made because the procedure is slow, complicated and expensive when compared to a voluntary arrangement made under the Insolvency Act 1986.

27. Insolvency Act 1986 ss.1–7

(a) *Introduction.* These sections provide a procedure by which a company may come to terms with its creditors by agreeing and implementing a scheme of arrangement or composition with the minimum of formality and court involvement.

(b) *The procedure.* A proposal for a composition or a scheme of arrangement of the company's affairs can be put to the company and its creditors by:

(i) The *liquidator*, if the company is in liquidation.
(ii) By the *administrator*, if an administration order is in force; and
(iii) By the *directors* in any other case.

An insolvency practitioner must act in relation to the arrangement and is referred to as the *nominee*. A liquidator or administrator acting as nominee may summons meetings of the company and its creditors as they think fit; any other nominee must report to the court within 28 days of their appointment and act on its directions.

The meetings must approve the proposal. However, no proposal or modification of it can be approved that affects the rights of *secured* or *preferential creditors*, unless the creditors affected agree.

Example

If the proposal involves the issue of more shares and the company's bank has taken the company's shares as security, the issue of more shares will devalue the bank's security.

Every person who had notice of and was entitled to vote at the meetings, whether or not they did so, is bound by the composition or scheme as though they were a party to it.

If the company is being wound up or is subject to an administration order when the proposal is approved, the court may stay the winding up or discharge the administration order and give such directions as it thinks will help implement the approved composition or scheme.

The decision of the meetings may be challenged by a member or creditor of the company (a bank for example), the nominee and (if applicable) the liquidator or administrator on the grounds that the approved composition or scheme unfairly prejudices the interests of a creditor, member or contributory of the company and/or that there had been some material irregularity at or in relation to either of the meetings.

When the proposal is approved and not subject to a challenge, the nominee becomes known as the *supervisor* of the composition or scheme and acts under the supervision of the court to whom the supervisor may apply for directions. The supervisor can also apply to the court to have the company wound up or made subject to an administration order.

Administration orders

28. Introduction

Administration orders are made: s.9. The procedure is intended to provide an alternative to liquidation where a company is in serious financial difficulties and the petitioning creditor cannot appoint a receiver because it does not hold a floating charge.

The mechanism is similar to appointing an administrative receiver under a floating charge and the protection of the court is gained while schemes of reconstruction are put forward. However, an administrative receiver acts on behalf of a particular *creditor* while an administrator acts on behalf of the *company and the (unsecured) creditors generally*.

29. Grounds for an administration order

The court may make an administration order following an application by a company, its directors or creditors where:

(a) It is satisfied that the company is, or is likely to become, *unable to pay its debts.*

and where it considers that doing so would:

(b) Promote the *survival of the company* as a going concern; or
(c) Lead to a *voluntary arrangement* being agreed; or
(d) Secure a more advantageous *realisation* (sale) of its assets than a winding up would produce.

> NOTE: An administration order cannot be made where a company has already gone into liquidation.

30. Notice of the application

Under s.9, notice of the application for an administration order must be given to any person who has appointed, or is or may be entitled to appoint, an administrative receiver of the company, i.e. the holder of a debenture secured by a floating charge. If there is already an administrative receiver of the company, an order will not be made *unless* either the person, such as a bank, on whose behalf the receiver was appointed consents or the floating charge is liable to be set aside: s.9 (*see* 16:2).

> NOTE: The application does not prevent the holder of a floating charge appointing an administrative receiver and, providing the charge is not liable to be set aside, the floating chargeholder can prevent an order being made by appointing one before the court reaches its decision on the application. A bank may therefore be tempted to step in earlier than it might otherwise have done, and before another creditor does so, in order to retain control of the situation and protect its interests. It also puts in jeopardy any informal rescheduling of debts. The adverse publicity this formal and more public intervention could cause at such a critical time might very well prejudice any chance of survival the company might have.

31. Effect of the order

An administration order restricts the rights of existing creditors, secured or unsecured: s.11. Specifically, it:

(a) Prevents the company from being wound up.
(b) Prevents any security given by the company (a fixed or floating charge to a bank, for example) being enforced without the consent of the administrator or leave of the court.

(c) Prevents goods subject to hire purchase, leasing or retention of title agreements (*Romalpa clauses*) being repossessed.

(d) Prevents an administrative receiver being appointed and removes from office an existing administrative receiver or receiver appointed under a fixed charge.

(e) Requires all documents issued by or on behalf of the company or the administrator to state the fact that an administration order is in force and give the name of the administrator.

The *application* for an administration order prevents the company being wound up or action taken to enforce securities that it has given.

On *appointment*, an administrator must inform the company and advertise details of it, file a copy of the order with the Registrar of Companies and inform all creditors within 28 days.

> NOTE: Although the making of an administration order prevents action being taken to enforce securities, the securities are not affected in so far as, on their sale by the administrator, the creditor secured is paid first. However, payment under a floating charge is subject to prior payment of the administrator's fees and expenses – and preferential debts. (Remember, if a bank holds a floating charge covering the whole or most of the company's property, it is in a position to prevent an administration order being made and therefore to preserve its freedom of action as a secured creditor.)

32. Administrator's powers

Essentially, the administrator can do anything that may be necessary for the management of the affairs, business and property of the company; the administrator has, in effect, the full powers of the directors of the company. For example:

(a) Carrying on the business of the company as its agent.

(b) Selling the business of the company.

(c) Borrowing money and granting security for it over the company's property.

(d) Making an arrangement or compromise with creditors.

(e) Drawing, accepting, making or endorsing any bill of exchange or promissory note in the name of or on behalf of the company.

(f) Disposing of property that is the subject of a floating charge, the proceeds of the disposal becoming the subject of the floating charge.

(g) With the court's consent, disposing of any other charged property or any goods in the company's possession under a hire-purchase, conditional sale, lease or retention of title agreement. (The net proceeds of the sale must be applied to the discharging of the debts owed to the chargeholder or the owner of the goods.)

These powers enable an administrator to reorganise the affairs of the company. As in dealings with an administrative receiver, a person who deals with an administrator in good faith and for value need not enquire whether the administrator acts within their authority. The administrator also has powers similar to those of a liquidator to collect assets, acquire information and apply for a disqualification order against a director.

33. Administrator's proposals
Within three months of the administration order being made, the administrator must send to all creditors proposals for achieving the purposes stated in the order and present them to a creditors' meeting. This meeting must approve them and may establish a *committee of creditors*. A creditor or member may petition the court if they believe that the administrator is not acting in their best interests. If the proposal fails, the company can be put into liquidation.

At the end of the administration, the administrator must account to the company or to a liquidator who may then be appointed.

Insolvency concepts common to individuals and companies

34. Preferences
A debtor makes a preference if the debtor does anything that has the effect of putting a creditor or guarantor for any of the debtor's debts in a *better position* in the event of the debtor's insolvency than that person would have been had that thing not been done: s.340 (individuals) and s.239(4) (companies).

For the preference to be actionable, the trustee or liquidator or administrator must prove the following.

(a) The debtor was unable to pay their debts at the time the preference was made or became so as a result of the preference having been made.
(b) The debtor was *influenced by a desire* to put the creditor or guarantor in a better position than they would have been in had the preference not been made. If the creditor or guarantor was an *associate* (individuals) of the debtor or a *connected person* (companies), it is presumed that the debtor was influenced by such a desire.

NOTE: Under s.435, a person is an *associate* of a debtor if that person is either the debtor's spouse, or is a relative or the spouse of a relative of the debtor or the debtor's spouse. A company controlled by the debtor or an associate (as defined above) of the debtor is an associate for this purpose.

Under s.249, a *connected* person is a director or shadow director, an associate of either or an associate of the company (for example, a director or other officer) or another company under the same control or controlling shareholders: s.435. Being employed by the company is not by itself sufficient for a person to be 'connected' with a company for this purpose.

(c) The preference was made within the prescribed periods before the bankruptcy or winding up petition was presented or, in the case of companies, before the resolution to wind up voluntarily was passed or a petition for an administration order was presented. A preference can also be challenged if it was made in the period between the petition for and the making of an administration order:

(i) Six months where the person preferred was not an *associate* (individuals) or a connected person (companies);

(ii) Two years where the person preferred was an *associate* or a *connected* person.

Example

In *Re M C Bacon* (1990), it was held that to be 'influenced by a desire' meant that the debtor positively wished to improve the creditor's position in the event of the debtor's own insolvent liquidation. Thus, pressure by a bank on the debtor to make repayment or (as in this case) to give security would seem to prevent the debtor being influenced by a desire to prefer the bank. If a debtor is given the choice of giving security or having an overdraft called in and chooses the former, the debtor does not 'desire' to improve the position of the bank.

However, being 'influenced by a desire' need not be the only factor or even the decisive one. The requirement is satisfied if it was just *one* of the factors that operated on the minds of those who made the decision.

It was further held that the time when this wish must have existed was when the decision to make the preference was made, not when it was actually made, e.g. the execution of a charge.

35. Preferences, guarantees and banks

A bank may receive a preference where its customer repays an overdraft or a loan or provides security for previously unsecured borrowing.

It can also find itself unwittingly involved in a preference where the debtor's payments to the bank are intended to reduce or extinguish the liability of a guarantor of the debtor's overdraft. Although the payments are designed to benefit the guarantor, the bank could receive a preference within the meaning of the Act (but *see Re M C Bacon* (1989) 6:**34**).

NOTE: A person who deposits securities to secure another's indebtedness is a guarantor for this purpose even though that person makes no *personal undertaking* (as is the case with a guarantee) to the bank: *Re Conley* (1938).

However, where the bank has to repay a preference, s.342 (individuals) and s.241 (companies) enable the court to revive the guarantee if it has been released or impose new obligations and require security to be provided for the discharge of any obligation imposed (*see* 6:**37**).

NOTE: Bank guarantee forms allow the bank to hold the guarantee undischarged for a period of at least two years after repayment has been made. This avoids the possible problem with a repayment later being held to be a preference and the court declining to reimpose the guarantee or impose alternative obligations. (Two years is the maximum period within which a preference can be set aside.)

36. Transactions at an undervalue

Under s.339 (individuals) and s.238 (companies), a debtor enters into such a transaction with another person if the debtor:

(a) Makes a *gift* to that person.

(b) Is to receive *no consideration* from that person under the transaction.

(c) Is to receive a consideration that is worth *significantly less* than the consideration provided by the debtor.

(d) In the case of an individual debtor, enters into the transaction in *consideration of marriage*.

To be actionable, the trustee or liquidator or administrator must prove that:

(a) The debtor was unable to pay its debts at the time the transaction was entered into or became so as a result of it.

NOTE: (1) Inability to pay debts is *not* required where an *individual* enters into such a transaction within two years of the presentation of the bankruptcy petition. (2) Where the transaction is between a *company* and a *connected person*, the company is *presumed* to be unable to pay its debts: s.240.

(b) In the case of an *individual debtor*, it was entered into in the *five years* prior to the presentation of the petition; in the case of a *company debtor*, it was entered into in the *two years* prior to commencement of winding up or the presentation of a petition for an administration order.

No intention to benefit the other party is required; the transaction is actionable merely because the transaction was entered into.

> NOTE: In *Re M C Bacon* (1989), it was held that giving security is not a transaction at an undervalue because the ownership of the assets charged has not changed. The company had merely appropriated the assets to meet liabilities that were due.

37. Powers of the court in relation to preferences and transactions at an undervalue

On the application of the trustee or liquidator or administrator, the court has wide powers to restore the position between the parties to what it would have been if the debtor had not made the preference or entered into the transaction at an undervalue. In particular, it can order that the property or benefits be returned to the trustee or liquidator. This can include the setting aside of charges associated with a preference or reviving the obligations of a guarantor released by a bank (*see* 6:**35**).

Certain protection is provided to innocent third parties however.

(a) A purchaser for value of the property that was the subject of a preference or a transaction at an undervalue who buys in good faith and without notice of the relevant circumstances, acquires a good title to it even though the vendor's title was voidable. The court cannot make an order that upsets the purchaser's interest.

> NOTE: A bank's interest as mortgagee in property that was the subject of preference or a transaction at an undervalue is protected if it was acquired for value, in good faith and without notice of the relevant circumstances.

(b) The court cannot order a person who received a benefit from the preference or transaction in the same circumstances to make any payment to the trustee or liquidator or administrator unless the payment is in respect of a preference given to that person at the time they were a creditor of the debtor, e.g. a bank that receives a payment into an overdrawn account, or that person was a party to the transaction at an undervalue: s.342 (individuals) and s.241 (companies).

(c) In the case of a transaction at an undervalue, the court will not make an order if it is satisfied that the debtor entered into the transaction in good faith and for the purpose of carrying on the business and that, at the time, there were reasonable grounds for believing that the transaction would benefit the company.

38. Transactions defrauding creditors

Such transactions are those entered into by a debtor with another person:

(a) At an *undervalue* ('undervalue' as in a transaction at an under-value).

(b) For the purpose of *putting assets beyond the reach* of actual or potential claimants against the debtor or with the intention to otherwise prejudice the interests of such claimants: s.423.

If the court is satisfied that this was the purpose of the transaction, it can make such an order as it thinks fit to restore the position to what it would have been if the transaction had not been entered into and/or to protect the interests of such claimants. An application for an order can be made by the Official Receiver or the trustee in bankruptcy or the supervisor of a composition or scheme of arrangement (individuals) or by the liquidator or administrator (companies).

NOTE: The court's power to set aside such transactions is not restricted to a particular period. A transaction entered into, say, 20 years earlier could, in theory, be set aside in the interests of creditors who had no dealings with the company at the time of the transaction. For example, in the case of an individual, the transfer of a house to the spouse as a precaution against insolvency.

Certain protection is provided to innocent third parties however.

(a) A purchaser for value of the property that was the subject of a fraudulent transaction who buys in good faith and without notice of the relevant circumstances, acquires a good title to it *even though* the vendor's title was voidable. The court cannot make an order that upsets the purchaser's interest.

NOTE: A bank's interest as mortgagee in property that was the subject of a transaction defrauding creditors is protected if it was acquired for value, in good faith and without notice of the relevant circumstances.

(b) The court cannot order a person who received a benefit from the transaction in the same circumstances to make any payment to the trustee or liquidator or administrator *unless* that person was a party to the transaction: s.425.

39. Extortionate credit transactions

A credit transaction is extortionate under s.343 (individuals) or s.244 (companies) if, having regard to the risk accepted by the person providing the credit, it requires grossly exorbitant payments to be made or otherwise grossly contravenes ordinary principles of fair dealing. The transaction is presumed to be exorbitant unless the contrary is proved.

To be actionable, the transaction must have been entered into within three years of the presentation of the bankruptcy petition or the commencement of winding up or the making of an administration order. On the application of the trustee or liquidator or administrator, the court may make an order setting aside or varying the transaction or the terms on which security is held.

NOTE: (1) It is clearly *possible* for credit transactions with a bank to be challenged as extortionate credit transactions. (2) It would seem that it is possible to challenge such transactions as being transactions at an under-value, in which case the operative period is five not three years.

Creditors

40. Proof of debts
Creditors must prove their debts before they can be paid. Proof is by a statement in the form required by the Bankruptcy Rules 1986 accompanied by an affidavit if the Official Receiver so requires.

NOTE: Proof may be dispensed with by the liquidator in a voluntary liquidation.

41. Provable debts
These are all debts and liabilities, present and future, certain and contingent, to which the individual or company is subject at the date of the insolvency order.

If the debts are *contingent*, that is dependent on the happening of a future event, their value must be assessed. If the creditor disagrees with the assessment, the creditor can appeal to the court.

If there have been dealings between the the debtor and another party (*mutual dealings*), an account is taken and only the balance is proved in the insolvency: s.323 (individuals) and the Insolvency Rules 1986, 4.90 (companies). It is not possible to contract out of this right of set-off, e.g. an agreement to keep separate a current account and a loan account, as it is with the common law right of set-off (combination of accounts). Set-off under the Act also applies to contingent and future liabilities, this is not so with the common law right. For example, if a bank holds a guarantee (a contingent liability) from a customer who has been made bankrupt or wound up for insolvency, it can set any credit balance(s) it holds against the value of the guarantee and prove in the customer's insolvency for the net amount of the guarantee (*see* 1:**16**.)

No set-off is possible if the creditor knew that insolvency proceedings were pending when credit was given to the debtor.

42. Non-provable debts.

(a) Unliquidated damages not arising out of a breach of contract or breach of trust, e.g. damages from an action in tort.
(b) Debts that, in the opinion of the court, are incapable of being fairly assessed.
(c) Statute-barred debts.

In the case of individuals:

(d) Debts due to any person who knew that a bankruptcy petition had been presented at the time the debt was incurred, e.g. a bank who advances money in such circumstances.
(e) Debts contracted after the commencement of bankruptcy, i.e., the date of the bankruptcy order.

In the case of companies:

(f) Debts contracted with knowledge of a petition for compulsory winding up.

43. Secured creditors

Secured creditors are those that hold a charge or lien over the debtor's property as security for the debt(s). They can:

(a) Rely on their securities and not prove for their debts.
(b) Realise their securities and prove as unsecured creditors for any deficiency.
(c) Surrender their securities and prove for the whole debts.
(d) Value their securities and prove as unsecured creditors for the balance.

If a secured creditor chooses to value their security, the liquidator or trustee may redeem the security at that value or require that the security be sold if they disagree with the valuation.

A secured creditor cannot both enter a proof and retain security.

NOTE: Guarantees and third-party charges or liens can be ignored when submitting a proof as these, if given up, would not increase the amount available for distribution to creditors. Money received from third-party securities will be placed in a suspense account and not to the debtor's account.

The validity of the security held from the debtor can be challenged in certain circumstances (*see* 6:**23**).

44. Preferential creditors

These receive preference over certain other creditors (*see* below) in the insolvency of a company or individual. Under Schedule 6 of the Act, the following are preferential debts.

(a) *PAYE income tax payments* due for the previous 12 months.

(b) *VAT* due for the previous six months.

(c) *Social security contributions*: for Class 1 and 2 contributions, those owing for the previous 12 months; for Class 4 contributions, those owing for any 12 month period.

(d) State and occupational *pension scheme* contributions.

(e) *Wages and salaries* of employees of the company for the previous four months, subject to a limit of (at present) £800 per employee (directors are not, as such, employees of their company).

(f) Accrued *holiday pay*.

(g) *Advances* made to make payments under (e) and (f) above, to the extent to which the advance is actually used to satisfy these preferential claims.

> NOTE: The advances to cover ordinary pay and holiday pay must be genuine advances. Thus, if the advances are only made after equivalent credits have been paid into another of the company's accounts, the advances will not be preferential debts: *Re E J Morel (1934) Ltd* (1962) *see* 5:**21**.

As between themselves preferential creditors rank equally (*pari passu*) but as a class they have priority over unsecured creditors and, in the case of a company's insolvency, creditors secured by floating charges. They do not have priority over creditors secured by fixed charges nor over the costs of the insolvency. Bank debentures normally give both fixed and floating charges and preferential creditors therefore only have priority over the assets covered by the floating charge.

> NOTE: Where a bank has both a preferential claim against and holds security from its customer, it may realise the security and apply the proceeds in satisfaction of any non-preferential debt and claim as preferential creditor for the preferential debt: *Re William Hall (Contractors) Ltd* (1967) (*see* 1:**16**).

45. Other creditors

(a) *Unsecured creditors*. The only action available to unsecured creditors is to enter proof for the amounts due to them from the debtor and await whatever dividend is ultimately paid. They rank *pari passu* (equally) among themselves. A landlord may, however, distrain for rent owed.

(b) *Deferred creditors*. These are only encountered in bankruptcy and are paid *after* all other creditors have been paid, in full. Such deferred claims include:

(*i*) Loans between spouses: s.329.

(*ii*) Loans to a business at a rate of interest varying with profits under the Partnership Act 1890 s.3.

(*iii*) A joint creditor's claim against the separate estate of a bankrupt partner (*see* 4:**19**).

46. Order of repayment

(a) *individual bankruptcy*.

(*i*) Creditors secured by fixed charges – from the securities charged to them. If the sale of the securities realises insufficient to repay the secured creditors, they must prove as unsecured creditors for the balance.

(*ii*) Costs and charges incurred in the bankruptcy, e.g. the expenses of the trustee and the trustee's remuneration (if any).

(*iii*) Preferential creditors.

(*iv*) Unsecured creditors.

(*v*) Deferred creditors.

(b) *corporate insolvency*.

(a) Creditors secured by fixed charges – from the securities charged to them. If sale of the securities realises insufficient to repay the secured creditors, they must prove as unsecured creditors for the balance.

(b) Costs of the liquidation, although in a compulsory winding up the court has a discretion to order payment of expenses in such priority as it thinks fit: s.156.

(c) Preferential creditors.

(d) Holders of floating charges.

(e) Unsecured creditors.

> NOTE: A company is not necessarily liquidated because it is insolvent. Where a solvent liquidation takes place, debts and liabilities can be settled in any order because every creditor will be paid in full. Surplus assets are distributed among the company's members according to their rights.

Insolvency and banks

47. Introduction

The purpose of this short section is to collect and summarise the protection a bank enjoys when it becomes involved in the insolvency of a customer. All the points identified are discussed fully elsewhere in this chapter.

48. Summary of the protection available

(a) *Rights as a secured creditor.* These cannot be affected without the bank's consent in any insolvency process or voluntary arrangement, although action against the security may be blocked (*see* 6:31).

(b) *Rights as a preferential creditor.* A bank will enjoy preferential creditor status in respect of advances to cover ordinary and accrued holiday pay (*see* 6:44). Operating a wages account will help a bank monitor its position (*see* 5:21).

(c) *Rights as the holder of a floating charge.* As a floating charge holder, a bank can appoint an administrative receiver. Such an appointment prevents other creditors successfully applying for an administration order and thereby taking the situation out of the bank's control (*see* 6:30).

(d) *Preferences, transactions at an undervalue and transactions defrauding creditors.* Where a bank has to repay a *preference*, the court is able to revive any obligation released, e.g. that of a guarantor, or impose new obligations and require security to be provided for the discharge of any obligation imposed. A clause in a guarantee form enabling the bank to hold the guarantee undischarged for a minimum period of 24 months after the principal debtor has made repayment will also protect the bank (*see* 6:37).

In the cases of a *preference*, a *transaction at an undervalue* and *a transaction defrauding creditors*, a bank's interest as mortgagee in property that was the subject of a preference or transaction is protected if it was acquired for value, in good faith and without notice of the relevant circumstances (*see* 6:34–38).

(e) *Void transactions.*

(i) *Bankruptcy.* In the period between the petition being presented and a bankruptcy order being made, a payment by the debtor into their overdrawn account is protected if the bank dealt with the debtor in good faith, for value and without notice that the petition has been presented (petitions are not published in the *London Gazette*): s.284(4).

A bank is also protected if it acquires an interest in property, such as taking a charge over it, from a person whose receipt of the property from the debtor was protected by s.284(4).

The protection of s.284(4) is lost after the bankruptcy order is made.

Payments from an account in credit are only protected if sanctioned or ratified by the court. If the bank did not have *notice* of the petition, it may prove for the payment. Payments from an overdrawn account are not dispositions of the debtor's property and therefore not void. A bank can prove for the debt *unless* it has notice of the petition.

After the bankruptcy order, all transactions are void, but s.284(5) may enable a bank to prove for a debt that it would not otherwise be able to (*see* 6:**4** and **8**).

(ii) Company liquidation. Any disposition of the company's property made after the commencement of the winding up is void unless *sanctioned by the court*: s.127. There is no statutory protection if the bank continues the account in ignorance of the petition; it must rely on the court sanctioning transactions retrospectively (*see* 6:**21**).

Progress test 6

1. Who can petition for a bankruptcy order against a debtor? (3)

2. Explain how a creditor establishes the inability of the debtor to pay their debts. (3)

3. On what grounds can a supervisor submit a petition? (3)

4. State and explain the effect of s.284(1). (4)

5. What is a protected transaction under s.284(4)? (4)

6. Explain the circumstances in which the court can make an order for summary administration. (4)

7. List the main consequences of the making of the bankruptcy order. (5)

8. Explain the role of the Official Receiver following the making of a bankruptcy order. (6)

9. When does bankruptcy commence and for how long does an individual remain an undischarged bankrupt? **(7)**

10. A debtor's account is overdrawn but the bank continues to make payments from the account. Considering the position both when the bank does *not* have notice of the presentation of the petition against the debtor and when it *does*: *(a)* are these payments void under s.284(1); *(b)* does the protection of s.284(4) apply; *(c)* are the debts created provable in the debtor's bankruptcy? **(8)**

11. Explain the protection afforded by s.284(5) in relation to transactions entered into after the making of the bankruptcy order. **(8)**

12. By whom is the trustee in bankruptcy appointed? **(9)**

13. List the main duties of the trustee. **(10)**

14. On what date does the trustee's title to the bankrupt's property commence and on what date does it vest? **(13)**

15. List the types of property that are unavailable for distribution to creditors. **(14)**

16. Property transferred under what kinds of transactions can be recovered by the trustee? **(15)**

17. Explain the difference between a scheme of arrangement and a composition with creditors as part of a voluntary arrangement. **(16)**

18. What is the effect of an interim order? **(17)**

19. List the steps that follow an interim order under a voluntary arrangement. **(18)**

20. Why is a voluntary arrangement under the 1986 Act preferred to a voluntary arrangement under the Deeds of Arrangement Act 1914? **(19)**

21. List the consequences of a compulsory winding up of a company. **(20)**

22. What statutory protection is available to persons entering into transactions with a company after the commencement of its insolvent liquidation? **(21)**

23. List the main duties of a liquidator. **(22)**

24. In what circumstances can a charge taken from a company that subsequently becomes insolvent be invalidated? (**23**)

25. Define and explain the difference between fraudulent trading and wrongful trading. (**24**)

26. Define a shadow director and explain whether or not a bank could incur liability as a shadow director of an insolvent company. (**24**)

27. By whom can a voluntary arrangement under ss.1–7 be proposed and in what circumstances? (**27**)

28. Explain when an administration order might be sought against a company. (**28**)

29. On what grounds must the application for an administration order be based? (**29**)

30. Explain the relationship between administration orders and the ability to appoint an administrative receiver. (**30**)

31. What is the effect of an administration order? (**31**)

32. Define a preference. (**34**)

33. What requirements must be fulfilled for a preference to be actionable? (**34**)

34. What is the importance of *Re M C Bacon* (1990) in relation to preferences? (**34**)

35. What statutory protection does a bank enjoy when it finds itself the innocent victim of a preference by the principal debtor under a guarantee and how can a bank protect itself? (**35, 37**)

36. Define a transaction at an undervalue. (**36**)

37. In what specific way does the court's power in relation to a transaction defrauding creditors differ to that available in relation to a preference and a transaction at an undervalue? (**38**)

38. When is a credit transaction extortionate within the meaning of the Act? (**39**)

39. State which debts are provable and which are not in insolvency. (**41, 42**)

40. What options are open to secured creditors in the insolvency of their debtor? (**43**)

41. What is the position in relation to third-party securities? (**43**)

42. List the categories of preferential creditors. (**44**)

43. How do preferential creditors rank among themselves? (**44**)

44. List the order of repayment of debts in bankruptcy and company insolvency. (**46**)

45. Summarise the protection available to a bank in its customer's insolvency. (**48**)

7

Regulated lending

The Consumer Credit Act 1974: an overview

1. Regulated agreements

The Consumer Credit Act 1974 s.189(1) defines a regulated agreement as a 'consumer credit agreement or consumer hire agreement other than an exempt agreement'. This chapter is concerned with the first and third of these categories.

Consumer credit agreements embrace all credit facilities up to £15 000 provided to private individuals, sole traders, partnerships and other unincorporated bodies unless the credit facilities are provided under an exempt agreement: s.8. Provision of credit to companies is *not* regulated.

Under s.9(1), credit is defined as a 'cash loan, and any form of financial accommodation', a wide definition.

The Act also regulates ancillary businesses, such as credit and mortgage brokers, debt collectors, debt adjusters and counsellors, and credit reference agencies.

All references in this chapter are to the Consumer Credit Act 1974 unless otherwise stated.

2. Purpose of the Act

The main purpose of the Act is to prevent the exploitation of individuals by unscrupulous suppliers of credit by providing an effective means of *controlling* a wide range of consumer credit transactions. From their perspective, and with some justification, banks consider the Act to be a sledgehammer to crack a nut, yet they must abide by its provisions in the same way as a moneylender advancing small sums to 'vulnerable' clients.

The Act seeks to achieve its purpose by:

(a) Supervising all those involved in granting credit through a licensing system;
(b) Regulating the contract between creditor and debtor;
(c) Controlling the advertising and canvassing of credit.

As an example, the contact must include terms relating to the amount of credit, the credit limit, the rate of interest and the repayments. If such *prescribed terms* are not included, the agreement is *wholly unenforceable*. Thus, the debtor is given (statutory) rights that are quite independent of the express terms of the contract.

3. Major provisions: an outline

(a) *Licensing*. All businesses that provide credit, lend money or hire goods within the Act's provisions or engage in ancillary credit activities must be *licensed*. Licences are issued by the Office of Fair Trading and it is a criminal offence to engage in such activities unlicensed.

(b) *Advertising*. The Act imposes restrictions on the *mode of advertising* for credit and gives potential borrowers the right to ask for quotations of the true cost of the credit available. This enables them to shop around, confident that they will get the best terms to suit their requirements.

> NOTE: Remember that, while banks compete with each other, there is, in practice, very little difference between the terms they offer borrowers. All banks are subject to the same market forces and the same legal regulations.

(c) *Canvassing*. Canvassing consists of attempting to persuade an individual to enter into regulated agreement by making *oral* representations to the individual when:
　(i) Not previously requested to do so in writing; and
　(ii) Where a visit is made in order to persuade the individual to enter into such an agreement.

(d) *Form and content of regulated agreements*. The Act prescribes the form and content of regulated agreements and provides that copies must be supplied to the prospective debtor.

(e) *Cancellation rights*. A regulated agreement can be cancelled by written notice within the five days (the 'cooling-off' period) after receiving a second copy of the agreement or a statutory cancellation notice in certain circumstances.

(f) *Charge for credit*. The total charge must include not only the *interest payments* but also *all other charges* payable under the agreement or transactions made in connection with it, e.g. a security arrangement. The total charge is converted into a rate of total charge for credit, the *annual percentage rate of charge* (APR).

(g) *Connected lender liability*. Under a debtor–creditor–supplier agreement (*see* 7:8), a creditor incurs joint and several liability with the supplier of the goods or services for the latter's misrepresentation or breach of contract.

(h) *Enforceability.* Failure to comply with the Act's regulations renders the agreement unenforceable without a court order. The court can vary or impose terms or suspend the agreement. These powers extend to any securities taken in connection with the loan.

Types of credit

4. Running-account credit and fixed sum credit

(a) *Running-account credit* is where a credit agreement enables the debtor to receive cash, goods or services from time to time under a continuing credit arrangement up to an amount that does not exceed the debtor's credit limit: s.10(1)(a). Typical examples are bank overdrafts, shops' budget accounts and credit and charge cards.

Running-account credit is regulated:

(i) If the permitted credit limit (the maximum debit balance) is no more than £15 000, disregarding any terms of the agreement that allow that maximum to be temporarily exceeded: s.10(2).

(ii) Where the credit limit exceeds £15 000 or there is no credit limit, if:

(1) No more than £15 000 can be drawn on any one occasion.

(2) The credit charge increases above a certain debit balance (not more than £15 000); or

(3) The debit balance is unlikely to exceed £15 000 at any time.

(b) *Fixed-sum credit* is credit provided under an agreement that fixed the actual amount of the credit from the start, such as a loan of £10 000. In other words, it is any form of credit other than running-account credit: s.10(1)(b).

It is still fixed-sum credit if it is to be received or repaid in instalments.

5. Restricted-use and unrestricted-use credit

(a) *Restricted-use credit* is where the credit is tied to a particular transaction. Under s.11(1), restricted-use credit encompasses the following.

(i) Credit to finance a transaction between the debtor and the creditor, whether forming part of that agreement or not. This covers cases where the supplier of goods or services and the creditor are the same person, such as when the company running the shop supplying the goods also provides the credit.

(ii) Credit to finance a transaction between the debtor and a person other than the creditor. This covers, for example, credit provided by a finance company or by a credit card company.

(iii) Credit to refinance any existing indebtedness to the creditor or to any other person.

(b) *Unrestricted-use credit* is credit that does not fall within s.11(1): s.11(2). Essentially, the debtor is free to use the credit provided as they please, e.g. an overdraft.

(c) *Points to note.*

(i) If a debtor is given a cash loan to buy specific goods, the loan is unrestricted-use credit because the debtor is free to use it as they please, even though, by so doing, the debtor may break the credit agreement: s.11(3).

(ii) A credit card purchase is restricted-use credit because the credit is provided solely for a specific transaction.

(iii) Withdrawing cash on a credit card is unrestricted-use credit. This makes a credit card agreement allowing cash withdrawals is a 'multiple agreement': s.18 (*see* 8:**11** below).

(iv) The distinction between restricted-use and unrestricted-use credit is important in relation to, first, debtor–creditor and debtor–creditor–supplier agreements and, second, the consequences of cancellation (*see* 8:**21**).

6.　Exempt credit

Certain forms of credit are exempt from regulation by the Consumer Credit (Exempt Agreements) Order 1989 made under s.16 of the Act. They are as follows

(a) *Mortgage lending.* This exemption covers debtor–creditor–supplier agreements for loans secured by land mortgages made by all major suppliers of consumer mortgage finance: s.16(2).

(b) *Lending in relation to land transactions.* This exemption covers debtor–creditor–supplier agreements to finance the purchase of land or buildings repayable in *four* instalments or less: s.16(5). The instalments must include all interest and other charges. The agreement does not have to be secured.

(c) *Debtor–creditor–supplier agreements subject to repayment by a prescribed maximum number of instalments.*

(i) Fixed-sum credit to be repaid in four or fewer instalments and within one year of the date of the agreement, e.g. trade credit where there is no running account.

(ii) Running-account credit where the credit advanced in any one

period must be repaid by a single payment, e.g. charge cards (but *not* credit cards), though interest and other charges can be subject to other payments.

(d) *Low-cost credit.* This exemption covers debtor–creditor agreements where the APR does not exceed the highest of the London and Scottish clearing bank's annual base rates plus 1 per cent or 13 per cent, whichever is the higher. (Most bank staff loans are within this definition of low-cost credit.)

(e) *Loan agreements to finance foreign trade.* This exemption covers credit agreements made to finance the import or export of goods and services.

> NOTE: Exempt agreements are not the same as credit agreements that are completely unregulated because they are not within the definition of a regulated agreement, e.g. loans in excess of £15 000 and any credit given to companies, nor partially regulated agreements, such as overdrafts.

7. Overdrafts

Overdrafts provide debtor–creditor, unrestricted-use, running-account credit. Their importance warrants emphasis and reiteration of their legal position in relation to the Act. Note the following points.

(a) An overdraft is a regulated credit agreement, but it is exempt from the *documentation requirements* of the Act (*see* further below).

(b) The wording of s.10(3) *prevents* a creditor avoiding regulation by the Act by either:

(i) Setting a credit limit above £15 000 or by not specifying a credit limit; or by

(ii) Providing that the interest rate will increase when the overdraft exceeds a given figure not exceeding £15 000 although the credit limit is higher than £15 000. Section 10(3) does this by providing that the overdraft will be regulated in such cases if the debtor cannot withdraw more than £15 000 on one occasion or if it is probable that the debit balance will not at any time exceed £15 000. A term of the agreement which allows the credit limit to be temporarily exceeded and which could result in the debit balance exceeding £15 000 will be ignored for the purposes of determining whether the credit limit is below £15 000.

(c) Under s.49(3) a bank can offer overdrafts to its existing current account customers by canvassing them away from the bank's premises without committing an offence (*see* 7:32).

(d) Overdrafts on current accounts are exempt from the documentation requirements of the Act by virtue of a Determination made under s.74 by the Director General of Fair Trading, but a bank is required under the same Determination to provide the following written details about the overdraft to its customer:

(i) The credit limit;

(ii) The annual interest rate and the charges and the conditions under which they may be amended;

(iii) The procedure required to terminate the overdraft. (This amounts to specifying that it is repayable 'on demand'.)

In the case of an *agreed overdraft*, these details must be given to the customer before or at the time the overdraft is granted. The provisions also recognise an *'unagreed' overdraft*. This is an overdraft that is subject to the bank's tacit agreement, specifically, one that was not agreed in advance, but which has continued for three months without the bank taking positive efforts to have it reduced or repaid. In such cases the details must be given before, or within seven days after, the end of the three-month period.

(e) On request by its customer, a bank must give the customer a copy of any document that embodies all or any of the terms on which the overdraft was granted, *providing* the document was signed by both parties: s.78. It must also provide its customer with regular statements (at least annually) showing the state of the account.

(f) The provisions of the Act regulating early termination and enforcement of agreements entered into for fixed periods will not apply unless the overdraft was granted for a fixed period. In this case, the bank cannot make a demand for repayment before the end of this period unless it has given its customer seven days' notice of termination in the prescribed form: s.98 (*see* 7:**23**). (Overdrafts are not usually entered into for fixed periods and they become repayable on demand not on a breach of their terms.)

Types of consumer credit agreements

8.   Debtor–creditor–supplier agreements

Under s.12, there are three kinds of debtor–creditor–supplier agreements.

(a) A restricted-use credit agreement to finance a transaction between the debtor and the creditor: s.12(a).

Only two parties are involved here: the *debtor* and the *creditor*. The creditor is also the supplier of the goods or services purchased with the credit it supplies itself, e.g. a retailer operating its own finance scheme – 'supplier finance'.

(b) A restricted-use credit agreement to finance a transaction between the debtor and a third-party supplier that is made under pre-existing arrangements, or in contemplation of future arrangements, between the creditor and the third-party supplier: s.12(b).

Here three separate parties are involved: the *debtor* who purchases goods or services from the *supplier* with credit provided by the *creditor*. Credit provided by finance companies and credit card schemes are examples of this type of debtor–creditor–supplier agreement. The creditor provides the money directly to the supplier.

The key phrases are 'pre-existing arrangements' and 'contemplation of future arrangements'. On the one hand, the name of a finance company on the windscreen of every car in a showroom and application forms readily available would surely be conclusive evidence of a 'pre-existing arrangement', whereas advice to 'Go and talk to the bank around the corner, I believe the new manager may be helpful' would clearly not be. In between these examples there are many less clear-cut possibilities. Each case would have to be decided on its facts, although the decision would tend to err on the side of the consumer as it is the consumer that the Act is intended to protect.

(c) An unrestricted-use agreement made by the creditor under pre-existing arrangements between the creditor and a third-party supplier knowing that the credit is to be used to finance a transaction between the debtor and the third-party supplier: s.12(c).

Here, the same three parties are involved as in s.12(b), but the credit is unrestricted-use. Whereas in s.12(b) the supplier is paid by the creditor directly, in s.12(c), although an arrangement between supplier and creditor exists to fund the purchase, a cash loan is made to the debtor. It is unrestricted-use because the debtor could, in theory, spend the money on anything they wanted.

9. Debtor–creditor agreements

Under s.13, there are, again, three kinds.

(a) A restricted-use credit agreement to finance a transaction between the debtor and a third-party supplier that is *not* made under pre-existing arrangements, or in contemplation of future arrangements, between the creditor and the third-party supplier: s.13(a).

The only difference between this type of agreement and a debtor–creditor–supplier agreement under s.12(b) is the absence of the 'pre-existing arrangements' or 'contemplation of future arrangements'; again, a question of fact.

(b) A restricted-use agreement to refinance an existing loan advanced by the creditor or any third party.

This would arise where, say, a finance company provides credit to repay credit card companies and other borrowing and makes the payments directly to the other creditors.

(c) An unrestricted-use agreement that is *not* made by the creditor under pre-existing arrangements between the creditor and a third-party supplier knowing that the credit is to be used to finance a transaction between the debtor and the third-party supplier: s.13(c).

Here the scenario is the same as in s.12(c) *except* that there is *no* pre-existing arrangement between creditor and supplier. Personal loans and bank overdrafts are examples of this type of agreement.

10. The importance of the distinction between debtor–creditor–supplier agreements and debtor–creditor agreements

It may seem that the definitions in 7:9 are rather involved because the Act is, essentially, distinguishing between transactions where the creditor also supplies the goods, or has a business arrangement with a third-party supplier who does so and those where the creditor does not or has not. The detail is necessary, however, because the distinction gives rise to different legal consequences.

(a) *Canvassing.* It is an offence to canvass most debtor–creditor agreements: s.49(1) (*see* 7:32 below);

(b) *Connected lender liability.* This only arises under debtor–creditor-supplier agreements.

NOTE: Bearing in mind that the distinction between the two types of agreement is primarily based on whether 'pre-existing arrangements' exist between creditor and supplier, the existence or absence of such arrangements is of the essence.

11. Other types of agreements

The following fall into this group.

(a) *Exempt agreements.* These agreements are exempt from regulation by the Consumer Credit (Exempt Agreements) Order 1989 made under s.16 of the Act (*see* generally 7:6). Note that the definitions found in ss.11–13 are used in the definitions of the categories of exempt agreements.

(b) *Small agreements.* These are regulated agreements for the provision of credit not exceeding £50 (other than hire-purchase and conditional sale agreements): s.17.

The documentation requirements of the Act do not apply to small agreements and a debtor under a small agreement cannot invoke the withdrawal and cancellation rights contained in the Act. Small agreements are, therefore, partly regulated agreements.

(c) *Multiple agreements.* An agreement for a credit card that allows the cardholder to make cash withdrawals which are debited to the account is an example of a multiple agreement under s.18. When used as a credit card, it provides restricted-use credit under a debtor–creditor–supplier agreement (there are pre-existing arrangements between the card issuer and the retailer) and unrestricted-use credit under a debtor–creditor agreement when used as a cash card.

The Act treats each use as a separate agreement for the purposes of regulation and applies the appropriate documentary requirements and formalities to each.

(d) *Linked transactions.* Under s.19, a transaction is linked to a regulated agreement, actual or prospective, if:

(i) It is entered into to comply with a term of the principal agreement; or

(ii) It is financed by a debtor–creditor–supplier agreement.

An example of the first type would be an insurance or maintenance contract entered into with a specified company at the insistence or suggestion of the finance company that provided the credit. An example of the second would be the contract of sale entered into when goods are purchased using a credit card or a loan from a finance company.

The concept of the linked transaction is intended to avoid the possibility of the protection afforded by the Act being undermined by virtue of extra charges that may be imposed in the linked transaction and to protect the debtor if the anticipated credit is not made available. Section 19 does this by providing that:

(i) In general, a linked transaction entered into before the regulated credit agreement is concluded shall have no legal effect until the latter contract is concluded, i.e. the debtor can cancel the purchase if the application for credit is turned down; and

(ii) Any rights of withdrawal, cancellation or early settlement under the credit agreement shall extend to the linked transaction.

NOTE: An agreement for the provision of security cannot be a linked transaction: s.19(1).

(e) *Non-commercial agreements.* A non-commercial agreement is a regulated credit agreement that the creditor does not make in the course of its business, e.g. a loan made to an employee in order to buy a season ticket. Such agreements are partly regulated agreements because the provisions relating to documentation and cancellation do not apply to them.

(f) *Credit-token agreements.* A credit-token agreement is a regulated agreement for credit to be provided by means of the use of a credit-token: s.14(2) (*see* 7:**12**).

Of the five payment cards discussed in 7:**13**, only an agreement for a credit card is a credit-token agreement within the meaning of the Act.

Credit-tokens

12. Definition

Section 14(1) defines a credit-token as a card, cheque, voucher, coupon, stamp, form, booklet or other document or thing given to an individual by a person carrying on a consumer credit business, who undertakes:

(a) that, on production of it (whether or not some other action is also required), they will supply cash, goods and services (or any of them) on credit; or

(b) that where, on production of it to a third party (whether or not any other action is also required) and the third party supplies cash, goods and services (or any of them), they will pay the third party for them (whether or not deducting any discount or commission), in return for payment to them by the individual.

The definition is important to banks in so far that if any type of payment card is a credit-token, the agreement for the card will be regulated by the Act, for example the documentary requirements will apply, as will s.51 (unsolicited credit-tokens) and s.84 (liability for the use of a credit-token by a third party).

Section 14(1) clearly contemplates that payment cards *can* be credit-tokens by including the reference to 'other action' in both subsections, e.g. credit card vouchers must be signed to authorise the transaction and money cannot be obtained from an ATM without the cardholder keying in the amount of money to be withdrawn and authorising the withdrawal by keying in their PIN.

13. Payment cards

The question to be answered is whether any of the five main types of payment cards is a credit-token. The definitions that follow are taken from *Good Banking*, the code of practice published by the Association for Payment Clearing Services, the British Bankers' Association, and The Building Societies Association in December, 1991.

(a) *Cheque guarantee card* – a card issued by a bank or building society that guarantees the payment of a cheque up to the amount shown on the card provided its conditions of use are followed.

A cheque guarantee card is *not* a credit-token because the bank guarantees the payment of the cheque used to purchase the cash, goods or services obtained; it does not pay for them itself.

(b) *Cash card* – a card used to obtain cash and other services from an ATM.

By s.14(4), activating an ATM by using a cash card is 'production' of it within s.14(1). However, this is academic for the following reasons.

(i) When a cash card is used in the issuing bank's own machines, credit is not obtained as required by s.14(1)(a) because the cash withdrawal is recorded immediately, even though the balance is not adjusted until later. If a withdrawal is made from an overdrawn account, it is the prior agreement and not the use of the card that results in credit being provided. If the use of the card results in an unauthorised overdraft (through the limitations of the ATM system), this is not 'credit' within the meaning of the Act because it was not previously agreed.

(ii) Use of a cash card in a different bank's ATM will *not* be producing the card to a 'third party' as required by s.14(1)(b) if that bank acts as the issuing bank's agent, which is probably the case. The position will be as in (i) above.

(iii) If the other bank does not provide cash as the issuing bank's agent, the credit-token agreement is *within* s.14(1)(b), but is *exempt from regulation* under the Act as 'an arrangement for the electronic transfer of funds from a current account at a bank' by virtue of the Banking Act 1987, s.89.

NOTE: Where a credit card or charge card incorporates a cash card facility with cash withdrawals being debited to the account, the cash withdrawn is supplied on credit within s.14(1)(a), *whoever's* ATM is used. The cash withdrawal facility will be a regulated debtor–creditor, unrestricted-use agreement. This will make the charge card agreement a 'multiple agreement' within s.18 and, therefore, partly regulated.

(c) *Debit card* – a card, operating as a substitute for a cheque, that can be used to obtain cash or make a payment at a point of sale. The customer's account is subsequently debited for such a transaction without deferment of payment.

As a debit card is used to obtain goods or services from a third party, it is a credit-token by virtue of s.14(1)(b). (In some large retail chains, a limited amount of cash can also be obtained when the card is used to purchase goods or services in the shop.) However, the credit-token agreement is exempt by virtue of the Banking Act 1987 s.89.

NOTE: A fuller discussion of cash cards and debit cards in the context of s.14(1) can be found in 10:7 and 12.

(d) *Credit card* – a card that allows customers to buy on credit and to obtain cash advances. Customers receive regular statements and may pay the balance in full, or in part, usually subject to a certain minimum. Interest is payable on outstanding balances.

A credit card is a credit-token providing running-account credit and use of the credit card to purchase goods or services is a fully regulated, restricted-use, debtor–creditor–supplier agreement within s.12(b). 'Connected lender liability' under s.75 applies (*see* 7:**28** and **29**).

(e) *Charge card* – similar to a credit card, it enables customers to pay for purchases and, in some cases, to obtain cash advances. When the monthly statement is received, the balance must be paid *in full*.

However, charge card agreements are not regulated because paragraph 3(1)(a)(ii) of the Consumer Credit (Exempt Agreements) Order 1989 exempts from regulation debtor–creditor–supplier agreements where the debtor must repay the *total* credit provided in a given period in *one* payment. As the balance on a charge card statement must be paid in full each month, paragraph 3(1)(a)(ii) exempts charge cards. As a result of exemption, 'connected lender liability' under s.75 does not apply.

NOTE: Although charge cards are not usually subject to a credit limit, they are not excluded from the Act on this ground because it is unlikely that the £15 000 credit limit in the Act will be exceeded in any one month (*see* 7:**4**).

(f) *Summary*.

(i) Cheque guarantee cards and cash cards used in the card issuer's ATMs are not credit-tokens. Cash cards used in third-party ATMs are not credit-tokens if the third-party bank acts as agent for the card issuer.

(ii) Debit cards, credit cards, charge cards and cash cards used in third-party ATMs (where no agency agreement exists with the card issuer) are credit-tokens.

(iii) Agreements for debit cards, charge cards (unless they incor-

porate a cash card facility) and cash cards used in third-party ATMs are exempt from regulation.

(iv) Only credit card agreements are fully regulated.

14. Unsolicited credit-tokens

Section 51(1) makes it an offence to give a person a credit-token unless that person has asked for it. Under s.51(2) the request must be *in writing* unless the agreement is a small debtor–creditor–supplier agreement, i.e. an agreement under which the credit limit is less than £50.

In practice, therefore, banks cannot send debit cards, credit cards, charge cards and cash cards that can be used in third-party ATMs to their customers unless requested in writing to do so. (*See* 10:6 for a fuller discussion of the position in relation to cash cards.)

The prohibition does not apply to renewal or replacement cards: s.51(3). However, a written request is still required for a renewal or replacement debit or charge card because s.51(3) only applies to cards used under a credit-token agreement, i.e. a regulated agreement and agreements for debit and charge cards are exempt from regulation by virtue of the Banking Act 1987 s.89. (The terms in the original agreement or application form are probably sufficient to satisfy the requirement for a written request.)

15. Third-party use of credit-tokens

As with a cheque, a card issuer (the bank) can only debit the cardholder's (the customer's) account with a payment if the cardholder authorised the payment, i.e. the card issuer has the cardholder's mandate to pay.

The position differs according to whether the payment is authorised by a signature or by a PIN.

(a) *Payment authorised by a signature.* This applies to credit card, charge card and most debit card payments. If the cardholder's signature is forged, the card issuer cannot debit the account.

(b) *Payment authorised by a PIN.* This applies to cash card withdrawals from ATMs and some debit cards (where a more advanced EFTPOS system is operated). Here the authorisation principle is different. The card issuer will have the cardholder's mandate to make the payment where either:

(i) The person using the card and PIN did so with the cardholder's express or implied authority; or

(ii) The conditions of use make the cardholder responsible for third-party use of the card.

To make third-party use the cardholder's responsibility, the conditions of use will impose on the cardholder a duty to safeguard the card and the PIN, e.g. by not writing the PIN on the card.

NOTE: Such provisions do not come within the Unfair Contract Terms Act 1977 because the bank is not seeking to exclude liability for its own breach of contract. Thus, the provisions could, in theory, be enforceable even though they were 'unreasonable'.

(c) *The position in relation to regulated credit-token agreements.* Of the five payment cards discussed above, this applies only to credit cards (*see* 7:**13**).

The Act limits a cardholders' liability to £50 (s.84(1)) for third-party use of such credit-tokens. Liability can only be incurred where:

(i) The third party acts as the debtor's (cardholder's) agent: s.83(1).
(ii) The third party has the debtor's (cardholder's) authority to use the credit-token (payment card): s.84(1).
(iii) The third party acquired possession of the credit-token with the debtor's consent: s.84(2).

NOTE: This section does not mention using the credit-token on behalf of or with the authority of the debtor and would seem to mean that the debtor is liable even if they have not voluntarily disclosed the PIN to the third party.

(iv) The credit-token has been lost or stolen, until such time as the creditor (card issuer) receives notice of the loss or theft: s.84(3).

By s.66, a debtor is not liable for any use of a credit-token before they have accepted it by signing it, signing a receipt for it or using it. This would cover misuse of a card that has been lost in the post before reaching the debtor.

NOTE: The statutory limit to liability of £50 in s.83(1) does *not* apply to cash cards and debit cards because neither are used under a regulated credit-token agreement. However, the provisions of the Code of Practice effectively extend the protection of the Act to their holders (*see* 10:**5** and **12**).

Form of the contract

16. Introduction
The Act and the regulations made under it prescribe many different forms and procedures. This section of the chapter and the next –

'Procedures' – are concerned only with regulated personal loan agreements for unsecured credit provided by a bank to an individual.

17. Compliance

Compliance is determined by s.61. This section provides that a regulated agreement must be:

(a) In the prescribed form;
(b) Embody all the terms of the agreement other than implied terms;
(c) Readily legible when presented or sent to the debtor for signature;
(d) Signed in the prescribed manner by the debtor and by the creditor or the creditor's agent.

The consequence of non-compliance is that the agreement becomes enforceable against the debtor only by order of the court: s.65. However, the court will only dismiss the enforcement application where it is just to do so, taking into account any prejudice suffered by the debtor and the degree to which the creditor is responsible for the non-compliance.

An enforcement order cannot be made if:

(a) The debtor did not sign the agreement in the prescribed manner or did not sign at all.
(b) The agreement that the debtor signed did not contain all the prescribed terms, whether or not it was in the required form.
(c) In the case of *cancellable* agreements, the copies and statutory notices required by the Act were not sent or given to the debtor (s.127).

18. Prescribed contents

The contents of the agreement are prescribed by the Consumer Credit (Agreements) Regulations 1983.

(a) *The heading.* This must indicate the nature of the agreement. The main statutory heading is 'Credit Agreement regulated by the Consumer Credit Act 1974'.
(b) The *full name and address* of each party.
(c) *The financial details.* These must appear together in the agreement without any other information being inserted in the section, specifically:

> *(i)* A description of the subject matter of the contract if the loan to purchase it is a restricted-use, debtor–creditor–supplier agreement for fixed-sum credit;
> *(ii)* The cash price;

(iii) The amount of credit advanced (fixed-sum credit) or the credit limit, if any (running-account credit);

(iv) The total charge for credit (fixed-sum credit) or the interest rate and charges (running-account credit and variable-rate fixed-sum credit);

(v) The timing and amounts of repayments;

(vi) The APR and, for variable-rate agreements, a statement that a variation in rate has not been taken into account in calculating the APR and a statement of the circumstances in which the rate might vary.

NOTE: This provision could have caused considerable practical difficulties to banks because much bank lending is subject to a variable rate. Fortunately, in *Lombard Tricity Finance Limited* v *Paton* (1989) (CA), it was held that the proviso is satisfied by a statement that the rate is subject to variation from time to time at the *absolute discretion of the creditor*.

The section of the agreement containing the financial details is sometimes known as the 'holy ground'.

(d) *Security.* Any security to be given by the *debtor* must be described and the security document referred to. Any third-party security is likely to be the subject of an express term inserted by the bank.

Any default payments must be described.

(e) *Cancellation rights (see 7:21).*

19. Other terms

(a) *Conditions for inclusion.* A bank or other creditor may include other terms in a regulated agreement provided they are:

(i) Not contrary to the provisions of the Act;

(ii) Not given greater prominence in the agreement than the statutory contents; and

(iii) Not inserted in the section covering the financial details.

(b) *Bank terms.* Typically a bank might include:

(i) A *repayment covenant*;

(ii) An acceptance of *joint and several liability* where there is more than one borrower;

(iii) A *right of combination*.

NOTE: Such additional clauses must be effectively incorporated into the contract by inserting a clear reference to them before the signature clause.

Procedures

20. Execution of the agreement

(a) *Signature.* The borrower must sign the agreement in the signature box, the specifications and contents of which are prescribed.

(b) *Copies of the agreement.* Under the Consumer Credit (Cancellation Notices and Copies of Documents) Regulations 1983, the borrower must be given a copy of the agreement immediately if it is presented personally to them for signature. If it is sent, a copy must accompany the agreement. If the agreement is sent *before* the lender signs it, which is usual, i.e. the 'agreement' signed by the borrower is actually a contractual offer to the lender, a second copy must be sent within seven days of the lender signing it (thereby accepting the borrower's offer). The second copy of a credit-token agreement can be sent before or at the time the credit-token is issued.

In the case of a cancellable agreement (*see* 7:**21**), the copy must contain a statutory notice of the borrower's right to cancel the agreement and how this right can be exercised. To make sure the borrower is aware of this right, a statutory cancellation notice must be sent within seven days of the borrower or the lender signing the agreement, whichever is the later, *unless* a second copy of the agreement containing the notice is sent (it must be sent by post) during this period.

21. Cancellation

(a) *Conditions.* Under s.67, A regulated agreement can be cancelled where:

(*i*) Face-to-face oral negotiations took place between the creditor and debtor *before* the contract was entered into by the debtor.

(*ii*) The debtor signed the agreement somewhere *other* than the trade premises of the creditor or those of a party to a linked transaction. In the latter case it would usually be the trade premises of the supplier and the agreement would be a restricted-use debtor–creditor–supplier agreement.

NOTE: Certain other agreements cannot be cancelled by virtue of their nature, not by virtue of the circumstances of their conclusion, e.g. agreements secured on land, restricted-use agreements to finance the purchase of land, a bridging loan to purchase land and non-commercial agreements.

(b) *Exercise of the right.* The debtor exercises the right to cancel the agreement by giving written notice to the creditor of their wish to do so during the *five days* after receiving the statutory cancellation notice or the second copy of the agreement containing the notice. This five-day period is known as the 'cooling off' period.

NOTE: The 'cooling off' period begins on the *day after* the notice or second copy containing the notice is received and the notice of cancellation is in time if it is posted on the fifth day and received later or never received at all: s.69.

(c) *Effect.* The effect of the debtor exercising their right of cancellation is to terminate the regulated agreement and any linked transaction. In consequence, the *debtor* must repay any money borrowed and return any credit-token issued; the *creditor* must refund any interest and charges.

NOTE: In order to avoid the problems raised by cancellable agreements, for example money being withdrawn before cancellation that the debtor is unable to repay, banks will normally ensure that cancellable agreements are either signed on bank premises or that no borrowing takes place under the agreement until the end of the five-day cooling off period.

22. Variation
Under s.82, a bank can include a clause in the agreement allowing it to vary interest rates and repayment instalments provided that the debtor is given written notice setting out particulars of the variation at least seven days before the variation takes effect. Variations not covered by the variation clause, e.g. an extension of the term because the debtor is in default, require a modifying agreement.

If the only variation is a change in the interest rate, the bank can notify the change by publishing it in three national daily newspapers and by notices in its branches. In this case the variation takes effect immediately.

23. Termination
Under s.98, a creditor must give the debtor at least seven days' written notice of termination of a regulated agreement, even if the agreement states that it will terminate at the end of a specific period. Termination may not necessarily be because of the debtor's breach of the agreement. The agreement may provide, for example, that it can be terminated if the debtor is sent to prison or loses their job.

If the creditor wishes to terminate for breach of the agreement, the debtor must, similarly, be given seven days' notice – a *default notice*. Additionally, the notice must specify the nature of the breach and either give the amount of compensation that must be paid or, if the breach can be remedied, what action is required by the debtor to do so. The debtor must be given at least seven days in which to remedy the breach of the agreement or pay the compensation: s.88.

Until written notice of termination has been given, a creditor is, *inter alia*, unable to demand early repayment, terminate, restrict or defer any of the debtor's rights or enforce security where the debtor is in breach of the agreement: s.87. If the creditor wishes to enforce early repayment or to terminate, restrict or defer any of the debtor's rights before the end of a *fixed-term* agreement where the debtor is *not* in breach of the agreement, the creditor must, again, give the debtor seven days' written notice: s.76.

> NOTE: The statutory provisions relating to termination do not apply to overdrafts because they are not fixed-term credit and because it is impossible to demand *early* repayment because the obligation to repay does not arise until a demand for repayment is made.

24. Voluntary early repayment

Whether or not the agreement permits it, s.94 gives a debtor the right to make early repayment of the whole debt (not part). If the debtor does so, they are entitled to a rebate of the credit charges proportional to the period of the loan that is unexpired.

To enable the debtor to exercise this right, s.97 entitles the debtor to a statement from the creditor showing the amount outstanding after the early repayment rebate has been deducted.

Secured lending

25. Introduction

This section of the chapter covers only *mortgages over land*, although the Act covers all forms of security.

26. Land-related lending

In practice, most lending secured by land mortgages will be completely unregulated simply because the sum involved is above the £15 000 limit for regulation. Much of what remains will be exempt by virtue of s.16 and the Consumer Credit (Exempt Agreements) Order 1989 made under s.16, which redefined the section. (This was mentioned in 7:6 and now needs to be considered in more detail.)

The exemption covers land-related lending by, among others, local authorities, many insurance companies and friendly societies and all building societies, banks and wholly owned subsidiaries of banks. Land-secured lending will also generally be unregulated if the loan is not made for a purpose related to the land.

The following loans are exempt by virtue of the 1989 order.

(a) A debtor–creditor agreement for a loan advanced for the purchase of land or for the provision of residential or business premises secured by a mortgage on *any* land.

(b) A debtor–creditor–supplier agreement for a loan advanced for the purchase of land or for the provision of residential or business premises secured by a mortgage on land *purchased with the loan*.

(c) A further loan by a lender under an existing agreement that is exempt under (a) above for the alteration, enlargement, repair or improvement of a building on the land purchased or built on with the initial loan, provided that both loans are secured by mortgages on that land.

(d) A debtor–creditor agreement for a loan made to refinance an existing loan that is exempt under (a) or (c) above whether with the same or a different lender.

> NOTE: The above exemptions do not require that the mortgage is given by the borrower.

27. Right of withdrawal

(a) *Introduction.* In order to avoid problems with conveyancing practice and the Land Registry, e.g. a mortgage might be registered before cancellation took place, a borrower's cancellation rights under s.67 do not apply to regulated agreements secured by mortgages over the land. In order not to negate the protection of the Act, an alternative is provided by s.58 – the borrower is able to *withdraw* from certain proposed credit agreements and withdraw from or cancel any linked transaction, e.g. the contract of purchase, and recover any money paid, for example survey fees on the property.

(b) *Application.* The right of withdrawal itself is very limited because it does not apply to restricted-use agreements to purchase the land mortgaged or a bridging loan in connection with its purchase. In practice, almost all loans to purchase property are restricted-use because the funds will usually only be made available to the borrower through one of the solicitors involved in the purchase. Furthermore, of course, if the loan is for more than £15 000, which would be usual, it will not be regulated in any case.

Thus, the right of withdrawal only applies to an unrestricted-use, secured, regulated agreement.

(c) *Procedure.* In such agreements, the lender must give the borrower a copy of the proposed agreement at least seven days before the borrower is given the actual agreement for signing: s.61(2). This advance copy must inform the borrower of their right to withdraw from the agreement and how to exercise this right: s.58(1).

There then follows the *consideration period.* This period begins on the day the advance copy is given to the borrower and ends seven days after the actual agreement is sent to the borrower for signing or, if earlier, seven days after the borrower has signed and returned it: s.61(3). During this consideration period, the lender must not communicate with the borrower in any way unless specifically requested to do so by the borrower (s.61(2)) and the borrower *may withdraw from the agreement* and withdraw from or cancel any linked transaction.

A regulated agreement secured by a land mortgage that fails to comply with the procedural requirements of the Act is unenforceable by the lender without a court order: s.65(1).

> NOTE: Under s.126, a land mortgage securing a regulated agreement is enforceable only by court order and only in so far as the agreement provides for its enforcement, i.e. the right to enforce must be expressly given by the agreement.

Connected lender liability

28. Section 75

(a) *Meaning.* Section 75(1) provides that, if the debtor has a claim against the supplier for *misrepresentation* or *breach of contract* under a debtor–creditor–supplier agreement (*see* 7:**8**), the creditor is jointly and severally liable with the supplier to the debtor.

(b) *Application.* Connected lender liability typically arises when purchases from the supplier are made (financed) by credit card or financed by a personal loan instalment finance agreement with a finance house.

> NOTE: Connected lender liability does not arise when a charge card or a debit card is used. Both are exempt from regulation (*see* 7:**13**).

A claim for misrepresentation by the supplier could arise if the supplier made untrue statements about the goods or services that resulted in the debtor buying them. An action for breach of contract could arise, for example, if the goods supplied were defective or a service was provided without due care and skill or not provided at all. Most purported exclusions of liability for such breaches are either rendered totally void or made subject to a test of reasonableness by the Unfair Contract Terms Act 1977, depending on the types of transaction involved.

Under section 75(3), connected lender liability does not apply:

(i) In respect of a non-commercial agreement: s.189(1); or

(ii) Where the claim relates to any single item the cash price of which is £100 or less or more than £30 000. This exclusion subsumes a 'small agreement': s.17.

NOTE: Section 75(4) enables the debtor to claim: s.75(1) *even if* the debtor broke the terms of the credit agreement by entering into the contract with the supplier.

29. The creditor's indemnity

Under s.75(2), the creditor is entitled to an indemnity from the supplier for loss suffered in satisfying their liability: s.75(1). The indemnity includes reasonable costs incurred in defending an action brought by the debtor.

Section 75(2) does not apply where the supplier successfully defends an action brought by the debtor or settles the claim without admitting liability. The creditor may, nevertheless, have incurred substantial costs. An indemnity in these cases would appear to be payable only where the agreement between the supplier and creditor provides for one.

Advertisements, quotations and canvassing

30. Advertisements

(a) *Scope of the regulation*. The advertisement provisions of the Act apply to any form of advertisement published for the purposes of a business carried on by the advertiser indicating that they are willing to provide credit: s.43(1). Both credit brokers and credit providers are covered.

A variety of exemptions under the Act mean that the statutory controls on advertising apply only to advertisements for:

(i) Regulated agreements;

(ii) Credit agreements with an individual that is secured on land.

(b) *Form and content*. Under s.44(1), the Secretary of State can make regulations governing the form and content of advertisements. These regulations cover not only *what* can and cannot be included but also *how* it should be set out. For example, the current regulations – the Consumer Credit (Advertisements) Regulations 1989 – provide that the charge for credit must be expressed as an annual percentage rate (APR) and be set out as prominently as any other credit-related information and more prominently than any other interest rate. They also provide that the term 'overdraft' can only be used in the context of an overdraft on a current account.

The overriding requirement is that any regulated advertisement conveys a fair and reasonably comprehensive explanation of the nature of the credit (or hire) facilities offered and their true cost.

To ensure this, s.47 makes it an offence, subject to certain defences, for any person to design, produce or cause the publication of an advertisement that infringes the Advertisement Regulations: s.47. The advertiser also commits an offence if the advertisement gives information that is materially false or misleading, including instances where this is so because the advertiser's stated or implied intentions are untrue: s.46.

(c) *Types of advertisements.* Advertisements will be one of three types: simple, intermediate or full. They differ in the amount of information that must be supplied.

(i) Simple. The advertisement *must* merely state the advertiser's name, logo, address, telephone number and occupation. It must *not* mention that the advertiser is willing to extend credit.

(ii) Intermediate. Besides containing details of the advertiser, the advertisement *must* state certain details about the credit offered, e.g. the APR, whether a credit-broker's fee is payable, where applicable, that security or insurance is required and that written details are available on request.

The statutory warning 'Your house is at risk if you do not keep up payments on a mortgage or other loan secured on it' *must* be included if a mortgage over a borrower's home is or may be required to secure the credit offered. Intermediate advertisements are the most common type.

(iii) Full. Full advertisements *must* provide a comprehensive and fair view of the credit facilities advertised. In addition to the requirements of an intermediate advertisement, the frequency of payments must be stated and whether the credit offered is restricted to a particular class or group of the public, e.g. 'Sorry, no tenants'.

31. Quotations

A provider of consumer credit must provide written information about the credit terms being offered to a prospective borrower who asks: s.52.

The form and content of quotations is governed by the Consumer Credit (Quotations) Regulations 1989. The content is similar to an intermediate advertisement with the addition of details of the credit limit and the amounts, number and frequency of payments.

32. Canvassing

(a) *Definition.* Under s.48(1), canvassing is attempting to persuade an individual to enter into a regulated agreement by making *oral* representations to the individual when:

(i) Not previously requested to do so in writing; and

(ii) Where a visit is made in order to persuade the individual to enter into such an agreement.

Under s.49(1), it *is* an offence to canvass *debtor–creditor* agreements *off trade premises.*

Note the following points.

(i) Canvassing a debtor–creditor–supplier agreement or an exempt agreement is *not* an offence.

(ii) Canvassing of overdrafts to *existing current account customers* is expressly permitted: s.49(3)(b).

(iii) The canvassing prohibition does *not* apply where the customer or prospective customer is a *company* or other corporate body, nor where the credit facilities under discussion *exceed* £15 000.

(iv) Restrictions do *not* apply to telephone conversations, letters, circulars and leaflets (other than to minors) and to situations where the customer or prospective customer initiates the discussion about credit facilities.

(v) It is an offence to send a circular or any document to a minor that invites the minor to borrow money or to use other credit facilities, including credit cards, or to apply for information or advice on borrowing money or otherwise obtaining credit or hiring goods: s.50(1). It is, however, a defence for the person charged to prove that they neither knew, nor had reasonable cause to suspect, that the intended recipient was a minor unless the document was sent to the minor at a school or other educational establishment for minors: s.50(2) and (3).

(b) *Trade premises.* In the context of a bank's likely involvement, trade premises are the normal business premises of the bank (temporary or permanent) or the business premises of the customer: s.48(2).

NOTE: As personal customers do not have trade premises, a bank can only legally canvass such customers on its *own* business premises, unless it has previously been requested in writing to do so elsewhere.

Credit brokerage

33. Definition

Credit brokerage is the business of introducing individuals requiring credit to persons that provide either consumer credit or goods under consumer hire agreements: s.145. It therefore applies to a wide range of businesses, e.g. insurance agencies and mortgage brokers, solicitors and accountants who arrange loans for clients, estate agents who introduce prospective purchasers to banks and building societies and retailers who introduce customers to a finance house.

A credit broker must be licensed under the Act by the Director General of Fair Trading.

Whether a person 'introduces' an individual to a provider of consumer credit is a question of fact. It would seem that a positive act is required, although the Act should be interpreted in the individual's favour. Thus, completing a loan application on behalf of an individual and sending it to the finance company or bank would certainly constitute an 'introduction', but merely displaying leaflets advertising providers of consumer credit would probably not.

34. Types of credit covered

Section 145 applies to the following types of credit:

(a) Regulated credit;
(b) Exempt credit, unless it is exempt because of the number of repayments involved (*see* 7:**6**);
(c) Credit secured on land where the individual wanting the credit requires it to purchase a residential property for occupation by themselves or by a relative;
(d) Credit that is to be provided by an agreement made under foreign law but which would be a regulated agreement if made under UK law.

35. Enforceability of agreements

If a regulated agreement results from an introduction of the debtor to the creditor by an unlicensed credit broker, the agreement will only be enforceable with the consent of the Director General of Fair Trading.

Factors that the Director General will consider include the extent to which the credit broker's conduct prejudiced the debtor and the extent to which the creditor is responsible for enabling the credit broker to carry on their business unlicensed.

Progress test 7

1. Agreements with whom are covered by the Act? **(1)**

2. Name the three methods by which the Act seeks to achieve its objective of controlling the provision of credit to consumers. **(2)**

3. In what circumstances is running-account credit above £15 000 regulated by the Act? **(4)**

4. Explain how a credit card provides both restricted-use credit and unrestricted-use credit. **(5)**

5. List the types of lending that are exempt from regulation by the Act. **(6)**

6. What type of credit is provided by an overdraft? **(7)**

7. Why is an overdraft agreement only partly regulated? **(7)**

8. What is an 'unagreed' overdraft under the Act? **(7)**

9. Distinguish between a debtor–creditor agreement and debtor–creditor–supplier agreement. **(8, 9)**

10. Explain the differences between the three kinds of debtor–creditor–supplier agreements. **(8)**

11. In what two main respects is the distinction between debtor–creditor agreements and debtor–creditor–supplier agreements important? **(10)**

12. Explain what is meant by a multiple agreement and by a linked transaction. **(11)**

13. Which common payment cards are credit-tokens? **(12)**

14. Which common payment cards are regulated credit-tokens? **(12)**

15. To what extent can a credit-token be sent unsolicited, if at all? **(14)**

16. Payment by credit-token can be authorised by signature or by PIN. Explain the different approaches to third-party use based on the nature of the authorisation. **(15)**

17. Explain the circumstances in which a credit card holder is liable for its use by a third party. **(15)**

18. What is the limit on a credit card holder's liability for unauthorised use of the card by a third party? Is this limit imposed by the Act or as a result of the Code of Practice? **(15)**

19. To be enforceable, a regulated agreement must comply with the Act. Name the four aspects in which compliance is required. **(17)**

20. List the contents of a regulated agreement that are prescribed by the Act. **(18)**

21. What restrictions are there on a bank including terms other than those prescribed by statute in the agreement? **(19)**

22. Explain the regulations relating to copies of the agreement. **(20)**

23. Under what circumstances can a regulated agreement be cancelled? **(21)**

24. Define the cooling off period. **(21)**

25. Explain the effect of cancellation. **(21)**

26. How may a bank communicate a variation in the interest rate to its borrowers? **(22)**

27. Explain how a regulated agreement can be terminated. **(23)**

28. Most land-related lending is unregulated. Why? **(26)**

29. Why is the 'right of withdrawal' a very limited right in practice? **(27)**

30. Explain the meaning and scope of connected lender liability. **(28)**

31. What is the overriding principle applied in the regulation of advertisements for consumer credit? **(30)**

32. Define canvassing under the Act. **(32)**

33. In what circumstances is canvassing an offence? **(32)**

34. In what circumstances is canvassing permitted? **(32)**

35. Define credit brokerage. **(33)**

8

Financial services regulation

Introduction

1. The Financial Services Act 1986
The Financial Services Act 1986 (FSA):

(a) Established a system for regulating the conduct of investment business with the aims of encouraging competition among financial organisations and promoting confidence among investors;
(b) Relies on a system of *self-regulation* by the financial services industry, controlled by the Securities and Investment Board (SIB);
(c) Requires all persons engaged in investment business to obtain authorisation for their activities.

> NOTE: The term 'persons' includes partnerships and corporate bodies.

All references in this chapter are to the Financial Services Act 1986, unless stated otherwise.

2. Authorisation

(a) *Primary methods*. Authorisation can be obtained in one of three main ways.
    (i) Direct authorisation by SIB – such authorisation makes the person subject directly to the rules of SIB.
    (ii) By membership of a Self-Regulatory Organisation (SRO) – a person is only expected to join one such SRO.
    (iii) Through membership of a Recognised Professional Body (RPB) – such authorisation places limits on the investment business that may be undertaken (*see* 8:**11**).
(b) *Other methods*.
    (i) Friendly societies – authorised under the Friendly Societies Act 1974.
    (ii) Insurance companies – authorised under the Insurance Companies Act 1982. (Authorisation by the 1982 Act covers long-term life assurance business and should an insurance company wish to undertake *unrelated* investment business it will require authorisation by being a member of LAUTRO.)

Both the above Acts provide appropriate controls of investment business.

(iii) By being an investment business *authorised in a member state of the EC.*

3. Exemptions

Some organisations and individuals engaged in investment business have partial or total exemption from authorisation.

(a) The *Bank of England* – total exemption.

(b) *Listed institutions* – the list is maintained by the Bank of England and allows the Bank to regulate the conduct of business in the money market on a non-statutory basis.

(c) *Lloyds and Lloyds underwriters* – in connection with investment business related to its own insurance business.

(d) *Recognised investment exchanges and recognised clearing houses* – for example, the International Stock Exchange and TALISMAN, its clearing house – exemption depending on recognition by the SIB.

(e) *Appointed representatives* – self-employed company representatives and tied agents who market investments on behalf of authorised persons, the latter being responsible for their conduct.

(f) *Certain public officials* – for example, the Public Trustee and official receivers.

4. Penalties

(a) *Lack of authorisation*. It is a criminal offence to conduct investment business without authorisation. It is a defence to show either that reasonable precautions and due care were being exercised when the offence was committed, e.g. authorisation was not sought on legal advice or that the accused reasonably believed that authorisation was unnecessary.

Investment agreements entered into by an unauthorised person are unenforceable unless the court considers that it is just and equitable to enforce them. The client can recover money paid or property transferred and can claim compensation from the unauthorised person, e.g. for loss of interest on investments.

(b) *Misleading statements*. It is an offence for a person to make a misleading statement, promise of forecast so as to induce someone to enter into an investment agreement or to exercise any rights conferred by an investment agreement or to refrain from doing so.

(c) *Misleading practices*. It is an offence to do any act or engage in any course of conduct that creates a false or misleading impression as to the price or value of any investment if it is done for the purpose of creating that impression and thereby inducing a person to deal in those investments.

5.   The Consumer Credit Act 1974 and FSA 1986 compared

(a) *Similarities.* Both:

    (i) Aim to protect the public;

    (ii) Rely on a licensing system to do this;

    (iii) Are implemented through secondary legislation.

(b) *Differences.*

    (i) The FSA protects companies as well as individuals.

    (ii) There are financial limits to the CCA's protection.

    (iii) The FSA provides a regulatory framework; the CCA sets out rules.

    (iv) Regulation under the CCA is directly by the Department of Trade and Industry; regulation under the FSA is self-regulation through the SIB and through it by SROs and recognised professional bodies.

Investment and investment business

6.   Investment business

There are five categories:

(a) Dealing in investments;

(b) Arranging deals in investments;

(c) Managing investments;

(d) Advising on investments;

(e) Establishing, operating or winding up collective investment schemes, e.g. unit trusts.

The Act covers investment business ranging from that undertaken by single individuals to that undertaken by the major clearing banks.

7.   Investments

The main categories covered are:

(a) *Securities*: stocks and shares, Eurobonds, debentures, certificates of deposit, government and local authority bonds and units in unit trusts; (Bills of exchange, bank drafts, letters of credit, mortgages, bank notes and trade finance instruments are specifically excluded.)

(b) *Traded options, currency options, precious metal options, and options over such options;*

(c) *Financial and commodity futures,* that is contracts where the price is agreed at the time of contract, but delivery of the subject matter is at a future date – but excluding contracts made for commercial purposes;

(d) *Long-term life assurance contracts* – personal health and injury insurance and term life assurance (up to 10 years) are excluded;

(e) *Contracts for differences* – for example, interest rate or currency swaps.

> NOTE: Investments do not include land, shares in a building society and 'commodities' such as jewellery, works of art and coins which are frequently bought as investments.

8.   Banks and investment business
This business affects banks in the following ways.

(a) *SRO membership.* Each bank must be a member of an SRO (*see* 8:**10**). Banks usually also have a number of subsidiary companies specialising in particular investment areas and each subsidiary will be a member of the appropriate SRO.

(b) *Polarisation.* Most banks sell only their own products and are, therefore, *tied agents.* Many, however, have subsidiaries that are independent intermediaries and so are able to advise on and sell the whole range of investment products. This enables a bank to offer a more complete service to its customers, branch staff acting as company representatives who are able to refer customers to one of the bank's subsidiaries if independent advice is required (*see* 8:**14**).

(c) *Know your customer.* Banks have developed questionnaires (*customer profiles*) to ensure that they find out sufficient information to enable them to satisfy the 'best advice' rule (*see* 8:**15**).

(d) *Compliance.* Banks have compliance officers (of a senior grade) whose task is to ensure that the bank and other companies in the group comply with the provisions of the Act and the rules of SIB and the relevant SROs. In particular, the compliance officer is responsible for ensuring the effectiveness of the complaints procedure.

(e) Banks, and other investment firms, must provide *safe custody facilities* for their customers' investments.

Regulatory bodies

The framework of regulatory bodies is shown in Figure 8.1.

9.   The Securities and Investment Board (SIB)

The SIB was established by the Department of Trade and Industry that, together with the Bank of England, appoints (and if necessary removes) its members. It has three main functions.

(a) To publish rules for the conduct of investment business.
(b) To recognise and regulate SROs and RPBs.
(c) To authorise persons to carry on investment business and maintain a Central Register of authorised persons.

Few investment businesses are directly authorised by SIB.

10.   Self-Regulatory Organisations (SROs)

At present, there are four SROs, each covering a particular area of investment business.

(a) *The Financial Intermediaries, Managers and Brokers Regulatory Association (FIMBRA)*. FIMBRA covers most independent financial advisers, mainly small firms, who deal directly with the public:

(i) Giving advice on life assurance and unit trusts;
(ii) Providing investment and management services to retail customers;
(iii) Advising on and arranging deals in securities for private clients other than for futures, options or contracts for differences (swaps).

(b) *The Life Assurance and Unit Trust Regulatory Organisation (LAUTRO)*. LAUTRO covers those involved in the retail marketing of life assurance and unit trust products.

NOTE: FIMBRA and LAUTRO plan to merge in 1993.

(c) *The Investment Management Regulatory Organisation (IMRO)*. IMRO covers investment advisers and managers, where this is the person's sole or main activity. It covers banks (investment management business only), pension fund managers, unit trust and trust fund managers and trustees of such collective investment schemes.

(d) *The Securities and Futures Authority (SFA)*. The SFA was formed in 1991 from the merger of The Securities Association (TSA) and the Association of Futures Brokers and Dealers (AFBD).

The SFA is responsible for regulating firms that deal in or advise

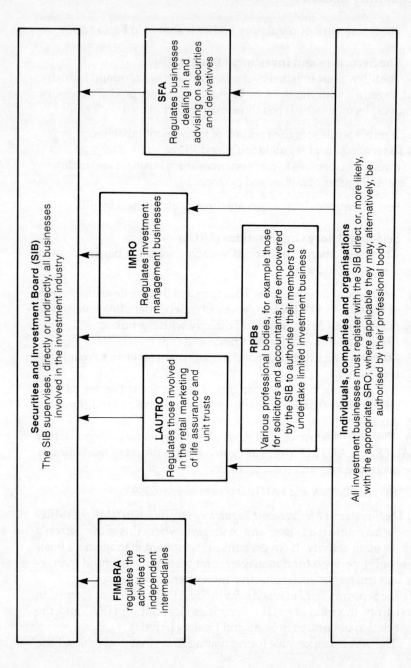

Securities and Investment Board (SIB)

The SIB supervises, directly or undirectly, all businesses involved in the investment industry

SFA

Regulates businesses dealing in and advising on securities and derivatives

IMRO

Regulates investment management businesses

LAUTRO

Regulates those involved in the retail marketing of life assurance and unit trusts

FIMBRA

regulates the activities of independent intermediaries

RPBs

Various professional bodies, for example those for solicitors and accountants, are empowered by the SIB to authorise their members to undertake limited investment business

Individuals, companies and organisations

All investment businesses must register with the SIB direct or, more likely, with the appropriate SRO; where applicable they may, alternatively, be authorised by their professional body

Figure 8.1 *The regulation of investment business*

on securities and derivatives where such dealing and advice are the main activities of the business, such as all securities houses and brokers. Its remit encompasses shares, bonds, financial and commodity futures and contracts for differences (swaps), as well as advice to corporate finance customers and investment management for private clients.

> NOTE: The SROs are required, *inter alia*, to (1) have a governing body that fairly balances the interests of its members and those of investors; (2) provide an acceptable level of investor protection; (3) have the power to intervene in the affairs of its members and operate an effective complaints procedure.

11. Recognised Professional Bodies (RPDs)

The SIB has delegated authority from the Secretary of State for Trade and Industry to grant 'recognised' status to professional bodies that are able to certify their members for the purposes of the Act. Not more than 20 per cent of a member's turnover, however, must be investment business and all of this must be incidental to its main business. Each RPD is able to specify the type and impose a limit on the amount of investment business its members can undertake. Regulation of its members by RPDs must satisfy SIB.

Examples of RPDs are the Law Society, the Institute of Chartered Accountants and the Institute of Actuaries.

Conduct of business rules

12. Introduction

(a) *Objectives.* The main objectives of the rules are to ensure that:
   (i) Investment business is conducted honestly and fairly.
   (ii) Those involved should act capably, carefully and to the best of their abilities.
   (iii) Those involved should be fair to their customers and avoid conflicts of interest.

(b) *Other rules.* In many respects, the conduct of business rules confirm and expand established rules of common law and principles of equity that impose the duties of care and skill, good faith, confidentiality and fiduciary duties on those involved in investment business. For example, the principal and agent relationship that is created imposes on the agent (the adviser) a duty to account. This means that the agent must disclose all relevant information, fees, commission and charges to the principal (the customer) (*see* 3:**5**.) However, the conduct of business rules are *additional* to these established and more general duties.

On the other hand, the customer (as principal) also owes the adviser (as agent) duties at common law, e.g. to indemnify the agent for liability incurred (*see* 3:**6**).

13. Advertising and unsolicited calls

(**a**) *Advertising.* The form and content of advertisements for investment services is controlled and only authorised persons may advertise. All advertisements must be accurate, concise and clear. If an advertisement that does not conform to the rules directly results in an investment agreement, the agreement is unenforceable and the advertiser can be prosecuted.

Well-known examples of rules regulating advertisements are that any risks associated with an investment must be declared and the requirement to include the phrase 'investments may go down as well as up in value' in any advertisement where this is so, such as in advertisements for unit trusts.

(**b**) *Unsolicited calls.* An unsolicited call is defined by the Act as 'a personal visit or oral communication made without express invitation'. 'Oral communication' includes telephone calls.

The practice of making such unsolicited approaches is usually known as 'cold calling'. Cold calling is not permitted except:

(*i*) In connection with life assurance and unit trust business;
(*ii*) To professional or business investors;
(*iii*) To solicit new business from existing customers;
(*iv*) On the premises of the caller.

Cold calling is not a criminal offence, but agreements entered into as a result will not be enforceable without a court order or at the instance of the investor, money and other property transferred is. recoverable and compensation can be sought. A court order may be granted, e.g. where the investor is shown not to have been materially influenced by anything done in the course of, or in consequence of, the call.

NOTE: A 14-day cooling off period, running from the date of receipt of documentation relating to the sale, applies to most life assurance and unit trust business. During the cooling off period, the investor can cancel the agreement and recover any money paid or property transferred. The cooling off period does not apply, *inter alia*, to unit trust investment and single-premium life assurance contracts entered into on an execution only basis (*see* 8:**15**).

14. Polarisation

An important distinction exists between an authorised person who sells only the products of one company – an appointed representative, better known as a *tied agent* – and one who is free to sell any product available – an *independent intermediary*. An authorised person may not be both.

A bank, as all other investment firms, must make it clear at the outset of its dealings with a customer whether it acts as a tied agent or as an independent intermediary.

An independent intermediary must only sell the product that best meets the customer's needs, although this can be the intermediary's own product. If a tied agent's 'best advice' to a customer is another company's product, the customer must be referred to an independent intermediary.

The company to which a tied agent is 'tied' is bound by the representations made by the agent during the course of a transaction. It is also responsible to its regulatory body for the tied agent's conduct.

15. Investment advice

(a) *Best advice.* The investment advice given must always be that which best satisfies the needs and circumstances of the customer, regardless of the benefit accruing to the firm. Thus, company representatives (and tied agents) must suggest the most suitable product from *their* company's range and independent financial advisers must suggest the most suitable product from the *whole range* of products available. Records of the reasons *why* a particular product(s) was recommended must be kept.

(b) *Know your customer.* An investment firm must find out sufficient information about its customer, e.g. ability to pay and tax position, to enable it to give best advice.

The information gained enables the firm to determine into which category of investor the customer falls and advise accordingly. The firm must, *inter alia*, not only advise on the risks but also ensure that the investor *understands* them.

The categories of investor are:

(i) Professional investor – one who is authorised to carry out investment business or who is exempted from authorisation.

(ii) Business investor – one who buys and sells a particular type of investment in the course of a business that cannot be authorised, e.g. a company whose treasury management function involves dealing in currency futures.

(iii) Experienced investor – one who has gained substantial experience in actively managing particular types of investments on their own behalf; an investor must agree to be treated as an experienced investor.

(iv) Ordinary individual investor – each investor is presumed to be an ordinary individual investor unless the adviser can prove otherwise. (The degree of knowledge that each type can be assumed to possess decreases from (a) to (d).)

NOTE: The 'know your customer' rule does not apply to professional investors, experienced investors or 'execution only' customers – customers who merely give instructions to be carried out and who do not seek advice on investment matters or those who are unwilling to provide relevant information.

(c) *Full disclosure.* An investment firm must disclose to its customer details of commission and any other benefit that will accrue to the firm as a result of buying or selling the investment product. Payments to the firm must be fair and reasonable.

16. Customer agreements

Customer agreements must be written. With certain exceptions, a customer agreement must be signed by the investor before the investment firm can provide the customer with services. The form of the agreement varies according to the type of customer.

(a) *Full customer agreements* must be used for ordinary individual investors.

(b) *Occasional customer agreements* may be used where the firm reasonably believes it is dealing with the customer on a 'one-off' basis.

(c) A *terms-of-business letter* can be used for business, professional and experienced investors.

NOTE: Signed customer agreements are not required for long-term life assurance or unit trust business, 'execution only' customers or 'market counterparties' – another firm in the same investment business that is dealing with you in the ordinary course of their business.

All customer agreements must detail the nature of the investment services provided and the basis, method and frequency of payments to be made by the customer to the firm. Among other things, full customer agreements must also contain a warning of the risks involved in the investment.

17. Best execution

Investment firms must take all reasonable steps to obtain the best deal they can for their customers when buying or selling investments. This rule will not apply to professional, business and experienced investors who agree in the terms-of-business letter that the duty is not owed to them.

18. Internal rules

(a) *Employee dealing.* Staff must be prevented from conducting investment business for themselves on the basis of confidential customer information as breaching such rules can lead to prosecution.

(b) *'Chinese walls'.* To prevent conflicts of interest between clients arising internally, an investment business must ensure that there is no flow of confidential information between different departments in the business. The barriers to the flow of information put in place are known as 'Chinese walls'.

Example

The Corporate Finance Department of a bank advises X Ltd, a quoted company; while the Personal Investment Department advises personal clients, some of whom hold shares or are considering buying shares in X Ltd. Knowledge of X Ltd's likely future performance gained by the Corporate Finance Department would be likely to influence advice given by the Personal Investment Department if it passed between the departments. Similarly a researcher's advice to a corporate client could be influenced by information gained from the Broking Department of the bank.

The flow of such information between departments could constitute 'insider dealing' and an offence under the Company Securities (Insider Dealing) Act 1985.

(c) *Record keeping.* Records of all investment business must be kept and retained for an appropriate period. They can be inspected by the relevant SRO or RPB.

(d) *Compliance.* An investment adviser must produce and distribute to all its branches/outlets a compliance manual detailing how compliance with the Act is achieved.

19. Complaints and compensation

(a) *Complaints.* All SROs and RPBs and their members must have formal procedures for handling complaints and customers must be informed of their rights to complain to the SIB or the relevant SRO or RPB. Records of complaints must be kept.

(b) *Compensation.* SIB maintains a compensation fund that provides payments of up to £48 000 to private investors who suffer loss as a result of the insolvency of an authorised investment firm. Each SRO pays a levy towards this fund. Each RPB maintains its own compensation fund.

20. Clients' funds

Clients' funds are held on trust for the client and must be held separately from the firm's own money. Statements must be issued and interest on funds held may be payable.

Banks must treat investment firms' clients accounts as they do other trust accounts. To enable the firms to comply with the rules of the SRO, banks are usually asked to formally acknowledge that they are not able to combine the firm's clients account with its office accounts.

Progress test 8

1. List the ways in which a firm can be authorised to conduct investment business. **(2)**

2. What individuals and organisations are exempt from authorisation under the Act? **(3)**

3. What constitutes a criminal offence under the Act? **(4)**

4. List the five categories of investment business regulated by the Act. **(6)**

5. What main categories of investments are regulated by the Act? **(7)**

6. State the main functions of the SIB. **(9)**

7. Name the SROs recognised by the SIB and briefly explain the type of investment business each covers. **(10)**

8. Give two examples of recognised professional bodies. **(11)**

9. State the main objectives of the conduct of business rules. **(12)**

10. What other general rules of law regulate the conduct of investment business? **(12)**

11. What test must all advertisements for investment business satisfy? **(13)**

12. What is 'cold calling' and when is it permitted? **(13)**

13. To what kind of investment business does the 14-day cooling off period apply? **(13)**

14. What is meant by 'polarisation'? **(14)**

15. Explain the 'best advice' rule and how it relates to 'polarisation'. **(15)**

16. Name the four categories of investor under the 'know your customer' rule. **(15)**

17. In what circumstances are investors not required to sign customer agreements? **(16)**

18. What is meant by 'best execution'? **(17)**

19. Explain and illustrate what is meant by a 'Chinese wall'. **(18)**

20. How must a bank treat investment firms' accounts? **(20)**

9
Cheques

What is a cheque?

1. Definition

The Bills of Exchange Act 1882 s.73, defines a cheque as 'a bill of exchange drawn on a banker payable on demand'. Section 3(1) of the Act defines a bill of exchange and, adapting s.3(1) to a cheque, we can say that, at law, a cheque is an unconditional order in writing, addressed by the drawer to their bank, signed by the drawer, requiring the bank to pay on demand a certain sum of money to or to the order of a specified person or to the bearer.

In simpler terms, a cheque is a written promise by the drawer that the bank on which it is drawn will pay the payee on demand the amount stated.

'Cheques' made out to 'cash' or to 'wages' are not cheques, although they may look like cheques and, indeed, be treated as such by banks. A cheque (as a bill of exchange) must be made payable to a specified person or to the bearer; such 'cheques' are payable to neither. Nevertheless, they are valid orders to the bank from the customer to pay the stated amount from the customer's account. In addition to being a negotiable instrument, a cheque is a mandate from the customer, authorising and directing their bank, according to the terms of the banker–customer contract, to pay the holder (the person entitled to payment). Needless to say, instruments made out to 'cash' or 'wages' are not negotiable.

For a different reason, a bankers' draft is not a cheque. Here it is because the draft is not an order by one person addressed to another, as required by the Bills of Exchange Act 1882. It is, instead, addressed by the bank to itself, all branches of the bank being part of one legal entity (a corporation) (*see* 9:**38**).

A cheque made payable to a non-existant or fictitious person is a bearer cheque: Bills of Exchange Act 1882 s.7(3) (*see* 9:**17**).

2. Parties to the transaction

Initially, three parties are involved:

(a) The *drawer* – the person who makes out the cheque.

(b) The *drawee* – the person to whom the order is addressed. By definition, this is always a bank.

(c) The *payee* – the person to whom the cheque is made payable.

If the cheque is transferred (negotiated), another person – the *endorser* – becomes a party to the transaction.

Above we have used the term 'party to the transaction' to mean anyone who was in some way connected with a cheque. However, the term 'party' has a stricter meaning at law. A party to a cheque is a person who has *signed* it and, by so doing, incurred liability on it: Bills of Exchange Act 1882 s.23. Thus, it covers the drawer (the customer) and any endorser.

Under the Bills of Exchange Act 1882 s.55(1) and (2) the drawer and endorser, respectively, promise that the cheque will be paid when presented and that they will compensate any holder or endorser (any subsequent endorser in respect of the endorser's promise) who has to pay if the cheque is dishonoured by the drawee bank. The drawer cannot deny to a holder in due course (*see* 9:**19**) the payee's existence and their capacity to endorse the cheque and an endorser cannot deny to a holder in due course the validity of the signatures of the drawer and any previous endorser.

> NOTE: Capacity to incur liability as a party to a cheque is co-extensive with the capacity to contract: Bills of Exchange Act 1882 s.22(1). Thus, for example, a cheque is unenforceable against a minor who either drew or endorsed it, even if the minor drew it in payment for necessaries ordered by and supplied to the minor. A cheque to which a minor is a party is, however, enforceable against any other party to it.

A person who signs a cheque as the agent of the drawer or endorser incurs no personal liability in the event of the cheque being dishonoured provided that that person adds words to their signature indicating that they sign for and on behalf of their principal (the drawer or endorser). However, merely describing themselves as an agent, without indicating who they sign for, will not exempt them from personal liability (*see* 5:**20**.)

A bank *never* becomes a party to a cheque and therefore never incurs liability to its holder, most likely the original payee. This is because a bank never *accepts* (agrees to the drawer's order to pay the payee) a cheque by indicating this on the cheque and signing it, although at law it could. Even if the bank wrongfully returns a cheque, the holder only has rights of action against the drawer and any endorsers. It is the drawer who has a right of action against the bank, for breach of contract, e.g. where it wrongfully debits the account or wrongfully dishonours the cheque.

NOTE: Banks frequently accept bills of exchange other than cheques.

The drawer is always the party primarily liable on a cheque and any endorsers are guarantors of the drawer's payment. As such they incur joint and several liability.

3.   A cheque as a contract

A cheque is subject to the ordinary rules of contract law with two important exceptions:

(a) *Consideration.* 'An antecedent debt or liability' will support the promise of payment: Bills of Exchange Act 1882 s.27(1)(b). As such this is an exception to the common law rule that 'past consideration is no consideration'. Many cheques are drawn in payment for goods and services already provided. The bargain in the underlying contract is goods or services in return for a promise of payment, the promise, of course, being enforceable. However, the issue of a cheque in payment is a fresh promise in return for the goods or services *having been supplied* and this fresh promise is therefore in return for an antecedent debt or liability, i.e. a pre-existing liability to pay for them. Thus, the promise contained in the cheque is separately enforceable.

(b) *Privity of contract.* Normally a contract is only enforceable by the parties to the contract. In the case of a cheque, these are the drawer and the payee. However, the principle of *negotiation* (*see* below) allows strangers to the contract to whom the cheque has been negotiated – endorsees in the case of an *order cheque* and the bearer in the case of a *bearer cheque* – to enforce the drawer's promise. Furthermore, the Bills of Exchange Act 1882 s.27(2) enables such third parties to rely on the consideration provided by a prior party (*see* 9:**18**).

NOTE: As between the immediate parties to a cheque, consideration must be provided for the promise to be enforceable. For example, if a cheque is drawn by A payable to B, who provides consideration for it, and B then negotiates it to C as a gift, although C can enforce the cheque against A, relying on B's consideration, C *cannot* enforce it against B because C gave B no consideration for it.

4.   Negotiation of a cheque

(a) *Definition.* Negotiation of a cheque takes place when it is transferred in such a way as to make the transferee the *holder* of it: Bills of Exchange Act 1882 s.31.

A bearer cheque is negotiated by delivery, an order cheque by endorsement of the holder, completed by delivery. ('Delivery' means the transfer of the instrument in such a way that the transferee is intended to become the holder of it.)

(b) *Transfer and negotiation distinguished.* The key to the distinction is to remember that the term 'negotiation' is a term unique to bills of exchange and other negotiable instruments and relates to the special attributes of negotiable instruments when title is transferred. Technically a negotiable instrument is transferred by *assignment* (*see* 9:5).

In the sense of physically transferring a cheque from one person to another, the terms tend to be used interchangeably but *negotiation* requires the transfer to be in accordance with the Bills of Exchange Act 1882 and usually there is the need for a valid endorsement, as explained above.

The more important point is the consequence of a negotiation to a *holder in due course* (*see* 9:19). Taking a negotiation of a cheque as a holder in due course means that the transferee (holder) takes it free from any defects of title that affected the cheque while it was in the hands of the transferor or any other prior parties and also free from any personal claims between prior parties. Examples of 'personal claims' are a right to claim damages for breach of contract and the right to set-off a debt owed by the drawer to the payee against a claim on the cheque by the payee against the drawer. (These prior defects and claims are referred to as *equities*.)

If the transferee does not take a transfer of the cheque as a holder in due course, *transfer* is the better term in relation to the passing of title. The reason is that although the cheque has been negotiated, the transferee, not being a holder in due course, does not enjoy the full benefits of negotiability, i.e. the ability to take free from prior equities. In a very general sense, therefore negotiation can be thought of as being an enhanced form of transfer. (More correctly negotiation is an enhanced form of *assignment*.)

NOTE: An order cheque is *assigned*, not negotiated, where its holder transfers it for value without endorsing it. The transferee only acquires such title to the cheque as the transferor had and cannot sue on the cheque in their own name (*see* 9:5). The transferee does, however, acquire the right to have the cheque endorsed to them by the transferor: Bills of Exchange Act 1882 s.31(4).

5.   Cheques as negotiable instruments

(a) *Legal characteristics.* A cheque as a negotiable instrument has four legal characteristics:

   (i) Transfer of title. Title to a cheque is transferred by delivery or, in the case of cheque payable to order (the majority), by endorsement, completed by delivery.

   (ii) Quality of the title. A person taking a transfer of the cheque in good faith, for value and without notice of any defect in the title of the transferor (a holder in due course) is unaffected by any defects in the title of prior parties as well as by mere personal defences, such as counter-claims or set-offs, available among them. Thus, the transferee *can acquire a better title* than that held by the transferor. For example, a person who acquired the instrument by fraud has only a voidable title to it, but a bona fide transferee for value from that person acquires a perfect title. Similarly, if the payee owed the drawer money under a separate transaction and the payee sought to enforce the cheque against the drawer, the drawer could set-off this debt to arrive at the net indebtedness. However, if the cheque is negotiated to a holder in due course, the drawer is liable for the full amount of the cheque.

   The ability of a person who takes a transfer of a cheque in good faith, for value and without notice of any defect in title of the transferor to gain a perfect title to it is, of course, quite opposite to the general position with regard to the transfer of title to goods.

Example

If, say, someone buys a stolen car, it matters not that the purchaser is completely *unaware* that it is stolen; the true owner can, at any time, reclaim the car and an action against the seller is the purchaser's only (often useless) remedy. On the other hand, while the true owner of stolen bank notes (negotiable instruments) can recover the notes from the thief, if the notes are used to purchase goods or services, the seller, providing they act in good faith and have no notice of the possessor's defect in title, obtains a perfect title to the notes and they cannot be recovered from the seller by the person from whom they were stolen.

   What is important in practice is that a holder in due course acquires an absolute right to payment of the full amount of the cheque and can enforce this right against all parties to the cheque if the cheque is not paid by the drawee bank.

NOTE: If an order cheque is transferred bearing a forged endorsement, the transferee gains no title whatsoever to the cheque, even though they satisfy the three criteria identified above (*see* 9:**12**).

(iii) Enforceability. The holder *can sue in their own name*, that is the holder does not have to join the drawer or any other prior parties in an action to enforce payment. As such, this is an important exception to the doctrine of privity of contract, i.e. that a contract can only be enforced by the parties to it (*see* 9:**3** above).

(iv) Notice of transfer. The holder *need not give notice of the transfer to prior parties* to establish their title.

NOTE: By adding a new section (s.81A) to the Bills of Exchange Act 1882, the Cheques Act 1992 s.1 introduced the 'not transferable cheque', one that is crossed 'account payee' (although the Act does imply that there are other ways of rendering a cheque not transferable). If a cheque is not transferable it is, by definition, also not negotiable. A not negotiable cheque is, of course, a contradiction in terms according to common law but the 'not transferable cheque' introduced by the 1992 Act is an *exception* to the general law intended to reduce the incidence of cheque fraud. Only characteristic (c) above applies to such cheques.

(b) *Origin of these characteristics.* The law relating to negotiable instruments developed from the practices of merchants in previous centuries and these distinctive legal characteristics can all be explained by their commercial origins. For example, merchants would be unlikely to accept negotiated bills of exchange instead of cash if they knew that their rights to obtain payment of them could always be prejudiced by some defect in the title of prior parties to the bills or a counter-claim of which they were completely ignorant. Again, it would be a ludicrous situation if each time a £5 note (a type of negotiable instrument) changed hands, notice and details of the transfer had to be given to the Bank of England!

(c) *Negotiation and assignment.* Negotiable instruments are an extension of the concept of assignment: the transfer of a right or interest in intangible property (a *chose in action*) to another person, e.g. the legal title to a life policy. Written notice of the assignment of a life policy has to be given to the issuing company and any defect in the assignor's title, such as that it is voidable for failure to disclose a material fact, is also transferred, as is any counter-claim for unpaid premiums. If a bank takes an equitable mortgage (assignment) of a life policy then, additionally, it is unable to enforce its rights in its own name (*see* Chapter 13).

6.   Inchoate cheques

An inchoate cheque is one that has been incompletely drawn but which can be completed subsequently to make it a valid cheque. For example, the payee's name or the amount of the payment may be omitted.

Unless it is proved otherwise, the person in possession of the cheque has authority to complete the cheque in any way that person thinks fit: Bills of Exchange Act 1882 s.20(1). However, under s.20(2), to enforce an inchoate cheque against a person who became a party to it before its completion, it must have been completed within a reasonable time and strictly in accordance with the authority given. To this the subsection provides an important *exception*. If the cheque is negotiated to a holder in due course after its completion, they may enforce it, even though it was completed in breach of authority and/or after an unreasonable delay.

Example

A signs a blank cheque and gives it to B with authority to complete it for £100. B completes it in favour of C for £200. C then negotiates it to D, who takes it as a holder in due course. D can enforce the bill against A for £200 *even though* B had exceeded the authority given to them by A.

Crossed cheques

7.   Definition

A crossing is a direction to the *paying bank* that the money proceeds of the cheque should be paid only to another bank as agent of the payee and not directly to the payee in cash. A crossing therefore *restricts payment* of a cheque.

NOTE: Where a crossing incorporates the words 'account payee' this has a different effect (*see* 9:9).

8.   Background

Crossings are the result of banking practice, specifically the practice of the Clearing House begun in the eighteenth century. So that each bank could make its accounts up and return cheques for lack of funds, the clerk of, say, bank X would write bank X's name between parallel lines on cheques that were left in, say, bank Y's drawer. Customers eventually began adding crossings to their cheques because making cheques payable only through another bank account reduced the chance of a third party fraudulently obtaining payment.

Today crossings are used to minimise the chances of persons

fraudulently obtaining payment of a cheque. Consider the position with an *uncrossed,* or, 'open' cheque. This can be paid over the counter. Thus, a person finding or stealing an uncrossed cheque would be able to obtain payment over the counter at the designated branch of the drawee bank, provided that person had reasonable identification as the payee and provided the payee was not personally known to the bank. The first proviso certainly would not be difficult for a determined rogue to satisfy and the second is most unlikely to apply.

As a crossed cheque can only be paid through another bank account, it therefore assumes that the rogue has a bank account or can persuade someone with a bank account to pay in the cheque suitably endorsed by the rogue and obtain the proceeds on the rogue's behalf. In itself it is not that great a protection against fraud because a determined attempt to open an account in a fictitious name using bogus referees if need be will often succeed. Taken with other factors, however, it, without doubt, makes it considerably more difficult for a fraudulent person to obtain the proceeds of a cheque. In particular, the consequences of a crossing increase the time available for discovering the fraudulent activity and gives the drawer more time to stop payment of any stolen cheque.

Furthermore, even if payment *has* been made before the loss or fraud is discovered, it can usually be recovered from the person for whom it was collected as that person would have to have an account at the collecting bank. The exceptions would be where the rogue had opened an account in a fictitious name and could not be traced or where a bearer cheque had been lost or stolen and the customer for whom it was collected had given value (something in return) for it to the finder or thief without knowledge of the circumstances. The customer would then be its true owner (its holder in due course) and entitled to the proceeds.

9. Types of crossings

(a) *General crossing.*

(i) A general crossing consists of two transverse parallel lines across the face of the cheque, with or without the words 'not negotiable' under s.76(1). The words 'and Company' (or '& Co') may be added between the lines although they are purely a traditional addition and have no legal effect.

(ii) Where the words *not negotiable* are added to the crossing, they deprive the cheque of its negotiability. This means that the person taking the cheque does not receive and cannot give a better title than that of the person transferring it: Bills of Exchange Act 1882 s.81. (The ability to transfer a better title is the very essence of negotiability.)

The words do not mean that the cheque cannot be *transferred*, however; a crossed cheque is just as transferable bearing these words as without them, the person to whom it is transferred is just in a far weaker position if the transferor's title proves to be defective.

In short, while the cheque is *still* transferable, the words prevent a transferee from becoming a holder in due course as the cheque is always transferred subject to any existing defect in title. Of course, if the transferor has a perfect title to the cheque, so will the transferor.

The effect of the words on an uncrossed cheque is uncertain as there is no statutory rule; they may merely deprive it of its negotiability, as on a crossed cheque, or prevent its transfer altogether, as they do on bills of exchange other than cheques. However, the point is relatively academic as uncrossed cheques are very unusual and uncrossed cheques bearing these words therefore extremely unusual.

(iii) The words *account payee* or *account payee only* frequently appear within the crossing. These words prevent title to the cheque being transferred: Bills of Exchange Act 1882 s.81A (added to the 1882 Act by the Cheques Act 1992 s.1). This means that the cheque is only valid between the immediate parties to it – the drawer and the payee; no other person can obtain title to it. The words are, therefore, a greater restriction on the cheque than 'not negotiable'; indeed, the addition of 'not negotiable' is redundant because title to the cheque cannot be transferred at all.

A cheque crossed 'account payee' is not, of course, a negotiable instrument. It follows that if the words 'or order' appear on the cheque, they are also redundant.

A general crossing incorporating these words is somewhat different to other crossings. The general crossing is still a direction to the paying bank, but the added words are, in practice, a direction to the *collecting* bank. They direct the bank to collect the cheque *only* for an account of the payee (*see* 9:**25**).

NOTE: The effect of the words 'not transferable' added to a general crossing is not expressly covered by statute or by case law. However the Cheques Act 1992 ss.2 and 3 amend s.80 of the Bills of Exchange Act 1882 and s.4 of the Cheques Act 1957 by mentioning cheques that are not transferable other than by virtue of adding 'account payee' to the crossing. This would seem to cover adding the words 'not transferable', deleting the words 'or order' and/or adding 'only' after the payee's name.

(b) *Special crossings.* A special crossing consists of the name of a *particular bank* and often a *particular branch* to which payment must be made. The name is itself the crossing and, while they would usually be present, two transverse lines (the essence of a general crossing) are unnecessary: Bills of Exchange Act 1882 s.76(2). The words 'not negotiable' and 'account payee' can be added to the crossing and they then have the same effect as on a cheque crossed generally.

(c) *Proposed changes.* The 1990 White Paper 'Banking Services: Law and Practice' proposes a number of important changes to crossings on cheques:

(i) A crossed cheque should cease to be a negotiable instrument, whether or not the words 'not negotiable' are written on it. Note that this means that it will still be possible to transfer title to crossed cheques by delivery (if a bearer cheque) or by endorsement completed by delivery (if an order cheque), but the full benefits of negotiability will *not* be available – it will not be possible for a transferee to become a holder in due course.

(ii) Special crossings should be discontinued.

(iii) An open cheque – at present very unusual – will continue to be a negotiable instrument presentable for cash (or payable through the clearing system) as at present.

10. Who may cross a cheque

(a) The *drawer* may cross a cheque generally or specially, adding the words 'not negotiable' if they wish.

(b) The *holder* may cross an uncrossed cheque generally or specially and, if it is crossed generally, the holder may cross it specially – in either case, the words 'not negotiable' may be added to the crossing.

(c) A *bank* to which a cheque has been specially crossed can cross it specially to another bank for collection and a bank may specially cross an uncrossed or generally crossed cheque sent to it for collection.

11. Miscellaneous points

A crossing is a material part of a cheque under the Bills of Exchange Act 1882 s.78 and an unauthorised alteration of a crossing will discharge the cheque: Bills of Exchange Act 1882 s.64 (*see* 9:**29**). A bank should therefore *not* pay a cheque when the crossing has been altered, unless the alteration has been signed by the drawer.

A bank is liable to the true owner of a cheque for any loss caused by paying a cheque contrary to its crossing: Bills of Exchange Act 1882 s.79(2). Furthermore, it cannot debit its customer's account with the amount of the cheque.

Although the Bills of Exchange Act 1882 does not provide for the removal of a crossing, banks allow their own customers or their known agents (but no other third parties) to cash crossed cheques over the counter. Sometimes the customer is required to open the crossing by writing 'Please pay cash' and signing the opening, but, more usually, an opening is not requested. The practice, although technically incorrect at law, is convenient and the risk involved slight.

Endorsement of cheques

12. Definition

An *endorsement* is the signature of the payee or a subsequent holder on the cheque. The signature indicates the payee's/holder's intention to transfer their rights in the cheque.

A *forged* endorsement is *no* endorsement because a forged signature is wholly inoperative: Bills of Exchange Act 1882 s.24.

13. Validity of an endorsement

To be valid, an endorsement must satisfy the following criteria:

(a) It must be *written on the back* of the cheque.

(b) It must be of the *entire cheque* and not part.

(c) If there are two or more payees, *all* must endorse, unless one is authorised to endorse for the others, such as a partner.

(d) It should *correspond exactly* with the drawing or the previous endorsement.

Example

If the payee's name is misspelt, the payee should endorse it with the same spelling, adding their proper signature if they wish.

An endorsement that does not correspond exactly with the previous designation on the cheques is not invalid, but any *irregularity*, a question of fact, will prevent a transferee from becoming a holder in due course (*see* 9:**19**).

NOTE: It is usual banking practice to refuse to pay cheques on which the endorsement does not correspond exactly with the name of the payee or previous endorsee. For example, an endorsement on a cheque that reads 'John Smith' when the payee is designated 'J. Smith' is an irregular endorsement.

14. Types of endorsement

There are three types.

(a) *An endorsement in blank* is where the holder merely signs the cheque on its back. The cheque becomes payable to the bearer.

(b) *A special endorsement* is where the holder adds a direction to pay a particular person. The cheque becomes payable to, or to the order of, the person specified, e.g. 'Pay X, Signed Y'.

(c) *A restrictive endorsement* can be one of two types.

(i) An endorsement that *prohibits further negotiation of the cheque*, for example, an endorsement 'Pay X only' enables X to enforce payment of the cheque but X is unable to transfer title to it.

(ii) An endorsement that gives authority to deal with the cheque as indicated but does not transfer title. For example, Pay X for the account of Y' entitles X to receive the sum paid, but only as agent for Y. Furthermore, such a cheque can only be *transferred* if express power to do so is given by the endorsement (which would be most unusual): Bills of Exchange Act 1882 s.35(2). If it is transferred, the transferee takes the cheque with the same rights and subject to the same liabilities as the first endorsee under the restrictive endorsement: Bills of Exchange Act 1882 s. 35(2). In short, the transferee cannot become a holder in due course.

NOTE: A condition added to an endorsement can be ignored.

15. Points to note

(a) Any endorsement on a *bearer cheque* drawn as a bearer cheque is irrelevant and of no effect in this context. It can be ignored. Thus, a cheque drawn as a bearer cheque remains as such; it cannot be converted into an order cheque by a special endorsement: Bills of Exchange Act 1882 s.8(3).

(b) Conversely, a cheque drawn as an *order cheque* and converted to a bearer cheque by an endorsement in blank *can* be converted back to an order cheque by any holder writing an order to pay a specific person above the signature of the endorser.

(c) The rule relating to bearer cheques drawn as bearer cheques can be important where an endorsement has been forged, for example. On an order cheque, the forgery prevents the transferee obtaining the right to payment, i.e. becoming the holder. On a bearer cheque, a forged endorsement does not affect the bearer's title because an endorsement is not required to transfer title and any endorsement can be ignored, the bearer is still the holder and is entitled to payment.

This would apply to a cheque drawn payable to 'X or bearer' on which X's signature was forged. The holder in due course of such a cheque could enforce it against the drawer but not, of course, against X.

> NOTE: A person who does endorse a bearer cheque becomes a party to it and incurs liability on it.
>
> A person who negotiates a bearer cheque by delivery alone is known as a *transferor by delivery*. As such, they are not liable on the instrument, but, if they negotiate the cheque for value, they are liable to the *immediate* transferee if the cheque is not genuine, if they have no right to transfer it and if they are aware of any fact that makes it valueless: Bills of Exchange Act 1882 s.58.

Types of holders

16. Introduction

The terms dealt with in this section are important whenever a cheque is negotiated and in a bank's role as agent for collection of its customers' cheques. Nevertheless, this section is less relevant to day-to-day banking than others. It applies in practice mainly to bills of exchange other than cheques. This is because most cheques are paid straight into the payee's account. However, the theory must be covered in order to understand and explain the practice.

There are three primary parties to the transaction: the *drawer*, the *drawee* and the *payee*. (Be sure you can define them before reading on.) The *holder* is, in a way, another party to the transaction, but, instead of being identifiable as an individual in the way the drawer, drawee and the payee are, the holder is identifiable by applying *legal criteria to a particular person's possession of a cheque*.

17. The holder

The Bills of Exchange Act 1882 s.2, defines a holder as 'The payee or endorsee of a bill who is in possession of it, or the bearer thereof'.

(a) *Payee*. This is the person to whom an order cheque is made payable.
(b) *Endorsee*. This is a specific person to whom the payee or subsequent holder of an order cheque transfers title by endorsing the cheque.
Example _____

Where a person wishes to negotiate (transfer) a cheque that is made out to them by name, e.g. 'Pay J. Smith' or 'Pay J. Smith or order', the cheque is an *order* cheque and can only be negotiated by J. Smith first signing (endorsing) the cheque on the back. J. Smith may wish to negotiate the cheque to a specific person, say, P. Brown, in which case the endorsement must read 'Pay P.

Brown' followed by J. Smith's signature. P. Brown is now the endorsee and, therefore, the holder of the cheque. If J. Smith merely signs the back of the cheque and does not specify to whom they intend to negotiate it, the endorsement is an *endorsement in blank* and the cheque becomes payable to bearer, i.e. payable to whoever has possession of it at any particular time, that person being its holder.

NOTE: To be the holder, the endorsee must be in possession of the cheque.

(c) *Bearer*. A bearer as defined by the Bills of Exchange Act 1882 s.2, means someone in possession of a bearer cheque. Essentially this is the opposite of an order cheque; a bearer cheque is payable to anyone in possession of it. A bearer cheque is negotiated by delivery alone. Specifically, a cheque is payable to the bearer if it is:

(*i*) Drawn payable to bearer;

(*ii*) Endorsed in blank; or

(*iii*) Drawn payable to a fictitious or non-existing person: Bills of Exchange Act 1882 s.7(3).

A *fictitious person* is someone the drawer never intended to receive payment, not necessarily someone who does not exist. A *non-existing person* is someone of whose existence the drawer did not know when they drew the cheque, even if a person of that name actually exists. Both situations are usually associated with fraud.

Section 7(3) is important because any endorsement, forged or otherwise, on a bearer cheque can be ignored.

Example 1

In *Clutton* v *Attenborough* (1897) (HL), a clerk dishonestly induced his employer, C, to draw cheques in favour of B by telling him that money was owed to B, although C did not know of B. The clerk then forged B's endorsement on the cheques and transferred them to A who received payment. C sought to recover the monies from A.

It was held that the cheques were bearer cheques as B was a non-existent payee. A was, therefore, the holder of the cheques and payment to him was payment in due course under s.59, which discharged the cheques.

Example 2

In *Bank of England* v *Vagliano Brothers* (1891) (HL), VG's clerk forged a number of bills of exchange drawn on VG using an existing client as the drawer and the name of a real company as the payee. He got the bills accepted by VG (they thereby incurred liability on them), forged endorsements on them and subsequently obtained payment in cash from VG's account with the Bank.

It was held that the Bank was entitled to debit VG's account because, *inter alia*, the bills were payable to the bearer and the endorsements could be ignored. The clerk was deemed to be the drawer of the bills and they were payable to a fictitious person because the clerk intended that he and not the named payee should receive payment of them.

NOTE: In *North & South Wales Bank Ltd* v *Macbeth* (1908) (HL), W fraudulently induced M to draw a cheque in favour of K, a person known to M and to whom he fully intended payment to be made. W obtained the cheque and forged K's endorsement on it and obtained payment through his account at the bank. The bank maintained that it had paid the bearer of the cheque as it was drawn payable to a fictitious person within s.7(3).

It was held that the cheque was not payable to a fictitious person within s.7(3) because M intended that K, a real person, should receive payment. It was therefore not payable to the bearer and the forged endorsement meant that the bank had collected a cheque to which its customer had no title. (As the drawer of a cheque will rarely not intend it to be payable to an identifiable person, the decision in this case means that 7(3) is of limited relevance to cheques.)

(d) *Further points.* It is worth exploring the term *holder* a little more fully. Note the following four points.

(i) The term includes an *unlawful holder*, that is, someone to whom the cheque is expressed to be payable but whose possession of it is unlawful. Examples include the finder or thief of a bearer cheque and the person who obtained the cheque's issue or transfer to themselves by fraud.

(ii) It follows from (i) above that anyone in possession of a bearer cheque is its holder. This includes a finder or a thief, although such a holder obtains *no rights* against the parties to the cheque and a claim brought by the finder/thief on the cheque will fail on proof of their defective title. The finder/thief can, however, transfer a good title to a holder in due course (*see* below).

(iii) The term does *not* include a *wrongful possessor*, for example, a person who has stolen an order cheque or a person holding under a forged endorsement – a forged signature is entirely inoperative, at law title has not been transferred: Bills of Exchange Act 1882 s.24.

(iv) Is the holder of a cheque its owner? It would be helpful if this was invariably the case but unfortunately this is not so. Tying together the points above, it follows that a thief of a bearer cheque is its holder but clearly not its owner. In addition, a holder's title can be defective as, e.g. where the cheque was acquired by fraud.

(e) *Legal attributes of a holder.* All three are important.

(i) A holder can enforce payment of a cheque in their own name against prior parties, although an action by the thief of a bearer cheque would obviously fail on proof of the theft.

(ii) Only a holder can transfer – by negotiation – the right to enforce the promise of payment against prior parties and to transfer that right to another party free from defects in title.

(iii) Payment to the holder discharges the cheque and therefore the obligations of the parties liable on it: Bills of Exchange Act 1882 s.59(1).

18. Holder for value

A holder for value is a holder of a cheque for which value (consideration) has at some time been given: Bills of Exchange Act 1882 s.27(2). This includes the situation where the holder has a lien on the cheque.

The value need not have been given by the holder personally. For example, if a cheque is issued in payment for goods, value is given for it. If the cheque is then transferred by the payee as a gift, the transferee (the holder) is a holder for value.

A holder for value can enforce payment of the cheque against all persons who became parties to the cheque *prior to the value being given*.

Example
_____

A draws a cheque in favour of B as a gift, B endorses it to C, also as a gift and C endorses it to D as payment for painting his house. D, in turn, endorses it to his daughter, E, as her pocket money. Consider the legal position.

A incurs no legal liability to either B or C and B incurs no legal liability to C, because of the lack of consideration between the parties. D, however, gave consideration and can enforce payment of the cheque against A, B or C because A, B and C became parties to the cheque before D gave value for it. Similarly, E, the current holder for value, can enforce payment A, B or C – the value given by D makes her holder for value – but she *cannot* enforce it against D because she gave D no value (consideration) for the cheque and, as between the immediate parties to a cheque, consideration is always required to make the cheque enforceable. (Remember that this series of transactions would be most unlikely to happen in practice. We have used it purely to illustrate the theory. We have also assumed that each time the cheque is transferred it has been specially endorsed.)
_____

Unless it can be proved otherwise, any holder is a holder for value but as such obtains no better title than that possessed by the transferor, a holder for value does not take title free from the defects of prior parties. Thus, a holder for value does not enjoy the full benefits of negotiability and as such differs from a holder in due course.

19. Holder in due course

(a) A holder in due course is defined by the Bills of Exchange Act 1882 s.29(1).

(b) *Requirements of s.29(1).*

   (i) Complete and regular. The cheque must be *complete* and *regular* on the face of it, i.e. technically correct. The rights of a holder in due course are such that the cheque must be above suspicion when it is taken in payment. This requirement can be explained by remembering that cheques are a substitute for cash payment. A person surely would not be prepared to take £50 in payment if a third of it was missing or it had been torn into a number of pieces and stuck back together or (apart from its obvious rarity value) if it lacked a serial number. The same thinking lies behind taking a cheque in payment.

An *incomplete* cheque is either undated or does not state an amount or lacks a required signature, such as an endorsement.

Irregularity usually applies to endorsements and would arise where there is a clear and serious difference between the name of the payee or endorsee and their endorsement. The discrepancy must be such that it raises doubts about the genuineness of the endorsement. A cheque is also irregular if it bears an unauthorised alteration.

> NOTE: The face of the cheque includes the back. For example, in *Arab Bank* v *Ross* (1952) (CA), the bank held two promissory notes (a type of negotiable instrument) drawn in favour of a firm 'Fathi and Faysal Nabulsy Company'. One partner had discounted them to the bank, endorsing them 'Fathi and Faysal Nabulsy'.
>
> It was held that omitting 'Company' from the endorsement made the notes irregular. The bank was, therefore, not a holder in due course of the notes, only a holder for value.

A cheque would also be irregular if it had been stuck back together after being torn up, but not if it had been accidentally torn – a question of fact.

   (ii) Not overdue. The holder must have taken the cheque *before it was overdue.* A bill payable on demand is overdue when it appears to have been in circulation for an unreasonable length of time. Thus, the holder of a cheque may find that they are not a holder in due course if they do not present it for payment within a *reasonable time* of its issue. What is a 'reasonable time' is a question of fact to be determined by the individual circumstances of each case; there are no modern decisions on the point.

If a cheque is held to be overdue, this does not mean that the cheque will not be paid, merely that the transferee does not take from prior defects in title.

NOTE: An *overdue* cheque is quite different from a *stale* cheque, i.e. one which, by banking custom and practice, is more than six months old. 'Overdue' relates to the negotiability of the cheque; 'stale' relates to a bank's refusal to pay. It is usual for a bank to refuse to pay a cheque that is stale. Instead, it would be returned marked 'out of date'. It would seem reasonable to assume that a cheque becomes overdue long before it becomes stale. The issue is how long is 'long'. (The Code of Practice s.10 requires a bank to inform its customers about its practice on out-of-date cheques.)

A person in possession of an undated cheque has prima facie authority to date it as they wish: Bills of Exchange Act 1882 s.20(1).

(iii) No notice of any previous dishonour. The holder must have had *no notice of any previous dishonour.* A bank marking a cheque with a reason for dishonour would clearly prevent subsequent parties from becoming holders in due course, although a transfer of such a cheque is unlikely to take place for obvious reasons.

(iv) Good faith. The holder must have taken the cheque in *good faith.* Negligence alone is not lack of good faith, the transferee must know or suspect that all is not as it should be concerning the cheque: Bills of Exchange Act 1882 s.90. For example, the transferee's knowledge that the cheque was endorsed to them in circumstances amounting to a preference under the Insolvency Act 1986 s.340 would prevent the transferee taking the cheque in good faith.

(v) Value. The holder must have given value for the cheque *personally;* it is not enough that value at some time has been given.

(vi) Negotiation. The cheque must be *negotiated to the holder.* This means that the *payee* of a cheque, while its holder, cannot be its holder in due course: *Jones Ltd v Waring and Gillow Ltd* (1926) (HL). A cheque is issued to a payee not negotiated.

(vii) No notice of defective title. At the time of the cheque's negotiation to them, the holder must have *no notice of any defect in title* of the person who negotiated it. Notice means *actual* knowledge of a defect in title or a suspicion of one followed by a deliberate failure to make reasonable enquiries. *Constructive notice* – where the transferee should have known of the defective in title – does not infringe s.29(1): *Raphael v Bank of England* (1855).

Example

In *Midland Bank Ltd* v *Reckitt* (1933) (HL), a bank was held to have notice that its customer had a defective title to cheques that it collected for the private account of the customer, a solicitor, drawn by the customer payable to himself on R's account under power of attorney. The bank had been pressing its customer to reduce his overdraft.

Under s.29(2) of the Bills of Exchange Act 1882 the title of the person negotiating the cheque is defective if that person obtained the cheque by, among other things, fraud, coercion or other unlawful means, for an illegal consideration and negotiating it in breach of faith or fraudulently. For our present purposes, misrepresentation and undue influence are good examples.

20. Points to note

(a) Every holder is *presumed* to be a holder in due course until fraud or illegality is admitted or proved in the issue or negotiation of the cheque. The holder must then prove that value in good faith has subsequently been given for the cheque.

(b) A person who takes a transfer of a *bearer cheque* from a thief can be a holder in due course.

(c) A person who takes an order cheque bearing a *forged endorsement* cannot be a holder in due course; that person is merely a *wrongful possessor*. This is because a forged signature is entirely inoperative (s.24) and, therefore, the cheque, at law, has not been endorsed at all. Thus, the person taking the cheque cannot be an endorsee, therefore, not a holder and, therefore, not a holder in due course.

(d) Section 55(2) of the Bills of Exchange Act 1882 states that an endorser of a cheque is *precluded* (prevented) from denying to a holder in due course the genuineness and regularity of their signature and all previous endorsements. However, as a person taking a cheque under a forged endorsement is not a holder and therefore cannot be a holder in due course, the term 'holder in due course' in s.55(2) has a special meaning. It means a person who *would have been* a holder in due course *but* for the forgery. In short, such a person has the *rights* but not the *status* of a holder in due course against *certain parties* to the cheque.

Specifically, when a question of liability arises in this situation, persons signing the cheque *after* the forgery are prevented from denying the genuineness of what is actually a forgery and are therefore liable to the person in possession of the cheque. Hence estoppel will render the cheque valid and enforceable between the parties *subsequent to the forgery*.

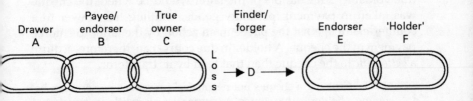

Figure 9.1 *The effect of a forged endorsement and s. 55(2) of the Bills of Exchange Act 1882*

This means that the ultimate possessor will usually be able to obtain payment from the person who transferred the cheque to them and they in turn will be able to claim from the person who negotiated the cheque to them and so on. The loss will eventually lie with the person who first took the cheque when it bore a forged endorsement, unless that person can trace and recover from the forger. This, of course, is unlikely.

Look at Figure 9.1. Here, the true owner of the cheque is C, but s.55(2) gives F, in fact a wrongful possessor, the rights of a holder in due course *provided* the requirements of s.29(1) *would have been* satisfied if it were not for the break in the chain of negotiation. While D's finding of the cheque and forgery of C's signature breaks the chain of negotiation and title, thereby preventing F from enforcing the cheque against A, B, or C, F *can* enforce the cheque against E because s.55(2) precludes E from denying that D's forgery of C's endorsement is genuine. C, still the *true* owner of the cheque, can bring an action in conversion against E or F for the value of the cheque or its return and E is most likely to stand the loss. If C can recover the cheque, C can still enforce it against A and B.

21. Rights of a holder in due course

The rights of a holder in due course are the practical application of the legal characteristics of a negotiable instrument. Thus, they are the very essence of the concept of negotiability (*see* 9:5). Specifically, a holder in due course:

(a) *Can sue in their own name* any prior party to a cheque.
(b) *Is unaffected by any defect in the titles of prior parties or from claims arising from previous dealings among them.*

An example of the former would be where the issue or transfer of the cheque was obtained by fraud, making the payee or endorser's title voidable. An example of the latter would be where the cheque was taken in payment for faulty goods, entitling the drawer to a counter-claim against the payee in an action by the latter to enforce payment of the cheque. A holder in due course can, therefore, acquire a *better title* to the cheque than that held by its transferor.

> NOTE: Crossing a cheque 'not negotiable' prevents a person from becoming a holder in due course. Any prior defects in title are transferred with the cheque.

(c) *Can transfer their title* as holder in due course to any person for value or as a gift, provided that that person was not a *party* to any defect that affected the cheque – mere notice of the defect is not enough.

Collecting cheques

22. A bank's duty to its customer

(a) *Presentation of cheques.* A bank acts as agent when it presents cheques for payment (collects) on its customer's behalf. If it fails to present a cheque in accordance with the requirements of the Bills of Exchange Act 1882 s.45 and established banking practice, it will be liable to its customer for breach of contract. In particular, s.45(2) requires that a cheque is presented within a *reasonable time* in order for it to be enforceable against its drawer. Clearly, presentation through the 'clearings' would almost, by definition, satisfy this duty.

> NOTE: A collecting bank's duty to its customer is not fully discharged until a cheque has physically reached the branch of the paying bank on which it is drawn: *Barclays Bank PLC and Others* v *Bank of England* (1985). Although the case involved a dispute between the clearing banks and the Bank of England over contributions by the latter to the cost of the clearing system, the decision would seem to establish that the collecting bank is liable to its customer for any financial loss caused should a cheque be delayed or lost within the clearing system. In turn, the collecting bank would seem to be able to claim against the clearing system.

(b) *Notice of dishonour.* If a cheque is dishonoured by the paying bank, for whatever reason, the collecting bank must inform its customer within a reasonable time in order that the customer in turn is able to give notice as required by the Bills of Exchange Act 1882 ss.48 and 49 to any endorser the customer (the holder) wishes to enforce the cheque against.

NOTE: The Act does not require notice of dishonour to be given to the cheque's drawer as the drawer is deemed to know of the cheque's dishonour.

Where the bank and its customer reside *in the same place*, interpreted as the same postal area (London districts would be considered as the 'same place' for example), under s.49 a reasonable time means that notice must be posted so as to arrive on the day after the cheque's dishonour. Where they reside in *different places*, notice must be sent off on the day after the cheque's dishonour, provided that there is a convenient post on that day and, if not, by the next convenient post thereafter. Note that the Act refers to the notice being *sent* rather than *arriving* – the bank cannot be held responsible for postal delays, provided the notice has been properly posted.

If the bank's delay in giving notice prevents its customer giving effective notice to any endorser and the customer thereby suffers loss because they lose the right to enforce the cheque against an endorser, the bank is liable to its customer for damages.

(c) *No duty is owed to advise a customer of risks associated with collecting a cheque.* In *Redmond* v *Allied Irish Banks* (1987), R paid into his account three cheques payable to G, crossed 'Not negotiable – account payee' and bearing G's general endorsement, apparently to assist G who did not want them to go through his account for tax reasons. R withdrew the funds and paid them to G, who then disappeared. The cheques had been obtained by fraud and R ultimately stood the loss. R argued that the banks had a duty to inform him of the dangers of paying in third-party cheques endorsed 'not negotiable' (*see* 9:**9**), but the court held *obiter* that no such duty was owed and R's action failed. The position may well be different if a customer seeks advice and is wrongly advised or where misleading advice is volunteered.

23. Liability to the cheque's true owner

(a) *At common law*. A bank commits the common law tort of *conversion* against its true owner if it collects the cheque on behalf of a customer who has no title to it.

Conversion is committed where a person deals with another's property in a manner that denies that other person's title and right to possess the property. It is *no defence* in an action for conversion to establish that the tort was committed innocently, it is a tort of *strict liability*, that is proof of intention or negligence is not required. This is partly the justification for the statutory protection banks enjoy.

The customer is the primary tortfeasor, of course, but an action against a bank may be the preferred option because of the bank's undoubted ability to pay the damages awarded.

> NOTE: A bank, as agent, has the right to be indemnified by its customer if it is held liable for conversion when collecting cheques, usually by redebiting the account with the amount of the cheque. Given that the customer's fraud may well have been the cause of the conversion, this right may be somewhat empty if it seeks to recover its expenses as well.

(b) *In equity.* A bank will become a constructive trustee of the proceeds, and therefore liable to the beneficiaries, if it collects a cheque in circumstances where a reasonable banker would realise that a breach of trust had been or was likely to be committed. This cause of action has the advantage that time does not begin to run in the bank's favour under the Limitation Act 1980 (the plaintiff's claim would become statute-barred after six years) although the plaintiff would be subject to the maxim 'delay defeats equity'.

24. The Cheques Act 1957 s.4

This provides that a bank incurs no liability in conversion to the true owner of the cheque where its customer had either a defective title or no title at all to it, merely because it received payment of that cheque.

Although s.4 is almost always invoked in connection with cheques (including cheques that are not transferable by virtue of an 'account payee' crossing: Bills of Exchange Act 1882 s.81A, or otherwise), it also covers 'cheques' drawn 'Pay cash/wages' (these are not cheques), most payment warrants issued by government departments and bankers' drafts: Cheques Act 1957 s.4(2).

Certain conditions must be fulfilled for the protection to apply.

(a) The bank must *act for a customer* or *for itself* having credited the customer's account with the cheque. Thus, the protection applies both when a bank collects as an agent, i.e. for its customer, and when it collects for itself (as holder of the cheque).

Collecting 'for itself' covers the usual practice of crediting the customer's account immediately a cheque is paid in for collection. The bank is therefore collecting 'for itself' but because the credit is purely an accounting entry the bank has given no value for the cheque. It is not collecting 'for itself' in the sense that it has 'bought' the right to enforce payment of the cheque. If a bank gives value for a cheque paid in for collection (*see* 9:**26**), it is not protected by s.4.

> NOTE: Payment in of a cheque at another branch of the customer's bank would seem to be still acting 'for a customer' because the bank is, at law,

a single entity. Payment in at a different bank would appear *not* to satisfy the condition and the 'collecting' bank would not be protected by s.4.

(b) The bank must act in *good faith*. Honesty is required, but negligence is not evidence of bad faith: Bills of Exchange Act 1882 s.90.

(c) The bank must act *without negligence*. Section 4(3) provides that a bank is not to be treated as negligent *purely* because the cheque collected was not endorsed or was irregularly endorsed, i.e. it failed to concern itself with these things, but in all other cases it must establish that it acted with reasonable care. This is justified quite simply in that s.4 deprives the true owner of the cheque of their common law right to compensation from the bank for conversion.

Negligence in relation to collecting cheques can only be explained by referring to decided cases that provide *guides* – not hard and fast rules – for the court's use. However, a number of general propositions can be stated.

(i) The *standard of care* required is that of an ordinary competent bank.

(ii) The criterion for this is *current banking practice*, rather than decisions dating back 50 or more years – times change – although it by no means follows that current banking practice will never itself be held to be negligent.

(iii) Under the Banking Act 1979 s.47, a bank can plead contributory negligence by its customer in any action where the bank pleads s.4 as a defence to an action against it for conversion. A successful plea will reduce the damages awarded. The defence would be applicable, for example, where the owner of cheques carelessly left them lying around, facilitating their fraudulent use or where carelessly drawn cheques are fraudulently altered.

Example

In *Lumsden & Co v London Trustee Savings Bank* (1971), where the Law Reform (Contributory Negligence) Act 1945 was the relevant statute at the time, L, the employers of the fraudster involved, had drawn cheques payable to 'Brown' intending the payee to be 'Brown Mills & Co'. A gap had been left before 'Brown' on the cheques. The fraudster inserted initials before 'Brown' and paid the cheques into an account opened in the same name and obtained payment.

It was held that, although, on the facts, the bank had been negligent in opening the account, its own procedures for taking and checking references not having been followed, the plaintiff was partly to blame for the fraud and their damages were accordingly reduced by 10 per cent. (Attractive though a plea of contributory negligence would seem to be, it appears only to have been successfully pleaded in this one reported case.)

NOTE: The *Rule* in *Macmillan and Arthur* (1918), discussed below, does not apply to a collecting bank. Conversely, the defence of contributory negligence is not available to a paying bank.

25. Examples of negligence and s.4

Each case is ultimately decided on its own facts but *common themes* have emerged in decisions against banks, specifically *absence of enquiry* where it was reasonably called for or the *unsatisfactory nature of the enquiries* that were made.

As s.4 affords a defence to an action for conversion, the onus is on the bank to establish that it acted *without* negligence.

NOTE: Many of the cases cited pre-date 1957. These were decided under the Bills of Exchange Act 1882 s.82, which was repealed and replaced by the Cheques Act 1957 s.4 – the two provisions affording very similar protection.

(a) *Failure to make reasonable enquiries* about a person's identity and circumstances before opening an account: *Ladbroke & Co v Todd* (1914). Traditionally the enquiries have taken the form of one or more references, although references are probably not required where the prospective customer is already known to the bank as a suitable person or introduced by a person of similar standing. Furthermore, unless the referee is personally known to the bank, for example where they are an existing customer, the authenticity of the reference should be checked, for example, through the referee's own bank: *Hampstead Guardians v Barclays Bank Ltd* (1923).

Example

Marfani and Co Ltd v Midland Bank Ltd (1968) (CA), concerned a carefully conceived fraud. The Office Manager of M contrived to make the acquaintance of A, a respectable restaurateur. The Office Manager introduced himself as E and, during the course of the acquaintanceship, A became interested in the fraudster's intentions to open a restaurant of his own. Knowing that the owner of M was leaving for Pakistan the following day, the fraudulent Office Manager prepared a cheque on the company's account for £3000, payable to E, one of the company's suppliers and, obtained M's signature on it. He opened an account at the bank with this cheque, using the name E, and, as one of his two referees, he nominated A, who already had a good account with the bank. The other referee did not reply, but A gave a satisfactory reference, whereupon the bank issued a chequebook to the new customer. Over the next two weeks, the entire balance was withdrawn from the account following which the Office Manager left the country. The company sued the bank for conversion, alleging negligence in opening the account.

It was held that the bank was protected by s.4 following evidence by other banks that the defendant had acted as a reasonable bank. In particular, the following circumstances were held *not* to constitute negligence in the case:

(a) opening an account after only one reference had been received without making further enquiries (the referee who replied was a respected customer and the second referee's failure to reply was satisfactorily explained by the mobility of the ethnic minority community to which he belonged);

(b) failure to ask the new customer for his passport; and

(c) collecting the cheque before receiving the reference.

The *Marfani* case shows that, while basic enquiries must be made, it is impossible to be categoric about what should make a bank suspicious and the nature and extent of its enquiries. These things will depend on current banking practice. It also indicates that current banking practice will not necessarily determine what the law expects of a reasonable bank. (Given this and the present high incidence of cheque fraud, which is facilitated by lax enquiries, it is perhaps interesting to speculate whether the decision would have been the same today.)

NOTE: The bank's duty is to make reasonable enquiries into a prospective customer's identity and suitability. Taking references is but one way of doing this. It is also time consuming and puts a bank at a competitive disadvantage if other banks are adopting more 'customer-friendly' procedures. In recent years, therefore, banks have developed alternative ways of apparently fulfilling this duty, e.g. documentary proof of identity, such as a passport and a search of a credit reference agency. It remains to be seen when and if such procedures are reviewed by the court whether they will be held to be reasonable enquiries.

(b) *Failure to obtain the name of its customer's employer* or, in the case of a married customer, the name of the *spouse's employer*. The point in making such enquiries is to avoid being innocently made party to conversion of cheques by your customer. The customer might, for example, steal cheques payable to their employer and pay them in for collection for their own account.

Similarly, a spouse's account could be used to collect cheques stolen by the other spouse payable to or drawn by that spouse's employer and fraudulently endorsed. The customer may even be in a position to draw cheques on behalf of their employer, making them payable to their spouse.

Example

In *Lloyds Bank Ltd* v *E B Savory and Company* (1932) (HL), two clerks, P and S, stole cheques from S, their employer. The cheques were payable to various stockbrokers or to bearer. All were paid in at City branches of the bank for the credit of accounts elsewhere, some by P for his own account and some by S for the credit of his wife's accounts. The 'branch credit' system, as it was then called, entailed the branches where the cheques were paid in sending the cheques through the clearing system for collection and passing on credit slips with a form of banker's payment to the account-holding branches. The credit slips bore no details of the items and thus the account-holding branches remained in ignorance of the payees and drawers of the cheques concerned. Even had this information been conveyed it would have been of no use as details of the employers of S and P had not been obtained.

It was held that the bank was liable in conversion because it had lost the protection of s.4 due to its negligence in failing to obtain details of the employers of the account holders or, in the case of Mrs S, of her husband.

The case law concerns married *women* customers, but there is no reason why the same precautions should not be taken when a married *man* seeks to open an account. Indeed, since the enactment of the Sex Discrimination Act 1975, any apparent discrimination against married women (or, indeed, married men) can no longer be maintained. As a result of the Act, banks often choose *not* to enquire as to the employer of the spouse of any married prospective customer.

Once the account is opened, there is no legal duty to keep employment details up to date.

Example

In *Orbit Mining and Trading Co Ltd* v *Westminster Bank Ltd* (1963) (CA), X, W's customer and co-director of OMT, had obtained the other co-director's signature on a number of blank cheques, ostensibly so that X could carry on the business while his colleague was abroad. X drew the cheques to 'cash', countersigned them with his own normal, but virtually illegible, signature and paid them into an existing private account at W. On opening the account with W, X had been asked for and had given details of his then employment, but this had subsequently changed and the bank was unaware of his employment with OMT.

It was held that an action for conversion against W failed. W were under no duty to make further enquiries as to X's employment after opening the account and, on the facts, it was not immediately obvious that X had co-signed the cheques. They had not, therefore been negligent in collecting the cheques.

The situations in (a) and (b) above illustrate negligence in opening an account. Other instances of negligence (below) involve collecting cheques where the bank has been negligent in relation to the drawer or payee of the cheque.

(c) *Failure to check the information required to be disclosed under the Business Names Act 1985 before opening an account in a trade name.* The Act requires that any one person, individual, partnership or company, who trades under a name different to their surname or surnames discloses their names on all business stationery and prominently displays details of ownership on all trade premises.

If enquiries are not made, it would be possible for a person who has wrongfully obtained a cheque payable to a business to open an account in the business' name and obtain payment of the cheque. Failure to make the enquiries would almost certainly result in the bank being unable to rely on s.4.

> NOTE: A similar situation arises where a *nom de plume* or pseudonym is used, e.g. by an author. A bank must ensure that a customer *is* the person actually entitled to it before it accepts a cheque payable in such a name for collection.

(d) Crediting cheques payable to *a company to the private account of an official of the company*. This applies even where it is a sole trader company.

Example

In *Underwood* v *Bank of Liverpool and Martins Ltd* (1924) (CA), the bank was liable to the company for conversion when it collected cheques payable to the company and endorsed by U for his personal account, even though U was the company's sole director and held all but one of its issued shares.

(e) Crediting the *private account of an agent or of an employee* with cheques drawn by them on the *account of their principal or employer*.

Example

In *Midland Bank Ltd* v *Reckitt* (1933) (HL), the bank was held to have acted negligently, and was therefore liable to R, when it collected for the personal account of a solicitor (which was overdrawn) cheques drawn by him under power of attorney on R's account. The power of attorney did not dispense with the need to make enquiries before collecting the cheques. A relevant factor was that the bank had previously asked the solicitor to reduce his overdraft.

(f) Crediting without satisfactory explanation a *cheque payable to a limited company for the account of another company* – see *London & Montrose Shipbuilding & Repairing Co Ltd* v *Barclays Bank Ltd* (1926) (CA).

> NOTE: The endorsement of such cheques would be unusual, but they could be collected where the payee company had specially endorsed the cheque to the other company – as in *Penmount Estates Ltd* v *National Provincial Bank Ltd* (1945) (CA) – or where general instructions are held concerning such credits. Such arrangements may exist where the compa-

nies are members of the same group, the bank taking indemnities from the companies concerned against any loss it may incur by so acting.

(g) Crediting an *agent's private account* with cheques expressly payable to the agent in the capacity of an *agent*.

Example

In *Marquess of Bute* v *Barclays Bank Ltd* (1955), the bank was held to have acted negligently in collecting for the private account of an agent three warrants made payable to him because in brackets on the cheques were the words 'for Marquess of Bute'.

(h) Crediting a *partner's private account with cheques payable to the partnership*: *Baker* v *Barclays Bank Ltd* (1955).

(i) Although a bank is under no general legal duty to examine for endorsement cheques paid in for collection, a bank *is* negligent if it collects a cheque that *lacks an endorsement* where one is necessary. This is partly based on the law, but mainly on banking practice, specifically a resolution of the Committee of London Clearing Bankers in 1957, which was adopted in spite of s.4(3) (*see* above). Examples include

    (i) Cheques paid in for an account other than that of the payee;

    (ii) Combined cheques and receipt forms marked 'R';

    (iii) Travellers' cheques;

    (iv) Cheques payable by banks abroad; and

    (v) Cheques made payable to joint payees and collected for an account to which all the joint payees are not parties, e.g. a cheque made payable to Mr and Mrs Patel and paid in by Mrs Patel for a sole account in her name.

NOTE: Cheques payable to one or more of a number of joint account holders may be collected for the credit of a joint account without first being endorsed; this includes the accounts of partners and trustees.

    Also, if the payee's name is misspelt or they are incorrectly designated, a cheque may be accepted for collection without endorsement *unless* there are circumstances to suggest that the customer is not the person to whom payment is intended to be made.

A third category of negligence is where cheques are collected without sufficient enquiry where unusual circumstances demand particular care. Some examples of this are explained below.

(j) Collecting without satisfactory explanation cheques, particularly third-party cheques, for *amounts inconsistent with its customer's activities*.

Example

In *Nu-Stilo Footwear Ltd* v *Lloyds Bank Ltd* (1956), N's company secretary opened an account in an assumed name, giving his real name as referee. The first cheque paid in was drawn in his own favour (under his assumed name) and for a modest sum, but the second cheque was a third-party cheque, apparently endorsed to him, for a large sum.

It was held that the bank had not been negligent in opening the account, nor in collecting the first cheque, but it was negligent in collecting the second and subsequent cheques, some of which were also third-party cheques, because the amounts were inconsistent with its customer's stated occupation as an agent newly started in business.

(k) Collecting *third-party cheques* without sufficient enquiry where the circumstances demand it, but the bank is not expected to play 'amateur detective'.

Example

In *Motor Traders Guarantee Corporation Ltd* v *Midland Bank Ltd* (1937), a bank lost the protection of s.4 when it collected without enquiry a third-party cheque fraudulently endorsed by its customer to himself because, in the six months the account had been opened, 35 cheques drawn on it had been dishonoured.

(l) Collecting with sufficient enquiry cheques crossed 'Account *payee*' *for someone other than the named payee.*

Under the Bills of Exchange Act 1882, s.81A, such a cheque is not transferable and therefore, by definition, anyone *other* than the payee is not its owner. However, the protection of the Cheques Act 1957 s.4 is extended to such instruments by s.3 of the Cheques Act 1992. Thus, providing the bank is satisfied that the payee *intended* the cheque to be collected for another's account, it would appear that the bank is protected.

> NOTE: The practice of banks has varied in relation to 'account payee' cheques, but the response to the Cheques Act 1992 has tended to be a decision not to collect 'account payee' cheques at all.
>
> There is no duty on a bank to make enquiries where it collects for a customer other than the payee a cheque crossed 'not negotiable'.

(m) Where a bank both pays and collects a cheque, it must be entitled to statutory protection in *both* capacities – ss.60 and 80 of the Bills of Exchange Act 1882 and s.4 of the Cheques Act 1957 – to avoid liability in conversion to the true owner of the cheque.

Example

In *Carpenters' Co* v *British Mutual Banking Co Ltd* (1938) (CA), BMB's customer X stole cheques drawn by C, his employer, payable to third parties. C also banked with BMB. X forged the endorsements of the payees and paid them into his own account.

It was held that, although BMB's payment satisfied s.60, it did not satisfy s.4 because it was negligent in failing to enquire *why* its customer (X) was paying his employer's cheques into his own account. BMB therefore also forfeited the protection of s.60 and was liable to C.

26. Protection as holder in due course

(a) *Introduction.* The Cheques Act 1957 s.4 does not protect a bank when it gives value (consideration) for the cheque it collects, it will then be collecting for itself as holder for value of the cheque and not as an agent. (Crediting the account before receiving the funds is purely a bookkeeping entry, it is not giving value and is, therefore, within s.4.) Nevertheless, establishing itself as holder in due course of a cheque in such circumstances gives a bank an alternative and perfect defence to an action for conversion of the cheque. At law it is the *true owner* of the cheque and it cannot commit conversion against its own property.

> NOTE: A bank cannot become a holder in due course of a cheque that it collects where the cheque bears a forged endorsement or where the words 'not negotiable' or 'account payee' (Bills of Exchange Act 1882 s.81A have been added to the crossing).

The defence afforded by satisfying s.29 of the Bills of Exchange Act 1882 (*see* 10:**25**) has the *advantage* of applying even where the bank may have acted negligently, but the *disadvantage* of not being available where the collecting bank took the cheque under a forged endorsement for this prevents the bank from becoming even a holder. The protection of s.4 of the 1957 Act is not lost in this latter situation.

Quite apart from the defence that it affords, the bank as holder in due course acquires the right to enforce the cheque, if it is dishonoured, against all prior parties – s.4 only affords a defence. An example of this would be where, having credited the customer's account and allowed the customer to draw against the uncleared effects (*see* below), the subsequent debit creates an overdraft that the customer is not in a position to repay. The bank could then enforce payment against the drawer and any endorser of the cheque.

(b) *Instances of giving value.*

(i) Where a bank allows the customer to draw against the cheque *before it has been cleared*. There must, however, be an express or implied agreement entitling the customer to do so, e.g. following the customer's specific request.

(ii) Where the cheque is paid in *specifically to reduce an existing overdraft* and not in the ordinary course of business as an overdrawn account. This would apply where the bank has specifically asked for the overdraft to be reduced and the customer pays in a cheque drawn by a third party in their favour or the customer's own cheque drawn on another bank. The consideration (value) provided by the bank is the existence of the overdraft – an 'antecedent debt or liability' supports a cheque: Bills of Exchange Act 1882 s.27(1).

(iii) Where the bank *buys* the cheque. For example, where a bank cashes a cheque drawn by a third party for its customer or where it cashes a cheque drawn on another branch or another bank without open credit arrangements. In both cases, the bank is acting in excess of its contractual duty and is therefore giving value.

(iv) Where the bank has a lien on the cheque, it is the holder for value of the cheque to the extent of the sum for which it has a lien: Bills of Exchange Act 1882 s.27(2). A lien arises automatically if a cheque is paid into an overdrawn account providing there is no agreement to the contrary.

NOTE: A lien is lost if the bank even temporarily gives up possession of the cheque to which the lien relates: *Westminster Bank* v *Zang* (1966) (HL).

(v) Although unlikely in practice, a bank would give value if it accepted a cheque for collection payable to its customer if it took it in payment for services such as foreign currency transactions or safe custody facilities.

(c) *Endorsement.* The Cheques Act 1957 s.2, provides that a bank is to be considered the holder of a cheque payable to order for which it has given value, or over which it has a lien, although the customer delivered it to the bank for collection *without endorsing it*.

This provision is necessary because an order cheque can only be negotiated by endorsement completed by delivery, while the Cheques Act 1957 s.1 removed the need for endorsement of an order cheque paid straight into the payee's account, i.e. the Acts would otherwise take away the possibility of a bank becoming the holder of a cheque that is paid in for collection.

(d) *Statutory requirements.* To be a holder in due course of a cheque received from a customer for collection, a bank must satisfy all the criteria in s.29(1) of the Bills of Exchange Act 1882 (*see* 9:**16**).

NOTE: If the proposal in the 1990 White Paper 'Banking Services: Law and Practice' that all crossed cheques should cease to be negotiable is made law, a bank will never be able to become holder in due course of a cheque that it receives for collection.

27. The defence of *ex turpi causa non oritur actio*

This can be translated as 'no right of action arises from a bad cause'. Although the defence appears only to have arisen once, it may protect the bank when it cannot rely on s.4 of the Cheques Act 1957 and the action for conversion arises from serious criminal activity. To allow the action to proceed, the court would have to condone the illegality and this is contrary to public policy.

Example
_____

In *Thackwell* v *Barclays Bank PLC* (1986), as a result of a fraud to which T was a party, a finance company issued a cheque for a large sum of money to T. T's endorsement was forged on the cheque and it was paid into another account.

It was held, on the facts, that the protection of s.4 was lost because the collection of the cheque was sufficiently unusual to warrant the making of enquiries. However, the defence of *ex turpi causa non oritur actio* succeeded because the cheque concerned was the result of the very fraud in which T was involved.
_____

Paying cheques

28. Introduction

A bank owes a contractual duty to pay its customers' cheques provided they are properly drawn, signed in accordance with the mandate and funds are available on the account. However, this authority can be revoked by the customer and, further, is terminated in a number of situations.

If the words and figures on a cheque do not agree, the bank can choose not to, and usually will not, pay it. However, it is entitled under the Bills of Exchange Act 1882 s.9(2) to pay the sum stated in words.

> NOTE: If the issue of a cheque was properly backed by a cheque card, the bank owes an additional duty to the *payee* to pay the cheque.

Payment of a cheque in due course by the drawee bank discharges the cheque: Bills of Exchange Act 1882 s.59.

29. Termination of authority to pay

(a) *Countermand of payment*: Bills of Exchange Act 1882 s.75. Here the customer revokes the bank's authority to pay the cheque. It is usually known as 'stopping a cheque'.

To be effective a countermand must:

(i) Be made by the *drawer*.

(ii) Be absolutely *unequivocal* – in effect, this means that it must be in writing, although there is no *legal* requirement that this should be so.

(iii) Be *communicated* to the *branch on which the cheque was drawn*: *London Provincial and South Western Bank Ltd* v *Buszard* (1918).

(iv) Give *complete details* of the cheque to be countermanded: the reference to the cheque must be unequivocal – in particular, the payee's name, the amount of the cheque and its number must be given. Of these, the cheque's *number* is the most important detail and a bank will not incur liability where a countermand gives the wrong number of the cheque and the bank accidentally pays the cheque that the customer intended to stop: *Westminster Bank Ltd* v *Hilton* (1926) (HL).

A bank can still stop payment when a countermand is received *after* the cheque has been presented but *before* it has been paid.

NOTE: It is generally considered that any party to a joint account can 'stop' a cheque; it does not have to be the party who drew the cheque, although, strictly speaking, it will depend on the application of the terms of the mandate to the facts of the case.

A customer cannot stop a cheque that was correctly backed by a cheque card. This is by virtue of the express terms in the contract made with the bank for the use of the cheque card.

Example

In *Curtice* v *London City and Midland Bank Ltd* (1908) (CA), a telegram countermanding payment of a cheque was delivered after banking hours and left in the bank's letter box. The next day, the countermand was accidentally overlooked and was found the following day. By this time the cheque had been paid.

It was held that a countermand was not effective unless and until it came to the *actual attention* of the drawee bank. Thus, the bank was entitled to debit the plaintiff's account with the amount of the cheque.

Although, in practice, a countermand must be in writing, telephone countermands are often made. These entitle a bank to postpone payment or dishonour of the cheque pending the customer's written confirmation of the verbal instruction. If, in the meantime, the cheque is returned, the bank must indicate that confirmation of countermand is awaited.

If the payee or a subsequent holder of a cheque loses it or has it stolen from them and contacts the bank to stop payment, the bank is in a legal dilemma, although there would usually be a simple practical solution. Without doubt, the bank would have no legal grounds to stop payment – only the drawer can countermand payment of a cheque – but it would risk losing its statutory protection under the Bills of Exchange Act 1882 s.60 and the Cheques Act 1957 s.1 (*see* 9:**34**). This is because it would seem not to be 'in the ordinary course of business' and, possibly, not 'in good faith' to pay the cheque if it is later presented knowing that it has been lost or stolen and therefore, almost by definition, to be in the hands of wrongful possessor. Fortunately, the problem would usually be resolved by asking the payee/endorsee to contact the drawer or by the bank itself contacting the drawer and asking for instructions.

> NOTE: Countermanding a cheque does not remove the drawer's liability on the cheque to the payee unless it was drawn as a gift or for a consideration that has totally failed. However, if the cheque had been negotiated for value, the drawer would be liable on it to a holder in due course.

(b) *Legal bars to payment.*

(i) *Garnishee order.* This is a court order that commands a debtor (in this instance the bank) to pay the debt, not to the immediate creditor (in this instance the customer), but to the court for the benefit of a person who has obtained a final court judgment against the creditor. The order attaches funds standing to the credit of the account at the moment the order is served and, depending on the amount specified in the order, if insufficient funds are left, it prevents the bank lawfully paying further cheques drawn on the account.

(ii) *Injunction.* This is a court order that forbids a person from doing or from continuing to do something. An injunction may be issued against a bank directly or, more usually, against a customer to freeze a bank account where, for example, the ownership of certain funds is disputed. The injunction's purpose is to prevent them from being paid away, possibly abroad and, therefore, outside the court's jurisdiction, before ownership is determined by the court. Such injunctions are known as *Mareva Injunctions* after a 1975 case involving a company of that name.

The legal effect of an injunction against the customer is that, if the customer draws a cheque in breach of it, the customer would be guilty of contempt of court and, if the bank honoured the cheque, it would be guilty of aiding and abetting the defendant's contempt. Thus, once a bank has notice of an injunction affecting money (or goods) in its hands it must not allow *anyone* to dispose of it *except* with the authority of the court.

(iii) Material alteration. The cheque is avoided except against a person who themselves made, authorised or assented to the alteration – most likely by signing over it – and any person who subsequently endorsed the cheque in its altered form: Bills of Exchange Act 1882 s.64(1). Section 64 operates, in effect, as a legal bar to the bank paying the cheque.

A material alteration is one that has the effect of changing the operation of the cheque or the liabilities of the parties. The alteration is usually a fraudulent increase in the amount, but it could be an alteration to the payee's name or to the crossing to enable the cheque to be cashed.

(iv) Outbreak of war between the country of the customer and that of the bank. This is an application of the general principle that the outbreak of war prevents the further performance of contracts between persons in this country and persons in enemy territory: *Arab Bank Ltd* v *Barclays Bank (Dominion, Colonial and Overseas)* (1954) (HL).

NOTE: The customer's right to be paid a credit balance on a current account survives the outbreak of war – it is merely suspended during the hostilities.

(c) *Notice of certain events affecting the customer*:

(i) The customer's *death*: Bills of Exchange Act 1882 s.75.

(ii) The customer's *mental disorder*, although the disorder must be such that the customer is incapable of managing their affairs.

(iii) A *bankruptcy petition* or *winding-up petition* against the customer.

(d) *Bankruptcy order or winding-up order.* Both orders have the effect of bringing the commercial activity of a business organisation to an end – the former applying to sole traders and partnerships, the latter to registered companies.

The point to note is that it is the *making* of the order, not notice of it, that terminates a bank's authority to pay. A bank, therefore, has no authority to pay the cheque even if it acts in complete ignorance of the order.

(e) *Third-party rights.* If a bank either *knows* or *should* know that a cheque has been issued for an illegal purpose or its payment would further an illegal purpose, it must not pay the cheque. The following are examples.

(i) A trustee who acts in breach of trust, such as a member of a firm of solicitors drawing cheques on the client account for their own purposes, or executors transferring monies from the

executors' account to private accounts, particularly if the latter are overdrawn. The bank must not pay such cheques *even* if the payment would be in accordance with the mandate.

NOTE: In *Lipkin Gorman* v *Karpnale and Another* (1989), the Court of Appeal emphasised that a 'lack of probity' (virtue/principle/honesty/uprightness) on the part of a bank is required before it will be liable as constructive trustee. It further emphasised that such conduct would probably also constitute a breach of the banker–customer contract – a more straightforward situation (*see* 1:**6**).

(ii) Agents who exceed their authority.

(iii) A company official who signs company cheques for the purchase of the company's own shares contrary to the Companies Act 1985.

(iv) An undischarged bankrupt who presents a cheque; the proceeds of the cheque probably belong to the bankrupt's trustee in bankruptcy.

(f) *Presenter has no title.* Should a drawee bank be aware that the presenter of a cheque has no title to it, the bank should postpone payment of the cheque until it receives instructions from the drawer. This is an unlikely situation, but it could arise if an open cheque is lost or stolen and presented over the counter by a stranger purporting to be the payee, the true payee having previously notified the bank of the loss.

30. Wrongful debit of an account

A bank is liable in damages to its customer if it wrongfully debits its customer's account. It may do so in one of five ways:

(a) *Countermand* – by debiting the account after its customer has countermanded payment (*see* 9:**29**).

NOTE: If the money cannot be recovered from the payee (*see* 9:**31**), the bank may exercise its right of subrogation and claim back from its customer goods purchased with the 'stopped' cheque that was wrongly paid.

(b) *Post-dated cheques* – by debiting an account with a postdated cheque before the proper date for payment. The customer is entitled to stop the cheque before the payment date and an early payment could result in other cheques being dishonoured for apparent lack of funds. Alternatively the customer may die or become insolvent before the date for payment.

(c) *Forgery of the customer's signature* – a forged signature is completely without legal effect: Bills of Exchange Act 1882 s.24. Thus, if its customer's signature on a cheque is forged, the bank has no authority to pay the cheque. This is so even if the forgery is undetectable. Nor can the bank debit the account if the drawer has purported to ratify a forgery of their signature as a forgery is incapable of ratification.

However, a customer may be estopped (prevented) from denying the genuineness of the signature, thereby enabling the bank to debit the account. Estoppel requires a representation about an existing fact, either by statement or by conduct, that is clear and unambiguous, that is intended to be acted on and which is, in fact, acted on by the bank to its detriment, e.g. that it is unable to recover the funds paid away.

Example 1

In *Greenwood* v *Martins Bank Ltd* (1932) (HL), G's wife held the chequebook for his account with MB and, over a period of time, drew a number of cheques by forging his signature. G subsequently discovered this but did not inform the bank. After his wife's death some eight months later, G sought to recover from MB the amount of the forged cheques.

It was held that his action was unsuccessful because his inaction after discovering that his wife had been forging his signature prevented him, at law, from denying their genuineness. The bank was entitled to debit his account by the value of the cheques.

Example 2

In *Brown* v *Westminster Bank* (1964), the bank had, on a number of occasions, drawn the attention of B, an old lady, to the number of cheques drawn on her account payable to C, her servant. B maintained that the cheques were genuine. Subsequently, the matter was discussed with her son, who held her power of attorney, which resulted in an action against the bank in respect of 329 cheques allegedly forged by C.

It was held that B's action failed. By virtue of her representations to the bank, she was estopped from denying the genuineness of the cheques.

On a 'both to sign' mandate, a bank is liable to the innocent account holder should it pay a cheque signed by one joint account holder who has forged the signature of the other: *Jackson* v *White and Midland Bank Ltd* (1967).

(d) *Breach of the mandate* – a bank will be liable if it does not adhere strictly to the terms of the mandate. For example, if it allows a withdrawal to be made by one account holder only on a 'both to sign mandate', it is liable to the other who can *independently* enforce repayment of the amount withdrawn: *Catlin* v *Cyprus Finance Corporation (London) Ltd* (1983).

The bank will have a defence for payments made in breach of the mandate where the payments extinguished the legitimate debts of the customer. The bank is subrogated to the rights of the creditors repaid (takes the place of creditors repaid) against the customer. Subrogation prevents the customer from being unjustly enriched.

Example

In *Liggett (Liverpool) Ltd* v *Barclays Bank Ltd* (1928), the bank wrongly paid L's cheques when they were signed by one director only but because they were drawn in favour of trade creditors an action by the company against the bank failed.

> NOTE: Refusal to pay a stale cheque would appear to be acting contrary to its customer's instructions. However, the practice of returning such cheques is so common and well-known that the right to do so would probably be held to be an implied term of the banker–customer contract.

(e) *Material alteration* – a bank is liable if it debits an account with a cheque that has been materially altered without the customer's consent.

If the alteration is *not apparent*, a holder in due course is entitled to the original amount for which the cheque was drawn. Any other holder presenting the cheque is entitled to nothing: Bills of Exchange Act 1882 s.64(1).

A bank has very limited statutory protection if it pays a cheque that has been materially altered, *whether or not* the alteration is apparent (*see* 9:**34**). However, a customer owes a duty to draw cheques with reasonable care to avoid fraudulent alteration of them and the bank may debit the customer's account where the latter's negligence has facilitated the fraud. This is known as the *Rule* in *Macmillan and Arthur* (1918) (HL). Here, a partner in the defendant firm signed a cheque payable to the payee or to bearer made out by a clerk for the sum of £2. The amount payable was shown in figures only. The clerk fraudulently altered the figure to read £120, wrote the amount on the cheque and obtained payment from the plaintiff, the firm's bankers. It was held that, because of the defendant's negligence, the plaintiff bank was entitled to debit the firm's account with the value of the cheque.

A bank will seldom be the 'innocent' victim of a fraudulently altered cheque. If a visibly altered cheque is paid without confirmation of the alteration, a bank has only itself to blame, while most non-apparent alterations will be facilitated by its customer's negligence, thereby enabling the bank to rely on the *Rule* in *Macmillan and Arthur*.

In *Tai Hing Cotton Mill Ltd* v *Liu Chong Hing Bank Ltd* (1985), the

Privy Council reaffirmed the customer's duty established in *Macmillan and Arthur* to draw cheques with reasonable care in order to prevent their fraudulent alteration, but held that there is no wider duty to take reasonable precautions in managing their business to *prevent* cheques being forged. Similarly, the customer's duty to inform their bank of any forged cheque drawn on their account of which they were aware, as in *Greenwood*, was affirmed, but no duty to check bank statements for unauthorised debit items was recognised.

Example

In *Slingsby* v *District Bank* (1932) (CA), a fraudulent solicitor drew a cheque payable to X for S's signature. After S signed, the solicitor added 'per Cumberbirch and Potts', his firm, to the payee's name and obtained payment of the cheque. S sought to recover the value of the cheque from the bank.

It was held that his action succeeded. Although the bank could not have been expected to detect the alteration because the whole cheque, apart from the drawer's signature, was in the solicitor's handwriting, the drawer owed no duty to draw a line after the payee's name to prevent any addition or alteration to this. Therefore, the cheque was invalid under s.64(1).

31. Recovery of money paid by mistake

(a) *By the bank*. If a bank pays a cheque:

 (i) Which has been *materially altered*; or

 (ii) After it has been properly *countermanded*; or

 (iii) On which the *drawer's signature is forged*; or

 (iv) As a result of some other breach of the mandate; or

 (v) If it makes the *same payment twice*;

it may be able to recover the payment from the payee as money paid by mistake.

To recover a payment the bank must have made it:

 (i) Under a mistake of fact, not of law (a notoriously problematic distinction);

 (ii) Without its customer's authority; and

 (iii) Not be estopped (prevented) from claiming repayment. An estoppel would arise where the payee is able to show that they relied on the representation of the bank (the payment of the cheque) that the money was due to them and altered their position to their detriment because of this, or at least be able to show that it would be inequitable to call for repayment. Whether the payee has so altered their position is a question of fact in each case.

Thus, funds cannot be recovered if payment is made merely because the bank mistook the balance on the account (there being no other reason requiring the bank not to pay the cheque) for here the bank still has its customer's authority to pay.

Example

In *Barclays Bank Ltd* v *Simms, Son & Cooke* (1979), a customer of the bank drew a cheque in favour of S in payment of a debt. S went into receivership the following day and the customer telephoned a countermand, confirming it in writing. S's receiver, unaware of the countermand, paid the cheque into S's account and had it specially cleared. By mistake, the bank paid the cheque.

It was held that the bank was entitled to repayment from the receiver.

NOTE: A mistaken payment can only be recovered from a collecting bank if the funds have not been withdrawn by the payee. After they have been withdrawn, an action can only be brought against the payee.

An alternative way to recover money paid by mistake is to seek a tracing order on the grounds that the money, in equity, still belongs to the paying bank. The recipient of the funds would be deemed to hold them as constructive trustee.

NOTE: Tracing would not be available where the cheque was paid into an overdrawn account for here the collecting bank would have purchased the cheque in good faith and for value.

(b) *By the customer.* A customer may seek to recover money paid to the payee under a mistake of fact where, for example, the bank has correctly debited their account with a cheque which had been materially altered through the fraud of, say, an employee and the customer's failure to exercise due care in drawing the cheque facilitated the fraud (*see London Joint Bank* v *Macmillan and Arthur* (1918) at **30** above). It is no defence that the funds paid by the bank are technically its own (*Foley* v *Hill* (1848)), because in substance the funds used belong to the customer: *Agip (Africa) Ltd* v *Jackson and others* (1992) (CA).

The customer is also able to trace funds paid in such circumstances from an account in credit because in *Lipkin Gorman* v *Karpnale Ltd* (1992) (HL) the House held that the customer owns the debt (the credit balance) due to them from the bank. It follows that even an innocent recipient of funds paid to them by mistake can be made to repay them where the recipient did not give full consideration for them and was thereby unjustly enriched at the expense of the true owner (the customer).

Example

In *Lipkin Gorman* v *Karpnale Ltd* (1992) (HL) the firm of solicitors owned the debt due to them by the bank and they could trace this property into its direct product, i.e. the money stolen from the client account by C (one of the partners), and follow it into the hands of the casino. On the facts the casino gave no consideration for the money because (1) the chips bought with it were valueless outside the casino and were merely gambling tokens within it and (2) each bet placed (bought) with a chip (which represented money) was void under the Gaming Act 1845. Since C lost the money the club did not suffer an injustice in having to repay it! (*See* also 1:**6, 7** (for Court of Appeal hearing) and **20**.)

32. Wrongful dishonour of a cheque

A bank may wrongfully dishonour a cheque for a variety of reasons, all normally associated with poor administration. For example it might wrongly mark the account as closed, wrongly believe there were insufficient funds on the account, perhaps because a post-dated cheque had been paid early, fail to mark the account with the correct overdraft limit or fail to lift a stop on a cheque.

NOTE: A bank is entitled to a reasonable time in which to complete bookkeeping entries after funds are credited to an account before those funds are available to meet cheques: *Marzetti v Williams* (1830). What is a reasonable time will depend on the nature of funds, where they are paid in and banking practice.

If there are insufficient funds available on the account on which the cheque is drawn but sufficient funds available on another account held by the drawer, the bank can, if it wishes, pay the cheque and debit the other account relying on its right of combination (*see* 1:**16**). Conversely, if there is a debit balance on another account, the bank can combine the accounts and *refuse* to pay the cheque if there is an insufficient net balance.

If a cheque is wrongly dishonoured, a bank can incur liability under two heads. First, for *breach of contract* and, second, for *libel*. The first needs no further explanation, the latter does.

Libel is a form of *defamation* and the cause of action is based on the statement made lowering the plaintiff in the eyes of right-thinking members of society generally or causing the plaintiff to be shunned and avoided. An action for libel following a wrongful dishonour of a cheque is based on the words used in stating the reason for dishonour.

Example

In *Jayson v Midland Bank Ltd* (1968), J was a garment manufacturer and retailer. The bank returned two of his cheques marked with the words 'Refer to drawer' because paying them would have resulted in his overdraft limit being exceeded. The bank successfully defended the libel action that resulted by showing that the dishonour of the cheques was justified, but the jury (defamation cases may involve a jury) held that the words were defamatory.

'Refer to drawer' is probably the most common defamatory phrase used when dishonouring a cheque, but the phrase 'Not sufficient' has also been held to be defamatory: *Davidson* v *Barclays Bank Ltd* (1940).

The phrase 'refer to drawer' is defamatory because it is generally understood to mean that the drawer of the cheque has no money in their account and this, it is argued, causes them to be lowered in the estimation of others. This is no doubt the case with business customers – the damage to their credit is obvious – and was no doubt the case some years ago when only the prosperous middle classes had bank accounts. Perhaps it could be argued today, however, that the phrase does not always have this effect as far as individuals are concerned – especially among student communities! Alternatively, the phrase could carry the connotation that the drawer has been acting dishonestly by drawing worthless cheques – in so far as the drawer knows that they will be dishonoured – to obtain goods and services. (There is no authority for this proposition, however, and the *Jayson* case reflects the accepted view until and if the point is judicially reviewed.)

Thus, when banks use, say, the phrase 'refer to drawer' they must be prepared to justify it by showing that they were under no obligation to honour the cheque. The problem is neatly avoided by stating a technical reason for dishonour, if such is the case.

NOTE: Quite possibly, a bank is liable whatever form of words are used if they carry a clear message that the bank is not paying because there are insufficient funds on the account.

For breach of contract, a *trader* is entitled to substantial damages (reasonable compensation) for injury to reputation and credit without proof of actual damage. A *non-trader* must generally prove actual, that is financial, damage to be awarded more than nominal damages: *Gibbons* v *Westminster Bank Ltd* (1939). If, however, a cheque is returned to its presenter stating a reason for dishonour that is subsequently held to be libellous, a non-trader's claim would not be limited to nominal damages.

33. Liability to the cheque's true owner

If a bank pays a person who is not the holder (the payee or endorsee of an order cheque or the possessor of a bearer cheque), it is liable at common law for conversion to the cheque's true owner. However, because a paying bank is seldom in a position to know whether the presenter is the holder of the cheque, it is given limited statutory protection against innocently committing conversion when paying cheques.

34. A paying bank's statutory protection

(a) *Payment in due course.* Payment in due course requires the bank to pay the cheque to its holder in good faith and without notice of any defect in the holder's title: Bills of Exchange Act 1882 s.59. Such payment discharges the cheque and all parties to it, i.e. the promise of payment cannot be enforced against any of them.

(b) *Forged and unauthorised endorsements.* A person in possession of an *order cheque* bearing a forged or unauthorised endorsement cannot be its holder, merely a wrongful possessor. However, s.60 protects a bank against liability to the holder (the true owner) if it pays a cheque (open or crossed) that bears a forged or unauthorised endorsement provided it pays:

(i) In *good faith*; and

(ii) In the *ordinary course of business*.

The protection is necessary because a bank will very seldom be in a position to know whether an endorsement on a cheque presented for payment is forged – it is almost certain to be the signature of a total stranger. Without s.60's protection, a bank would have to make a second payment to the cheque's true owner, having already paid the person presenting it (without any certainty of being able to recover the funds), but would not be able to debit its customer's account.

NOTE: Section 60 affords the bank no protection where its customer's signature is forged.

If a bank cashes an open cheque at its counter, it must, in addition, obtain the endorsement of the holder in order to pay in the ordinary course of business (*see* below).

The Stamp Act 1853 s.19 provides similar protection against paying a banker's draft that bears a forged or unauthorised endorsement but s.19 does not require the bank to have acted in good faith and in the ordinary course of business. (Few banker's drafts are endorsed.)

Consider the following situation. A draws a cheque payable to B and B negotiates it to C. D steals the cheque from C, forges C's endorsement on it and transfers the cheque to E, who obtains payment. (Figure 9.2 represents this situation as a chain.)

In Figure 9.2, C is the holder and the true owner of the cheque, while E is the wrongful possessor. D and E have committed conversion of the cheque against C, as will the bank if it pays it. The bank,

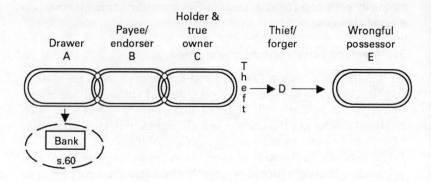

Figure 9.2 *Forgery and unauthorised endorsements and s.60 of the Bills of Exchange Act 1882*

however, is protected by s.60, but D and E have no protection (D obviously deserves none) and are liable at common law to C. If E, who has no right to receive payment in due course, has to compensate C, E, in turn, can seek compensation from D, provided E can find D and D proves to have the money to pay. However, C can take no action against A or B because the bank's payment within s.60 is deemed to be payment 'in due course' under s.59 and this discharges the liability of parties to the cheque, i.e. A and B. In short, it is a question of which of two innocent parties, C or E, should suffer because of the fraud of a third, D.

Payment of a cheque *knowing* that an endorsement on it was a forgery would not be a payment in *good faith*, but a *negligent* payment is still a payment in good faith under s.90 and is, therefore, protected by s.60. Thus, payment in good faith means an honest payment.

Payment in the *ordinary course of business* means payment according to current banking practice and within normal banking hours. For example, a crossed cheque should be paid only through a bank account and an open cheque cashed over the counter must appear to be properly endorsed (*see* below). Payment of an open cheque to an *unusual presenter*, for example, to an apparent office junior, particularly if drawn for a substantial amount, would probably not be payment in the ordinary course of business, although payment of cheques for large sums over the counter is not in itself outside the ordinary course of business.

Example

In *Baines* v *National Provincial Bank Ltd* (1927), it was held that a bank is allowed a reasonable period in which to complete its business after its advertised closing time. Thus, in this case, the bank was allowed to debit its customer's account with a cheque cashed five minutes after closing time and a countermand the following morning was ineffective.

It is generally considered that negligence does not prevent a bank acting in the *ordinary course of business*. This was the view of the majority of the Court of Appeal in *Carpenters Company* v *British Mutual Banking Co Ltd* (1938). Where there are suspicious circumstances, presumably each case must be taken on its own facts to determine whether a bank acted within the s.60.

NOTE: Although the point has not been before the court, it would seem that s.60 protects the encashment of a cheque under an open credit by another branch or by another bank, in the latter case because the bank making the payment acts as agent of the paying bank.

The Cheques Act 1957 s.1 (*see* below), has greatly reduced the practical significance of s.60, but it remains important wherever endorsement of a cheque is still necessary. Without s.60's protection, a bank would have to make a second payment to the cheque's true owner (C in Figure 9.2), having already paid the person presenting it (E), but would not be able to debit the customer's account (A).

(c) *Crossed cheques*. Statutory protection when a bank pays a crossed cheque is given by the Bills of Exchange Act 1882 ss.79(2) and 80.

Section 79(2) protects the bank where it pays a cheque in good faith and without negligence on which the crossing is not apparent or on which the crossing has been obliterated, added to or altered and this is not apparent.

NOTE: Section 79(2) affords no protection against other material alterations of a cheque.

Section 80 protects a bank against liability to the true owner provided it pays a cheque:
  (i) In *good faith*;
  (ii) *Without negligence*; and
  (iii) In *accordance with the crossing*.

NOTE: The Cheques Act 1992 s.2 extends the protection of s.80 to cheques bearing the words *account payee* in the crossing by providing that a bank is *not* to be treated as having been negligent in the context of s.80 by reason *only* of its failure to concern itself with the purported endorsement – the addition to the crossing means that the monies are being paid to someone other than their true owner, so the endorsement is ineffective.

Provided the requirements of s.79(2) or s.80 are fulfilled, a bank is placed in the same position as if it had paid the cheque's true owner. It follows that it can debit its customer's account with the amount of the cheque.

The protection of s.80 has seldom, if ever, been relied on. A forged or unauthorised endorsement is by far the most likely defect on a cheque that will involve a bank and s.60 already provides adequate protection where this occurs. In practice, therefore, s.80 virtually duplicates the protection of s.60, while applying only to crossed cheques and requiring a bank to act without negligence. Section 60 requires the bank merely to have acted in good faith, in practice a lower standard of care.

However, s.80 *also* protects the *drawer* if the bank's payment fulfils the requirements of the section. Once a crossed cheque has actually or constructively (to an agent for example) been delivered to the payee, the *drawer* is also regarded as being in the same position as if the true owner had been paid. The drawer is thus discharged from liability on the underlying transaction, the original consideration given for the cheque. In other words, the drawer cannot be made to make a second payment.

In fact, the situation here is analogous to payment in cash. Once a debt is paid in cash, the former creditor cannot demand a second payment because the money paid has been lost or stolen. As most cheques are crossed and most payments of crossed cheques are within s.80, most drawers are protected if the cheque is lost by or stolen from the payee and payment obtained by the finder or thief.

(d) *Unendorsed or irregularly endorsed cheques.* Sections 60 and 80 of the Bills of Exchange Act 1882 deal with endorsed cheques; s.1(1) of the Cheques Act 1957 deals with cheques that are irregularly endorsed or not endorsed at all.

Under s.1(1), a bank that pays a cheque drawn on it that is not endorsed or which is irregularly endorsed is deemed to pay the cheque in due course if it pays:

(i) In *good faith*; and

(ii) In *the ordinary course of business*.

In practice, the section means that a bank does not have to check the endorsement. The protection of s.1(1) is necessary because the paying bank will normally have no knowledge of whether the collecting bank's customer is the payee or a third party to whom the cheque should have been endorsed and was not.

Example
_____

If D in Figure 9.2 opened an account posing as C and obtained payment from A's bank (instead of forging C's endorsement and transferring the cheque to

E), A's bank would have a good statutory defence against an action for conversion brought by C. (C's most profitable course of action would probably be to bring an action against the (collecting) bank at which D opened the account. It would then be up to that bank to successfully plead s.4 of the Cheques Act 1957 *see* 9:**24** above.)

An irregular endorsement must be distinguished from a forged or unauthorised endorsement. An *irregular endorsement* is genuine, it merely does not conform to banking practice, while a forged or unauthorised endorsement is one written on the cheque without the holder's authority. Thus, an endorsement on a cheque 'John P. Smith' by John Smith when the cheque was payable to him as 'John Smith' would be irregular, but an endorsement 'John Smith' in the same situation by Tom Jones who had stolen the cheque would be forged and unauthorised.

Section 1(1) means that, if a bank pays a cheque on which an endorsement is necessary, it cannot rely on the section because it would not be paying in the *ordinary course of business*. If, however, a cheque is endorsed as required, e.g. a negotiated order cheque, but the endorsement proves to be *irregular*, it may rely on s.1(1) and, further, if it proved to be *forged or unauthorised*, it can rely on s.60 of the Bills of Exchange Act 1882.

As with the Bills of Exchange Act 1882 s.60, payment under the Cheques Act 1957 s.1(1), is deemed to be payment in due course. Therefore, it protects a paying bank from an action for conversion brought by the true owner of the cheque and entitles it to debit its customer's account. The cheque is discharged and with it the liabilities of the parties to it.

Section 1(2) similarly protects the payment of a banker's draft that is unendorsed or irregularly endorsed.

(e) *Exceptions to s.1.* Banks have never fully relied on the Cheques Act 1957 s.1 and, by a resolution of the Committee of London Clearing Bankers in 1957, the following instruments, among others, still require endorsement before payment and the paying bank must examine them accordingly.

(i) Cheques and other instruments cashed at the counter. (This includes the situation where customers present their own cheques for payment, although the rule is seldom enforced. If, however, the 'cheque' is made payable to 'Cash' or to 'Pay' no endorsement is required – such a cheque is not a cheque remember.)

(ii) Combined cheques and receipt forms marked 'R'. (Although discouraged by banks, a few customers still insist on the payee's receipt before payment.)

(iii) Travellers' cheques.

Payment of the above cheques *without* an endorsement would not be payment in the ordinary course of business and so the bank would lose the protection of s.1.

NOTE: The 1990 White Paper 'Banking Services: Law and Practice' proposes that ss.60 and 80 of the Bills of Exchange Act 1882, s.1 of the Cheques Act 1957 and s.19 of the Stamp Act 1853 should be repealed and be replaced by a single section protecting a paying banker.

Cheque cards

35. Introduction

Essentially, cheque cards are a means of identification that:

(a) Enable customers to *cash cheques* up to a prescribed limit at branches or banks other than the ones at which they have accounts; and

(b) *Guarantee* that a cheque taken in payment backed by a card will be honoured, whatever the state of the customer's account, subject to a prescribed limit per cheque and provided that the card is properly used.

NOTE: The use of a cheque card does not involve the bank paying for the goods and services, merely honouring its customer's cheque. Thus, a cheque card is not a credit-token within the meaning of the Consumer Credit Act 1974 s.14.

The use of cheque cards to back cheques, their more important function, involves three separate contracts:

(a) A contract between the *bank's customer and the supplier* (the payee). This contract does not concern us here, save to mention that it will most probably be regulated by either the Sale of Goods Act 1979 or the Supply of Goods and Services Act 1982.

(b) A contract between the *bank and its customer*. In this contract, the customer agrees to use the card in accordance with the conditions of its issue and use and acknowledges that payment of a cheque guaranteed with the card *cannot be countermanded*. The customer also undertakes not to use the card to create an unauthorised overdraft. The bank for its part *undertakes to honour* any cheque backed by the card taken in payment by the payee subject to the prescribed limit.

(c) A contract between the *bank and the payee*. In this contract, the customer acts as the bank's agent. Under it, the bank gives an undertaking to the payee to honour a cheque up to the prescribed limit taken in payment provided the payee takes it relying on the card and according to the instructions printed on it or otherwise made known to the payee. The payee gains a direct right to claim payment from the bank and, in return, the bank receives the benefit of greater acceptability of cheques drawn on itself.

36. Backing a cheque

The conditions of use of a cheque card will specify that:

(a) The cheque must be signed in the presence of the payee in the UK and that the signature must agree with that on the card or, perhaps, actually be that of the cardholder.

(b) The card must not be out of date, altered or defaced.

(c) The bank's standard printed cheque must be used and it must bear the same name, sort code number and account number as the card.

(d) The cheque card number must be written by the *payee* on the reverse of the card.

(e) The cheque must not exceed the stated guaranteed amount.

The prescribed limit is a limit per *single transaction*. Say, for example, the limit is £100 and the value of the transaction is £175. If two cheques are made out in payment, one for £100 and one for £75, the guarantee will only cover *one* of them. However, it could be argued that drawing two cheques in this way is a breach of the conditions of use, which nullifies the guarantee on *both*. If a cheque card is used to back a cheque, in this case, for more than £100, the guarantee is also nullified; it does not even apply to the first £100.

37. Unauthorised use of cheque guarantee cards

(a) *Introduction*. Cheque cards offer great potential for misuse, both on the part of the customer to whom a card is issued and a thief or finder of a chequebook with the relevant cheque card. Thus, cheque cards are not normally issued until customers have proved to be responsible in the operation of their accounts or their integrity and responsibility is undoubted or they are willing to provide the bank with acceptable security beyond the potential risk, that is the number of cheques multiplied by the prescribed limit.

Furthermore, the conditions of use will specify that the card:

(*i*) Remains the property of the bank;

(ii) Does not entitle the customer to overdraw the account without prior agreement; and

(iii) Should be kept separately from the chequebook in order to prevent fraud if one or the other is lost.

These terms put the bank in a strong position as against its customer should the card be misused, although whether action is taken is essentially a practical rather than a legal decision.

The position of three parties in relation to the fraudulent use of cheque guarantee cards must be considered, that of: the *payee*; the *customer*; and the *bank*.

(b) *The payee.* The payee's position is secure provided that the instructions for the use of the card have been followed, then the bank guarantees that the cheque will be paid. The most likely situation where the bank can refuse payment is where the signature on the cheque does not agree with that on the card, for here the possibility of fraud arises and the payee would be wrong to accept the cheque without further enquiry or proof of identity. This, however, does not give a bank a great deal of protection against the determined and professional rogue. Indeed, because of rising losses through fraudulent use of cheque cards, banks have begun to take a stricter view of their obligations, provided the terms of the guarantee allow. In such a case they may refuse to pay a cheque because the *signature is not that of the customer*, despite the forgery being indistinguishable from the real thing.

(c) *The customer.* The customer's position is also secure where a chequebook and cheque card have been misused, for without the customer's signature on the cheque the bank has no authority to debit the customer's account. However, the customer's own behaviour is relevant. If the customer has been negligent in the care of the chequebook and cheque card and this negligence was responsible for the fraud being perpetrated, the bank would have a counter-claim against the customer for the amounts of the cheques that they had to honour. (Whether or not a bank would wish to pursue this course of action is another matter.)

The misuse of a cheque card to obtain an unauthorised overdraft, which the bank is obliged to grant because it must pay the cheque, is, besides being a breach of contract, the criminal offence of dishonestly obtaining a pecuniary advantage by deception under the Theft Act 1968 s.16 – the pecuniary advantage being the overdraft that might not otherwise have been granted.

Example

In *Metropolitan Police Commissioner* v *Charles* (1976) (HL), the defendant, who had been granted an overdraft limit of £100, issued 25 cheques each for £30 with each properly backed by a cheque card during the course of one evening at a gambling club. The bank was obliged to honour all 25 cheques, even though the defendant's overdraft now stood at £750.

It was held that the issue of a cheque combined with the production of a cheque guarantee card constituted a representation by the drawer that he had authority between himself and the bank to use the card in order to oblige the bank to honour the cheque. If the representation should be false, as it was on the facts, an offence is committed.

(d) *The bank.* As a bank is obliged to pay if the payee has followed the instructions for the use of the cheque card, the bank's interest is in recovering some or all of the money from its customer.

Clearly, it would not be in a bank's interest to try to recover a small sum from its customer when a chequebook and a cheque card have been either lost or stolen with no blame attaching to the customer. However, where the customer has been grossly negligent in the care of their chequebook and cheque card or has been unnecessarily slow in reporting a loss or theft, the customer has broken their contractual *duty of care* to the bank and it would be possible to commence a civil action to recover the monies. This would probably be the course of action followed by a bank if the customer had misused the cheque card and there appeared to be a reasonably cost-effective prospect of the customer being able to repay the overdraft thereby created.

Other payment orders

38. Bankers' drafts

A bankers' draft is defined by the Cheques Act 1957 s.4 as being 'Any draft payable on demand drawn by a banker upon himself, whether payable at the head office or some other office of his bank'. As the drawer and the drawee are the same person, a banker's draft is not a bill of exchange because the Bills of Exchange Act 1882 s.3 requires that a bill be addressed by one person to another. Bankers' drafts are generally regarded in business as being the equivalent of cash and are often used in transactions that involve the transfer of title to valuable property, e.g. cars and land.

In the same way that a bank can be sued for conversion if a cheque is collected for or paid to a person other than its true owner, the collection and payment of bankers' drafts can also give rise to liability for conversion. Thus, banks *collecting* bankers' drafts are protected by the Cheques Act 1957 s.4 (*see* 9:**24**) and banks *paying* them are protected by the Cheques Act 1957 s.1 and the Bills of Exchange Act 1882 s.80 (by virtue of the Cheques Act 1957 s.5) (*see* 9:**34**) on the same conditions as for cheques. The Stamp Act 1853 s.19 protects the payment of a bankers' draft on a forged or unauthorised signature, s.60 of the Bills of Exchange Act 1882 only applies to cheques.

A bankers' draft must *not* be drawn payable to bearer because such a draft would be a banknote and the Bank of England has the exclusive right to issue notes in England and Wales under the Bank Charter Act 1844.

39. Dividend and interest warrants

A *dividend warrant* is an unconditional order addressed to a bank by a company to pay on demand a sum of money to a shareholder in respect of a dividend due to that member. An *interest warrant* is an unconditional order addressed to a bank by a borrower to pay on demand a sum of money to a lender in respect of interest due to that lender.

These warrants are therefore within the definition of a cheque and the legal rules relating to cheques apply to them. These include the statutory protection afforded to a collecting and paying banker (*see* 9:**24** and **34**). This is so *even* if a dividend warrant states that it will not be honoured after a specified period from its date of issue; it is still unconditional within the meaning of the Bills of Exchange Act 1882 s.73: *Thairlwall* v *Great Northern Railway Co.* (1910)

40. Direct debits

Direct debiting is a system that enables the payee to claim payment via their bank (the originating/collecting bank) from the payer via their bank (the paying bank). In contrast to a standing order, which is initiated by the payer, a direct debit is *initiated by the payee* and can be used to pay varying amounts at varying intervals as well as fixed amounts on fixed dates. A mandate detailing the nature of the payments is required by the payee (the originator) and the paying bank from the payer. This can be revoked by notice from the payer to both parties. Payment of direct debits is usually through BACS.

Direct debits can only be initiated by an organisation (not an individual) sponsored by its bank. A standard agreement is used by all banks. This includes an indemnity clause that enables the paying bank to debit the originator's account through the clearing process as soon as it advises the originating bank that the wrong amount has been claimed or the payer has revoked their mandate.

If a debit is paid by the paying bank *after* the payer has revoked their mandate, the paying bank must recredit the payer's account. If the funds credited to the originator are still in the originator's account, the paying bank can seek to recover them from the originating bank as payments made under a mistake of fact: *Barclays Bank Ltd* v *Simms, Son & Cooke* (1979) (*see* 9:**31**). If they have been withdrawn by the originator, the paying bank can seek to recover them from the originator themselves under this principle as an alternative to claiming repayment under the standard indemnity.

Should the originator make a fraudulent claim and the payer's mandate is for an unspecified amount (which is not uncommon), the mandate protects the paying bank from an action for breach of contract by the payer and enables the payer to sue the originator for fraud in addition to claiming recovery of the money as a payment made under a mistake of fact. If the mandate is for a definite amount and the paying bank pays an unauthorised sum, it must recredit its customer's account with the excess paid and seek to recover the sum under the standard indemnity or as a payment made under a mistake of fact.

If a debit is dishonoured by the paying bank's branch for lack of funds, it must notify the relevant branch of the originating bank by 12 noon on the day following the receipt of the debit and return the debit voucher. The sum, having already been paid by the head office of the payee bank, is recovered by sending an unpaid claim through the clearing process. No action can be taken against the bank for wrongful dishonour.

Progress test 9

1. Define a cheque. (**1**)

2. Why is a 'cheque' made payable to 'cash' not a cheque? (**1**)

3. Why is a bankers' draft not a cheque? (**1**)

4. Who is a party to a cheque? (**2**)

5. Why is a bank never liable on a cheque? (**2**)

6. When and how is a cheque negotiated? (**4**)

7. State the legal characteristics of a cheque as a negotiable instrument. (**5**)

8. What is the difference between a general and a special crossing on a cheque? **(9)**

9. What are the effects of adding the words 'Not negotiable' or 'account payee' to a crossing? **(9)**

10. What is the effect of a forged endorsement on an order cheque? **(12)**

11. State the requirements for a valid endorsement. **(13)**

12. Distinguish between general, special and restrictive endorsements, explaining the effect of each. **(14)**

13. Distinguish between a holder and a holder for value. **(17, 18)**

14. What is meant by a 'fictitious or non-existing person' in the Bills of Exchange Act 1882 s.7(3)? **(17)**

15. List the three legal attributes of a holder? **(17)**

16. What conditions must be satisfied for a holder to be a holder in due course? **(19)**

17. State the rights of a holder in due course. **(21)**

18. What duties does a bank owe customers when collecting their cheques? **(22)**

19. State the requirements of the Cheques Act 1957 s.4. **(24)**

20. Explain ten specific examples of situations which have been held to constitute negligence under the Cheques Act 1957 s.4. **(25)**

21. Explain why collecting a cheque as its holder in due course may offer better protection to a bank than relying on s.4. of the Cheques Act 1957. **(26)**

22. In what circumstances will a bank give value for a cheque it collects? **(26)**

23. What is meant by the defence of *ex turpi causa non oritur actio*? **(27)**

24. State the circumstances in which a bank's authority to pay its customer's cheques is terminated. **(29)**

25. When is an alteration of a cheque 'material'? Give examples. **(29)**

26. List the situations in which a paying banker could wrongly debit its customer's account. (**30**)

27. State the *Rule* in *Macmillan and Arthur* (1918). (**30**)

28. In what circumstances can money paid by mistake be recovered? (**32**)

29. Explain the nature of a bank's possible liability if it wrongly dishonours a cheque. (**32**)

30. Define 'payment in due course' of a cheque. (**34**)

31. What is the protection afforded to a paying banker by the Bills of Exchange Act 1882 s.60? (**34**)

32. What is the protection afforded to a paying banker by the Bills of Exchange Act 1882 s.80? (**34**)

33. What is meant by 'good faith' in the Bills of Exchange Act 1882 s.60? (**34**)

34. When is an endorsement considered to be irregular? (**34**)

35. Explain the relationship between the Bills of Exchange Act 1882 s.60 and the Cheques Act 1957 s.1. (**34**)

36. What protection has a bank if it pays a crossed cheque on which the crossing has been altered? (**34**)

37. List the instruments on which an endorsement is still required before payment is made. (**34**)

38. Explain the three contracts involved in the use of a cheque card. (**35**)

39. List the conditions that must be fulfilled for a cheque card to guarantee payment of a cheque. (**36**)

40. Why is misuse of a cheque card to obtain an unauthorised overdraft a criminal offence? (**37**)

41. Define a bankers' draft. (**38**)

42. State the protection available to bank collecting or paying a bankers' draft. (**39**)

43. Is a bank collecting a dividend warrant for a customer protected by the

Cheques Act 1957, s.4 if it states that it will only be honoured within three months of its issue? **(39)**

44. How does a direct debit differ from a standing order? **(40)**

45. Under what circumstances can the paying bank seek to recover the amount of a direct debit paid in error from the originating bank? **(40)**

10
Electronic payment systems

The topic outlined

1. Introduction

There are a range of electronic payment systems – BACS (Bankers' Automated Clearing Services), CHAPS (Clearing House Automated Payments System), SWIFT (Society for Worldwide Interbank Financial Telecommunications), ATMs (automated teller machines) and EFTPOS (electronic funds transfer at point of sale) networks in particular. This chapter is concerned with the legal implications of just two of these: ATMs and EFTPOS networks.

There is little directly relevant case or statute law on electronic banking. The present statutory framework regulating payment systems is based on mid-nineteenth century commercial practice and a paper-based payments system dealing with many times fewer transactions than today. Even the Cheques Act 1957 became law at a time when computers were in their infancy and certainly had not been applied by banks to financial record keeping to any great extent. Change in the banking industry, particularly advances in and the application of technology, has outpaced the law's ability to evolve in parallel.

The use of 'plastic', however, is extremely widespread. Many people find that using cash/debit/cheque guarantee cards (cards are usually multifunctional) is more convenient and/or safer than using cash or cheques. Similarly withdrawing money from their accounts via a machine outside the bank or in its foyer is certainly similarly quicker than at its counter – a view supported and encouraged by the banks.

Unlike the underlying banker–customer contract, most aspects of electronic banking are subject to express contracts that comprehensively detail the rights and liabilities of the parties involved. The contracts between banks and their customers covering ATM and debit cards are subject to written conditions of use and the legal relationship between banks undertaking electronic funds transfer (EFT) is governed by the rules (be they expressly stated and agreed or established by custom and practice) of the clearing systems (such as BACS and CHAPS) to which they belong. There is, therefore, less opportunity for disputes to arise that would result in a body of rules derived from case law and arguably, at least at present, little need for comprehensive statutory intervention and regulation.

This is partly because the Unfair Contract Terms Act 1977 subjects any limitation or exclusion of liability in such contracts to a judicial test of reasonableness and mainly because 'Good Banking', the Code of banking practice, covers most, if not all, of the issues that could otherwise be the subject of legislation. The Supply of Goods and Services Act 1982 also assists in resolving disputes.

2.   The Code of banking practice

The Code of Practice was covered generally in Chapter 1 (*see* 1:**21**) and it is important to remember that it is not 'law' as such. It is *possible* that, at some future time, ATM and debit card agreements will be held to incorporate the Code's provisions, i.e. the provisions will become *implied terms* of the contract. Alternatively, the provisions may be incorporated in the 'conditions of use' of cards and, thereby, become *express terms* of the contract. In this way the Code may become legally enforceable without becoming 'law'.

Nevertheless, the Code will probably have the same effect as if it were an Act of Parliament. There are four interrelated reasons for this.

(a) All major banks and building societies (card issuers) have agreed to be bound by the Code.
(b) It is on the basis of the Code that the Banking Ombudsman will primarily resolve disputes between banks and customers.
(c) It is highly probable that customers will prefer to pursue claims against banks through the Banking Ombudsman than the courts.
(d) The Banking Ombudsman can make an award of up to £100 000 to an individual (corporate customers are not covered by the scheme) and banks have accepted that an award is binding on them.

In other words, most, if not all, disputes will be resolved by reference to the Code rather than by reference to law. The effect of this is likely to be that otherwise important legal issues regarding ATM and debit cards will be rendered largely academic – until such time as a judicial decision is made that contradicts the Code.

NOTE: The Code of Practice only applies to *personal customers*, that is to private individuals and *not* companies, partnerships, sole traders, clubs and societies. Thus, only personal customers enjoy the greater protection afforded by the Code than that afforded by the law.

ATMs

Introduction

referred to as *cash dispensers*, ATMs are essentially what suggests – an automated (electronic) method of withdrawy. To do this an ATM card is needed, containing information hine-readable magnetic strip. This information includes the 's account number and PIN (personal identification number), which is keyed into the machine to authorise the withdrawal request. The machine, in turn, can access the customer's account details to decide whether to allow the withdrawal.

The capability of ATMs is governed largely by the banks' investment in the existing hardware and general systems costs, not by software or other technological limitations. For example, if the card slot merely allowed for thicker cards 'all things would be possible', particularly perhaps electrical connections that would activate new generations of cards known as *smart cards*. However, the system works pretty well and appears to satisfy the needs of most customers.

In addition to cash withdrawal facilities, ATMs offer at least some of the following additional facilities:

(a) Ordering cheque books and statements;
(b) Balance enquiries (*see* below);
(c) Making deposits;
(d) Transfers between different accounts held by the cardholder.

In relation to *balance enquiries*, the balance shown is a representation by the bank on which the customer is entitled to rely. If the customer relies on a representation that *overstates* the credit balance and withdraws the money as a result, the bank may not be able to recover the money withdrawn if it would be inequitable for it to do so: *United Overseas Bank* v *Jiwani* (1976) (*see* 1:**20**). A further point is that ATM displays should not make it easy for others to see the balance on the account. If they do, an action for breach of the duty of confidentiality could be possible (*see* 1:**13**).

As with all services, in offering these facilities a bank must obey its customer's mandate and abide by the general duty of care and skill embodied in the Supply of Goods Act 1982 s.13. Any attempted limitation or exclusion of liability in the contract with its customer in this respect is subject to a test of reasonableness under the Unfair Contract Terms Act 1977. If a bank wishes to rely on an exemption clause, the onus is on the *bank*, under s.11(5) of the 1977 Act, to *prove* that the clause is reasonable. The *court* decides that which is reasonable, and such a clause is interpreted *contra proferentem* that is, against the party seeking to rely on it, in our case the bank.

4.   A bank's duties to its cardholders in relation to ATMs
Three duties are owed.

(a) To ensure that its ATMs respond correctly to the commands of authorised cardholders.

(b) To maintain its ATMs in working order.

(c) To ensure that its ATMs provide sufficient information to enable its cardholders' accounts to be correctly debited.

Let us look at these each in turn.

(a) *To ensure that its ATMs respond correctly to the commands of authorised cardholders.* This duty merely amounts to the bank obeying its customer's (cardholder's) mandate. It corresponds to a bank's duty to pay its customer's cheques, provided that they are properly drawn, there are funds on the account and there is no bar to payment. The duty to pay is absolute.

If a machine dispenses *more* money than the customer requested, the customer holds it on trust for the bank. If necessary, the bank can take action for its return as money had and received, the overpayment being as a result of a mistake of fact.

If the machine dispenses *less* than requested, this constitutes a breach of contract by the bank. However, it is unlikely that the customer could prove financial loss over and above the shortfall on the amount dispensed, particularly given the customer's common law duty to mitigate their loss – the customer would, for example, be expected to try another machine or obtain funds over the counter by cheque until the machine error is sorted out. If the customer's account is debited with the full sum requested, the bank must correct the entry and refund any interest lost. Wrongly retaining the customer's card is also a breach of contract, but, again, it is unlikely that the customer would be able to show financial loss sufficient to justify legal action.

NOTE: The Code of Practice s.18.2 supports this approach by providing that a card issuer's liability is limited to those amounts wrongly charged to a customer's account and any interest on those amounts.

(b) *To maintain its ATMs in working order.* This duty is one of *reasonable care.* It would be unreasonable to impose an absolute duty on a bank to ensure that *all* its ATMs are properly functioning *all* of the time.

In practice, a bank is unlikely to incur liability for breach of this duty as ATMs not in use automatically display a notice indicating this and the Code of Practice s.18.1 provides that card issuers are only liable for direct loss caused to customers if the fault was not obvious or not advised by a message or notice displayed on the machine (*see* 10:2 for the role of the Code *vis-à-vis* the contract and legal rules in this respect).

Where the failure is that of *another bank's* ATM that accepts the cardholder's card, the cardholder's bank is only liable if it can be established that it failed to select a reliable third-party bank as its agent, for example where the other bank's machines have proved to be unreliable or it fails to maintain or refill them. This is unlikely to be the case.

If a bank is liable for breach of its duty to properly maintain its ATMs, it can plead *contributory negligence* by the cardholder if the latter misused the card or the machine. In addition, the cardholder would be expected to mitigate their loss and, in practice, it is unlikely that a cardholder would, once again, be able to prove reasonably foreseeable financial loss sufficient to make an action for breach of contract worthwhile.

NOTE: No action for defamation can arise when a cardholder's request is wrongly rejected because no reason for the rejection is displayed on the ATM screen, even if another person witnesses the rejection. (Defamation requires that a statement is communicated to at least one other person than the person defamed.) Reasons other than lack of funds will also result in a withdrawal request being rejected, for example using an incorrect PIN or requesting funds exceeding the daily permitted maximum withdrawal.

(c) *To ensure that its ATMs provide sufficient information to enable its cardholders' accounts to be correctly debited.* This is a particular application of the bank's *duty to account* and is supported by s.19 of the Code of Practice, which states that a bank must provide customers with a written record of all payments and withdrawals on their account. ATMs use tally-rolls to record details of all transactions and attempted transactions and these are admissible as evidence in legal proceedings under the Bankers' Books Evidence Act 1879 (as amended) and the Civil Evidence Act 1968.

5.   Authorised and unauthorised use of cash cards

A bank can only debit a cardholder's account with a cash card withdrawal if it was made by the cardholder or with the cardholder's authority. If the tally-roll shows that the card was used, the cardholder could presumably only avoid liability by showing either that they and the card were elsewhere at the time of the withdrawal or, perhaps, that the card had been lost or left somewhere else. In other circumstances the cardholder must have expressly or impliedly authorised the withdrawal.

In practice the position will be governed by the Code of Practice because the cardholder is in a stronger position under the Code than at law. Three situations are possible.

(a) *Express or implied authorisation by the cardholder.* The cardholder is fully liable for authorised withdrawals by third parties. Implied authorisation is a question of fact.

(b) *Fraud or gross negligence by the cardholder.* Under s.18.4 of the Code, the cardholder will be *fully liable* for unauthorised withdrawals that are the result of their fraud and maybe liable for losses which can result from the their *gross negligence*. Fraud is an established legal concept but *gross negligence* has not been judicially defined. It will be necessary for the courts to do so in the context of the Code should it be held that the Code, or relevant sections of it, have been incorporated into the contract. An interesting point is, perhaps, that the Banking Ombudsman could interpret gross negligence differently to the court as the Banking Ombudsman Scheme is entirely separate from the court system.

Clearly gross negligence means more than ordinary carelessness and would presumably include the cardholder writing the PIN on the card or writing it down without making a reasonable attempt to disguise the number, both specific points that card issuers must emphasise to cardholders under s.16.2 of the Code. Under s.18.5, the burden of proving fraud or gross negligence lies with the card issuer.

> NOTE: Where a card issuer is unable to establish gross negligence by its cardholder, it could seek to establish that the third party had implied authority to use the card (*see* above).

(c) *Absence of consent, fraud or gross negligence by the cardholder – accidental loss of the card or disclosure of the PIN.* Under s.18.1 of the Code, the card issuer is liable for all transactions not authorised by the cardholder after the card issuer has been told that the card has been lost or stolen or that someone else knows or may know the PIN. The cardholder's liability for unauthorised transactions up until the card issuer is notified is limited by s.18.3 to £50, provided the withdrawals were not facilitated by the cardholder's fraud or gross negligence. In effect, s.18 of the Code extends the protection available to holders of credit-tokens such as credit cards under ss.83 and 84 of the Consumer Credit Act 1974 to the holders of ATM cards (and debit cards) (*see* 7:**12–15**).

The card issuer may waive the right to this £50 either generally in the contract with the cardholder or in specific cases. The sum is small and likely to involve disproportionate effort to recover and would almost certainly prove counter-productive where the cardholder is a valued customer.

(d) *Summary.* Under the Code of Practice, the liability of the cardholder for the use of a cash (or debit) card can be summarised as follows.

(*i*) The cardholder is liable for all authorised use, whether the authorisation is express or implied.

(*ii*) The cardholder's liability for unauthorised use is limited under the Code of Practice s.18.3 to £50, unless the cardholder has acted fraudulently or with gross negligence, until such time as the card issuer is notified of the loss or theft of the card or a third-party's knowledge of the PIN.

(*iii*) The cardholder *will* be held liable for all losses if they have acted fraudulently. The cardholder *may* be held liable for all losses if they have acted with gross negligence: s.18.4.

(*iv*) A bank's *conditions of use* for a card (the express terms of the cash card contract) can exempt the cardholder from liability for misuse of the card even where the Code does *not*. The reverse is not true, however. The conditions of use cannot, in practice, impose liability on the cardholder where the Code does not. *If* cash cards are credit-tokens (*see* 10:**7**), the same would apply to the relationship between the conditions of use and ss.83 and 84 of the Consumer Credit Act 1974.

NOTE: If cash cards are issued to non-personal customers, for example 'company cash cards', the Code of Practice does not apply and the liability of, say, a company or a partnership for unauthorised use of the card will be determined according to law and not according to the provisions of the Code. As it is generally agreed that a cash card is *not* a credit-token (*see* 10:**7**), the £50 limitation of liability in s.84 of the Consumer Credit Act 1974 does not apply and non-personal customers can, in theory, incur unlimited liability for the unauthorised use of the card until such time as the card issuer is notified of the loss, theft or a third-party's knowledge of the PIN. Furthermore, even if a cash card *is* held to be a credit-token, *companies* and other corporate cardholders would still not be protected because the Consumer Credit Act 1974 regulates credit provided to individuals and not to corporate bodies. (Remember also that the Banking Ombudsman Scheme does not apply to corporate bodies.) It is unusual for non-personal customers to be issued with cash cards.

6.   Unsolicited cash cards

It is generally considered that a cash card is *not* a credit-token within the meaning of the Consumer Credit Act 1974 s.14(1) *unless* it can be used in a third party's ATMs where the third party is not the card issuer's agent (*see* 10:**7**). Thus, s.51 of the 1974 Act, which makes it an offence to send a credit-token to a person without a written request to do so, does not apply unless the cash card can be used in third-party ATMs. This is usually the case.

Section 15.1 of the Code of Practice relegates the distinction between cash cards that can and cannot be used in third-party ATMs to one of academic importance in this particular context because it provides that, with the exception of a renewal or replacement card, a cash card must *only* be issued following a written request to do so. Further, s.18.1 provides that if the card is misused after it is posted but before it is received by the cardholder, the card issuer must bear the full loss. As all major banks and building societies (card issuers) have agreed to be bound by the code, s.15.1 (reinforced by s.18.1) is an effective prohibition on unsolicited cash cards.

7.   Are cash cards credit-tokens?

This question is important because, if a cash card is a credit-token within the meaning of s.14(1) of the Consumer Credit Act 1974, agreements for its use could be *regulated agreements*. This would mean that the documentation required by the Act (clearly a matter of considerable practical importance) and statutory limitation of the cardholder's liability for unauthorised use of the card (ss. 83 and 84) would apply. (As to this latter point, *see* 10:**5**.)

Applying s.14(1) to this particular situation, a credit-token is defined as 'a card ... given to an individual by a person carrying on a consumer credit business, who undertakes:

(a) that on production of it he will supply cash ... on credit, or

(b) that where, on production of it to a third party, the third party supplies cash ... , he will pay the third party for (it), in return for payment to him by the individual'.

The issues are (1) whether cash is supplied 'on credit' within subsection (a) when a cash card is used in the card issuer's own ATM or (2) whether there is a 'third party' who supplies the cardholder with cash within subsection (b), which the card issuer has agreed to reimburse. It is considered that the former is definitely *not* the case and the latter is *probably* not so. The following reasoning is put forward:

(a) *Using a card in the card issuer's own ATM:*

(i) Clearly no cash is supplied on credit when a withdrawal is made when the account is in credit and there is a delay – perhaps a maximum of 24 hours – in debiting the account. This delay cannot be considered to be providing credit. (This delay in debiting the account normally occurs even when the system is on-line – the on-line facility usually being used to monitor the withdrawal request in relation to the last updated balance and the maximum daily withdrawal limit.)

(ii) A withdrawal from an account on which there is an available agreed overdraft facility is providing credit in the wider sense, but it would seem clear that, for the purposes of the Act, the credit is supplied by virtue of the *overdraft agreement*, not through the use of the cash card.

(iii) Where accounts are debited some time after the withdrawal, it is clearly possible that a cash card withdrawal could result in an unauthorised overdraft – a previous withdrawal on the same day perhaps being the most likely cause. Once again, 'credit' in the wider sense is supplied. However, the Consumer Credit Act 1974 regulates *agreements* and, for two reasons, the credit supplied in this situation cannot be considered to be credit *agreed* by the card issuer. First, and simpler, the limitations of the ATM system effectively stop the card issuer preventing the withdrawal; second, the conditions of use will 'prevent' (in the sense that to do so would be a breach of the conditions) the cardholder using the card to obtain an unauthorised overdraft. (Where an overdraft facility is agreed, (ii) above applies.)

(b) *Using a card in a third-party ATM.* The acceptability and viability of cash card schemes is largely based on the availability of ATMs in which particular cards can be used. As it is far cheaper for card issuers to arrange for their cards to be accepted in the ATMs of other card issuers than to provide additional machines themselves, major cash cards can be used in the ATMs of a variety of card issuers.

These arrangements involve a third party providing cash within the meaning of s.14(1)(b). The third party is reimbursed by the card issuer and the *undertaking* to do so is deemed to be supplying credit to the cardholder: s.14(3). The cardholder, in turn, reimburses the card issuer through a debit to their account. This situation may appear to make any cash card that can be used in a third party's ATM a credit-token and its issue subject to the Act. The following would, however, seem to be the actual position.

(i) If the third party is acting as the card issuer's agent, no third party is, at law, involved. The position is exactly the same as using the card in the card issuer's *own* ATM. As no credit is provided in this case, the card *cannot* be a credit-token.

(ii) If the third party is *not* acting as the card issuer's agent, a withdrawal from one of the third-party ATMs is a restricted-use debtor–creditor–supplier agreement under s.12(b) of the Consumer Credit Act 1974 (*see* 7:8) and the cash card is a credit-token. (It is a restricted-use agreement under s.11(1)(b), and not an unrestricted-use agreement, because the card issuer's undertaking to reimburse the third party supplier constitutes the credit and this undertaking is restricted to the particular cash withdrawal(s). If the provision of credit related to the cash withdrawn, it would be an unrestricted-use agreement.)

However, s.89 of the Banking Act 1987 exempts from regulation by the 1974 Act 'arrangements for the electronic transfer of funds from a current account at a bank'. (A 'bank' includes a building society for the purposes of s.89.) This exemption covers such withdrawals.

NOTE: The legal status of a debit card as a credit-token is exactly the same as a cash card used in a third-party ATM when the third party is not the card issuer's agent. It is a credit-token within s.14(1)(b), but exempt by virtue of the Banking Act 1987 s.89.

(c) *Summary.* The answer to the question 'Are cash cards credit-tokens?' would therefore appear to be as follows.

(i) If cards are used in the card issuer's own machine, they are *not* credit-tokens – no credit is provided: s.14(1)(a).

(ii) If cards are used in a third-party machine and the third party is acting as an agent of the card issuer, they are *not* credit-tokens – at law no third party is involved and no credit is provided.

(iii) If cards are used in a third-party machine and the third party does *not* act as agent of the card issuer, they *are* credit-tokens because credit is provided by the card issuer under ss.14(1)(b) and 14(3), but such transactions are exempt from regulation under the Consumer Credit Act 1974 by virtue of the Banking Act 1987 s.89.

NOTE: A cash card *is* a credit-token where the cash card is combined with a credit or charge card and the credit or charge card account is debited with the withdrawal.

EFTPOS

8. EFTPOS explained

EFTPOS is a payment system that enables a person (the cardholder) to pay for goods or services by using a debit card. The debit card is 'swiped' through a terminal that reads the details of the cardholder's account imprinted on the card's magnetic strip on the card. The retailer then enters the amount to be paid and the cardholder confirms the transaction by entering their PIN. The retailer's bank account is then immediately credited with the amount and the cardholder's account immediately debited by the same amount.

At least that is the theory. At present, the term EFTPOS is rather misleading. Mainly because of the cost of the necessary hardware, most EFTPOS transactions are paper-based, a signature rather than a PIN is used to authenticate the transaction and the crediting and debiting of accounts takes place some time after the transaction. In addition, funds are never actually transferred, balances on the relevant accounts are merely adjusted. However, the explanation of the legal principles governing EFTPOS assumes a true EFTPOS scheme.

Besides the cardholder and the retailer, the other parties involved in an EFTPOS scheme are the *card issuer*, the bank or building society that issued the debit card, and the *retailer acquirer*, the bank that is responsible to the retailer for processing the retailer's EFTPOS transactions. The retailer acquirer and the card issuer may be the same bank.

9. The payment process

'Swiping' the card through the retailer's terminal and the cardholder's confirmation of the transaction by entering their PIN have been described above. If the value of the transaction exceeds the retailer's *floor limit* set by the retailer acquirer, the transaction must first be authorised by the latter. This is done by telephone or automatically via the retailer's terminal. An authorisation code is given to show that the transaction has been approved. Should the value also exceed the *interchange limit* (a higher figure agreed for the retailer between the retailer acquirer and the card issuer), the retailer acquirer must obtain the card issuer's authorisation of the transaction. The card issuer must authorise the transaction if funds or overdraft facilities are available to meet the debit or may exercise its discretion if there are not (the position is analogous to that regarding the payment of cheques).

In a purely electronic system, a processing unit then sends a credit instruction to the retailer's bank and a debit instruction to the cardholder's bank where they are, in turn, processed automatically. This processing unit may be owned by the retailer acquirer, the retailer or by a separate company (the *processor*), acting as agent for one of them.

In practice, the credit and debit are not effected immediately, but, depending on the card scheme and the agreements made by the retailer acquirer and card issuer, between one and four days after the transaction. Where the retailer acquirer is not the retailer's bank, the former will send the latter a credit for the retailer's account. The net position between the card issuer and retailer acquirer is established each day through a central automated system and the balancing payment is made through BACS or CHAPS.

10. The contracts involved
These are as follows:

(a) *Cardholder and card issuer* – governed by the written conditions of use of the debit card.

(b) *Cardholder and retailer* – a contract for the sale of goods (governed by the common law and the Sale of Goods Act 1979) or a contract for the supply of services (governed by the common law and the Supply of Goods and Services Act 1982).

(c) *Retailer and retailer acquirer* – governed by the agreements for (1) the hire and maintenance of the terminal, if applicable, and (2) the operation of the debit card scheme. (Note that it is possible for the retailer to obtain the terminal and processing facilities from a third party.)

(d) *Retailer acquirer (the payee bank) and card issuer (the paying bank)* – governed by the terms of the agreement for the operation of the debit scheme. (In contrast to cheque clearing, in some debit schemes these terms are contained in formal agreements signed by the parties.)

(e) *Retailer acquirer and retailer's bank* – arises where these are different parties and is governed by the rules regulating credit transfers.

(f) *Retailer acquirer/Retailer and processor* – arises where the former uses the services of the latter to process the credit and debit instructions and is governed by the terms of processing agreement.

(g) *Processor and polling company* – arises where the retailer's terminal accepts cards from different schemes, including credit and charge cards, and involves sorting the electronic credit and debit instructions (known as *polling*) and sending them to the appropriate processor. The contract is governed by the terms of the polling agreement.

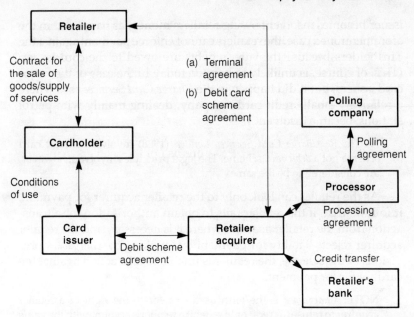

Figure 10.1 *EFTPOS: the contracts involved*

These contracts are shown diagrammatically in Figure 10.1.

11. The position of the retailer

(a) Once the retailer has contracted with the retailer acquirer, the retailer must accept payment by the debit card from a customer who wishes to use it. In return, the retailer acquirer must pay the retailer the amount of the transaction by directly crediting the retailer's account with them or by credit transfer to the retailer's bank.

(b) *Payment by debit card discharges the cardholder's payment obligations to the retailer: Re Charge Card Services Limited* (1988). More precisely, the acceptance of the debit card in payment under the contract between the retailer and the retailer acquirer includes acceptance of the retailer acquirer's promise of unconditional payment. The effect of this is to substitute the retailer acquirer for the cardholder as the debtor of the retailer and, therefore, to completely discharge the cardholder's personal obligation to pay. The cardholder's obligation to pay is owed to the *card issuer*, i.e. the cardholder must pay the minimum amount specified on their statement each month. Undoubtedly the most important possible consequence of this is that if the card issuer becomes insolvent owing retailers money, as happened in the aforementioned case, the retailers cannot enforce payment against the cardholders because the latter's debts are owed to the card issuer. (This, of course, is unlikely to happen today in the case of the major card issuers, but it did happen in the *Charge Card Services* case where a relatively small credit card company, dealing mainly with petrol stations, became insolvent.)

NOTE: *Re Charge Card Services Limited* (1988) involved a *credit* card scheme not a *debit* card scheme. The legal principles involved, however, are considered to be the same.

As the retailer can look only to the retailer acquirer for payment, it follows that, if the retailer fails to obtain authorisation for a transaction from the retailer acquirer where it is necessary and the retailer acquirer rejects liability for payment by invoking the *chargeback* provisions of the scheme, the retailer is unable to take action against the cardholder for payment.

NOTE: *Chargeback* is the term used to refer to the right of a retailer acquirer to refuse to credit or to redebit a retailer's account with the value of a transaction that has not been processed according to the agreement.

The position is the same where the retailer fails to enter the correct details, for example a lesser sum than the true value of the transaction, or fails to follow the correct procedures or where the retailer is the victim of fraud or forgery by the cardholder or someone purporting to be the cardholder. (The position in this last case is the same as with a cheque bearing a forged signature – the retailer could not take action against either the drawee bank or the account holder, the 'drawer'.)

NOTE: Although the retailer has no action in contract against the cardholder, the retailer *is* able to bring an action in tort for deceit against the customer where fraud was involved or for restitution of the goods or their value.

(c) *Equipment failures and processing errors.* The party contractually responsible for the equipment and/or processing is liable for the consequences of failure or errors. For example, if the retailer owns the equipment or rents it from a third party and an equipment failure results in the retailer acquirer not receiving the details of the transaction, the retailer acquirer is not liable to pay for the transaction. Conversely, the retailer acquirer will be liable to the retailer for any loss caused by defective equipment or processing errors where the former provides the terminal, processing or polling.

NOTE: Any exclusion or limitation of liability by the retailer acquirer in its contract with the retailer is subject to the *reasonableness test* under the Unfair Contract Terms Act 1977.

A back-up scheme, involving stand-by equipment or paper vouchers that can be paid in at the retail acquirer's branches or by post, may be part of the debit card scheme. Such a scheme will reduce the likelihood of loss resulting from hardware and software failures and, therefore, reduce the likelihood of resultant legal action.

12. The position of the cardholder

(a) *A debit card as a credit-token.* A debit card is a credit-token within the Consumer Credit Act 1974 s.14(1)(b) because it is used to obtain goods and services from a third party and the card issuer undertakes to pay the third party for them (*see* 10:**7** and 7:**13**). It follows that:

(*i*) Sending a debit card to a customer unsolicited is an offence except where a renewal or replacement card is sent: s.51(3)(b).

However, as debit cards are exempt from regulation by the Act by virtue of the Banking Act 1987 s.89 (which exempts electronic transfer of funds from a current account at a bank):

(b) Connected lender liability (the incurring of joint and several liability with the retailer by the card issuer) under s.75 does not arise.

(c) Sections 83 and 84 do *not* apply. However, s.18 of the Code of Practice in practice extends ss.83 and 84 to *all* payment cards *unless* the cardholder has been grossly negligent or fraudulent (*see generally* 10:**5** – the position of debit and cash cards is the same in this respect).

(b) *Wrongful refusal to authorise a transaction.* Wrongly refusing to authorise a transaction above the interchange limit for apparent lack of funds constitutes a breach of contract by the card issuer. However, an action for breach of contract would require actual financial loss to make the claim worth pursuing and, also, that the loss suffered was a reasonably foreseeable consequence of the breach of contract.

By analogy to returning a cheque marked 'refer to drawer', wrongly making known to the retailer that there are apparently insufficient funds to meet the debit also constitutes defamation. However, as this would be slander, not libel, the cardholder would have to establish *actual* damage to succeed in a claim. (Libel is actionable *per se* (without proof of damage), but slander is not.)

(c) *Hardware or software failure.* Despite the fact that the display of the debit scheme logo constitutes an undertaking to accept payment by the card, it would seem unreasonable for the retailer to be held liable for hardware or software failures that make it impossible to obtain authorisation for the transaction or to process it. In any case, it is highly unlikely that the cardholder could prove sufficient financial loss as a result of the failure to make an action for breach of contract worthwhile. The cardholder must also mitigate their loss and, therefore, could reasonably be expected to pay by cash, by cheque or by credit card in such circumstances.

Where the retailer's terminal and the processing and polling of transactions are provided by a third party, the card issuer has no control over them and, thus, would not seem to be liable in contract law for any failure. However, s.18.1 of the Code of Practice makes the card issuer liable for direct loss caused by faults in its own or a retailer's equipment and systems *unless* the defect was obvious or advised to the cardholder.

Progress test 10

1. How does the typical contract for the use of ATM and debit cards differ from the underlying banker–customer contract? **(1)**

2. Explain the relationship between the Code of banking practice and the law. **(2)**

3. Why is it that the Code is likely to have the force of legislation in all but name? **(2)**

4. What three general duties does a card issuer owe to its cardholders in relation to its ATM network? **(4)**

5. If an ATM machine dispenses *less* than the amount of money requested or retains a cardholder's card without valid reason, the card issuer has broken its contract with the cardholder. Why is it seldom, if ever, worthwhile for the cardholder to bring an action for breach of contract? **(4)**

6. In what circumstances could a card issuer be liable for a third-party bank's failure to maintain its own ATMs? **(4)**

7. In what circumstances can a bank debit a cardholder's account with a cash withdrawal? **(5)**

8. What would be the point of the card issuer establishing that a cardholder had been fraudulent or grossly negligent in relation to the use of their card? **(5)**

9. What, if anything, limits the liability of a cash card holder where the loss of the card or disclosure of the PIN was accidental? **(5)**

10. Explain why the position of a company in relation to its cash cards is different to that of a private individual who uses exactly the same card. **(5)**

11. Why is it, in practice, academic whether or not s.51 applies to unsolicited cash cards? **(6)**

12. Can a cash card be a credit-token? **(7)**

13. Explain the importance of the Banking Act 1987 s.89. **(7)**

14. Explain the legal importance of the 'interchange' limit in the context of debit cards. **(8)**

15. In an EFTPOS scheme, which is the payee bank and which is the paying bank? **(10)**

16. State the principle established in *Re Charge Card Services Limited* (1988). **(11)**

17. Explain the consequences of the *Charge Card Services* decision for retailers. **(11)**

18. What redress has a retailer against a cardholder in an EFTPOS scheme? **(11)**

19. The Consumer Credit Act 1974 s.75 applies to credit cards but not to debit cards. Explain the importance of s.75 and why it does not apply to debit cards. **(12)**

20. Can the rejection of a debit card by the retailer acquirer/card issuer ever constitute defamation? **(12)**

11

Security: an introduction

Security generally

1. Meaning of security

The term *security* means the acquisition of rights over property taken to support a borrower's personal undertaking to repay. These rights can be exercised if the borrower (debtor) does not make repayment. An example is a power of sale.

Both real and personal property (*see* 11:37) may be charged to secure the repayment of a debt.

2. Function of security

(a) *Introduction*. Security is *insurance* against unforeseen and unforeseeable circumstances. The bank as lender acquires some right over and above the basic contractual right to sue the customer if repayment is not made according to the terms of the contract.

Loans should not be made on the strength of the security offered – quite the reverse in fact. You should have decided that you want to make the loan before you even look at the security available. If the proposition does not seem viable *in its own right* then it is wrong to lend against good security *knowing* that it will probably have to be relied on as the source or repayment.

This is not to underrate the importance of security in the lending decision, however, as the provision of suitable security is a major factor. Indeed, customers frequently do not fully appreciate its importance, even its basic function and, in particular, the full ramifications of having given it.

(b) *Specific functions*. There are two specific functions of security.

(i) Should the customer become insolvent, it enables the bank to avoid the *full consequences of its customer's bankruptcy* (if an individual or a partnership) or *liquidation* (if a limited company). Provided suitable security has been taken, the whole debt can be recovered by its realisation, with any surplus being paid over to increase the assets available to other creditors. If the advance was unsecured, the bank would only be able to prove for the amount owed in competition with the other unsecured creditors receiving, perhaps, just a very small percentage (so many pence in the pound) of the debt after the total assets available for distribution have been divided by the total liabilities.

(ii) It is neither good banking practice nor kindness to your customer to allow the bank to be thought of as an easy source of money, to be repaid when the *customer* wants to repay. Of more importance is that advances should be 'turning over' continually. Taking suitable security avoids these possible problems – it can be sold to effect repayment – and also avoids the expense and general problems involved in litigation.

3. Attributes of good security

Although this book is written for a law course, law should not be considered in a vacuum. It would be quite possible to cover different types of security – how they are taken, protected and so on – from a *purely* legal perspective, but this would paint a somewhat incomplete picture of the role of security in the business of banking. Bankers have wider perspectives. For this reason we briefly consider below the basic attributes of *good security*. You should treat this as an introduction, but be prepared to explain the attributes of different types of security in an examination as these arise partly from legal principles and procedures and partly from the wider commercial world that the law regulates.

(a) *Value.* Security should have a value that is stable and easy to check. The value should be *at least* that of the advance, but, usually, a sufficient margin is required, especially where the value can fluctuate, as is the case with shares. Checking the value can involve merely consulting a table in the schedule of a life policy or an analysis of financial statements when shares in a private company are offered as security.

(b) *Checking title and charging the security.* This should not be too costly or complicated. It is no good being offered excellent security for an urgent loan if you cannot check title and charge the security before the repayment date.

The possible complexity of a charge over unregistered land can be compared with the simplicity of a charge over bearer securities in this respect; the latter are negotiable instruments and title to them therefore passes by delivery (*see* 9:**5**).

(c) *Protecting the security.* How easy is protection effected and how effective is it? A mortgage of land can be protected absolutely, for example, but protection is relatively complicated. Conversely, protection of a legal mortgage of a life policy is simple but not total. Your customer could develop a sudden fascination with some bizarrely dangerous activity and possibly invalidate the policy by killing themselves.

(d) *Realisation.* The security should command a ready market and be easy to realise. Commercially this is of the essence. It is commercial nonsense to lend over a two-year term and then have to rely on a security that takes three years to realise. Besides the attributes of specific types of security, you will see that property over which a legal charge is taken is usually easier to realise than that covered by an equitable charge.

(e) *Third-party security.* It can be better to take security for a loan to Mr X from Ms Y or Mr Z rather than from Mr X himself. Technically this is known as taking *third-party* or *collateral* security. *Direct* or *first-party* security is when the customer (the borrower) charges their own assets as security.

The advantage of third-party security is that it gives the bank completely separate rights against the debtor and the surety (as the third party is known). If the debtor will not pay, the bank can sue the debtor and threaten insolvency proceedings. If the debtor cannot, the bank can prove for the debt in the insolvency proceedings, receiving whatever dividend is finally paid. The important point, however, is that the bank's action against the debtor does not affect its rights against the security taken from the surety. These are still available to the bank. Thus, the bank is able to recover its money from two sources, independently or in combination.

Third-party security can take one of three forms.

(i) A *guarantee*, which involves only a personal obligation (*see* 11:**10**).

(ii) A *third-party mortgage*, where the third party (the surety) charges property as security for the customer's indebtedness.

(iii) A *supported guarantee*, which combines both of the above, the bank acquiring a personal right against the guarantor under the guarantee and an action against the property under the charge.

Technically, there is little difference between (i) and (ii) above except where an unlimited guarantee is taken – bank guarantees are 'all monies' securities (*see* 11:**26**), but usually contain an actual limit on the guarantor's liability. Under an unlimited guarantee, the guarantor is liable for the principal debtor's borrowing, whatever the amount, to the full extent of their personal wealth. Under a third-party mortgage, the mortgagor is only liable to the value of the property charged.

NOTE: In *Deutsche Bank AG* v *Ibrahim and Others* (1992), it was held that the deposit of title deeds with a bank as security for a customer's overdraft is, in effect, a guarantee of that liability to the extent of the value of the property. To be enforceable it must be evidence in writing in accordance with the Statute of Frauds 1677. A bank would, however, be entitled to retain the deeds under a contract to secure an overdraft, provided consideration moved from the bank to the depositor and not merely to the customer.

Types of security arrangement

4.   Introduction

Besides classifying and discussing securities by physical type, such as land, life policies and so on, we can classify them according to the nature of the arrangement entered into and then go on to give some specific definitions. These, as you will see, are, to some extent, independent of the nature of the actual property taken as security.

5.   Whole ownership

The customer (the debtor) can transfer the whole ownership of the property to the bank (the creditor) under a contract in which the bank agrees to retransfer it to the customer if the debt is repaid on the due date. A legal mortgage of shares and an assignment of a life policy take this form.

6.   Possession

The customer can give the bank mere possession, not ownership, of the property. Clearly this stops the customer disposing of the property, but it does not directly assist the bank unless it also acquires the right to sell it. Pledges and liens (*see* 11:**12** and **13**) take this form.

7.   Documents of title

Documents of title, such as title deeds to land or share certificates, can be deposited by the customer with the bank. This gives the bank the right to retain the documents until repayment is made. This is sometimes referred to as giving the bank a lien on them, but this is incorrect because, here, the right to retain the documents is given by an express agreement, whereas a lien arises by operation of law.

The effect of the deposit is that the property represented by the documents cannot be dealt with without them and therefore provides the customer with a strong inducement to make repayment. In addition, a bank will normally give itself direct rights against the property in a contractual memorandum of deposit, primarily the right to sell the property, if repayment is not made.

8.   Rights against property

Without giving any rights of ownership, possession or documents of title, the customer may give the bank certain rights against property. The right to apply to the court for an order for sale if the loan is not repaid is the essence of this type of security. Such rights are given by the customer executing a *charge* over the property.

We must cover two other security arrangements. The first, a floating charge, is peculiar to companies and the second, a guarantee, involves a personal obligation and not rights over specific property.

9.   Floating charge

A floating charge is an equitable charge over the fluctuating assets of a company, such as its stocks and raw materials, without attaching to specific assets until crystallisation, i.e. until it becomes *fixed* (*see* 16:9).

10. Guarantee

A guarantee is a personal undertaking to repay a debt if another person who should make repayment does not.

NOTE: Guarantors are normally required to charge specific property in support of their personal undertakings.

Definitions

11. Mortgage

A mortgage is *the creation or transfer of an interest in property* as security for the payment of a debt or the discharge of some other obligation with a *provision for redemption*, that is, on repayment or discharge of the obligation it will become void or the interest reconveyed.

Possession of the property remains with the *mortgagor* (the borrower/customer), while the *mortgagee* (the lender/bank) obtains some or all of the rights of ownership or the right to obtain ownership if the borrower defaults in repayment. In other words, if repayment is not made, the bank (or other lender) can take action against the property, directly or indirectly depending on the type of mortgage, to recover what is owed.

NOTE: The term *mortgage* is used very loosely. For example, legally, a customer *gives* a mortgage to the bank and does not get one from the bank; it is also frequently taken to mean the money lent.

Legal mortgages of *land* are almost invariably created by *legal charge* under the Law of Property Act 1925 and not, since 1925, by creating a lease. The legal charge does not give the mortgagee an estate in the land mortgaged as a lease would (*see* 12:4), but does confer the same protection, powers and remedies.

Land is the form of property most usually mortgaged but choses in action (*see* 11:38), such as life assurance policies, can be mortgaged by assignment and goods by a conditional bill of sale, both subject to a condition that, on repayment, the property will be reassigned to the mortgagor. A mortgagor of goods is rare.

A mortgage may be either legal or equitable. A *legal mortgage* creates rights against the property itself whereas an *equitable mortgage* creates only personal rights against the mortgagor. A legal mortgagee is therefore in a stronger position than an equitable mortgagee (*see* 11:16).

12. Pledge

A pledge is a *deposit of goods*, or documents of title to them, or *negotiable instruments* with a lender as security for a debt. It confers the power of sale if repayment is not made. (Pawnbroking is an example of utilising a pledge as security.)

It differs from a mortgage in that the lender obtains possession of the property while the borrower retains ownership.

13. Lien

A lien is a creditor's right to *retain possession* of property belonging to the debtor until a debt is paid.

It differs from a mortgage or pledge in that it arises by *operation of law* from certain situations, a garage, for example, would be entitled to a lien over its customer's car until a bill for repairs was paid. Mortgages and pledges are both the result of express agreements between borrowers and lenders.

A lien may be either particular or general. A *particular lien* gives the right to retain possession only to secure payment of money owing in respect of the particular property over which the lien is exercised. A *general lien* gives the right to retain possession until any amount outstanding is repaid.

Normally, a lien only confers the right to retain possession of property but, by mercantile custom, a *banker's lien* is a general lien that confers the right of sale and recoupment. A bank can exercise a lien over any of its customer's documents in its possession other than those deposited for safe custody.

In practice, this means that the lien can be exercised over cheques paid in to be collected and credited to the customer's account if the account is overdrawn, although the lien is lost when they are presented for payment. Other documents, such as life policies and share certificates, are likely to be held under a specific agreement – either for safe custody or as security – and, therefore, a lien cannot arise over them while they are so held. However, if a life policy, say, was originally held as security but the debt has been discharged without the customer asking for the return of the life policy, a lien could arise over the policy in respect of subsequent borrowing.

NOTE: *Safe custody* facilities give rise to a *contract of bailment*. This is wholly inconsistent with a lien which can, therefore, never arise over articles held in safe custody. A *safe custody agreement* may provide, however, that the items held may be retained until charges incurred have been paid, but this is not a true lien.

As mentioned in 11:7, taking possession of documents of title under a security arrangement gives rise to the right to retain them until repayment is made. This is sometimes referred to as *contractual lien*, but, because such a lien does not arise by operation of law but by agreement, this is not a lien in the legal sense.

14. Charge

A charge is usually regarded as a type of mortgage. However, a mortgage creates or conveys an interest in the property mortgaged subject to a right of redemption, whereas a charge merely gives certain rights over the property charged as security, e.g. the right to ask the court for an order for sale of the property.

NOTE: A *legal charge* over land under the Law of Property Act 1925 s.87(1) does create an interest in land and to avoid confusion is better considered in practice as a mortgage rather than a charge because it creates the same rights in the land as would be created by a mortgage (*see* 12:**34** and **35**).

In the same way that it is common to use the term 'mortgage' to cover a variety of security arrangements, so too is it common to use the term 'charge'.

15. Assignment

Assignment is the transfer of title to a chose in action.

A legal mortgage of a life policy is taken by assignment. The assignment has to be in writing and written notice must be given to the life assurance company (*see* 13:**7**).

Types of mortgage

16. Legal and equitable

The terms *legal* and *equitable* are a historical legacy from the time when different courts operated different systems of law based on different principles. Today there are four practical distinctions between these two types of mortgage:

(a) *Ownership.* With a *legal charge* some or all of the rights of ownership are transferred to the mortgagee together, in some cases, with possession of the asset. An *equitable charge* does not transfer any rights of ownership, only rights against the asset charged should repayment not be made.

NOTE: Whether or not possession of the asset charged is transferred to the bank depends on the type of asset rather than on the type of charge.

(b) *Remedies.* Because a *legal charge* transfers some or all of the rights of ownership, it gives the mortgagee rights *in rem*, that is rights against the property itself. The most important of these is the absolute right to sell the asset charged if the mortgagor defaults. These rights *in rem* are in addition to the personal action available against the mortgagor for the principal and interest due.

NOTE: A possession order must be obtained from the court before a mortgagee can exercise the power of sale over residential property.

An *equitable charge* gives only rights *in personam*, that is rights against the person who charged the asset. Thus, although the mortgagor has given the mortgagee rights *against* the asset charged, the mortgagee has no rights of ownership and therefore cannot, say, sell the asset without the consent and assistance of the mortgagor or a court order. In other words, the mortgagee's rights against the asset can only be realised through the mortgagor or the court.

An equitable mortgagee's principal right is to share in the proceeds of sale when the property is sold and a right to seek the court's aid in enforcing this right.

NOTE: If an equitable charge is executed by deed, the mortgagee's power of sale is not dependent on the mortgagor's consent, the mortgagee has a statutory power of sale (also a statutory power to appoint a receiver) on default by the mortgagor: Law of Property Act 1925 s.101 (*see* 16:**32**).

(c) *Form.* While the exact form of the mortgage will depend on the type of asset to be charged, we can generally say that a *legal charge* is executed by deed or by whatever method must be used to transfer legal title.

At its simplest, an *equitable charge* is taken by a deposit of the asset, or documents of title to it, together with the mortgagor's grant of rights against the property for the purpose of security. A bank will rarely take the deposit of the asset alone as an equitable charge, it will require the mortgagor's express declaration of the charge in a *memorandum of deposit.*

NOTE: An equitable charge over land cannot be created by the mere deposit of documents of title, the Law of Property (Miscellaneous Provisions) Act 1989 requires a written contract (in this case a memorandum of deposit) signed by both parties.

A memorandum of deposit is taken for three main reasons.

(i) It puts the purpose of the deposit of the asset or documents of title to it beyond doubt, i.e. as security and not for safe custody.

(ii) It includes a range of clauses designed to strengthen and protect the bank's position.

(iii) If taken by deed, it enables the bank to exercise its power of sale without the consent and cooperation of the mortgagor or court order should the mortgagor default in repayment.

(The memorandum of deposit is discussed in more detail in the context of specific types of security in later chapters.)

NOTE: In theory, an equitable charge can be created merely by the borrower declaring that a lender has rights against a certain asset in return for value given such as a loan, i.e. no deposit or supporting written evidence is actually required. The obvious problem of enforceability that would arise means that banks would never take a charge in this way.

(d) *Prior equitable interests.* An *equitable* mortgage is always subject to prior equitable interests even if the mortgagee is unaware of them. (Where the equities are equal, the first in time shall prevail.) With certain important exceptions, a *legal* mortgagee takes free of equitable interests, provided they are unaware of them (*see* 12:**13** and **17**).

This principle may affect a bank taking an equitable mortgage over shares because the shares may be held in trust, i.e. the beneficiaries will have a prior equitable interest.

17. Legal or equitable mortgage: which to take?

Here it is possible only to generalise. Much depends on the type of loan sought, the individual circumstances of the borrower, their relationship with the bank and, possibly of most importance, the type of asset(s) offered as security.

In purely legal terms, a *legal mortgage* offers the better security to a bank, but the charging procedure is usually more complicated, takes longer to complete and is more expensive, although all costs are usually passed on to the borrower in one way or another. An *equitable mortgage* is usually easier, quicker and cheaper to take but, unless taken by deed, does not enable the bank to take action directly against the property charged to recover the advance. In short, the choice will be dictated mainly by bank policy and partly by professional judgement. (We consider the attributes of legal and equitable mortgages in the context of different types of security elsewhere in this book.)

18. Second mortgages

It is possible for any number of charges, legal or equitable, to exist at the same time over an asset, although second or subsequent mortgages are usually associated with land. A bank may be prepared to accept a second mortgage as security for an advance if the value of the property is sufficient to repay both the first mortgage and the proposed second mortgage, i.e. there is sufficient *equity* in the property.

The main disadvantage of a second mortgage is that the first mortgagee may exercise their legal remedies without reference to, and therefore to the possible detriment of, the second mortgagee.

A second legal mortgage is usually created by a legal charge and a second equitable mortgage by a general equitable charge. No deposit of documents will be possible because these will be held by the first mortgagee.

Taking security from private individuals

19. Introduction

The topics we discuss in this section are of general application to all customers. However, they are particularly relevant when taking security from private individuals because, as a generalisation, private individuals are in a weaker position *vis-à-vis* their bank or, possibly the principal debtor, and have less understanding of security arrangements than trading customers. Trading customers are also more likely to have professional advisers.

20. Undue influence

(a) *Introduction.* Where one party to a contract is subject to the dominant position of the other, undue influence, an equitable principle, can arise. If it is proved, it renders the contract *voidable* at the option of the weaker party and the contract may be rescinded (set aside) by the court. As you will see below, however, the relationship between the parties, and even proof of actual dominance, is not enough alone to avoid the contract.

In certain, well-defined relationships, known as *fiduciary relationships,* a dominant position is presumed to exist, for example, between solicitor and client, doctor and patient and parent and child. In other relationships, the dominant position must be established by the party wishing to avoid a contract for undue influence. The banker–customer relationship falls into this latter category.

Example

In *Lloyds Bank Ltd* v *Bundy* (1975) (CA), the defendant, an elderly farmer of little business sense, twice mortgaged his home, his only asset, to the bank to secure the overdraft of his son's company. The bank knew that the company was in financial difficulties but did not explain this fully to the defendant, although it knew that he relied upon them totally for advice in such matters. The son's company became insolvent and the bank eventually sought possession of the house.

It was held that the bank's action failed, the bank had been seeking a benefit from the defendant and there was a conflict of interest. The relationship between the bank and the defendant was one of trust and confidence that imposed a duty on the bank to ensure that the defendant received informed independent advice before entering into the commitment. The bank was in breach of that duty of care and could not be allowed to benefit from the transaction. While this 'special relationship' is unlikely to arise frequently, banks must be aware of the possibility.

(b) *The basis of undue influence.* The leading case is *National Westminster Bank PLC* v *Morgan* (1985) (HL). Mr and Mrs Morgan were joint owners of their home. They mortgaged it to the bank to secure the refinancing of a previous loan from a building society, on which they had fallen behind with the repayments when Mr Morgan's business got into difficulties. Mrs Morgan did not want the new mortgage to extend to advances for her husband's business activities and she was assured, wrongly, but in good faith, by the bank manager that it did not. The bank sought possession of the house when the couple fell into arrears with the repayments. Mr Morgan died soon afterwards without any business debts to the bank and Mrs Morgan appealed against a possession order on the grounds that she had signed the legal charge because of undue influence from the bank manager. It was held that the appeal was dismissed and the possession order was upheld by the House of Lords. The mortgage Mrs Morgan had signed was not to her disadvantage because it had enabled her to remain in her home. Nor, indeed, had the bank exploited its position. On the facts, no special relationship had arisen.

The legal principle of the case is that a contract will only be set aside for undue influence where:

(i) The weaker party was subject to the dominance of the stronger party; and
(ii) They suffered a real and obvious disadvantage as a result.

In a rare case, the dominance will be exercised by the bank directly but, more likely, it is exercised by someone who is considered to be acting as agent for the bank, e.g. a debtor who persuades, say, a relative to guarantee their proposed borrowing from the bank or one joint owner of a house who persuades the other joint owner – typically a husband persuading his wife – to execute a mortgage deed over it.

Example 1

In *Avon Finance Co Ltd* v *Bridger* (1985) (CA), Mr and Mrs B bought a retirement home partly with a mortgage and partly with money from their son. What they did not know was that their son had raised a loan from AV to help him provide his contribution. This loan was secured by a second charge on the property and the son persuaded his parents to execute the charge at the office of AV's solicitor by misleading them as to its nature and by exerting influence over them. The son later defaulted on the loan and AV sought possession of the house.

A possession order was refused because AV had used the son as its agent to obtain the Bs' signatures on the charge. Clearly, the Bs had also suffered a real disadvantage as a result of the transaction.

Example 2

In *Bank of Credit and Commerce International SA* v *Aboody* (1989) (CA), a different view was taken. Here the matrimonial home was in Mrs A's sole name and Mr A persuaded her to charge it to secure a loan to a company controlled by Mr A of which Mrs A was an officer. In fact, Mrs A never took an active part in any business affairs and signed any document her husband put in front of her. The company defaulted on the loan and BCCI sought a possession order.

The order was granted. Although Mrs A had acted under her husband's dominance and he, in turn, was acting as agent for the bank, Mrs A could not show that she had suffered any real disadvantage. On the contrary, she had benefited from the support the loan had given to the company's business. (But *see Barclays Bank PLC* v *O'Brien* (1992) (11:**22**) remembering that equity's intervention is discretionary on the individual facts of each case.)

Example 3

In both *Avon Finance* and *Aboody*, the person exercising undue influence was held to be acting as agent of the mortgagee. This was not the case in *Coldunell Ltd* v *Gallon* (1986) (CA). Here C advanced short-term business finance to the son of the Gs on security of a charge over their home executed by Mr G, the registered proprietor, and consented to by Mrs G. C's solicitor prepared the necessary documents and intended to post them to the Gs, together with a letter advising them that they should obtain independent legal advice before signing. However, the son intercepted the letters at some stage, withheld the solicitor's advice from his parents and persuaded them to sign the charge and the consent respectively. The son defaulted on repayments and C sought a possession order against the Gs.

It was held that, although the Gs had clearly signed the documents under the influence of their son and had suffered a real disadvantage as a result, their son was equally clearly not acting as C's agent. The solicitor had not handed the letters to him and, even if they had, this in itself would not necessarily have constituted his appointment as their agent. The possession order was therefore granted.

(c) *Independent legal advice.* It is common banking practice to insist that a person providing security, particularly a third-party surety, such as a relative of the borrower, obtains independent legal advice on the nature of and the obligations incurred under the charge before executing it and further that it is executed in the presence of the adviser. This practice is designed to prevent a subsequent plea of undue influence when the bank seeks to enforce the security.

In almost all cases, this will prevent the plea but, for two interdependent reasons, it is not absolute protection.

(i) All equitable remedies and intervention are *at the discretion of the court* – this is one of the fundamental tenets of equity – and it follows from this that a court may still be prepared to set aside a charge on the facts of the case, even where independent advice was given.

(ii) The dominance may be so powerful that it may transcend the advice and the court may take the view that whatever advice is given and whoever gives it, the dominance is so great that the advice will be ignored.

NOTE: Independent legal advice is also protection against a plea of misrepresentation by the mortgagor (*see* 11:**21**).

It is perhaps worth concluding by noting that in *National Westminster Bank PLC* v *Morgan* (1985), Lord Scarman stated that '... there is no precisely defined law setting limits to the equitable jurisdiction of a court to relieve against undue influence'.

21. Misrepresentation

(a) *Definition.* Misrepresentation occurs where one party to a contract is misled by the other as to the true facts of the situation – fraudulently, negligently or innocently – with the result that they enter into the contract.

Misrepresentation makes the contract *voidable* and always entitles the innocent party to rescind (set aside) the contract and, where made fraudulently or negligently, always to an action for damages at common law. An action for damages is also available for innocent misrepresentation in certain circumstances under the Misrepresentation Act 1967.

(b) *Misrepresentation and banking.* It is reasonable to assume that only rarely has a bank deliberately misrepresented the truth to a customer or other contracting party. Professional standards should ensure that negligent misrepresentation (the bank should have known the statement were untrue) is also relatively uncommon. Innocent misrepresentation? Well human or system error means that this will happen. Banks may attempt to protect themselves with disclaimer clauses against possible liability, but the Misrepresentation Act 1967 subjects any such disclaimer to a test of reasonableness – the forerunner of the test found in the Unfair Contract Terms Act 1977.

Misrepresentation could affect *any* contract a bank enters into with *any* customer – from the opening of a current account to taking property into safe custody. In practice, however, it is most likely to be relevant when security is taken, the customer later arguing that the bank misled them as to the true facts or consequences. The misrepresentation may be committed by either the bank or its agent.

Example 1

In *Kingsnorth Trust Ltd* v *Bell* (1986) (CA), Mr B required his wife's consent to a charge on the matrimonial home to secure borrowing to buy a business property. (Technically, she had an overriding interest in the property:*see* 12:**16**.) KT's solicitor sent B's solicitor the necessary documents, which the latter gave to B for signature by himself and his wife. Mr B misled his wife as to the purpose of the loan. Furthermore she was accustomed to sign anything her husband asked her to sign.

It was held that Mr B was acting as KT's sub-agent – in effect he had been entrusted by KT with obtaining his wife's signature – and his actions were held to amount to fraudulent misrepresentation which prevented KT obtaining a possession order when Mr B defaulted on the loan. The charge was also voidable for undue influence. Note that if KT's solicitor had instructed B's solicitor *not* to give the charge to Mr B to obtain his wife's signature, the decision might well have been different. Mr B could not then have been said to be acting as agent of KT.

Example 2

An unusual example of misrepresentation occurred in *Lloyds Bank PLC* v *Waterhouse* (1990) (CA) where W guaranteed a loan to his son from L to enable his son to buy a farm. The guarantee was in the bank's standard form and contained an 'all monies' clause, which meant that it covered not only the borrowing to buy the farm but also any other borrowing the son might make. The son borrowed far more than was necessary to buy the farm and, eventually, W was called upon to pay under his guarantee. At this point W disclosed that, while he may have appeared to be familiar with business matters and, indeed, was reasonably successful in business himself, he was illiterate and had no idea what terms the guarantee contained although he realised what it was.

On the facts, W was able to avoid the guarantee because he had asked about its terms and the bank had merely told him that it was intended to provide security for the loan to his son to buy the farm. W was able to establish that he would *not* have signed the guarantee if he had known that it contained the 'all monies' clause. In short, the bank had negligently misrepresented the terms of the guarantee.

NOTE: Where a security contract is not voidable for misrepresentation – because the misrepresentation was not the cause of the contract being entered into – damages may nevertheless be recoverable in the tort of negligence under the *Hedley Byrne* principle (*see* 1:**18**) for the loss that results from a negligent misrepresentation, e.g. a misrepresentation as to the purpose or scope of the security. In practice, the result would be that the security would be devalued, if not worthless.

Example 3

In *Cornish* v *Midland Bank PLC* (1985) (CA), the bank failed to make clear to C that the charge she had signed with her former husband to secure funds advanced to renovate a farm they had purchased contained the usual all 'monies clause'. She was under the impression that the bank would not lend more than the agreed limit of £2000. After she and her husband separated, which fact the bank knew, her husband continued to operate the account alone until it was overdrawn well beyond the agreed limit.

It was held that, although the charge was valid, the bank had broken its duty to C and she recovered damages for the loss she had suffered as a result.

22. Providing information

Here a variety of related issues are involved.

(a) *Confidentiality.* A bank owes a duty of confidentiality to its customer (*see* 1:**13**) and, therefore, if third-party security is to be taken, the bank must be very careful when answering questions from the prospective mortgagor/guarantor. Potential problems can normally be avoided by a meeting at which all parties are present.

(b) *Disclosure.* A security contract is not a contract *uberrimae fidei* (*see* 13:5). This means that a bank is not bound to disclose information that might affect the prospective mortgagor's/guarantor's judgment. However, if the mortgagor/guarantor is under an obvious misapprehension as to, say, the debtor's financial position, the bank is under a duty to correct it. Failure to do so may give grounds to avoid the security.

Banks will often avoid problems arising by obtaining the customer's written authority to disclose relevant information to a prospective guarantor.

(c) *Duty to explain.* It is clear that no general duty to explain a security document is owed to a provider of security who is not a customer of the bank: *O'Hara* v *Allied Irish Banks Ltd* (1984).

The position is not so clear when the security is provided by a personal customer of the bank. *Obiter dicta* in *Cornish* v *Midland Bank PLC* (1985) (CA) suggests that such a duty may exist when third-party security (a guarantee) is taken. The duty was recognised in relation to direct security by the High Court in *Midland Bank PLC* v *Perry* (1987). However, in *Barclays Bank PLC* v *Khaira* (1992), the High Court held that a bank owed *no* duty of care in tort or contract to offer explanations or to advise the taking of independent advice to those who came to its premises (customers or non-customers) to sign securities. The court further held that if an explanation is given the bank is under a duty not to advise negligently on the effect of the documentation and to ensure that it is reasonably accurate.

If such a duty is held to exist, its breach entitles the customer to sue the bank in negligence for damages although the *security remains valid.*

More recently, the Court of Appeal in *Barclays Bank PLC* v *O'Brien* (1992), while upholding the general rule that a creditor does not owe a proposed surety a duty to explain the effect of the transaction, held that a bank has a duty to explain surety documents to *wives*, recognising that, in practice, the degree of emancipation of women in society varies. Married women who provide security for their husband's debts must be specially protected. Thus, a bank will only be able to enforce such security against a wife if it took reasonable steps to ensure that she understood the transaction. (Elderly parents – shades of *Bundy* (*see* 11:20) – were identified as also being capable of being accorded the same special protection.)

The Court stated that this special protection would arise where:

(i) The relationship between the debtor and the surety, and, therefore, the likelihood that the latter would rely on the former, was known to the bank;

(ii) The surety's consent to the transaction was obtained by undue influence or misrepresentation by the debtor and the surety failed to fully understand the nature and effect of the transaction; and

(iii) The bank failed to take reasonable steps to ensure that the surety fully understood the nature and effect of the transaction and that the surety's consent to the transaction was true and informed.

The facts of the case were that Mrs O'B had executed, jointly with her husband, a legal charge over their jointly owned matrimonial home to secure the overdraft of a company in which her husband had an interest. Her husband pressurised her into signing and falsely represented to her that the limit of the security was £60 000, not the overdraft limit of £135 000, and that it would be released in a few weeks. The security was executed at a sub-branch where the clerk failed to follow the instructions of the branch manager (perhaps the real key to the decision) to explain to her the nature of the overdraft and to advise her to take independent legal advice before executing it. Mrs O'B signed the charge without reading it and the clerk merely witnessed her signature.

Eventually, the bank sought to enforce its charge, but the Court of Appeal held that it was unable to do so. Although Mr O'B did not act as the bank's agent and, therefore, undue influence could not be raised against the bank, nor was it responsible for his misrepresentation as to the amount and nature of the security, in equity the charge was only enforceable for £60 000, the amount falsely represented to her by her husband.

The Code of Practice s.12 provides that banks (and building societies) will advise private individuals proposing to give them a guarantee or other security for another person's liability that, by so doing, they might become liable instead of or as well as that other person and that they should seek independent legal advice before entering into the guarantee or other security contract. It also provides that guarantee and other third-party forms will contain a clear and prominent notice to this effect. Thus, irrespective of their common law rights, aggrieved guarantors can seek compensation from the Banking Ombudsman who will base a decision on s.12.

An interesting issue is whether, by following the Code to the letter, banks will automatically satisfy their (decidedly imprecise) duty at common law.

23. Mistake

(a) *Mistake generally.* Occasionally, a contract will be totally null and void where one or both parties make a mistake. However, most types of mistake have no effect at all. For example, the law will not assist customers if they underestimate their capacity to repay a loan or if a bank wishes to avoid a contract for the purchase of expensive computer equipment because it wrongly assessed its need for it.

Where, however, the mistake either prevents any agreement being reached at all, or where an agreement is reached that lacks any foundation because of the mistake, the contract will be *void*. Most such situations occur in contracts of sale that obviously are of limited relevance in banking. A situation that is, theoretically at least, is known as *non est factum*.

(b) *Non est factum.* Literally translated, this means 'it is not my deed' (not what I intended to do) but it carries the more general meaning of a document mistakenly signed.

For a party to a contract, e.g. a guarantor under a contract of guarantee, to avoid the contract on the grounds of *non est factum*, two things must be established.

(i) The document they actually signed was fundamentally different from the one they *intended* to sign. An example could perhaps be a person signing a guarantee in the mistaken belief that they were witnessing a will or where the guarantee was for a substantially greater amount.

(ii) They acted without negligence. Thus signing a document without reading it would defeat the plea. In one leading case an old lady could not read the document in question because her glasses were broken but her plea of *non est factum* nevertheless failed: *Saunders* v *Anglia Building Society* (1970) (HL).

Possible problems with *non est factum* can easily be avoided by ensuring that a guarantee is signed and witnessed at the bank or attested (certified as valid after having been explained) by a solicitor. Thus, from what we have said above about legal theory and what you know about banking practice, you could reasonably conclude that *non est factum* is of more academic interest than practical importance.

Example

In *Lloyds Bank PLC* v *Waterhouse* (1990) (see 11:21), W clearly thought he was signing a guarantee that was substantially different in its terms from that which he did sign. Nevertheless, his plea of *non est factum* failed. (You will recall, however, that the guarantee was held to be voidable for misrepresentation.)

24. Forgery

Occasionally a signature on a security form will be forged. In general, a forged signature is without effect and, therefore, the person whose signature it purports to be incurs no liability. However, where the security is provided jointly by two or more persons, the forgery can have different effects depending on the type of security taken.

(a) *Guarantee.* A forged signature of one of the parties to a joint guarantee releases *all* the parties from liability under it, the guarantee is completely unenforceable: *James Graham & Co (Timber) Ltd* v *South-gate-Sands* (1985) (CA).

(b) *Legal charge.* A forged signature by one of two co-owners on a mortgage deed prevents a *legal charge* arising, but the mortgagee obtains an *equitable charge* over the share of the asset owned by the genuine signatory: *First National Securities* v *Hegarty* (1985). Such situations have occurred (as in *Hegarty*) where a husband or wife is accompanied by a person who pretends to be the other spouse and the parties execute a charge for fraudulent purposes.

In all situations where there is any possibility of fraud being perpetrated in this way, it should be avoidable by ensuring that the security forms are signed and witnessed in the presence of a bank official or a solicitor.

Bank security forms: standard clauses

25. Introduction

Bank security forms epitomise the standard form contract. A customer's freedom to negotiate the terms of a security contract are, at best, extremely limited and, usually, non-existent. Each clause is there for a purpose, the overall aim being to put the bank in the strongest possible position in relation to the borrower and the asset charged.

Each type of security form has its own specific clauses, but the following are common to *all* security forms. We consider them generally here and in specific contexts in later chapters.

26. All monies

This clause means that the charge secures all amounts outstanding on any account, including interest charges and commission payments and any expenses incurred by the bank in taking and enforcing the security.

In addition, where third-party security is taken, the clause prevents the mortgagor proving in the insolvency of the principal debtor or claiming subrogation unless the debt has been fully repaid.

27. Continuing security

This clause ensures that the mortgage secures the outstanding balance at any time and not the specific sum advanced. It thereby avoids the operation of the *Rule* in *Clayton's Case* (1816) to the bank's detriment. Without this clause, every payment in would reduce the amount secured by the charge and every payment out would constitute a new debt that would not be covered by the charge.

> NOTE: This clause affords no protection if the bank receives notice of a second mortgage from another lender over the asset. Unless the bank's first charge imposes an obligation to make further advances (which is very rare), the notice terminates the charge as a continuing security and any further advances will be postponed to the second mortgage. Furthermore, unless specific protection is included in the charge (*see* 11:**28**) or the account is broken, *Clayton's Case* (1816) will operate to the bank's detriment: *Deeley* v *Lloyds Bank Ltd* (1912) (*see* 1:**15**).

28. Avoidance of *Clayton's Case*

Banks make excellent use of the law. Generally speaking, if there is more than one way to protect their position, they will take advantage of each way. In the situations where the *Rule* in *Clayton's Case* (1816) can work to a bank's detriment (*see* 1:**15**), the simple expedient of breaking (ruling off) the account and passing all subsequent entries through a new account will afford protection. However, where a security form contains a specific exclusion of the Rule, either in so many words or by stating that if notice of a second mortgage is received the account is deemed to have been ruled off, actually breaking the account would not seem necessary. (The Rule in *Clayton's Case* is an implied term in the banker–customer contract and can therefore be excluded by an express term to the contrary.)

A similar clause was held to be effective in a bank guarantee in *Westminster Bank* v *Cond* (1940), but the more general efficacy of the device has not been judicially tested. Thus, rather than leave anything to chance, banks will usually include such a clause *and* rule off the account.

29. Repayable on demand

Under the Limitation Act 1980, an action on a contract must be commenced within six years of the cause of action arising otherwise the right of action is lost. Including this clause ensures (though it is probably not strictly necessary with the continuing security clause included) that the bank's right of action arises, and the six-year period begins to run, when a demand for repayment is made, not when the security is taken.

30. Change in the constitution of the parties

During the period of the loan, it is quite possible that the principal debtor may change in constitution, e.g. a sole account may become a joint account or trustees change. Less commonly, the bank may change its constitution, e.g. by merger. This clause ensures that, despite any such change, the charge remains enforceable against the mortgagor/guarantor.

31. Conflict of laws

This clause provides that the security contract is subject to the laws of England and Wales. It prevents a claim by a foreign national that the contract was made according to their own country's laws, laws that might not be to the bank's advantage and which could quite possibly give rise to difficulties in enforcing the security.

32. Third-party security

Where security is taken from a third person, additional clauses will be included. These will, for example.

(a) Give details of the account secured.
(b) Allow the bank to vary arrangements with the debtor without prejudicing its security.
(c) Allow the bank to put any money received under the mortgage into a suspense account, thereby enabling it to proceed against the principal debtor (its customer) for the full amount.

These clauses are covered in detail in 15:9.

Securities for current account borrowing

33. Introduction

Here we are concerned with overdrafts and the effect of certain events and the Rule in Clayton's Case on the bank's position. This section outlines situations discussed more fully elsewhere.

34. Notice of a second mortgage

Notice of a second mortgage fixes the debit balance covered by the bank's charge. It ceases to be a continuing security (*see* 11:**27**) and further lending will be postponed to advances made by the second mortgagee.

35. Notice of events affecting the account

Such events include the death of a partner or a joint guarantor. Even though joint and several liability will have been accepted, this only preserves the liability of a deceased's estate, the actual liability is fixed by the notice of death. Thus, any personal assets charged from the deceased partner or guarantor only cover the debit balance at notice of death; they do not cover further advances (*see* 2:**10**). In such cases (and also where notice of a second mortgage is received), the account should be broken and fresh entries passed through a *new* account. If advances are made, fresh security should be taken unless the bank is satisfied with its remaining security.

It is possible, of course, that the bank will not wish to seek to preserve the liability of the deceased account holder's estate, in which case the account can simply be continued. The standard clause dealing with changes in the constitution of the parties would, for example, ensure the continuing liability of the remaining co-guarantors when one of their number dies.

36. *Clayton's Case*

We have discussed 'appropriation' and the *Rule* in *Clayton's Case* in detail in Chapter 1 (*see* 1:**15**). You should recall that, unless specific appropriations are made or the *Rule* is excluded or prevented from operating (*see* 11:**28**), payments into a current account clear outstanding debits in chronological order (a debit balance or overdraft consists of a series of separate debts).

The situations outlined in 11:**32** and **34** are made worse by the operation of *Clayton's Case*. Unless the account is broken or a suitable exclusion of the *Rule* is included in the security form, not only will the bank's claim to recover further advances be postponed or negated entirely, but also the amount for which it is secured will be progressively reduced by each and every payment into the account, despite equal or greater payments out.

Types of property

37. Real and personal property

Our legal system classifies property into 'real' and 'personal', the former comprising *only* freehold interests in land and the latter every-thing else, including leasehold interests in land. In fact, freehold and leasehold interests in land are treated in much the same way and it is usual to refer to leaseholds as *chattels real* when classifying property, to distinguish them from *chattels personal*, that is other forms of personal property. Look carefully at the categories shown in Figure 11.1.

38.   Choses in action and choses in possession

A *chose in action* is property that does not physically exist and, consequently, cannot be effectively protected by physical means, only by court action. Thus, it is often referred to as intangible property. Examples include rights in negotiable instruments (such as cheques), patents, copyrights and the goodwill of a business. Apart from land, banks nearly always take charges over choses in action as security for loans, life policies and shares being obvious examples. ('Chose' is an old French legal term for 'thing'.)

A *chose in possession* is property with a physical existence and that can, therefore, be physically possessed and protected – this book or your clothes for example.

39.   The historical background

These somewhat strange-sounding categories are a legacy of the very rigid procedural rules that the common law courts (the Royal

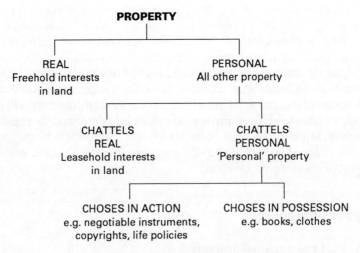

Figure 11.1 *Types of property*

Courts) developed early in our legal history. If a man's freehold land (a woman could not own land at that time) was wrongfully taken from him (this happened quite frequently in a society where might was largely right), he could recover the actual land by bringing a *real* action (technically an action *in rem*, Latin for 'against the thing') in the common law courts. If, however, he was dispossessed of anything else, he could not recover the actual property and was only entitled to bring a *personal action* (technically an action *in personam*, Latin for 'against the person') for money compensation against the person who had taken it.

So, where do leaseholds fit in? The answer is simple, the concept of the leasehold interest, essentially a commercial creation, developed rather later than the freehold, by which time legal procedure had become so rigid that the real action available to the freeholder could not be adapted to a leaseholder's claim. In time, however, a remedy developed that enabled a leaseholder to recover his land if he had been wrongfully dispossessed.

Progress test 11

1. What is the function of security? Give two specific reasons why it is taken. (**2**)

2. List the attributes of good security. (**3**)

3. How does a guarantee differ from other types of security arrangement? (**10**)

4. Define and distinguish between a mortgage, a pledge and a lien. (**10–13**)

5. Explain assignment. (**15**)

6. Explain the practical differences between a legal mortgage and an equitable mortgage. (**16**)

7. What is a second mortgage? (**18**)

8. In what circumstances will a contract be set aside on the grounds of undue influence? (**20**)

9. What was unusual about *Lloyds Bank Ltd v Bundy* (1975)? (**20**)

10. What is the most usual method a bank can adopt to avoid its customer seeking to rescind a security contract for undue influence? **(20)**

11. What effect does misrepresentation have on a contract? **(21)**

12. To what extent does a bank owe a legal duty to explain a security document to the provider of security? **(22)**

13. What is a plea of *non est factum*? Why is a successful plea unlikely, but, what is its effect if successfully pleaded? **(22)**

14. What effect does a forged signature have on a security form? **(24)**

15. Explain the purpose of the 'all monies' and 'continuing security' security clauses found in standard bank guarantee forms. **(26–7)**

16. Give examples of clauses specific to third-party security forms. **(32)**

17. Explain the effect of notice of a second charge on a 'continuing security' clause. **(34)**

18. State the *Rule* in *Clayton's Case* (1816). **(36)**

19. Distinguish between real and personal property. **(37)**

20. Distinguish between a *chose in action* and a *chose in possession*. **(38)**

12

Land as security

An introduction

1. What is land?

(a) *Land*. At law the term 'land' embraces not only the visible surface of the Earth, but also, in theory, everything above and below the surface and rights over land.

When the term is used in Acts of Parliament, the Interpretation Act 1978 defines it as including, 'buildings and other structures, land covered with water, and any estate, interest, easement, servitude or right in or over land'.

Hence, in addition to the visible surface of the Earth, land can be said to include minerals, buildings, fixtures in buildings, reasonable rights in the airspace above the surface and rights over another person's land, such as a right of way.

(b) *Fixtures*. Fixtures are things that, at law, have become part of the land or building to which they are attached.

In deciding whether an object is a fixture, the court looks at the degree to which it is attached to the building (the greater the degree of annexation, the more likely it is to be a fixture) and, more importantly, the purpose of the annexation. If the intention was to permanently improve the building and not merely to enjoy the object itself, it is a fixture, e.g. fitted cupboards in a house and permanent installations in a factory are fixtures, while pictures hung on walls and moveable machinery are not.

Example

In *Berkley* v *Poulett* (1976) CA, it was held that pictures fixed in the recesses of panelling in rooms, a marble statue (weighing half a tonne and standing on a plinth) and a sundial resting on a stone baluster outside a house, were not fixtures that passed to the purchaser of the house. They were *chattels personal* (*see* 11:37) and, accordingly, the seller of the house was entitled to remove them.

As what is in a building can be very valuable, whether or not an item is a fixture could affect the value of a bank's security. This is particularly true of industrial and commercial property, fixed plant and machinery, for example.

(c) *Real and personal property.* *Real* property consists only of freehold interests in land, while *personal* property is everything else, including leasehold interests in land (*see* below).

2.   Registered and unregistered land

Registered land is land the title to which has been investigated and is guaranteed by the state. *Proof* of title is the registers held at one of a number of district land registries and *evidence* of title is a land certificate issued by the appropriate district land registry.

Unregistered land is all other land, title to which is evidenced by a collection of deeds and documents (*see* 12:**23**).

Eventually, title to all land in the UK will be registered.

3.   Ownership of land: the historical background

Since the Norman Conquest in 1066, all land in England has been theoretically owned by the Crown and the same has been true of the rest of the UK for many centuries. The most that anyone else can own is one of the two legal estates that now exist: a freehold estate or a leasehold estate.

At one time, an estate was held on a certain *tenure* – originally the provision of goods and services of some kind and later the payment of a sum of money.

Tenancies and rents are very much part of modern land law, but they are very different from the original feudal ideas of tenure. These have now almost entirely disappeared.

As new demands from a rapidly changing society were made upon it, the system of land law was altered and added to. It was not reformulated. By the early twentieth century it had become completely archaic and extremely complicated as a result.

The Property Legislation of 1925, consisting of seven statutes, completely reformed the system of land law and *conveyancing* (the transfer of estates and interest in land). Specifically, it:

(a) Reduced all remaining feudal tenures to one common form – *common socage,* which may now be regarded as identical to the term *freehold;*

(b) Removed outdated concepts, in particular feudal rights;

(c) Introduced a system of registration and transfer of title to land based on that used for shares;

(d) Reduced the number of possible *legal estates* to two and the number of *legal interests* to five with the aim, in conjunction with (c), of simplifying conveyancing.

Estates and interests

4.   Legal estates

(a) *Definition.*A legal estate is a measure of a person's interest in a particular piece of land in terms of *tenure*. It gives the *right to the land* itself, i.e. possession.

A legal estate is an abstract idea and it is quite separate from the land itself. It can be bought or sold, transferred by gift or by will without affecting the actual land itself or the possession of it. It is possible, for example, to buy the freehold of a block of flats without in any way affecting the rights of occupation of the tenants in the flats. Similarly, a legal mortgage of the freehold, while conferring rights sufficient to ensure its adequacy as security, does not affect the use of the land or the rights of occupation until and unless the terms of the charge are broken, normally by non-payment.

By the Law of Property Act 1925, the number of legal estates was reduced to *two*: *fee simple absolute in possession* and *a term of years absolute*.

(b) *Fee simple absolute in possession (freehold).* All land in this country is now ultimately held on freehold tenure. For all practical purposes, this amounts to absolute ownership. A freeholder may, for example, dispose of the estate to anyone.

Nevertheless, there are important restrictions on the rights of freeholders to do as they please with their land. At *common law*, the law of torts prevents a person from using their land in a way that would cause an actionable nuisance to the neighbours and the right to develop land is restricted by the Town and Country Planning Acts.

Before 1925, there were a variety of freehold estates that the common law recognised, but, since the Law of Property Act 1925, only the fee simple absolute in possession is recognised as a *legal* freehold estate.

All the former freehold estates can now only exist as *equitable interests* in land (*see* 12:**5** below).

The words used in the term have the following meanings

(i) *Fee* – an estate of inheritance, i.e. one that may be inherited or may pass by will.

(ii) *Simple* – the inheritance is not limited to a particular class of the freeholder's heirs, e.g. males only, or the offspring from a particular marriage. (An estate where the inheritance was limited was known as a *fee tail*.)

(iii) Absolute – not subject to any conditions, as a *life estate* would be for example.

(iv) In possession – takes effect immediately and not, say, from 1 January 2000. The words include not only the right to immediate possession but also the immediate right to receive rents and profits where the land is leased to a tenant.

(c) *Term of years absolute (leasehold).* The owner of a freehold estate may create from it an estate of limited duration: a leasehold. This can be illustrated diagrammatically, as shown in Figure 12.1. The *freehold* of Whiteacre is owned by A. A leases it to B for 99 years (the head lease) for £5000 a year. B, in turn, leases most of it to C for 90 years at, say, £4500 a year and so on down the chain until a small part is let to F. Alternatively, the *whole* of Whiteacre could be sublet a number of times, often at a profit, leaving F as the last sublessee and the present occupier. Yet again, B could transfer (assign) the lease to C, who transfers it to D and so on. Here there only ever exists the *one* lease. In all three cases, the right to occupy the land normally reverts back to A (the freeholder) when the (head) lease expires, i.e. at the end of 99

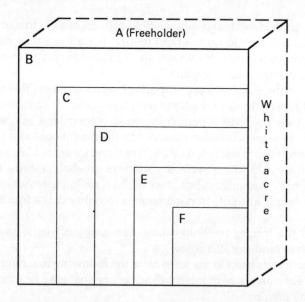

Figure 12.1 *Creation of leases*

years. The points to note from this are, first, that leaseholders are usually able to sublet their land and, second, provided each successive sublease is for a shorter period, a number of legal estates can exist at any one time over the same piece of land.

The words used in the term have the following meanings:

(i) Term of years – this includes not only leases for a specific number of years, but also those for less than a year or from year to year, although short leases are commonly referred to as tenancies.

(ii) Absolute – not subject to conditions.

The essential features of a leasehold estate are:

(i) It gives the right to exclusive possession.

(ii) It is for a definite term, i.e. the start of the term and its duration are fixed or can be determined.

NOTE: This is the essential distinction between a lease and a freehold, for the latter is of unlimited duration.

(iii) It creates the relationship of landlord and tenant.

At common law, the land reverts back to the freeholder at the end of the lease. However, the Leasehold Reform Act 1967 gives a leaseholder of a house, originally let for 21 years or more (a long tenancy) at a low rent, and who has held it for at least five years, the right to buy the lessor's freehold estate or to demand a new lease of 50 years when the original expires. This is known as *leasehold enfranchisement*.

(d) *The creation of a lease.* A lease for more than *three* years must be granted by deed to create a *legal estate*: Law of Property Act 1925 s.52(I).

A legal estate for a term not exceeding three years may be created orally or in writing, however, provided it takes effect in possession (immediately) and at the best rent that can reasonably be obtained.

A deed is required to effect a *legal assignment* of a lease, no matter how short the term (*see* 12:20).

NOTE: A contract to grant a lease, except for a short lease (*see* 12:20), must be in writing, contain all the terms agreed between the parties and be signed by both parties: Law of Property (Miscellaneous Provisions) Act 1989. A tenant who holds under an enforceable agreement to grant a lease will be in the same position against the landlord as they would have been had a deed been executed. Hence, provided specific performance of the contract can be granted, a written lease for a term *exceeding* three years confers an equitable term on the tenant.

5. Interests in land

(a) *Definition.*An interest in land is any estate, interest or charge in or over land or in or over the proceeds of sale of land: Law of Property (Miscellaneous Provisions) Act 1989 s.2(6). Thus, while an estate in land is also an interest in land, an interest in land is primarily a *claim against the land of another* less than actual possession.

Interests in land are either *legal* or *equitable*. The former must be created by deed:

(b) *Legal interests.* Legal interests are rights against the land itself (rights *in rem*) and are, therefore, enforceable against the 'whole world'. Thus, whoever acquires the land is bound by any legal interest that exists over it, whether or not they had knowledge of it.

NOTE: A legal interest must be held in fee simple absolute in possession or for a term of years absolute.

Under the Law of Property Act 1925 (as amended), there are five types of legal interest.

(i) An *easement, right* or *privilege* in or over land – such an interest may be a bare right over the land of another (an *easement*), for example a right of way, or a right to take something from the land of another (a *profit à prendre*), for example fishing or shooting rights.

(ii) A *rentcharge* – this charges a piece of land, quite independently of any lease or mortgage, with the payment of a periodical sum of money to the owner of the rentcharge. (For historical reasons, rentcharges are restricted to a few areas of the country, primarily Greater Manchester.)

NOTE: Under the Rentcharges Act 1977, the creation of rentcharges is prohibited subject to certain exceptions. Any remaining rentcharges will be extinguished at the end of a 60-year period beginning in July 1977, or on the date on which the rentcharge first became payable, whichever is the later.

(iii) A *charge by way of legal mortgage*, which is the interest of most practical importance to bankers and was introduced by the Law of Property Act 1925.

(iv) A *charge on land* that is not created by an instrument but *imposed by law* (such charges are of little practical importance today).

(v) A *right of entry* in respect of a legal term of years absolute or in connection with a legal rentcharge. (A landlord usually has a right

to re-enter if the tenant fails to pay rent or comply with the obligations (*covenants*) in the lease.)

(c) *Equitable interests.* An equitable interest was originally treated as a right enforceable against only the person who granted it (a right *in personam*), but was finally established as being enforceable against any person except a bona fide purchaser of a legal estate for value without notice of the interest or somebody claiming through such a person.

The Property Legislation of 1925 provided that all estates, interests and charges in or over land, both legal and equitable, other than the fee simple absolute in possession, the term of years absolute and the five legal interests listed above, would subsequently only take effect as *equitable interests.* For example, a life estate became a life interest, a fee tail became an entailed interest and a future fee simple absolute (that is, not in possession) became a *future interest.* All such interests must be created behind a *trust* (an arrangement whereby property is held by one person – a *trustee* – who must use it for the benefit of another – a *beneficiary*).

There are four important equitable interests that may exist independently of any trust.

(a) *A restrictive covenant* – an agreement whereby one person promises to restrict the use of their land for the benefit of another's adjoining land, e.g. an agreement preventing the land being used for the purposes of trade.

(b) *The equity of redemption* – the right of a mortgagor to redeem the mortgaged property on payment of the outstanding principal and interest.

(c) *An equitable charge* – an interest in land given as security for the payment of a sum of money. The chargee is entitled to take legal action for the sale of the land if payment is not made.

(d) *An estate contract* – this arises where the estate owner contracts to convey the estate to the other contracting party or to create a term of years in their favour from it. (The equitable interest arises at the time of the contract, but the legal interest does not pass until an actual conveyance or lease has been executed.)

Types of ownership

NOTE: This section might at first appear to fall more naturally under 'Title and its transfer', but you will see on closer examination that it is here because you need to be familiar with some of the concepts and terms covered in this section in order to be able to understand other parts of this chapter easily.

6. Legal and equitable ownership

There is both legal and equitable ownership of a legal estate in land. Legal ownership gives legal title to the estate and the equitable (or beneficial) interest in it gives the right to benefit from the estate. Usually the two forms of ownership are exactly combined and here the distinction is irrelevant. Where they are *not*, a trust arises – specifically a *trust for sale*, the legal title being owned by the trustee(s) and the equitable interest by the beneficiary(ies).

An equitable interest *distinct* from legal title would arise where someone other than the legal owner paid part or all of the purchase price for the land or where, under a family arrangement, the land *must* be used for the benefit of various family members, often children (who are unable to hold legal title themselves). The former situation is an example of an implied trust for sale (as arose in *Boland*), the latter an example of an express trust for sale (as arose in *Flegg*). (These cases are discussed in 12:**17**.)

Only a maximum of four joint owners can share legal title to land and where there are more joint owners a maximum of four must hold on trust for all. An example of this is where (up to four) partners hold legal title to partnership property for the benefit of all the partners, including themselves.

The legal owner can transfer title free from the beneficial interest (unless it is also an *overriding interest* in registered land: *see* 12:**17**), the beneficial owners being entitled to the appropriate share of the proceeds of the sale. This is known as *overreaching* (*see* 12:**13**).

NOTE: Overreaching of beneficial interests is important to a bank when it takes a mortgage over the land subject to them. Such a transfer may, of course, be a breach of the trust and, therefore, give the beneficiaries a right of action against the trustee, but this is not the concern of the bank.

7. Shared ownership

Shared ownership can take the form of a joint tenancy or a tenancy in common. If property is owned by X and Y under a *joint tenancy*, on Y's death, X automatically becomes the sole legal owner of the property. This is known as the *right of survivorship*. If, however, the property is owned under a *tenancy in common*, Y's share would pass according to the terms of Y's will or, if Y had not made one, according to the rules of intestacy.

Another important difference is that only joint tenants can hold a legal estate: Law of Property Act 1925 s.34. A tenancy in common only gives rise to equitable interests that must exist behind a trust for sale. Thus, if a tenancy in common is created, the legal estate must be held by the tenants as joint tenants (as legal owners) who, in turn, hold the property on trust for sale for themselves as tenants in common (the equitable or beneficial owners). The point of this is that it simplifies the transfer of the legal estate and taking charges over the property. Purchasers or mortgagees can deal with the joint tenants without concerning themselves about the beneficial interests that may or may not exist; these are overreached.

NOTE: Although legal and equitable ownership and shared ownership are normally associated and encountered in relation to land, both concepts can apply to any type of property.

Registration and protection of interests in unregistered land

8. Introduction

From a banking operations perspective this is more important to you than a knowledge of the interests themselves because it dictates the procedure used when taking a charge over land as security and the value of that security when charged.

9. Before and after 1925

With the considerable number of *legal* estates and interests existing *before 1925*, the purchasers of land took the risk of there being an estate or an interest in existence about which they were completely ignorant at the time of purchase but that would affect their possession *after* the purchase. On the other hand, the position of the holder of an equitable estate or interest was even worse. Their position was secure *only* if the purchaser had notice of their estate or interest; their equity (as it was and is known) would be lost if the legal estate was purchased in good faith and for value without notice of the equity.

After 1925, the position of a purchaser of land was greatly improved, the number of legal estates and interests had been reduced, but this, in turn, meant that many more equitable interests would now exist and the *doctrine of notice* was no longer adequate protection for them. The Land Charges Act 1925 (now consolidated with later amendments in the Land Charges Act 1972) introduced a state system of registering interests over *unregistered land* and this is the key to their protection. A registrable right is void against a purchaser ('purchaser' includes a mortgagee) of the legal estate *unless it is registered*, even if the purchaser had notice of the interest.

> NOTE: The discussion so far has concerned only *unregistered land*, but, in fact, most urban land in the country is now registered and, in due course, *all* will be. Where title to land is *registered*, such interests (called *minor interests* under the registration scheme) must be protected by an entry on the *charges register* and not under the Land Charges Act. The effect is the same, however, and the old rules on notice similarly do not apply.

10. Land charges register

(a) *Introduction.* Under the Land Charges Act 1972, there are five registers of registrable interests, the register of land charges being the most important. This, in turn, is divided into six classes: A to F. Of these, classes C and F are the most important to you and are the ones you must remember.

(b) Register of land charges.

(i) *Classes A and B*. These contain charges arising under certain Acts of Parliament.

(ii) *Class C*. Included in this class are:

(1) A puisne mortgage, a class C(i) charge (*see* 12:**12**).

(2) A general equitable charge, e.g. an equitable mortgage of a legal estate not protected by a deposit of the title deeds with the mortgagee, a class C(iii) charge.

(3) An estate contract, a class C(iv) charge.

(iii) *Class D*. Included in this class are:

(1) A charge registered by the Inland Revenue for inheritance tax due.

(2) Certain charges relating to restrictive covenants and equitable easements.

(iv) *Class E*. Certain annuities, few exist.

(v) *Class F*. A spouse's right to occupy a house owned by the other spouse under the Matrimonial Homes Act 1983.

(c) *Register of pending actions.* Bankruptcy petitions are registrable actions.

(d) *Register of writs and orders affecting land.* Writs and orders registrable here are those that enforce judgments and orders of the court, e.g. a bankruptcy order.

(e) *Register of deeds of arrangement.*

(f) *Register of annuities.* Very few registered annuities now exist.

> NOTE: A legal or equitable mortgage of unregistered land supported by

a deposit of the title deeds with the mortgagee and the rights of beneficiaries under a trust for sale are *not* registrable.

11. Other registers
These are in addition to the national registration system.

(a) *Local land charges register* – these are kept at the registering local authority and record charges acquired by the local authority under statutory authority, e.g. charges for making up roads or laying drains and intended compulsory purchase orders;
(b) *Company registers* – if a company creates a fixed charge over its land or a floating charge over the whole of its undertaking, such a charge must be entered in its register maintained by the Registrar of Companies.

12. Puisne mortgages
The system of registering interests in land applies mainly to equitable interests, for these are the more vulnerable. However, some important legal interests are also registrable, in particular a *puisne mortgage* (pronounced 'puny').

A puisne mortgage is a *legal mortgage of unregistered land that is not supported by a deposit of the title deeds with the mortgagee*. It is a common security taken by banks to secure overdrafts.

Normally a bank would take a deposit of the title deeds as security, but with a second or any subsequent mortgage, the deeds will already be in the possession of the first mortgagee (for example, a building society or another bank) and therefore unavailable.

NOTE: A second mortgage and a puisne mortgage are not the same thing. A second mortgage is just by far the most common example of a puisne mortgage but there are other circumstances in which the title deeds are not available for deposit.

13. Overreaching

(a) *Meaning.* On the sale or mortgage of unregistered land, equitable interests incapable of registration in the Land Charges Registry can be *overreached* under the Law of Property Act 1925. This means that a purchaser or mortgagee (such as a bank) of the legal estate takes free from the interests *whether or not the purchaser or mortgagee is aware of them*. The interests overreached now attach to the proceeds of the sale and can be enforced against the trustees; they can no longer be enforced against the land itself. In other words, the interests still exist, but are represented by different rights, while title to the land can be freely and safely transferred because it is uncluttered by interests that could frustrate this.

(b) *Two trustees or a trust corporation.* Trusts for sale are not land charges and, therefore, the equitable interests arising under them cannot be registered. Thus, if land subject to a trust for sale is sold or mortgaged by at least two trustees (overreaching requires there to be at least two trustees or a trust corporation to be involved) the interests of the beneficiaries (the equitable owners) are overreached even if the beneficiaries are in occupation and even if the purchaser or mortgagee knew of the interest. In short, it is quite safe for a bank to take a mortgage from two joint owners (the trustees) of unregistered land.

(c) *Single trustee.* A sale or mortgage by a *single trustee* does not overreach the equitable interest, but a purchaser or mortgagee without *actual or constructive notice* of the interest still takes free from it at common law.

This principle would affect a bank where, say, A and B are married and A has an equitable interest in property of which B is the legal owner and B, without A's knowledge, grants a mortgage over it to the bank to secure personal borrowing. A's equitable interest is not overreached and the position depends on whether or not the bank has *actual or constructive knowledge* of the interest. If the bank has, its mortgage is subject to the interest; if it has not, it takes free of the interest.

Contrast the position if A and B were joint legal owners and a parent who lived with them had an equitable interest in the property by virtue of having contributed to the purchase price. In this situation, a mortgage by both A and B would overreach the interest of the parent because the mortgage would be taken from two trustees. As you saw above, this would be so *even if* the mortgagee knew of the interest. (The parent's interest would still exist, of course, but would be an interest in the proceeds of the sale of the property and not in the property itself.)

Actual notice is straightforward, but *constructive notice* (where notice should have been gained from the circumstances) is more complicated.

Constructive notice of the interest exists in the following circumstances.

(i) If the legal owner/mortgagor is not in actual occupation and the purchaser/mortgagee does not make enquiries of the person(s) in occupation.

(ii) If the legal owner/mortgagor is in occupation, but the circumstances are suspicious (a question of fact): *Caunce* v *Caunce* (1969).

Example

In *Kingsnorth Trust Ltd* v *Tizard* (1986), a mortgagor dishonestly stated that he was single. An inspection of the property, at a pre-arranged time when his wife arranged to absent, disclosed evidence of occupation by children, which he explained by stating that he and his wife were separated.

It was held that the circumstances were suspicious and the mortgagee was therefore deemed to know of the wife's existence. This being the case, enquiries should have been made as to her rights. As they were not, the mortgagee had constructive notice of them. The mortgagee's charge was therefore postponed to the wife's interest.

(iii) Possibly, where the legal owner/mortgagor is in occupation and there are no suspicious circumstances, if the existence of someone who may have an interest, such as a spouse, is known, whether or not that person is in occupation.

NOTE: the judicial trend towards giving spouses who are not legal owners greater protection suggests that (c) rather than (b) above may better reflect the way the law will develop on this issue.

Registration of title to land

14. Introduction

So far, this chapter has been primarily concerned with unregistered land. However, it was noted that title to all land in the UK will eventually be registered at one of a number of district land registries.

15. The registration system

This is governed by the Land Registration Act 1925, as amended. Essentially, the system replaces title deeds as proof of title to unregistered land and the separate investigation of title necessary on every conveyance of unregistered land with a title investigated and guaranteed by the state and proved by a state maintained register. Many charges and encumbrances affecting the land are also shown on the register. However, whether title to land is registered or not, charges acquired by statute by any local authority must still be registered in the local land charges registers and charges on land given by companies must be registered on the company's register to be valid.

NOTE: If title to land is registered, the system of registering land charges in the Land Charges Register *does not apply*.

16. Registered interests

Only the two legal estates – freehold and leasehold – can be registered.

17. Overriding interests

(a) *Definition.* Overriding interests are those interests that could be discovered by making enquiries of the occupier or by an inspection of the land itself and not, if title to the land was unregistered, from the title deeds and documents relating to the land: Land Registration Act 1925 s.70. They do *not* appear on the register.

Examples include:

(i) Legal easements and *profits à prendre*;

(ii) Rights of a person in actual occupation, except where enquiries are made of such a person and the rights are not disclosed;

(iii) Leases for terms of 21 years or less.

NOTE: Spouses' statutory rights of occupation under the Matrimonial Homes Act 1983 are *not* overriding interests. They are minor interests and must therefore be protected by a notice on the Register.

Overriding interests bind the purchaser or a mortgagee of registered land even though the purchaser has no notice of them and they are not mentioned on the register. The effect of overriding interests means that it is imperative for any would-be purchaser or mortgagee to make enquiries or undertake an actual investigation of the land and its occupancy, through a solicitor or surveyor perhaps, to ensure that no overriding interest exists.

NOTE: There are no age restrictions on holding an overriding interest and a bank's standard occupancy questionnaire will, therefore, require all present or prospective occupiers to be identified. However, the problems that would be associated with minors postponing their interests to those of banks mean that, in practice, banks only concern themselves with adults who are in actual occupation or likely to be so.

(b) *Rights of persons in actual occupation:*

(i) The basic position. A person who has a beneficial (equitable) interest in property and who is also in actual occupation of the property within the meaning of the Law of Property Act 1925 s.70(1)(g), has an overriding interest in it.

NOTE: No overriding interest arises if enquiries are made of a person in occupation and that person does not disclose their interest.

This interest cannot be overreached (*see* 12:**13**) on a subsequent sale or mortgage by a *sole registered owner* (sole trustee) and a possession order will not be granted against the occupier: *Williams & Glyn's Bank v Boland* (1980). If, in the same circumstance, title to registered land is registered in joint names, i.e. *two trustees*, then a purchase or a mortgage from the trustees overreaches even the overriding interest of the beneficiary: *City of London Building Society v Flegg* (1987). (These cases are fully discussed below.)

The rights of a person in actual occupation are the type of overriding interest of most practical importance to banks. If an overriding interest is proved, a legal charge is invalid – a legal mortgage can only be over the whole of the property – and the bank only has an equitable charge over the legal owner's beneficial share of the property, if any. Furthermore, the bank is unlikely to be able to enforce the sale of the property to realise its interest.

(ii) The beneficial interest. A beneficial interest will arise where a person contributes to the purchase price of the property but is not registered as a joint legal owner and where there is a common intention, express or, more usually, implied, that the registered owner is holding the property on behalf of both of them.

In most cases, there is a direct financial contribution to the purchase money by the person claiming the beneficial interest, which itself is evidence of the necessary intention, but, in some cases, the evidence of contribution put forward is less clear-cut and it is then a question of fact whether the contribution gives rise to a beneficial interest.

Example

In *Lloyds Bank PLC v Rossett* (1990) (HL), Mr R bought a house in his own name and with his own money. He and his wife were allowed to take possession before contracts were exchanged and Mrs R undertook, but did not fund, a significant part of the necessary renovations. Before completion, Mr R borrowed on overdraft from Lloyds and charged the property as security. Mrs R knew nothing of the arrangement. Later, Mr R exceeded his overdraft limit and L eventually sought to enforce their charge. By this time, the Rs had separated and Mr R was no longer living in the house. Mrs R, however, defended the claim, arguing that she had an overriding interest in the house.

It was held that the work done by Mrs R was neither evidence of a common intention that she should have a beneficial interest in the property nor sufficient contribution to establish such an interest. Nor could the necessary intention be implied by the mere fact of marriage or cohabitation. She, therefore, had no overriding interest in the property.

(iii) Actual occupation. Whether or not a person is in actual occupation is usually a straightforward question. However, when a

mortgagor's claim to possession is disputed, circumstances other than, say, living in the property may be put forward as constituting actual occupation. It is then a question of fact in each case.

Examples

In *Lloyds Bank PLC* v *Rossett* (1990) (HL), it was held that Mrs R was in actual occupation (but did not have a beneficial interest) by virtue of visiting the property daily to decorate, clean and supervise the renovations. Similarly, in *Kingsnorth Trust Ltd* v *Tizard* (1986), an ex-wife who visited the former matrimonial home every afternoon and stayed overnight in the property once a fortnight was held to be in actual occupation. Conversely, in *Abbey National Building Society* v *Cann* (1990) (HL), a mother whose personal belongings were moved into a house bought by her son some 35 minutes before the society's charge was completed, and who was abroad at the time, was held not to be in actual occupation.

Whatever is held to constitute actual occupation, it must exist *at the time the mortgage is completed* by transfer and payment of the purchase money, not when it is registered, which may be a month or so afterwards: *Abbey National Building Society* v *Cann* (1990) (HL).

(iv) The extent of the problem. Until recently, the problem of overriding interests of persons in actual occupation arose both when a person moved into a house newly purchased partly with funds from the mortgagee and also when funds were advanced at a later date. The effect of the decision in *Abbey National Building Society* v *Cann* (1990) (HL) is that the problem should only arise in the *latter* situation – a charge to secure advances made some time after the property is purchased. *Cann* decided that the time for determining the existence of an overriding interest is the time the mortgage is completed, *not* when it is registered. (As you read above, this is also the time at which actual occupation must be established.)

In the situation that occurred in *Cann*, where the purchase is partly funded by the mortgagor, partly by the purchaser and partly by a third party (C's mother in *Cann*) of whom the mortgagor is ignorant, the third party's beneficial interest arises at the same moment as both the mortgage and the purchase are completed, i.e. all three at the same moment. In practice, however, the mortgage monies are advanced to the purchaser's solicitor a few days before completion and this gives the mortgagee an equitable charge over the property that has priority over the third party's beneficial interest. (Remember also that in *Cann* C's mother was, anyway, unable to establish that she was in actual occupation.)

Contrast this with the position that would occur if the relevant time was the date of registration. By the time the mortgage was registered, the third party's beneficial interest would exist and very likely so too would actual occupation. This is, of course, exactly the position a bank still faces when it takes a charge to secure an advance *after* the property charged has been acquired; bringing the operative time forward to the completion of the mortgage instead of its registration makes no difference in this situation.

(v) Protection available. There are five methods by which a bank can protect itself against overriding interests when taking a mortgage as security.

(1) It can require the legal owner or prospective legal owner to complete a questionnaire and, in addition, inspect the property to satisfy itself that there are no persons in actual occupation.

NOTE: The questionnaire itself affords no protection but should disclose details of other actual or prospective occupants against whom the bank can take steps to protect itself.

(2) It can make enquiries of any person found to be in occupation; if that person does not disclose their rights, they are not good against the bank's charge: Land Registration Act 1925 s.70.

(3) It can require a person in occupation to become a party to the mortgage.

(4) It can require a person in occupation to postpone their rights to those of the bank – by a *deed of postponement*. (In both (3) and (4) possible problems of undue influence would have to be avoided: *see* 11:**20**.)

(5) It could require that the sole registered proprietor appoint a second trustee before the mortgage is taken: *City of London Building Society* v *Flegg* (1987). Note, however, that requiring the appointment of a second trustee in order to avoid a beneficial interest of which the bank has notice is likely to be considered as acting in bad faith, good faith being required for the overreaching principle to operate. This can be contrasted with the situation where a bank requires the appointment of second trustee merely as a precaution.

Of these five methods, (1) a questionnaire and inspection, should be used in every case but (4) is probably the most common device employed.

(c) *Boland and Flegg.* In *Williams & Glyn's Bank* v *Boland* (1980) (HL), Mr and Mrs B had bought a house with their joint earnings, although it was conveyed to Mr B alone and he appeared as the sole registered proprietor on the Land Registry register. Mr B's company borrowed money from the bank and he gave his personal guarantee as security. Without telling his wife, he also mortgaged the house to the bank under a registered charge to support the guarantee. The bank did not ask either of the Bs whether Mrs B had an interest in the house. Subsequently Mr B's company ran into difficulties and the bank called upon Mr B to pay under his guarantee. When he could not do so, it sought possession of the house with the intention of selling it to recover the money owed. Mrs B resisted the bank's claim. The House of Lords held that the bank's action for possession must fail. Mrs B's financial contribution to the purchase of the house gave her an equitable interest in the property and, because she was in actual occupation when the bank took the legal charge from her husband, her interest was an overriding interest: Land Registration Act 1925 s.70. The bank's rights under the mortgage were therefore subject to Mrs B's right of occupation.

The decision is of great importance in land law and of direct significance to banks. Furthermore, the decision goes far beyond the actual facts. It applies to all forms of registered property, not just to matrimonial homes and other dwelling houses, and it protects *any* person with a financial stake in the property who is in actual occupation at the time the mortgage is completed or the legal estate transferred (in the case of a purchase).

In *City of London Building Society* v *Flegg* (1987), Mr and Mrs F bought a house with their daughter and son-in-law, the Maxwell-Browns, but the property was conveyed into the sole names of the M-Bs on an express trust for sale for themselves as joint tenants. The M-Bs mortgaged the property to the plaintiff and subsequently defaulted on the repayments. The plaintiff commenced proceedings to enforce the mortgage against both the M-Bs and the Fs. The former conceded defeat and the issue was whether the mortgage bound the Fs. The House of Lords held that it did and a possession order was granted against them. The crucial distinction from the *Boland* case was that in *Flegg*, title to the property had been registered in joint names. (Note, however, that the Fs' interest was not ignored by the law, but it was an interest in the proceeds of the sale of the land, not an interest enforceable against the land itself.)

When decided, the *Boland* case alarmed banks because of its apparently wide application. However, the decision in *Flegg* clearly shows that the overriding interest arising under *Boland* is an exception to the general principle, that a beneficiary's interest under a trust for sale is overreached on a sale or mortgage of the property. Nevertheless, the decision in *Boland* is established law and it gives a clear warning. When a bank intends to take a charge over land from a sole registered proprietor it must identify all occupiers, ascertain their financial stake, if any, in the property and secure their agreement to the registered proprietor's mortgage.

18. Minor interests

These consist of all interests in registered land other than registrable interests (freehold and leasehold estates) and registrable charges, such as legal mortgages, and overriding interests. Examples include:

(a) The rights of a spouse to occupy residential property under the Matrimonial Homes Act 1983;
(b) Equitable mortgages;
(c) The rights of a beneficiary under a trust;
(d) The rights of creditors when a bankruptcy petition has been presented against the registered proprietor.

A registrable interest or charge that is not registered within two months of its creation also takes affect as a minor interest. For example, failure to register a legal mortgage on the charges register within the two months means that it only takes effect as an equitable mortgage.

Minor interests – which can only be equitable interests – broadly correspond to those charges registrable under the Land Charges Act 1972 in the case of unregistered land. Minor interests require protection by an entry on the Register and, as with registrable interests in unregistered land, knowledge of the interest is completely immaterial because registration has completely superseded the doctrine of notice. However, even when registered, some interests can still be *overreached* by a purchaser or mortgagee. One such interest is that of a beneficiary under a trust for sale.

Minor interests can be divided into four types.

(a) Those protected by entry of a *notice* on the charges register (*see* below) of the title effected. These automatically bind the transferee of the land. Examples include restrictive covenants and a spouse's rights in the matrimonial home.
(b) Those protected by entry of a *caution* on the proprietorship register. This ensures that the cautioner receives notice of any proposed dealings with the land and gives them a specified period (usually 14

days) in which to object. Examples include equitable mortgages, whether or not protected by a deposit of the land certificate, and interests under a trust for sale.

(c) Those protected by entry of a *restriction* on the proprietorship register. The entry is made by or with the consent of the registered proprietor and restricts their power to dispose of the property without first fulfilling some specified requirement. (Such minor interests would rarely affect a bank.).

(d) Those protected by entry of an *inhibition* on the proprietorship register. The entry can only be made by court order or by the Registrar and prevents any dealings with the land during a specified period. An example is a bankruptcy inhibition entered when a bankruptcy order is made against the registered proprietor.

19. Overreaching

The principle of overreaching applies to equitable interests in both registered and unregistered land. From the perspective of a bank as a mortgagee, the position with regard to a beneficiary's interest under a *trust for sale* is the most important. It is as follows.

(a) If the beneficiary's interest is not registered – and most are not – the bank is unaffected by it, *unless* the interest proves to be an overriding interest that cannot be overreached because the mortgage is taken from only one trustee, as in the *Boland* situation.

(b) If a mortgage is taken from at least two trustees or a trust corporation, even an overriding interest is overreached, as in the *Flegg* situation.

(c) If the interest is protected by a caution on the Register, it is still overreached and the bank's mortgage is unaffected by it, provided, again, that the mortgage was taken from at least two trustees or a trust corporation. The beneficiary's interest becomes an interest in the proceeds of the notional sale of the property, it is no longer an interest in the land itself.

20. The Register

This is divided into three parts.

(a) *The Property Register*. This describes the land and the estate for which it is held, refers to a map or plan showing the land and notes any interest held for the benefit of the land, such as easements or restrictive covenants.

(b) *The Proprietorship Register*. This gives the nature of the title (*see* below) and the name, address and occupation of the registered proprietor. It sets out any cautions, inhibitions or restrictions affecting the proprietor's right to deal with the land such as bankruptcy or liquidation matters pending. (*See* 12:**18** above.)

(c) *The Charges Register*. This contains entries relating to rights against the land, such as mortgages and restrictive covenants and notices protecting rights over the land, e.g. a spouse's right of occupation in the matrimonial home (*see* above).

Each registered proprietor is given a *land certificate* containing a copy of these entries. This is the document of title that is kept until the land is sold or changed. Proof of title is, however, the Register itself because the land certificate may become out of date through subsequent entries on the Register.

21. Registered titles

Four types of registered title exist. (This section is included for information only.)

(a) *Absolute*. This title is state-guaranteed and subject only to entries on the charges register and overriding interests.

(b) *Qualified*. This title is granted following an application for registration of an absolute title where the title can only be established for a limited period or subject to certain reservations. A qualified title is very rare.

Under the Land Registration Act 1986, it may be converted to title absolute or good leasehold (as appropriate) at any time and must be on an application by the proprietor, provided the Registrar is satisfied as to the title.

(c) *Possessory*. This arises where the proprietor has produced only *prima-facie* evidence of title. The title is not guaranteed prior to its first registration and must, therefore, be investigated by a prospective purchaser as though the title was unregistered.

Provided that the proprietor satisfies the Registrar that they are in possession of the land, the Registrar must convert a possessory title to absolute title on an application by the proprietor, provided that the Registrar is satisfied that the title or the land has been registered with possessory title for at least 12 years.

(d) *Good leasehold*. This applies only to leaseholds. It is evidence that the leaseholder's title is good, but it does not guarantee title to the freehold from which the lease was granted.

A good leasehold title may be upgraded to title absolute at any time and must be on an application by the proprietor, provided the Registrar is satisfied as to the freehold and any intermediate leasehold title.

Title and its transfer

22. Unregistered land

(a) *Freehold.* The freehold title to unregistered land is evidenced by a collection of deeds and documents. Together these show a chain of title concluding with that of the present owner. They are known as the *title deeds*.

Transfer is effected in two stages.

(i) The *contract* – this binds the vendor and purchaser to complete the transfer.

(ii) The *conveyance* – this transfers the legal estate to the purchaser. (By the Law of Property Act 1925 s.52(1), the conveyance must be by deed.)

A contract for the sale of land is subject to the usual rules of contract law, although it must be *in writing*, incorporate *all the terms* the parties have expressly agreed and be *signed by both parties* to be enforceable: Law of Property (Miscellaneous Provisions) Act 1989 s.2.

NOTE: Section 2 of the Law of Property (Miscellaneous Provisions) Act 1989 does not apply to (1) a short lease, that is one taking effect in possession for a term not exceeding three years and at the best rent that can reasonably be obtained; (2) a contract made in the course of a public auction; (3) contracts concerning investment business within ss.1 and 2 of the Financial Services Act 1986; and (4) a legal mortgage, because this constitutes an actual disposition in land, not a contract to do so, and therefore must be by deed.

The vendor must produce for the purchaser's inspection an abstract of title showing evidence of title going back at least 15 years to a good root of title. This may be a *conveyance*, a deed transferring the legal estate to freehold land from the existing freeholder to a purchaser or donee; a *mortgage*; or an *assent*, a signed document transferring the legal estate from the personal representatives of a deceased holder to the person who inherits the land under a will or the rules of intestacy.

NOTE: A 15-year good root of title is equally required for unregistered land to be acceptable as security. Banks will obtain a report on title from a solicitor where they are unable to satisfy themselves as to the prospective mortgagor's title.

From the time that the contracts are exchanged, the purchaser becomes the equitable owner, as an order for specific performance of the conveyance will normally be granted if the vendor refuses to execute it voluntarily.

Following the exchange of contracts, the purchaser (usually their solicitor) will examine the deeds, making such enquiries as they consider to be necessary.

Arrangements are then made for completion, at which the conveyance executed by both parties is handed over with the title deeds (of which the conveyance now forms part) in exchange for the purchase price – usually in the form of a bankers draft.

NOTE: The system of unregistered conveyancing has the disadvantage that the process of investigating the title has to be repeated each time it is transferred.

(b) *Leasehold.* A leaseholder can dispose of the legal estate by assigning to another person the whole of the remaining term unless prohibited from doing so by the terms of the lease. (An *assignment* is a deed transferring the legal estate in leasehold land. It is similar to the *conveyance* used to transfer title to unregistered freehold land.)

Subject to the same proviso, a leaseholder may grant a *sublease* for a term shorter than that which the leaseholder holds. Leases frequently contain restrictions on the lessee's right to assign or to sublet. It is quite usual for the lessor's prior permission to be necessary.

A leasehold title to unregistered land is also evidenced by title deeds, but the lease itself may be the only document.

Completion is similar to completion on a sale of freehold land. The lease will be delivered against a banker's draft for the consideration monies or payment of the rent. A copy of the lease will be placed with the title deeds. An assignment of an existing lease will, similarly, be delivered with other relevant documents against payment.

23. Registered land

Transfer of a registered title is effected by a short, simple form of registered transfer. This replaces the conveyance or assignment necessary to transfer title to unregistered land.

At completion, the vendor hands to the purchaser the land certificate and a signed registered transfer form against payment.

The land certificate and transfer are sent to the district land registry where the new proprietor is entered on the Register and on the land certificate. The land certificate is then returned to the new proprietor as evidence of title.

Mortgages of land

24. Introduction

We discussed the nature of a mortgage in Chapter 11 (*see* 11:**11**). We also distinguished in general terms between a legal and an equitable mortgage (*see* 11:**16**). The distinctions concern (1) the rights of ownership acquired; (2) the mortgagee's remedies; and (3) the form the mortgage must take. (Revise these important aspects before reading further.) The next sections deal in detail with the form mortgages must take, how mortgages are protected, the remedies a bank has if repayment is not made and the redemption and discharge of mortgages.

25. Legal mortgages

A legal mortgage of land can be effected in two ways – both *by deed*. By the Law of Property (Miscellaneous provisions) Act 1989 s.1, the deed must clearly be intended to be a deed and must be signed and witnessed. (A seal is no longer required.) The two ways are as follows.

(a) *By a lease to the mortgagee for a term of years,* subject to a proviso that the lease will terminate on repayment of the debt (cessor on redemption).

If it is a leasehold to be mortgaged, there must be a sublease for a term less by one or more days than the head lease. It is usual to make the term ten days shorter in order to allow for second and subsequent mortgages.

The term granted is long, normally 3000 years, but, on repayment, the term automatically ceases.

(b) *A charge by deed expressed to be by way of legal mortgage.* This is commonly known as *a legal charge.* It is a creation of the Law of Property Act 1925 s.85(1).

A legal charge does not give the mortgagee a term of years, but does give the same protection, powers and remedies as a legal mortgagee by grant of a term of years. A legal charge has the following advantages.

(i) Freeholds and leaseholds can be conveniently mortgaged together so duplication of forms is avoided and the security can be taken by merely listing the properties in the schedule to the charge.

(ii) A charge of leasehold property creates no sublease and therefore does not infringe any covenant against subletting in the lease.

(iii) The form of a legal charge is short and simple.

Banks invariably take a legal charge and not a term of years as security.

(c) *Keeping the mortgage deed.* In the case of *unregistered* land, the mortgage will normally be retained by a bank with the other title deeds, which will have been previously obtained from the prospective borrower. In the case of *registered* land, the mortgage (charge form) must be sent with a duplicate and the land certificate to the Land Registry. The Registrar will enter the charge on the charges register, retain the land certificate and issue a charge certificate, which includes one 'sewn-in' copy of the mortgage.

26. Equitable mortgages

A bank can obtain an equitable mortgage in one of two ways:

(a) By taking a *deposit of the title deeds or land certificate* together with a *written memorandum of deposit (contract)* incorporating all the terms of the mortgage and signed by the bank and the mortgagor. (Before the Law of Property (Miscellaneous Provisions) Act 1989 changed the law by requiring all contracts relating to land to be in writing and signed by both parties, a deposit of the land certificate *alone* created an equitable mortgage.)

(b) By taking a *general equitable charge.* Such a charge is unusual as it would be unaccompanied by the title deeds, but it can be created by any written memorandum (contract) signed by the parties in which the terms of the agreement, including the security arrangements, are detailed. The charge creates no actual interest in the property, but the bank can seek the court's sanction for the sale of the property if repayment is not made.

As an equitable mortgage does not convey a legal interest in the property to the mortgagee, the mortgage cannot be enforced without the consent of the court. In other words, an equitable mortgagee (unless the mortgage was taken by deed, *see* below) cannot sell the property without the court's permission while a legal mortgagee can. It is for this reason that the bank's standard *memorandum of deposit* includes an undertaking to execute a legal mortgage as and when called upon to do so by the bank.

27. Bank forms of mortgage

(a) Bank mortgages are not intended to be investments and, therefore, they must possess as far as possible the same degree of liquidity found in other forms of security taken by bankers. Hence, they will be made repayable on demand and enable a bank to realise the security with a minimum of formality on the mortgagor's default in repayment.

(b) *Legal mortgages.* It is usual for the mortgage form to contain the following clauses (*see* 11:**26–32**).

(i) *All monies.*

(ii) *Repayable on demand.*

(iii) *Continuing security.*

(iv) *The mortgagor's undertaking to keep the property in good repair and insured against fire.*

NOTE: In *Halifax Building Society* v *Keighley* (1931), it was held that the mortgagee was not entitled to sums paid to the mortgagor for fire damage under an insurance of the mortgaged property effected quite separately from his statutory and mortgage obligations to insure. Thus, the clause will expressly provide that the mortgagor's obligation to use moneys received under an insurance policy on the property to make good the relevant loss or damage, or in discharge of the mortgage debt, applies whether or not the mortgagor is bound to maintain the insurance policy under the terms of the mortgage deed.

(v) *An undertaking to observe all the provisions of the lease* (in the case of a mortgage of a leasehold) and if so directed by the bank to issue instructions to any tenant of the mortgaged property to pay all rents to the bank.

(vi) *A provision excluding s.103 of the Law of Property Act 1925.* This allows the bank to exercise its power of sale or power to appoint a receiver immediately, or after a minimum period of notice – usually one month – should a demand for repayment be unsatisfied. Under s.103, a period of three months must elapse between the *demand* for repayment and the *exercising* of the power.

(vii) *An exclusion of s.93 of the Law of Property Act 1925.* If not excluded, s.93 would prevent the bank from consolidating two or more mortgages on different properties taken from the same mortgagor. (Consolidation prevents the mortgagor from redeeming a valuable mortgage while unsatisfactory ones are left outstanding. The bank can therefore prevent the mortgagor redeeming one mortgage in advance of others.)

(viii) *An exclusion of ss.99 and 100 of the Law of Property Act 1925.* This deprives the mortgagor of the right to grant or surrender leases without the bank's consent. The grant of a lease on the mortgaged property would clearly prejudice a sale of the security and a surrender of an existing lease could lessen its value. A lease granted in contravention of the clause does not bind the bank. The clause does not, however, apply to a mortgage of agricultural land, provided the lease is granted in good faith: Agricultural Holdings Act 1948.

NOTE: If a bank (or any other mortgagee) is relying on the vacant possession value of the security, for example when making a temporary advance to enable its customer to complete the purchase of a house with a building society mortgage, it is important to ensure that the premises are not let on or before the date on which the mortgage is executed. In *Universal Permanent Building Society* v *Cooke* (1952) (CA), for example, C exchanged contracts for certain premises but had no right to possession before the completion date. She nevertheless let the premises, the tenant taking possession before completion. The day *after* completion, C mortgaged the premises to the plaintiff, the mortgage excluding her power to grant leases. C defaulted on repayments and the plaintiff sought possession of the premises.

It was held that the tenancy was protected because the tenant's title was completed in the one day in which C had a right to grant a lease free from the restriction of the mortgage.

(ix) A power to grant leases at a premium. This could be of considerable value where the mortgage is over a block of newly constructed flats, as selling the flats individually may be easier than selling the freehold or leasehold of the entire block.

(x) On receipt of notice that the mortgagor has entered into a contract for the disposition of the mortgaged property, the bank is *entitled to close the current or loan account(s) and open a new account(s)* with the mortgagor. Further, no money paid in or credited to the new account shall be appropriated towards or have the affect of discharging any part of the amount due to the bank on the closed account(s). (This clause deprives the mortgagor of the right to appropriate payments and, specifically, gives the bank the right to take the simple step of closing the account to ensure that the *Rule* in *Clayton's Case* (1816) does not operate to its disadvantage.)

(c) *Equitable mortgages.* A bank will take an equitable mortgage by a deposit of the title deeds or land certificate accompanied by a written memorandum of deposit containing all the terms and signed by the parties.

A memorandum of deposit will avoid any possible dispute over the nature of the deposit, i.e. that the deposit was purely for safe custody purposes, and include the same or similar provisions to those contained in the usual legal mortgage form (*see* above).

In addition, the customer usually undertakes to execute a legal mortgage of the property to the bank when requested to do so, thereby extending the remedies available to his banker.

A memorandum of deposit by deed may be taken. This will incorporate either an irrevocable power of attorney or a declaration of trust in the bank's favour. The former enables a bank to sell or execute a legal mortgage of the property in the mortgagor's place if the mortgagor proves to be uncooperative. Incorporated in a suitably worded deed, the latter empowers a bank to replace the mortgagor as trustee with its own nominee, thereby enabling it to deal with the property should the mortgagor be similarly uncooperative. The irrevocable power of attorney is the more common.

If the memorandum of deposit is not by deed and does not contain such provisions, the mortgagee must seek the court's aid in any action against the property.

28. Second mortgages

(a) It is possible for any number of mortgages – legal or equitable – to exist at the same time over one piece of land. A bank may be prepared to accept a second mortgage as security for an advance if the value of the property is sufficient to repay both the first mortgage *and* the proposed second mortgage, i.e. there is sufficient *equity* in the property.

The main disadvantage of a second mortgage is that the first mortgagee may exercise their legal remedies, e.g. their power of sale, without reference to, and therefore to the detriment of, the second mortgagee.

A sale of the mortgaged property by the first mortgagee extinguishes the second mortgage and, while the second mortgagee is entitled to the surplus proceeds of the sale, it might not realise sufficient monies to repay both debts in full.

NOTE: A second mortgagee can obtain complete control of the security by paying off the first mortgage.

(b) *Creation of second mortgages.* A second *legal* mortgage is created by:
(i) A charge by deed; or
(ii) A lease for a term longer by one day than the term granted to the first mortgagee in the case of a freehold; or a sublease for a term longer by one day than that granted to the first mortgagee in the case of a leasehold.

A second *equitable* mortgage is created by a general equitable charge. No deposit of title deeds or land certificate is possible as the former will be in the possession of the first mortgagee and the latter will be lodged at the Land Registry.

29. Procedure on taking a bank mortgage

NOTE: This section is intended as an introduction only; no attempt is made to detail the practice of different banks.

(a) *Investigation of title.* It is essential to ensure that the prospective mortgagor has a good title to the property that is offered as security. If there is any doubt or if the process of investigation could prove to be complicated, the investigation should be entrusted to a solicitor. This is more likely to be the case where the title to the property offered is not registered.

A search must be made of:

(i) The land charges register (unregistered land) or the Land Registry registers (registered land);

(ii) The local land charges register; and

(iii) The Registrar of Companies register of charges (where applicable), to ensure that the proposed security and the customer's title to it are not subject to unacceptable adverse claims, e.g. a spouse's right of occupation. Remember also the importance of ensuring that no overriding interests exist by use of a questionnaire and inspection of the property. If such an interest is disclosed, it must be postponed to the interest of the bank.

(b) *Valuation.* The value of the property to be mortgaged must be sufficient to cover the advance. If a bank is considering taking a second mortgage on the property, it is essential to ensure that there is sufficient *equity* in the property after the first mortgage has been repaid in full.

The valuation may be undertaken by the manager or a senior member of staff, but a professional surveyor is usually employed, particularly when business or unusual property is offered as security.

A mortgage of leasehold property requires particular care. The inevitable drop in value as the lease nears expiry must be taken into account. There should be no onerous conditions in the lease and rents and receipts must be checked.

(c) *Insurance.* A bank's mortgage form imposes an obligation on the mortgagor to maintain adequate fire insurance on the property with a company approved by the bank and to produce receipts for payment when requested to do so.

The mortgage will further provide that, if the mortgagor fails to maintain adequate insurance, the bank can do so at the mortgagor's expense. Notice of the bank's interest must be given to the company concerned.

(d) *Execution of mortgage.* On a mortgage of *unregistered* land, the mortgagor must sign the bank's appropriate mortgage forms and acknowledge receipt of the advance in writing. The title deeds to the land, if available, must be deposited with the bank. If the deeds are not available, e.g. where a second mortgage is taken, the bank must register the mortgage as a class Ci charge at the land charges register.

On a mortgage of *registered* land, the mortgagor must execute the appropriate charge and stamp it. The charge must be registered at the Land Registry.

(Registration and protection of mortgages is considered generally in 12:**31–32**.)

A *deed of postponement* must be taken from any person with an apparent overriding interest in the property, declaring that the bank's rights (to enforce the security) are free from their overriding interest and, where a property is registered in the sole name of one spouse, a waiver from the other spouse of rights registered under the Matrimonial Homes Act 1983. The opportunity to take independent legal advice before such a postponement or waiver is executed should be offered.

If the property to be mortgaged is vested in the names of joint tenants, e.g. husband and wife, and one signs a legal charge, forging the other's signature, the genuine signature creates an equitable interest over the signatory's interest in the property. The other co-owner is not liable on the mortgage: *First National Securities Ltd* v *Hegarty* (1982).

NOTE: Where the mortgage is third-party security from an individual or where the bank is uncertain that the prospective mortgagor fully understands the nature and consequences of the charge, the opportunity to take independent legal advice should be given (*see* 11:**19–23**).

(e) *Second mortgages.* Title, value and fire insurance arrangements must be investigated and approved. This is normally done by sending a list of relevant questions, together with the customer's written permission to answer them, to the first mortgagee.

The answers will usually be accepted without further investigation if the first mortgagee is another bank, a building society, an insurance company, a local authority or other similarly reputable organisation.

A bank must give formal notice of its mortgage to the first mortgagee, requesting confirmation of the amount outstanding and that the mortgage does not impose on the first mortgagee an obligation to make further advances. This last enquiry is made because the Law of Property Act 1925 s.94(1) entitles a mortgagee under such an obligation to *tack* (add) these advances on to the original advance in priority to the second mortgage, irrespective of notice of it.

Such an obligation must be a term of the mortgage. It does not arise merely because the first mortgage is expressed to be a continuing security as is the case in bank mortgages.

NOTE: In a bank mortgage the obligation is unusual but may be encountered where the mortgage secures an advance to finance the construction of a building or a residential development, its payment being made in stages. Without such a right, notice of a second mortgage when the development is still incomplete would prevent the bank gaining priority on subsequent advances while holding an almost certainly unsaleable security.

Notice to the first mortgagee is important for two reasons.

(i) Further advances. It prevents a first mortgagee – other than one under an obligation to make further advances – from making further advances that will rank in priority to the second mortgage. In particular, a first mortgagee whose charge includes a continuing security clause is not under an obligation to make a search before increasing the mortgage advance: Law of Property Act 1925 s.94(2). This would be the case in a bank mortgage securing an overdrawn current account or a fluctuating loan account.

NOTE: This concession applies only to mortgages, registration of a bankruptcy petition or a bankruptcy order, for example, would constitute actual notice.

If a search is made and discloses a second mortgage in these circumstances, the first mortgagee is considered to have had actual notice of the second mortgage.

Where title to the property is registered, the Registrar will have sent prior notice of the second mortgage to a first mortgagee whose security expressly covers further advances.

(ii) Documents of title. When the first mortgage is discharged, notice of the second mortgage imposes a duty on the first mortgagee to hand over the title deeds or land certificate to the second mortgagee. Direct notice is necessary to ensure that this is done because a mortgagee is under no obligation to make a search for subsequent mortgages on the discharge of their own mortgage.

(f) *Notice of a second mortgage.*

> NOTE: This important matter is considered here a little out of context to achieve greater coherence in the consideration of second mortgages.

As a standard bank mortgage never imposes an obligation to make further advances, it is not possible for a bank to tack further advances onto existing borrowing once notice of a second mortgage has been received. The bank's mortgage is terminated as a continuing security and action must be taken to protect its interests. The mortgagor's account must be broken and a fresh account opened through which all subsequent transactions must be passed.

This action will preserve the priority of the debt existing when the notice was received over the subsequent mortgage by preventing the *Rule* in *Clayton's Case* working to the bank's detriment.

> NOTE: The mortgage may contain an express exclusion of *Clayton's Case*, in which case breaking the account is probably not necessary (*see* 11:28).

Under the *Rule,* further advances on the original account cannot be charged against the security in priority to the second mortgage and subsequent credits to the account would reduce and perhaps ultimately extinguish the amount secured by the mortgage, although the actual amount outstanding might remain the same or increase.

Example

In *Deeley* v *Lloyds Bank Ltd* (1912) (HL), the bank had advanced money against a second mortgage and was held to have had notice of a third mortgage to X, its customer's sister. The bank did not break the account as its own procedure required, however, and subsequent credits totalled more than its customer's debt to the bank. Its customer was subsequently made bankrupt and the bank sold the property for a sum just sufficient to repay the first and second mortgages.

It was held that the payments to the credit of the account after notice of the mortgage to X wiped out the advance outstanding at the time of the notice, that X's mortgage had priority over fresh advances, and that X was, consequently, entitled to the proceeds of the sale after repayment of the first mortgage.

A spouse's right of occupation, registered according to the Matrimonial Homes Act 1983, has the same effect for the purposes of s.94 of the Law of Property Act 1925 as a second or subsequent mortgage. Hence, a bank must protect its position as first mortgagee in the same way.

30. Advantages and disadvantages as security

(a) *Advantages*

(i) A mortgage of land possesses one overriding advantage: land never completely loses its value – indeed, a first legal mortgage of freehold land is the surest security that a banker can take.

(ii) Land has historically always appreciated in value.

(b) *Disadvantages.*

(i) Land is sometimes difficult to value for security purposes. For example, where the value depends heavily on planning permission, the possibility of this lapsing must be considered.

(ii) Greater difficulty and formality attach to a mortgage of land than to other forms of security.

(iii) Problems can arise with overriding interests and other rights of occupation.

(iv) Land is not an easily realisable security and realisation can possibly bring bad publicity to the bank (*see* 12:**34**).

(v) A second mortgage is subject to the rights of the first mortgagee.

(vi) An equitable mortgagee must seek the court's sanction in any action for realisation of the security.

(vii) Mortgages of leaseholds have specific disadvantages. The value of the security decreases as the term expires and the lease may impose restrictions on the leaseholder's ability to charge the property. The lease may also state that the lease is automatically forfeited if the leaseholder is declared bankrupt, thereby nullifying the bank's security.

Registration and protection of mortgages

31. Unregistered land

(a) *Accompanied by a deposit of the title deeds.* A mortgage of unregistered land, whether legal or equitable, accompanied by a deposit of the title deeds *cannot* be registered.

An exception exists where the mortgage is given by a company. In this case it *must* be registered in accordance with s.395 of the Companies Act 1985.

(b) *Not accompanied by a deposit of the title deeds.* Any mortgage that is unaccompanied by a deposit of the title deeds requires registration at the Land Charges Registry. If legal, it is registered as a *puisne mortgage*, if equitable, as a *general equitable* charge (*see* above). Most such mortgages are second mortgages.

NOTE: If the mortgage is a *floating charge* created by a company, it can only be registered with the Registrar of Companies.

With the important proviso that the first mortgagee in time holding the title deeds ranks first, priority among mortgagees is determined by the date of registration of the mortgages, whether they are legal or equitable.

A puisne mortgage or a general equitable charge is *void* against a subsequent mortgagee of the land charged *unless* it is registered before completion of the subsequent mortgage: Land Charges Act 1972 s.4. This emphasises the importance of registering the mortgage as soon as possible. It remains valid against the mortgagor, however.

NOTE: A prospective mortgagee can lodge a *priority notice* of the intention to register a charge with the Registrar. Provided the *actual* registration takes place within 30 days of lodging the priority notice and refers to it, the charge will be deemed to have been registered at the time the charge was executed.

32. Registered land

(a) *Legal mortgage.* This must be protected by sending to the Land Registry the land certificate, the original charge certificate and a duplicate, an application form and the Land Registry fee.

The Registrar will register the charge, retain the duplicate and the cover of the land certificate and return the charge certificate to the bank. This consists of the remainder of the original land certificate sewn in with the original charge form.

A second or subsequent mortgage is similarly protected by a charge at the Land Registry, a search certificate being sent in place of the land certificate. Details of earlier charges will appear on the charge certificate. Priority among mortgages is determined by the order of their registration on the charges register.

NOTE: A subsequent mortgage can only be registered with the consent of all prior mortgagees because all existing charge certificates must be returned to the Land Registry for updating. This gives a prior mortgagee the options of refusing to allow the registration altogether or to agree to registration providing the subsequent mortgagee agrees to a suitable postponement of their rights if the prior mortgagee wishes to continue lending against the security. This postponement avoids the *Rule* in *Clayton's Case* working against the bank (*see* 12:**29**). Should a prior mortgagee not agree to registration, the subsequent mortgage can still be protected by entering a caution on the register. It then takes effect as an *equitable* mortgage (whatever its form) and will rank *after* all legal registered mortgages and against any other equitable mortgage according to the dates of registration.

(b) *Equitable mortgage.* This is usually created by a deposit of the land certificate with the bank together with a memorandum of deposit. The bank acquires a contractual 'lien' on the land certificate and the charge then takes effect subject to overriding interests, registered interests and any existing entries in the Register: Land Registration Act 1925 s.66.

The mortgage must be further protected by sending a *notice of deposit of a land certificate* to the Land Registry, signed by the mortgagor or their solicitor. The land certificate should also be sent so it can be endorsed with the notice of deposit. After endorsement, it will be returned to the bank.

Having lodged a notice of deposit, the Registrar must give the mortgagee 14 days' notice of any proposed dealings with the land. In this period, a bank can take further steps to protect its interests, e.g. by taking and registering a legal mortgage, the mortgagor having undertaken to execute a legal mortgage on the bank's request in the memorandum of deposit.

However, entry of the notice is itself complete protection of the bank's equitable interest because subsequent chargees cannot claim to be without notice of it.

NOTE: A bank may be prepared to have a legal charge form executed but hold it unregistered to save its customer the Land Registry fees. Such an arrangement creates only an equitable mortgage, however, and must be protected by a notice of deposit of a land certificate. The legal charge can, nevertheless, be registered at any time. This would be done within 14 days of the Registrar giving notice to the bank of any proposed dealings with the land.

Protection of an equitable mortgage where the land certificate is temporarily unavailable is effected by lodging a notice of intended deposit at the Land Registry. This situation would arise, for example, where transfer of title to the mortgagor has not been completed.

When available, the land certificate will be sent direct to the bank. The original notice of intended deposit still stands and a bank need take no further action unless it considers it advisable to take a legal charge on the property.

Where the land certificate is not going to be available at all, an equitable mortgage must be protected by a notice or caution on the Proprietorship Register. This would be the case where a bank takes a second equitable mortgage. Until protected in this way, it is capable of being overreached as a minor interest (*see* 12:**18**).

An equitable mortgage by a company must also be registered with the Registrar of Companies.

The remedies of a mortgagee

33. Introduction

Bank mortgages ensure that all possible remedies are available to a bank should its security have to be realised. In particular, provisions are included to exclude certain sections of the Law of Property Act 1925, which would otherwise delay the realisation (*see* 12:2).

A legal mortgagee's rights are superior to those of an equitable mortgagee. A legal mortgage confers a right *in rem*, that is a right to the property itself, in addition to the right *in personam*, that is a personal right, against the mortgagor, while an equitable mortgage gives only a right *in personam*. Thus, an equitable mortgagee cannot take action against the property itself without the mortgagor's co-operation or the court's sanction and help.

34. Legal mortgagee

A legal mortgagee has five available remedies. These remedies are *cumulative* and *concurrent*. In other words, they may be used in combination at the same time to ensure that the full debt (but not more) is recovered.

(a) *An action for the debt.* This is an action to enforce the mortgagor's personal covenant to repay the capital sum and any interest owed. It avoids the delay and effort involved in realising the security, but is only suitable where non-payment is the result of unwillingness rather than inability. This remedy is, of course, a general remedy and it is available to an unsecured creditor. Strictly speaking, there are two separate rights of action – under the terms of the loan agreement and for breach of the covenant to repay contained in the mortgage.

After judgment is obtained a banker may serve a *statutory demand* on the mortgagor. The threat of bankruptcy proceedings can be an effective method of ensuring payment.

(b) *Sale of the property.* Every mortgage made by deed (legal or equitable) confers on the mortgagee a statutory power to sell the mortgaged property: Law of Property Act 1925 s.101.

Under s.103, however, the power may not be exercised until a demand for repayment has been made and the borrower has been in default for three months; some interest under the mortgage is two or more months in arrears; or the mortgagor has broken some other term of the mortgage. You have seen, however, that bank mortgages exclude s.103 and provide for repayment on demand or after a minimum period of default. A bank thereby strengthens its position as mortgagee against its customer.

There are statutory restrictions on a mortgagor's ability to exercise the statutory power of sale. These restrictions can relate to the power itself or gaining possession prior to exercising the right. Under the Criminal Law Act 1977 it is an offence to threaten violence against any person present on any premises to gain entry. Under the Protection from Eviction Act 1977, a court order is required to gain possession of residential premises, even if the mortgagor is temporarily absent, unless it has been abandoned. Any co-occupier must be joined as co-defendant in an action for possession. The court may suspend an order for possession if it appears that the mortgagor is likely to be able to repay the arrears within a reasonable time.

NOTE: A spouse's interest registered under the Matrimonial Homes Act 1983 will afford no protection *unless* it was registered *before* the charge under which the possession order is sought. A tenant protected against eviction by the mortgagor under the Housing Act 1988 is also unable to resist a possession order if the mortgage pre-dated the tenancy.

Where the legal mortgage is taken over residential property under a transaction regulated by Consumer Credit Act 1974, a court order is required before the property can be sold *unless* the mortgagor consents to the sale. The Insolvency Act 1986 also imposes restrictions on the power of sale (*see* 6:**14**).

The conveyance can be completed by the bank and a purchaser obtains a valid title free from any second or subsequent mortgage that may be outstanding: Law of Property Act 1925 s.104(1). Second or subsequent mortgages are extinguished.

NOTE: A mortgagor cannot prevent the sale by repaying the loan once the bank has entered into a binding contract with the purchaser: *Waring* v *London & Manchester Assurance Co.* (1935).

A mortgagee has considerable discretion with regard to the arrangements for the sale, but must act in good faith, e.g. the mortgagee cannot buy the property personally. Where there is a conflict of interests, however, the mortgagee can give preference to their own: *Bank of Cyprus (London)* v *Gill* (1979) (*see* below). They are not trustees of the power of sale for the mortgagor: *Cuckmere Brick Co Ltd* v *Mutual Finance Ltd* (1971) (*see* below).

NOTE: If there is a second mortgage on the property, it is usual practice for a bank to invite the second mortgagee to take over the first mortgage before exercising its power of sale.

A mortgagee owes a duty to the mortgagor to take reasonable care to obtain the true value of the property.

Example

In *Cuckmere Brick Co Ltd.* v *Mutual Finance Ltd* (1971) (CA), a piece of land with planning permission for houses and, subsequently, for flats was mortgaged to the defendants. In exercising their power of sale, the defendants did not state in advertisements for the property that planning permission for flats existed. This permission made the land more valuable.

It was held that the defendants had been negligent and their counterclaim for the balance of the advance was unsuccessful.

However, a mortgagee, in exercising their power of sale over mortgaged property, does not owe a person with a beneficial interest in the property of which it had notice, an independent duty over and above that owed to the mortgagor to take reasonable care to obtain a proper price: *Parker-Tweedale* v *Dunbar Bank PLC* (1989) (CA). (A beneficiary does, of course, have a claim against the trustee if the selling price is such that it constitutes a breach of trust.)

Banks usually prefer to obtain a professional valuation of the property and sell at or near the valuation price rather than sell the property by auction at which there is no certainty of a reasonable market price being obtained. Although the bank is always liable if the court holds the price to be too low, if it sells at or near the professional valuation price it will at least have a claim by way of indemnity against the valuer.

There is no obligation on the bank to wait for an improvement in the market or keep a business running pending sale: *Bank of Cyprus (London)* v *Gill* (1979).

A bank, however, is *trustee* of the proceeds of the sale, which must, therefore, be applied:

(i) To the costs of the sale;

(ii) In repayment of the mortgage debt and interest;

(iii) If surplus proceeds remain, in payment to subsequent mortgagees or, if there are none, to the customer.

It is necessary, therefore, to search the land charges register for second mortgages where title to the property is unregistered, because registration of a charge is equivalent to actual notice of it.

If title to the property is registered, a search is unnecessary provided the bank's mortgage was drawn to cover further advances by including a continuing security clause. This is because the Registrar is required to give a mortgagee notice of a subsequent charge in such circumstances.

(c) *Appointment of a receiver.* A receiver is appointed to collect the income from the mortgaged property. (The appointment must be in writing.)

A bank would appoint a receiver where a sale is impracticable, e.g. where the property is let or where the property market is depressed and a sale would be unlikely to realise sufficient monies to repay the advance.

Under a standard bank mortgage, power to appoint a receiver arises when the debt becomes due, i.e. when a demand for repayment is made.

The receiver is the agent of the mortgagor, not the mortgagee. Therefore, the mortgagor is responsible for the receiver's actions and stands the cost of the receivership. For this reason the appointment of a receiver is a more attractive remedy to pursue than entry into possession (*see* below).

However, should the bank interfere in the receivership and instruct the receiver, it may be liable for the receiver's actions: *Standard Chartered Bank* v *Walker & Walker* (1982) (CA).

Example

In *Standard Chartered Bank* v *Walker & Walker* (1982) (CA), the defendants had guaranteed substantial borrowing to 'their' company. This was not repaid and the bank appointed a receiver under its debenture and instructed the receiver to arrange for the quick sale by auction of the company's machinery. The sale was badly advertised and held during extremely bad weather. This resulted in the sale producing less than half the estimate. The bank was held to be liable to both the debtor (the company) and the surety (the defendants) for the shortfall because it had interfered with the receivership.

NOTE: It is usual practice for receivers to require an indemnity from the mortgagee for any liability in negligence they may incur during the course of the receivership.

The income collected by the receiver is applied:

(*i*) In payment of outgoings such as rates and taxes;

(*ii*) In payment of interest on prior charges (if any);

(*iii*) In payment of insurances required by law or by the mortgage and of their own commission;

(*iv*) In payment of interest due to the bank;

(*v*) If directed in writing by the mortgagee, towards repayment of the principal debt due (such a direction is always included when a bank appoints a receiver).

NOTE: If a receiver is appointed under a mortgage granted by a company, the appointment must be filed at Companies House within seven days.

(d) *Foreclosure.* Foreclosure deprives the mortgagor of the equitable right to redeem the mortgaged property (*see* 12:37) and the property becomes the mortgagee's absolutely. It makes no difference if the value of the property greatly exceeds the debt outstanding.

Under a bank mortgage, the right to foreclose arises after a demand for repayment has been made and a reasonable time has elapsed without repayment having been made. Foreclosure requires the court's consent.

In practice, this remedy is no longer used. While the term foreclosure is sometimes encountered, it invariably means that the mortgagee has entered into possession and exercised their statutory power of sale. In the late 1980s and early 1990s a fall in property values and an economic recession saw an increase in the number of mortgagors either unable to meet their repayments or with properties worth less than their mortgage debt or both. Sometimes properties were simply abandoned. It is probably to these cases that the term foreclosure is most commonly applied.

(e) *Taking possession of the property.* A mortgagee has the power to take possession of the property because a mortgage by demise gives a term of years and a mortgage by legal charge gives the same protection, powers and remedies as a mortgage by demise: Law of Property Act 1925 s.87(1).

Theoretically, a mortgagee can exercise this right even if there has not been a breach of the mortgage. It is usual, however, for the mortgagee to provide that the right shall not be exercised unless the mortgagor defaults in repayment.

Whether a mortgagee takes possession directly or constructively, i.e. by receiving income where the property is let, possession is at the mortgagor's own expense. The mortgagee is also accountable to the mortgagor for any income that would have been received but for the former's actions.

Example

In *White* v *City of London Brewery Co* (1889), the defendants took possession of the plaintiff's public house and let it as a *tied house*. A higher rent would have been obtained had it been let as a *free house*, that is one that could order supplies from any source and not just from the defendants.

It was held that the defendants were accountable to the plaintiffs for the higher rent that could have been obtained.

A bank will prefer not to take possession of mortgaged property because appointing a receiver (*see* above) achieves the same results without the expense and accountability involved in taking possession.

> NOTE: In addition to accountability to the mortgagor, entering into possession also involves accountability to third persons who enter the premises if they are empty under the Occupiers Liability Acts and possibly to the local authority for maintenance of the premises.

35. Equitable mortgagee

(a) *Mortgage under hand (in writing).* An equitable mortgagee who holds a mortgage executed under hand has only a right *in personam* (a personal right) against the mortgagor. Thus, a bank holding an equitable mortgage under hand cannot take direct action against the property; the court's sanction and aid to realise the security must be obtained if the customer is uncooperative.

A bank has the following remedies.

(i) An action for the money due.

(ii) An action for specific performance of the mortgagee's undertaking to execute a legal mortgage when requested to do so by the bank.

(iii) An action for the sale of the property.

(iv) The right to apply to the court for the appointment of a receiver.

(v) An action for foreclosure.

(vi) A possible right to take possession: this right only exists if expressly given in the mortgage because an equitable charge conveys no legal estate in the property to the mortgagee.

(b) *Mortgage by deed.* For practical purposes, an equitable mortgage by deed puts the mortgagee in the same position as a legal mortgage because s.101 of the Law of Property Act 1925 provides that any mortgage by deed gives the mortgagee the power of sale and the power to appoint a receiver. These are the two most useful remedies to a banker.

However, an equitable mortgagee is unable to transfer the legal estate in the mortgaged property because they themselves have only an equitable interest in it. Thus, by itself, the statutory power of sale is insufficient. To overcome this problem a bank's equitable mortgage by deed will always contain an *irrevocable power of attorney* clause and/or a *declaration of trust* clause – the latter including the power to replace the mortgagor as trustee. The former enables the bank to transfer the legal estate on behalf of the mortgagor; under the latter the mortgagor acknowledges that the property is held to the benefit of the bank, i.e. it will be sold by the mortgagor if the bank so demands.

NOTE: Any equitable mortgage is subject to prior equities. These cannot be overreached in the way that is possible when a legal mortgage is taken. An example that would affect a bank would be where one spouse gives an equitable mortgage over the matrimonial home held in his or her sole name when the other spouse has an equitable interest in it by virtue of having contributed to its purchase. An equitable mortgage is, of course, also subject to overriding interests (*see* 12:**17**).

36. Second mortgagee

A second mortgagee's remedies are very similar to those of the first mortgagee.

Theoretically the property can be sold without recourse to the first mortgagee but this is likely to be impossible in practice because the land would still be subject to the first mortgage. Therefore, a second mortgagee will usually seek to join the first mortgagee in the sale, the proceeds being applied in discharge of both mortgages.

NOTE: Under s.50 of the Law of Property Act 1925, a second mortgagee can apply to the court to free the property from the first mortgagee after paying a sum of money sufficient to repay the first mortgage into court.

Should a receiver be appointed, interest on the first mortgage must be paid *before* that on the second mortgage. The same applies to income received by taking possession of the property.

Redemption and discharge of mortgages

37. Redemption of mortgages

(a) *Introduction.* A mortgage is redeemed by the mortgagor repaying the advance. Once the mortgagee acknowledges receipt of the money, the mortgage automatically terminates: Law of Property Act 1925 s.115.

(b) *The equity of redemption.* A mortgagor has a legal (contractual) right to redeem the property on the date stipulated in the mortgage (if, in fact, a date is stipulated). After that date the contractual right to take back the property is lost.

Equity (the principles developed and applied in the old Court of Chancery), however, began to recognise a mortgagor's right to redeem the mortgaged property by giving *reasonable notice* and paying off the principal, interest and costs, even though the legal redemption date had passed. This became known as the *equity of redemption*.

Equity took the view that the mortgage was given only as a *security* and it was never intended to transfer the land to the mortgagee unless the mortgagor had no reasonable chance of repaying the loan.

The equity of redemption is an *equitable interest in land*. It can be sold, left by will or otherwise assigned.

NOTE: The equity of redemption is of academic interest only in relation to bank mortgages because they are expressed to be repayable on demand, not on a specified date.

38. Discharge of legal mortgages

(a) *Unregistered land.* A legal mortgage of unregistered land can be discharged by a *simple receipt* for the principal and interest: Law of Property Act 1925 s.115. This may be endorsed upon or attached to the mortgage deed. Bank mortgages usually include a printed form of receipt ready for completion when required.

Should a *third party* repay the advance, the receipt will acknowledge this. It will then operate as a transfer of the mortgage to the third party, e.g. where a guarantor pays off the whole debt and thereby becomes entitled to all securities deposited by the principal debtor.

Alternatively, the mortgagor can ask for a *formal reconveyance* of the property. This form of discharge is most likely to be used where several properties were mortgaged together and only one is being released or where only a part of the amount outstanding is being repaid.

If the mortgage to be discharged was unsupported by a deposit of the title deeds, it will have been registered as a puisne mortgage (a Ci charge) on the Land Charges Register. This registration must be removed by filing the appropriate form.

A bank that holds the title deeds may return them to its customer unless it has had express notice of a subsequent charge. It is not required to make a search for subsequent charges. Having received such notice, a bank must deliver the title deeds to the second mortgagee when its own first mortgage is discharged.

NOTE: This must be distinguished from a mortgagee's duty to make a search for subsequent charges when it has exercised its power of sale (*see* 12:**41**).

A legal mortgage, even though discharged, remains part of the chain of title to unregistered land and it must be retained with the other deeds by the owner of the property.

(b) *Registered land.* A mortgage of registered land is discharged by completing the Land Registry's Form 53 and sending this with the charge certificate to the Registry Office. The entry on the Register is then discharged. The charge certificate is cancelled and the land certificate, written up to date, is re-issued in its place.

Suitably amended, Form 53 can also be used where only part of the security is to be released.

Bank mortgages expressly cover further advances and the Registrar is therefore required to give a bank notice of any subsequent charge: Land Registration Act 1925 s.30(1). Thus, it is unnecessary for a bank to search the charges register before returning the land certificate or the surplus proceeds, if it has exercised its power of sale, to its customer.

39. Discharge of equitable mortgages

(a) *Method*. Equitable mortgages, whether by deed or under hand, are discharged by cancelling the memorandum of deposit. This is not a link in the chain of title and it can be retained by the mortgagee.

The title deeds or land certificate are then returned to the customer.

(b) *Removal of entries on relevant registers*.
   (i) *Unregistered land*. An equitable mortgage unsupported by a deposit of title deeds, e.g. a second equitable mortgage, must be registered at the Land Charges Registry as a general equitable charge (*see* 12:**31**). This entry must be removed.
   (ii) *Registered land*. An equitable mortgage of registered land will have been protected by a notice of deposit of a land certificate (*see* 12:**32**). This notice is removed by the Registrar on receipt of the mortgagee's written request to do so, accompanied by the land certificate. A bank makes this request by signing the reverse of its copy of the notice.

40. Discharge of mortgages given by companies

Company mortgages must be registered at Companies House. This entry must be removed in addition to any relevant entry considered in 12:**31** and **32**.

The company can file a *memorandum of satisfaction* with the Registrar and, although this is not obligatory, it is clearly advisable. The memorandum must be accompanied by a statutory declaration by the secretary and one director attesting the truth of the details it contains.

Progress test 12

1. Define land. (**1**)

2. Distinguish between real and personal property. (**1**)

3. State and explain the full legal terminology for freehold and leasehold estates. (**3**)

4. Distinguish between an estate in and and an interest in land. (**4 and 5**)

5. How may a leasehold estate be created? (**4**)

6. Distinguish between legal and equitable interests in land. (**5**)

7. List the five types of legal interests in land. (**5**)

8. What is a restrictive covenant? (**5**)

9. Distinguish between legal and equitable ownership of land. (**6**)

10. Shared ownership of land can take two forms; what are they and what is the difference between them? (**7**)

11. Which classes of land charges are most important to a bank? (**10**)

12. In addition to the land charges register, what other registers must a bank search before it takes a mortgage over land? (**11**)

13. What is a puisne mortgage? (**12**)

14. What is overreaching? (**13**)

15. With regard to overreaching, how does the position differ if there is a single trustee involved rather than two trustees or a trust corporation? (**13**)

16. Define an overriding interest, give examples of such an interest and explain the position of a bank that has taken a mortgage over land subject to an overriding interest. (**17**)

17. What form must the required beneficial interest in land take when a person claims an overriding interest by virtue of their occupation of property? (**17**)

18. Explain the decisions in *Lloyds Bank PLC* v *Rossett* (1990); *Kingsnorth*

Trust Ltd v *Tizard* (1986) and *Abbey National Building Society* v *Cann* (1990). (**17**)

19. In what ways can a bank protect itself against overriding interests? (**17**)

20. Distinguish between and explain the importance of *Williams & Glyn's Bank* v *Boland* (1980) and *City of London Building Society* v *Flegg* (1987). (**17**)

21. What are minor interests and how can they be protected? (**18**)

22. Name the three sections of the land register. (**20**)

23. Outline how title to land is proved and transferred. (**23**)

24. How does a bank take a legal mortgage of land and an equitable mortgage of land? (**25** and **26**)

25. List and explain the purpose of the usual clauses in a bank mortgage form. (**27**)

26. Why does the memorandum of deposit associated with an equitable mortgage contain an undertaking by the borrower to execute a legal mortgage when asked to do so by the bank? (**27**)

27. From a bank's point of view, what is the main disadvantage of a second mortgage? (**28**)

28. Briefly outline the procedure adopted by a bank when taking a mortgage. (**29**)

29. What is 'tacking'? (**29**)

30. When a bank takes a second mortgage, why is it important for it to give direct notice of the mortgage to the first mortgagee? (**29**)

31. Why must the mortgagor's account be broken when notice of a second mortgage is received? (**29**)

32. State the main advantages and disadvantages of a mortgage of land as a security. (**30**)

33. With respect to protecting a legal mortgage of unregistered land, what difference does possession of the title deeds make? (**31**)

34. How is a mortgage of registered land protected? (**32**)

35. In what circumstances would a bank lodge a notice of intended deposit of a land certificate? **(32)**

36. List the remedies of a legal mortgage. Which of these are usually pursued by banks? **(32)**

37. What statutory restrictions exist on a bank's power of sale? **(34)**

38. Why is the appointment of a receiver to be preferred as a remedy to taking possession of the mortgaged property? **(34)**

39. Explain the decisions in *Cuckmere Brick Co Ltd* v *Mutual Finance Ltd* (1971), *Bank of Cyprus (London)* v *Gill* (1979), *Parker-Tweedale* v *Dunbar Bank PLC* (1989) and *Standard Chartered Bank* v *Walker & Walker* (1982). **(34)**

40. Why is a bank in a stronger position if it takes an equitable mortgage by deed rather than merely under hand? **(35)**

41. How can an equitable mortgage overcome the problem of not being able to transfer the legal estate in the mortgaged property? **(35)**

42. What is meant by saying that an equitable mortgage is subject to prior equities? **(35)**

43. How do a second mortgagee's remedies differ from those of a first mortgagee? **(36)**

44. What is the equity of redemption and why is it of no practical importance in relation to bank mortgages? **(37)**

45. How is a mortgage of land discharged? **(38–40)**

13

Life policies as security

Life policies: the general law

1. Definition

A life insurance policy is a contract in which the insurer, in return for the payment of premiums, agrees to pay to the proposer a given sum of money on the death of the person whose life is insured or on a specified date before this.

> NOTE: To be strictly correct, a life policy is one of *assurance* not insurance because the latter term refers to contracts of indemnity, such as motor or fire insurance, under which a claim may never arise. Payment at some time is *assured* under a life policy.

2. Types of life policies

(a) *Whole life policies.* The sum assured is only payable on the death of the person whose life is insured. Premiums are lower than for an endowment policy (*see* below) because a claim will not usually arise for many years.

(b) *Endowment policies.* The sum assured is payable on a certain date or on the death of the life insured, whichever occurs first.

(c) *With profits or without profits.* Both whole life and endowment policies can either be with profits or without profits policies. The former type share in the profits of the issuing company, while the latter type do not. The premium for a with profits policy will be the higher of the two, for considerably more will be payable on maturity.

Although it is impossible to do so accurately, insurance companies will usually give an estimate of the maturity value of with profits policies based on the continued payment of bonuses at the current rate.

(d) *Policies covered by the Married Women's Property Act 1882 s.11.* Policies covered by s.11 are usually effected by a husband on his own life for the benefit of his wife or vice versa, his/her children or both.

NOTE: These policies must be considered separately because of the problems that can arise if one is offered as security (*see* 13:8).

Policies under s.11 create *trusts* in favour of the persons named in them. The proceeds of such a policy do not, therefore, form part of the policyholder's estate.

Any mortgage of a policy to which s.11 applies requires the consent of the beneficiaries and their signatures on the mortgage.

3. Parties to a life policy
There are three parties to a life policy.

(a) *The proposer.* The proposer is the person who wishes to take out the life assurance – the person who completes the proposal form. The proposer is usually also the life assured and/or the beneficiary under the policy.

(b) *The life assured.* The life assured is the person on whose life the policy is taken out and on whose death the policy monies become payable.

The proposer must have an insurable interest in the life assured (*see* 13:4).

(c) *The beneficiary(ies).* The beneficiary is the person entitled to receive the policy monies on the death of the life assured.

It is from the beneficiary(ies) that an assignment of a life policy must be taken (*see* 13:7).

Example
If a person takes out a life policy on their own life for their own benefit, the proposer (policyholder), the life assured and the beneficiary are one and the same person. If, however, policy monies are to be paid to persons other than the proposer, a trust is created and the beneficiaries must join in the assignment of the policy (*see* 13:7).

4. Insurable interest

(a) *Introduction.* The person intending to take out the policy (the proposer) must have an *insurable interest* in the life insured: Life Assurance Act 1774 s.1. A policy is void if no such interest can be shown.

A person always has an insurable interest in their own life and in that of their spouse, but in other situations the insurable interest required must be a *pecuniary interest*, that is the financial loss that would be suffered by the proposer on the death of the person whose life they insure: *Halford* v *Kymer* (1830).

The sum assured in such cases is limited to the amount of the pecuniary interest: s.3 of the 1774 Act; but where a person insures their own life or that of their spouse, i.e. where the insurable interest is *not* a pecuniary interest, the policy may be for any amount.

> NOTE: The insurable interest distinguishes a life policy from a *wager*, for they are similar in so far as they both provide for the payment of a sum of money on the happening of a future uncertain event. However, a wager *creates* the risk of loss, while a life assurance contract *guards against* the consequences of a loss.

A life policy may be *assigned* (*see* 13:7) to someone who has no insurable interest in the life insured: *Ashley* v *Ashley* (1892). (This rule is important because sale of the policy may be a more profitable alternative to surrender if the policyholder wishes or is compelled to realise the value of the policy before its maturity.)

(b) *Examples of insurable interests.*

(*i*) The interest of a creditor in the life of the debtor – to the amount of the debt; (This would include a bank insuring its customer, although this would be unusual.)

(*ii*) The interest of a guarantor in the life of the principal debtor – to the amount of the debtor's guarantee;

(*iii*) The interest of an employer in the life of their key employees.

> NOTE: A parent has no insurable interest in the life of a child, nor vice versa, purely on the grounds of parentage: a pecuniary interest must be shown. A parent would, for example, have an insurable interest in the life of a daughter who acted as their housekeeper. A parent may, however, effect a policy for a child in the child's name.

(c) *Termination of the insurable interest.* As the Life Assurance Act 1774 s.1 only requires an insurable interest to exist at the time the policy is taken out, the policy is not invalidated if the insurable interest subsequently ceases, e.g. when an employee leaves their employment or when a debtor repays an advance guaranteed by the proposer: *Dalby* v *India and London Life Assurance Co.* (1854).

5. Uberrimae fidei

(a) *Meaning.* All insurance contracts are contracts *uberrimae fidei* (of the utmost good faith). Both the proposer and the insurer are under a duty to disclose all *material facts* (*see* below) and failure by one party to do so makes the contract voidable at the option of the other, i.e. it is not sufficient merely to answer the questions asked, although the terms of the policy may vary this principle (*see* below). This rule applies however innocent is the failure to disclose.

In practice, it is the proposer who is most affected by the rule, since they alone are in a position to know all the facts that might influence their insurer.

(b) *Material facts.* A material fact is, therefore, one that would influence the judgment of a prudent insurer in fixing the premium or in determining whether or not to accept the proposal: Marine Insurance Act 1906 s.18. (This Act applies to all types of insurance contract: *Locker and Wolff* v *Western Australian Insurance Co.* (1936).) Whether or not a particular fact is material is a question of fact.

Example

In *Woolcott* v *Sun Alliance and London Insurance Ltd* (1978), the defendants issued a block policy of insurance to a building society. The insured were the building society and their mortgagors. The building society application form asked no specific question about applicants' characters but asked, 'Are there any other matters which you wish to be taken into account?' The plaintiff, in applying for a mortgage advance, answered that there were not, failing to disclose that he had served a long prison sentence for robbery. A claim arose on the policy. The defendants satisfied the society's claim to the extent of their interest but refused to pay the plaintiff's claim because he had not disclosed his criminal record.

It was held that they were entitled to do so. It also made no difference to the duty of disclosure that the policy was effected through a block proposal and not through individual proposal forms.

(c) *Modifications of the rule.* The common law rule on non-disclosure may be modified by the proposal form. This may provide that the inaccuracy of *any* statement made by the proposer will constitute grounds on which to avoid the policy, whether or not the statement is material to the assessment of the risk. Conversely, it may be provided that only fraudulent non-disclosure will constitute grounds for avoiding the contract.

It is usual, however, for the proposal form to specify that the questions it contains are to be the basis of the contract. Where this is so, the duty of disclosure is limited to these questions.

Insurance contracts are excluded from the Unfair Contract Terms Act 1977 and, therefore, the *uberrimae fidei* rule is unaffected by the 'reasonableness test', as are 'accuracy clauses' or others that exclude or limit the company's liability under the policy.

The rule is important to the use of a life policy as a security. Should a policy held as security be invalidated for nondisclosure of a material fact, the mortgagee's interest is similarly invalidated. Hence, a life policy can never be an absolutely safe security. However, most insurance companies, having accepted notice from a mortgagee, will honour the policy to the extent of the mortgagee's interest.

6. Suicide

It is a general principle of insurance law that a policyholder cannot claim for deliberately self-inflicted loss. Although suicide is no longer a crime under the Suicide Act 1961, this principle would defeat a claim on a policy by the representatives of a policyholder who commits *suicide while sane*, unless the policy expressly provides otherwise: *Beresford* v *Royal Insurance Co Ltd* (1938) (HL). *Insane suicide* is not considered to be a deliberate act and so does not affect the personal representatives' claim.

Most life policies do, in fact, expressly provide that suicide will not affect a claim, providing it takes place a given time after the policy is taken out.

Whether or not a particular policy contains a suicide clause is a relevant factor for a bank to consider should it be offered as a security. It is, however, quite common for a policy not containing a suicide clause to expressly permit an *assignee for value* to claim on it to the extent of their interest should the policyholder commit suicide while sane. A bank that accepts a life policy as security for an advance *is* an *assignee for value*.

7. Assignment of life policies

(a) *Introduction.* The right to claim under the policy may be transferred by the policyholder to another person, i.e. it may be *assigned*. The assignee is not required to have an insurable interest in the life insured: Life Assurance Act 1774 s.1.

> NOTE: The assignment must be taken from the *beneficiary(ies) of the policy,* that is the person(s) who will receive the policy monies on the death of the life assured. The beneficiary(ies) may or may not be the same person(s) as the proposer/policyholder and/or life assured.

(b) *Policies of Assurance Act 1867.* An assignment of a life policy must comply with this Act. Section 5 requires that the assignment must be by either an endorsement on the policy itself or by a separate document of assignment in the form laid down in the Act. The assignment must be signed and witnessed.

An assignee of a policy may sue in their own name for the policy monies (s.1), but this right is subject to two conditions:

> (i) *The assignee takes subject to equities.* This means that any defence which would have been available against the policyholder (the

assignor) is available against the assignee, e.g. invalidation of a policy by non-disclosure of material facts or a set-off for unpaid premiums: s.2. (A bank must bear this in mind when it is offered a life policy as a security.)

(ii) Notice in writing of the assignment must be given to the company that issued the policy under s.3. to vest legal title to the policy in the assignee.

(c) *Priority of assignments*. If there are *second or subsequent assignments,* priority between assignees is determined by the date on which notice of assignment was received by the issuing company: *Dearle* v *Hall* (1828).

Exceptions to this are as follows.

(i) A mortgagee who has *actual* or *constructive notice* of a prior assignment is postponed to it even though notice of the prior assignment was not given to the issuing company.

Example
_____

In *Spencer* v *Clarke* (1978), the plaintiff took as security an assignment of a policy that the defendant said he had left at home but would produce the following day. Notice of the assignment was duly given to the issuing company. The defendant had, in fact, already deposited the policy under a previous assignment, of which notice had not been given.

It was held that the first mortgagee's claim had priority because the mortgagor's failure to produce the policy constituted *constructive notice* of the prior assignment. On the facts, *possession* of the policy was more important than *notice* to the issuing company.

A bank must, therefore, insist on the production of the policy before accepting a mortgage of a life policy as security.
_____

(ii) An assignee loses their claim against the issuing company if it pays the policy monies in good faith to the assignor before notice of an assignment is received.

A life policy will state where notices of assignment are to be given – usually the company's principal place of business. The issuing company is bound by the Act to give written acknowledgement of the notice if requested in writing to do so by the assignee. A small fee is payable for this acknowledgement, although it is often waived.

NOTE: An assignment by way of charge by a company of a life policy on the life of one of its directors does not require registration: Companies Act 1985 s.395.

Life policies as security

8.   Inspection of the policy

Policies offered as security must be inspected in the following respects.

(a) *The life assurance company.* Most policies offered as security will have been issued by a reputable company that will present few problems. Policies of little known or recently formed companies are not favoured as securities. Any policy issued by a foreign company must be made payable in sterling at its London office:

(b) *Special restrictions in the policy.* These may relate to:

(i) Suicide (*see* 12:**6**);

(ii) Foreign travel;

(iii) Hazardous occupations;

(iv) Sporting activities;

(v) Residence.

Any restrictions on assignment in a life policy will prevent its use as a security. However restrictions on assignment are only common in *industrial policies* and these are not suitable securities as small weekly premiums are payable on them involving a bank in disproportionate effort to check that they have been properly paid.

(c) *Financial provisions.* A bank is primarily interested in the *surrender value* of a policy, for this represents its security. This will be checked, along with the capital sum assured and the amount and frequency of the premiums.

Endowment policies are preferred to whole life policies because they mature on a specified date. A *paid-up policy* is an even better security because no further premiums are payable and it will steadily increase in value.

(d) *Admission of age.* A policy will normally state either 'Age admitted' or 'Age not admitted'. This refers to the formal production of the insured's birth certificate to the issuing company as proof of their age (the mere mention in the policy of the age or date of birth of the insured does not mean that age has been admitted).

The insured's age *must* be admitted before the company will make any payment under the policy as premiums are related to age. The value of the policy is affected by an incorrect statement of the insured's age.

If a bank accepts as security a policy in which age is *not* admitted, it should obtain a copy of its customer's birth certificate and send it with the policy to the life office for admission of age to be endorsed on the policy.

(e) *Beneficiaries.* All the beneficiaries named in a policy to which the Married Women's Property Act 1882 s.11 applies (*see* 13:2) – often referred to as a settlement policy – must join the policyholder in effecting the assignment to the bank.

If all the possible beneficiaries are not identified with reasonable certainty or if any are under 18 years of age, no effective charge can be taken.

A plea of *undue influence* is always a possibility should a bank seek to realise such a policy. To avoid the risk of losing its security, a bank should ensure that a wife or 'child' receives independent legal advice on the effect of a proposed mortgage before they join in the assignment. At the very least, a *free will clause* should be added to the charge.

(f) *Ancillary matters.* A bank must also check that premiums have been paid up to date and whether or not there are existing charges on the policy.

If a previous assignment (the document of charge duly reassigned) comes with the policy, it forms a link in the chain of title to the policy and it *must* be kept with it.

9. Legal mortgage

A bank will take a legal mortgage of a life policy as follows.

(a) An assignment by deed of the mortgagor's rights to policy monies. Note, however, that a deed is not a legal requirement – the Policies of Assurance Act 1867 s.5 merely specifies that there be an assignment in writing.

(b) Giving written notice of the assignment to the insurance company, as required by the Policies of Assurance Act 1867 s.3.

This is done to:

(i) Vest legal title to the policy in the bank;

(ii) Enable the bank to sue in its own name;

(iii) Bind the insurer to pay the policy monies *only* to the assignee (the bank);

(iv) Prevent the insurance company raising a counterclaim or set-off for obligations arising after the notice;

(v) Acquire priority over earlier assignees who have not given notice, provided the bank had no actual or constructive notice of them when the advance was made; and

(vi) Preserve the bank's priority should there be subsequent assignments.

NOTE: The assignment must be taken from the beneficiary(ies) of the policy, i.e. the person(s) who will receive the policy monies on the death of the life assured (*see* 13:3).

A typical bank mortgage will contain the following clauses.

(a) An assignment of the policy to the bank, together with any accrued bonuses attaching to it.
(b) A clause providing for the reassignment of the policy to the customer (the mortgagor) when the advance has been repaid.
(c) An all monies clause.
(d) A clause making the advance repayable on demand.
(e) A continuing security clause.
(f) An undertaking by the customer to abide by the terms of the policy and to do nothing that would invalidate it. This includes the punctual payment of premiums and the production of receipts for them. If the premiums are not paid, the mortgage gives the bank the power to pay them and debit the customer's account accordingly.
(g) A clause giving the bank power to exercise its statutory rights under the Law of Property Act 1925 and under the policy itself (*see* 13:**11**) without the customer's consent.
(h) Exclusions of ss.93 and 103 of the Law of Property Act 1925.
(i) Where the mortgage secures the account of another person (a *third-party charge*), clauses:
    (i) Giving details of the account secured;
    (ii) Granting the bank the right to vary arrangements with the debtor without prejudicing its security;
    (iii) Allowing the bank to put any money received under the mortgage into a suspense account;
    (iv) Enabling the bank to give a valid discharge for the proceeds of the policy.

Many of these clauses are identical or very similar in purpose to those contained in a banker's form of legal mortgage over land. They are discussed fully in 11:**26–32** and 12:**27**.

NOTE: When a legal mortgage of a *duplicate policy* is offered as security, the possibility of fraud always arises, even though the issuing company will have made its own enquiries before issuing the duplicate. For example, a legal assignment of the original policy may exist of which notice, as required by the Policies of Assurance Act 1867, was not given, the assignment thereby creating an equitable interest only (*see* 13:**10**). Thus, a bank *must* receive a very good explanation for the policy's destruction to avoid being fixed with *constructive notice* of the prior charge: *see* 13:**7**, *Spencer* v *Clarke* (1878).

10. Equitable mortgage

A bank will take an equitable mortgage of a life policy by deposit of the policy, usually supported by a memorandum of deposit. The memorandum (the written contract between the bank and the borrower) is important because it will set out the purpose of the deposit, the terms of the mortgage (*see* 13:**9**) and the rights of the bank as mortgagee (*see* 13:**11**). An equitable mortgage by deed puts the bank in a particularly strong position (*see* 13:**11**).

In particular, the mortgage will be made a continuing security, it will contain the customer's undertakings to execute a legal assignment on the banks' request and to pay the premiums as they fall due, the bank being empowered to pay them if the borrower does not.

NOTE: An equitable mortgage of a life policy can be created by oral agreement or by deposit of the policy without a memorandum of deposit. Such mortgages are good against the mortgagor's trustee in bankruptcy because the policy vests in the trustee, subject to all equities existing at the date of the commencement of the bankruptcy: *Re Wallis* (1902). Banks, however, would never willingly take an equitable mortgage without a memorandum of deposit.

There is no legal requirement for notice of an equitable mortgage to be given to the issuing company, nor for the company to recognise an equitable interest. However, most companies will acknowledge notice if it is sent. This will give the mortgagee priority over previous equitable mortgagees, provided that it did not have actual or constructive notice of the prior interest at the time the advance was made. The company may also tell the bank of any prior problems with the policy, e.g. irregular payment of premiums. A bank will, therefore, always give notice of any equitable mortgage that it takes.

Where notice is *not* given, priority between equitable mortgages is determined by their date.

NOTE: An equitable mortgage of a life policy is comparatively rare because a legal mortgage is easily effected and provides a much better security (*see* 13:**14**).

11. Remedies of a mortgagee

(a) *Introduction.* Enforcing the security will never realise the potential value of the policy and it will inevitably involve the mortgagor in considerable loss. A bank will, therefore, allow a customer every latitude before exercising its rights as mortgagee.

(b) *Legal mortgagee.* If the policy monies have become payable, i.e. the insured has died or the policy has matured, the mortgagee can claim the policy monies from the company, proof of death being required.

If the policy monies are not yet payable, the mortgagee may do one of the following.

(i) Surrender the policy to the company. This right is expressly given in a bank's mortgage form.

(ii) Obtain a loan from the insurance company against the policy. The mortgagor's cooperation is necessary to do this because they must make the application to the company and authorise payment of the loan direct to the bank in exchange for the policy and the mortgage duly discharged.

(iii) Sell the policy. Sale is an alternative to surrender of the policy and it may realise a considerably larger sum. As s.103 of the Law of Property Act 1925 is excluded in bank mortgages, the power of sale can be exercised as soon as the customer defaults in repayment.

(iv) Convert the policy into a paid-up policy for a smaller capital sum. This remedy is useful when the customer is unable to pay the premiums. The surrender value of the policy is seldom affected.

(c) *Equitable mortgagee.* If the policy monies are payable, the insured or, if they have died, their personal representatives must join with the bank in a receipt for the policy monies. This is because the *legal title* is still vested in the insured or became vested in their personal representatives on their death.

If the policy monies are not yet payable, the mortgagee may do one of the following.

(i) Ask the mortgagor to execute a legal assignment of the policy. The customer's undertaking to do this is included in a bank's memorandum of deposit. (This would enable a bank to exercise the more extensive rights of a legal mortgagee.)

(ii) Seek the mortgagor's agreement to the sale or surrender of the policy.

(iii) Apply to the court for an order of sale or a foreclosure order if the customer proves to be uncooperative. An order for sale is far more common than a foreclosure order, but, should the latter be granted, the policy becomes the mortgagee's absolutely (subject to prior equities) and they can then surrender it.

A sale must be effected in good faith and reasonable care must be taken to obtain the best possible price for the policy.

(iv) Seek the mortgagor's consent and aid in converting the security into a paid-up policy or in obtaining a loan from the issuing company sufficient to pay off the advance. This course of action keeps the policy alive.

NOTE: If the mortgage was by deed, the statutory power of sale on default will arise: Law of Property Act 1925 s.101. If an irrevocable power of attorney is included, this will enable the bank to surrender or sell the policy in the name of the assignor.

12. Discharge of the mortgage

In general terms, the security is released by reversing the procedures used to effect the security.

(a) *Legal mortgage.* The policy must be *reassigned* by deed. Bank mortgages of life policies generally have a standard form of reassignment printed on them ready for use. Notice of the reassignment must be given to the issuing company.

NOTE: The discharged mortgage forms a link in the chain of title to the policy. It must be retained with the policy for production when a claim is made on it.

(b) *Equitable mortgage.* Cancellation of the memorandum is a sufficient discharge of the mortgage. No reassignment is necessary because legal title to the property remains with the mortgagor throughout.

If notice of the mortgage was given to the issuing company, notice of the discharge must also be given.

The policy is returned to the mortgagor.

13. Notice of a subsequent charge

The customer's account must be broken to prevent the *Rule* in *Clayton's Case* (1816) working to the bank's detriment (*see* 1:**15**). A new account must be opened through which all transactions must pass. This account must be kept in credit or fresh security taken.

If a bank is forced to *realise* the security, it must pay surplus proceeds to the second assignee after repaying itself. If the advance is *repaid*, it must reassign the policy and deliver it with the original assignment to the second assignee.

NOTE: As a bank will retain the policy and the assignment of it when taking the security, its customer will find it difficult to find anybody willing to take a second assignment of the policy as security. It is, therefore, uncommon to receive notice of a second charge on a life policy.

14. Advantages and disadvantages

(a) *Legal or equitable mortgage?* Life policies are both a very common and a very acceptable type of security. However, it is uncommon for a bank to take an equitable mortgage of a life policy because a legal mortgage can be effected easily and cheaply (compare land) and offers considerable advantages, particularly the following.

(i) The issuing company *must recognise* a legal assignment if requested to do so by the assignee; it need not recognise equitable interests.

(ii) A legal assignee has an *absolute right to surrender or sell the policy*; an equitable mortgagee, unless the mortgage was by deed, needs the cooperation of its customer or the consent of the court.

(iii) A legal assignee can *give a valid discharge for the policy monies in their own name*; an equitable mortgagee must join with the insured or their personal representatives in the discharge.

NOTE: These latter two advantages of a legal mortgage arise because title to the policy vests in a legal assignee.

(b) *Advantages.*

(i) The *value* of a life policy can be easily ascertained, rarely fluctuates with market forces and steadily increases.

(ii) *Title* to the policy can be easily checked.

(iii) The security can be *easily taken*.

(iv) Realisation of the security by a legal mortgagee is quick and simple.

(c) *Disadvantages.*

(i) The mortgagor's *possible inability to pay the premiums.* A bank must continue to pay these in order to keep the policy alive if the advance has been allowed to exceed the current surrender value of the policy.

(ii) *Possible invalidation of the policy* and hence the loss of the security, either through the customer's breach of the *uberrimae fidei* obligation, or of the conditions in the policy, or because of the customer's lack of an insurable interest when the policy was effected, although this is very unlikely to arise in practice.

(iii) Some life policies are linked to unit trust investments and these can and do *fluctuate in value* in line with the general value of stock market investment, so their surrender values can be reduced if stock market values are particularly depressed.

Progress test 13

1. Define a life policy. (1)

2. Distinguish between whole life and endowment policies. **(2)**

3. To what policies does the Married Women's Property Act 1882 s.11, apply? How does this section affect the use of such policies for security purposes? **(2)**

4. Explain the roles of 'proposer', 'life assured' and 'beneficiary' in relation to a life policy. From whom must the assignment be taken? **(3)**

5. Explain what is meant by an insurable interest. Give examples. **(4)**

6. Explain the principle of *uberrimae fidei* as applied to life policies. How can it affect a bank holding a life policy as security? **(5)**

7. What is a material fact in the context of the *uberrimae fidei* principle? **(5)**

8. Does an assignee for value lose its claim on the policy if the insured commits suicide while sane? **(6)**

9. What is meant by assigning a life policy? **(7)**

10. State the provisions of the Policies of Assurance Act 1867 in regard to assignments of life policies. **(7)**

11. What form does a bank's legal mortgage of a life policy take? **(9)**

12. List the usual clauses to be found in a bank's legal mortgage of a life policy. Explain the purpose of each. **(9)**

13. How does a bank effect an equitable mortgage of a life policy? **(10)**

14. Why should a bank send notice of an equitable mortgage to the issuing company? **(10)**

15. List a legal mortgagee's rights if the policy monies have not become payable. **(11)**

16. List the remedies of an equitable mortgagee. How do they differ from those of a legal mortgagee? **(11)**

17. How are a legal mortgage and an equitable mortgage, respectively, of a life policy discharged? **(12)**

18. Outline the procedure that a bank should follow after receiving notice of a second mortgage of a life policy. Explain why the procedure is necessary. **(13)**

19. Why does a bank prefer a legal mortgage of a life policy to an equitable mortgage? **(14)**

20. List the main advantages and disadvantages of life policies as security. **(14)**

14

Stocks and shares as security

Types of stocks and shares

1. Introduction

The term 'stocks and shares' is used in this chapter to embrace a variety of securities taken by banks in addition to those issued by companies. Included are unit trust holdings, shares in building societies, National Savings securities and government and local authority stock.

> NOTE: Bearer bonds, shares registered in good marking names, National Savings securities and unit trusts are not included in the current CIB syllabus. They are dealt with in this chapter to provide a comprehensive coverage of the topic.

2. Company securities

(a) *Stocks and shares*. The number of shares or the amount of stock a person holds in a company is the measure of their interest in that company.

A company must initially raise its financial capital by the issue of shares but, once issued, paid-up shares may be converted into stock. Each shareholder then receives an amount of stock equivalent to the nominal value of their shares.

(The different types of shares are considered in 5:**16** and the distinction between shares and stock in 5:**17**. You should now refer to these sections.)

(b) *Debentures and debenture stock*. This is *loan* capital, not invested capital. Hence, debenture holders are creditors of the company and not members of it.

(Debentures are discussed fully in 16:**3–7** and debenture stock in 5:**17**. You should once again refer to these sections at this point.)

3. Unit trust holdings

A unit trust is established by a trust deed. It is a *trust* in the true legal sense of the word.

The trust's investments are handled by *managers*, often a limited company formed for the purpose, and the investments are held on behalf of the unit holders by a *trustee*, usually a bank or an insurance company.

The units are not bought on a stock exchange but direct from the managers to whom they may be resold. Daily *bid* and *offered* prices are quoted by them. These are the prices at which the managers will buy and sell the units.

The managers invest the funds of the trust in a portfolio of securities in accordance with the provisions of the trust deed. Some trusts are set up to hold a general portfolio, others concentrate on either high income or capital growth and others are mainly devoted to one particular sphere of investment e.g. banking or environmentally 'friendly' commercial and industrial activities.

Unit trusts enable investors to have an indirect holding in a wide portfolio of investments. They also gain the advantage of having their investments managed by persons with a specialist knowledge of the stock market.

4.   Building societies

A person can either *subscribe for shares* in or *lend money on deposit* to a building society.

Depositors are entitled to priority in repayment of their investment should the society be wound up. They therefore receive a marginally lower rate of interest on their accounts.

Building societies are a very popular investment with 'ordinary people' because they offer easy realisation of the investment, a good rate of interest and excellent security.

5.   Government and local authority loan stock

These may be *dated*, that is repayable on or by a specific date, or *undated*, but they always bear interest at a fixed rate on the nominal value of the stock.

Such stocks are always repaid at their nominal value. Thus, a person who buys at less than the nominal value and holds the stock to maturity will receive a capital profit in addition to regular interest.

British Government stocks are known as *gilt edged* stock and they are guaranteed by the state. Their value does fluctuate, however, in particular undated stock which carries a low rate of interest.

The stock issued by local authorities and major Commonwealth governments is regarded as being almost as safe as *gilts*. Confidence in stock issued by other foreign governments is determined by the market's assessment of the *risk* involved.

6. National Savings securities
The most important securities in this category are:

(a) National Savings Certificates;
(b) Premium Savings Bonds;
(c) British Savings Bonds.

These securities are guaranteed by the state.

Title and its transfer

7. Introduction
The types of stocks and shares were classified above according to the type of organisation that issued them. Alternatively, they can be classified by the method by which title to them is established and transferred.

A bank must view these classifications as being complimentary, rather than mutually exclusive, because both are important when 'stocks and shares' are offered as security for an advance.

8. Registered securities
These are the most common type.

(a) *Title.* The company or other organisation issuing the securities maintains a register in which the holder's name and address and the amount of their holding is recorded. This is proof of ownership of the legal title. The registered holder receives a certificate in their name. This is *prima facie* evidence of title: Companies Act 1985 s.186.

> NOTE: The share certificate provides no evidence of equitable ownership of the shares – they may be held in trust.

Every company maintains its own register of shareholders and stockholders. The holders of British Government Stock and National Savings Securities are registered on either the National Savings Stock Register, and receive a certificate issued by the Director of Savings, or in books kept at the Bank of England and receive a certificate issued by the Bank.

Although the certificate issued is not a document of title, it must be surrendered when the shares are sold. A duplicate can only be issued when the original is lost or destroyed and proper inquiries must first be made. In most cases an indemnity from the holder is required before a duplicate will be issued.

(b) *Transfer of title.* Legal title to transferable registered securities is effected by lodging the transfer form (*see* below) signed by the transferor (and sometimes the transferee) and the relevant certificate with the issuing organisation for appropriate entries to be made on the Register. A new certificate is then issued in favour of the transferee.

NOTE: National Savings Securities and the shares in some building societies are not transferable.

The form of transfer used is nearly always the *stock transfer form*. This form contains a statement of the consideration given (the price paid) for the shares, the names of the issuing company or other corporation, the number and value of the securities involved and details of the registered holder and their signature. It is not signed by the transferee.

NOTE: The introduction on the Stock Exchange of a computerised accountancy system led to the introduction of the *Talisman* transfer form, a variant of the stock transfer form. This is used on a transfer by sale of shares in public companies.

In a few cases the stock transfer form cannot be used e.g. on the transfer of partly-paid shares, and a transfer must be *by deed* or by a *common form of transfer* signed by both parties. These alternative methods are almost identical to one another.

The *stamp duty* on the transfer of registered stocks and shares is at the rate of 0.5 per cent.

NOTE: The introduction of Taurus (transfer and automatic registration of uncertificated securities) will replace paper share certificates with computer entries for shares in listed public companies. While the company register will remain proof of title, any transfer will be effected by means of a simple book entry in the Taurus computer; no collection and exchange of paper share certificates will be necessary.

Units in *unit trusts* can be transferred by any method approved by the trustees. It is usual, however, for the holder to realise their investment by selling the units back to the managers of the trust by completing the form of renunciation on the back of his certificate.

9. Bearer securities

(a) *Introduction.* Governments may issue *bearer bonds* and, if authorised by their Articles of Association, companies may issue *share* *warrants* to the bearer in respect of paid-up shares or stock. They can also issue *bearer debentures*. No records are kept of the holders of bearer securities.

Bearer securities attract initial *stamp duty* of 1.5 per cent and their issue requires the Treasury's consent.

(b) *Transfer of title.* Bearer securities are *negotiable instruments* (*see* 9:5). As such, title to them passes by mere delivery and a person who takes a transfer in good faith and for value acquires a good title, even though the transferor had either a defective title or no title at all.

(i) Scrip certificates and letters of allotment. Subscribers for Government stock receive a scrip certificate until all instalments have been paid. The certificate is then exchanged for the actual stock. Companies now use *letters of allotment* instead of scrip certificates for the same purpose when issuing shares or debentures.

Scrip certificates are fully negotiable, but the form of renunciation contained in the letter of allotment must be completed and signed in order to pass title to the shares or debentures that the letter of allotment represents. The renounced allotment letter is treated as a bearer instrument and the transferee is able to complete the form of application and send it with the renounced allotment to the company within the period stated to have the share certificate issued in their name.

(ii) American-type share certificates. These are a cross between registered securities and bearer securities.

On the one hand, title to them is registered with the issuing organisation, usually in the name of a London stockbroker or trust company known as a *good marking name*. On the other hand, by including a form of transfer and power of attorney signed by the registered owner, they are effectively *endorsed in blank* (*see* 9:14). They thereby become *quasi-negotiable* in that title to them is transferred by delivery.

They are not fully negotiable because a holder cannot enforce the rights represented by them in their own name.

Stocks and shares as security

10. Registered stocks and shares

(a) *Introduction.* These are the usual types of stocks and shares taken as security, stock exchange securities in particular.

Either a legal or an equitable mortgage can be taken. In both cases, a memorandum of deposit setting out the terms of the mortgage will accompany the deposit of the certificate because it serves to clarify the purpose of the deposit.

The memorandum taken for a legal mortgage may list the securities held, or may be phrased in general terms. This would be done where the mortgagor frequently changes their shareholding and the bank is willing to substitute new shares for those originally taken.

NOTE: It is not strictly correct to call the document a memorandum of deposit when it accompanies a legal mortgage. This is because *legal title* is transferred to the bank (usually its nominee company) by a legal mortgage and therefore a bank does not rely on the deposit as its security. In addition, it can realise the securities without the need for any express written statement of its power to do so.

(b) *The contents of the memorandum.* A memorandum will usually contain the following clauses.

(i) An all monies clause.

(ii) A clause making the advance repayable on demand.

(iii) A continuing security clause.

(iv) An exclusion of s.103 of the Law of Property Act 1925.

NOTE: These clauses have been discussed fully in 11:**26–32** and 12: **27**. You should now refer back to these sections.

(v) The mortgagor's undertaking to complete on demand any formalities necessary to perfect the bank's title to the securities.

(vi) A power of attorney clause enabling the bank to sell the securities.

NOTE: Clauses (v) and (vi) are only found in equitable mortgages.

(vii) A specified margin of cover clause. By this clause, the customer undertakes to maintain the value of the shares deposited at a given level above that of the advance secured.

(viii) In the memorandum for an equitable mortgage, the mortgagor charges and undertakes to deliver to the bank all bonus and rights issues received (*see* 14:**15**). (These would automatically be received by the bank when a legal mortgage has been taken.)

(ix) The mortgagor's agreement not to insist on redelivery of the actual shares mortgaged on repayment of the advance. (A bank can therefore redeliver shares of the same type and value. This avoids potential inconvenience.)

(x) A declaration that the shares are held as security, thereby avoiding a claim that they are held in safe custody.

(xi) Where the account secured is that of a third party, the memorandum will include clauses similar to those in guarantees e.g. a clause allowing the bank to vary arrangements with the debtor without prejudicing its security.

(xii) A re-pledge clause, enabling the bank to use the securities deposited to secure its own borrowing. (This clause is associated with the memoranda of *merchant banks.*)

NOTE: A memorandum signed by joint holders of securities must impose joint and several liability if the bank wishes to take security over separately owned securities as well as over jointly owned securities.

(c) *Legal mortgage.* A legal mortgage is effected by transferring legal title to the shares to the bank or, more usually, its nominee company. This is done by taking the share certificate and a signed and completed share transfer form from the customer and sending these to the company. A transfer for security purposes attracts nominal stamp duty of 50p (*see* 14:8).

Letters of allotment are occasionally taken as security, provided that they are in favour of the customer and fully paid.

When the form of renunciation is signed, the allotment letter effectively becomes a bearer security and can be mortgaged by deposit with the usual memorandum of deposit. A bank is then able to complete the acceptance form and obtain a legal mortgage of the shares by having them registered in the name of its nominee company.

Alternatively, if repayment is not made, the bank is able to sell the shares by delivering the letter of allotment with renunciation in blank to the purchaser, who is then able to complete the form of acceptance and acquire legal title to the shares.

NOTE: Most banks will prefer to take an equitable mortgage and a blank transfer (*see* below) rather than a legal mortgage. This avoids the administrative cost that would follow from being registered as the holder of the shares and therefore receiving all communications from the company to its shareholders.

(d) *Equitable mortgage.* An equitable mortgage is created by a mere deposit of the share certificates. It is, however, standard practice to take a memorandum of deposit.

In addition, a bank will often take a *blank transfer* in order to strengthen its position should the advance not be repaid. The blank transfer will usually bear only the mortgagor's signature as transferor and details of the securities concerned; the transferee will not be stated.

A blank transfer enables a bank to transfer legal ownership of the securities to its nominee company by inserting its name as transferee (thereby completing the document) and registering the transfer whenever it considers it necessary to do so. Alternatively, the transfer may be completed in favour of a purchaser if the bank exercises its power of sale under the mortgage. Should the mortgagor die, however, the blank transfer form is unenforceable.

A bank holding an equitable mortgage *without* a blank transfer would have to obtain a court order for the sale of the securities if its customer was uncooperative.

NOTE: Until completed and registered, a blank transfer is subject to prior equitable interests. An example would be where the registered owner of the shares holds them as trustee; the beneficiary has a prior equitable interest in them. Once notice of any such interest is received, priority cannot be obtained by completing and registering the transfer i.e. by acquiring legal title to the securities.

In the very few cases where transfer of title must be by deed (*see* 14:8), a blank transfer cannot be used. This is because a deed must be completed at the *time of its delivery*.

A deed completed subsequently will only transfer an equitable interest and the transferee will take subject to prior equities, for example where the securities turn out to be trust property, those of the beneficiaries of that trust.

Should such circumstances occur, the bank's equitable interest would be good against the mortgagor's trustee in bankruptcy, who would probably be willing to repay the advance in order to obtain the securities and thereby augment the estate available for distribution.

NOTE: The introduction of Taurus (*see* 14:8) will not affect taking legal mortgages over shares in private companies at all and probably have little effect on the procedure for taking legal mortgages over shares in listed public companies. However, the method by which equitable mortgages over shares in listed public companies is taken *must* change, unless the shares are withdrawn from Taurus. It is likely to be possible to register some form of 'caution' against the owner of the shares on the company's register and make appropriate amendments to the memorandum taken as evidence of the mortgage. Equitable mortgages over shares in private or unlisted public companies, as well as those withdrawn from Taurus, will presumably be taken in exactly the same way as at present.

An equitable mortgage is taken of letters of allotment by deposit accompanied by a memorandum of deposit. The form of renunciation need not be completed by the mortgagor because the shares can only be exchanged for the letter and a bank can therefore easily obtain possession of them.

A blank transfer may also be taken to strengthen the bank's position when the actual shares are obtained.

(e) *Protecting an equitable mortgage.* In practice, a bank will never accept an equitable mortgage of stocks and shares where there is any doubt about its customer's ability to repay the advance; it would insist on a legal mortgage in such circumstances. Thus, when an equitable mortgage is taken, it is unlikely to be protected.

Two methods of protection for an equitable mortgage of *company securities* do exist, however, although neither is completely effective.

(i) Notice of lien. This is given by letter, informing the company of the interest and requesting acknowledgment of it. In the letter, a bank will enquire whether prior equitable interests exist over the securities and whether the company's Articles of Association give it a first and paramount lien over them for any debts owed to it by the shareholders.

NOTE: A company whose paid-up shares are quoted on a stock exchange cannot have such a lien. Thus it is restricted to those securities that are the least likely to be accepted as security by a bank i.e. *unquoted* or *partly-paid* shares.

The company can ignore or acknowledge the notice or state that, under the Companies Act 1985 s.360, it cannot record a notice of a trust on its register. Nevertheless, three advantages are gained by sending notice of a lien.

(1) On receipt, the company is prevented from exercising its own lien in priority to the bank's interest: *Bradford Banking Co Ltd* v. *Henry Briggs, Son and Co Ltd* (1866).

(2) Prior equitable interests will be discovered if the company keeps a record of them.

(3) If the company records equitable mortgages of its shares, protection is gained against the possibility of the mortgagor fraudulently obtaining duplicate certificates and then selling them to the detriment of the bank's interest.

(ii) Stop notice. This is a legal process by which a bank applies to the High Court for a notice to be served on the company requiring it to give it eight clear days' notice of any proposed transfer of the shares. This period enables the bank to take steps through the court to protect its position.

The cost and technicality of the process mean that it is seldom used.

(f) *Realising the security.*

   (i) Legal mortgage. The memorandum (or letter) of deposit gives the bank the right to sell the securities on default in repayment.

   (ii) Equitable mortgage. If a blank transfer was not taken with the security, either the mortgagor's consent and cooperation or a court order is required for the sale of the security.

   The memorandum will, however, contain the mortgagor's undertaking to effect a legal mortgage when requested to do so by the bank.

   If a blank transfer was taken, realisation is much easier. Merely depositing share certificates with a blank transfer confers an *implied* power of sale on the lender, the power being exercisable after reasonable notice to the borrower. If a memorandum of deposit was also taken, this will confer an *express* power of sale on the bank.

   If the memorandum of deposit was in the form of a *deed*, the bank has a statutory power of sale: Law of Property 1925 s.101 if a demand for repayment is not met. An alternative is to include an irrevocable power of attorney in the memorandum that will enable the bank to sell as agent.

(g) *Discharging the mortgage:*

   (i) Legal mortgage. Title to the shares must be re-transferred from the bank or its nominee company to its customer. Nominal stamp duty and the company's own registration fee are payable.

   (ii) Equitable mortgage. The certificates are returned and the memorandum of deposit is cancelled. If a blank transfer was taken, this must be destroyed. Notice of lien or a stop notice if lodged, must be discharged.

11. Bearer securities

(a) *Taking the security.* Bearer securities are charged by *pledge* (*see* 11:**12**) and not by mortgage.

   Bearer securities are negotiable instruments and their deposit alone is sufficient to transfer legal title to them. However, a bank will usually take a memorandum of deposit because this sets out its rights in the transaction.

   Provided that the securities are taken in good faith and for value (this includes securing an *existing* debt: Bills of Exchange Act 1882 s.27), and without notice of any defect in the customer's title, a perfect legal title is obtained.

   The doctrine of *constructive notice* does *not* apply to negotiable instruments. This means that a bank is under no duty to enquire into the pledger's title unless it is aware of suspicious circumstances that merit investigation.

Example
_____

In *London Joint Stock Bank* v *Simmons* (1892), a stockbroker pledged bearer securities belonging to S, a client, to secure his own overdraft. S sued the bank for their return. He argued that, knowing the business of its customer, the bank should have enquired into their ownership before accepting the pledge.

It was held that the bank had a perfect title to them. On the facts, there were no suspicious circumstances involved in the transaction and the bank was, therefore, under no duty to make enquiries.

_____

(b) *American-type certificates.* As these are only *quasi-negotiable* (*see* 14:9), a deposit as security is an equitable mortgage and not a pledge.

A legal mortgage is effected by transferring the certificates into the name of the bank's nominee company – normally it would be a *good marking name*.

(c) *Discharging the security.* This is achieved by cancelling the memorandum of deposit.

12. National Savings securities

These are *not transferable* and, therefore, only an equitable mortgage of them is possible.

Thus, a bank is largely dependent on the honesty of its customer because it is possible to obtain duplicates of the securities deposited and obtain repayment.

Equitable mortgages are obtained over:

(a) *British Savings Bonds* by the deposit of the bond book accompanied by a memorandum of deposit (an *encashment note* should also be signed by the customer);

(b) *Premium Savings Bonds* by their deposit with a memorandum of deposit and a *repayment form* signed by the holder;

(c) *National Savings Certificates* by the deposit of the certificates with a memorandum of deposit and a *repayment form* signed in blank by the holder.

13. Unit trusts

Only an *equitable mortgage* of unit trust certificates is possible because the holder's interest is only equitable.

The mortgage can be created in two ways.

(a) *By transferring the units* into the name of the bank's nominee company and taking a memorandum of deposit; or

(b) *By depositing the certificates* with a memorandum of deposit.

The form of renunciation on the back of the certificate should be signed by the mortgagor because this will enable the bank to send the certificates to the managers of the trust and obtain repayment.

Notice of the charge should be sent to the managers who will acknowledge and record it.

14. Building society shares

(a) *Legal mortgage.* Providing the rules of the building society allow the transfer of its shares, a legal mortgage is obtained by transferring the shares to the bank or to its nominee company on the society's appropriate form. A memorandum of deposit will also be taken.

(b) *Equitable mortgage.* This is effected by depositing the passbook or share certificate and taking a memorandum of deposit. A repayment form, completed in the bank's favour, save for the date, may also be taken.

Notice of the deposit should be sent to the society, enquiring if it claims a *lien* on the account for money owed to it by the shareholder whether it has received *notice of withdrawal* and whether it has received *notice of any prior claim* on the account.

15. Advantages and disadvantages as security

(a) *Legal or equitable mortgage?* A *legal mortgage* has the following important *advantages*:

(i) It ranks before a prior equitable interest, provided the bank did not have notice of it when the charge was taken.

(ii) All dividends will be paid directly to the bank.

(iii) All rights and bonus issues will be made directly to the bank (the importance of this is explained below).

NOTE: A *rights issue* is the sale of shares to existing shareholders at less than their market price. A *bonus issue* is the issue of shares paid-up to existing shareholders, i.e. no payment is made for them. A bonus issue usually takes place where a company capitalises its reserves to make its shares more marketable – the issue will lower their market price.

(iv) Should the customer not make repayment, the bank has the right to sell the shares and transfer legal title to them to the purchaser.

A *legal mortgage* has the following *disadvantages*. These are not nearly so significant, however, and should be avoidable by good banking practice.

(i) The customer may be unwilling to pay the registration fees involved.

(ii) The customer may be reluctant to let the company know about the mortgage. This would most likely arise on the mortgage of shares in a private company.

(iii) Where the shares qualify the customer for a directorship, re-registration in the name of the bank's nominee company would disqualify the customer.

(iv) Extra administration in so far as the bank's nominee company as registered owner of the shares receives all communications from the company and these must be passed to the customer.

(v) The payment of calls on mortgaged partly-paid shares. The customer may not be able to reimburse the bank.

(vi) Possible forgery of the share certificate or the transfer form. This latter problem can be avoided by insisting that the transfer be signed at the bank. A bank is liable to indemnify a company for any loss resulting from the registration of a forged transfer presented by the bank: *Sheffield Corporation* v *Barclay* (1905).

NOTE: Further complications can arise where the bank holds more than 50 per cent of the company's shares. It may be deemed a bank subsidiary and its VAT position may be affected. If it is part of a group, group accounting may be affected. Smaller holdings may be caught by disclosure of interests regulations, but this problem can be avoided by disclaiming voting rights attached to the shares.

The main advantage of an *equitable mortgage* is the ease and cheapness with which it can be taken; the mere deposit of a share certificate gives an equitable interest. This attribute is particularly useful where the customer's portfolio of shares is actively traded. Provided the customer maintains the security to an acceptable value, the bank will usually be prepared to release particular shares when asked to do so. The bank is not involved in any transfer or registration procedures.

In the case of partly-paid shares, an equitable mortgage would usually be preferred to a legal mortgage as the customer remains liable to pay calls and not the bank.

A private company's Articles of Association may restrict the transfer of its shares and thereby enable only an equitable mortgage of them to be made.

Equitable mortgages have significant *disadvantages*.

(i) The mortgage will be postponed to any prior equitable interest in the securities, whether or not the bank had notice of it when taking the mortgage. There is no method of protection against this risk. For example, the shares may have been held by the mortga-

gor as trustee, in which case the equitable interest of the beneficiaries would rank before that of the bank. (Shares held in joint
names indicate a possible trust.)

NOTE: Completing and registering a previously taken blank transfer
does not give a bank priority over equitable interests once it has knowledge
of them: *Coleman* v *London County and Westminster Bank* (1916) (*see* 14:10).

(ii) The bank's interest would be similarly postponed if the company has a *lien* on the shares for money owed to it by its shareholder. (This is very unlikely to be encountered in practice,
however, and can only arise over shares in *private* companies and
unquoted public companies.)

(iii) There is a possible loss of title, either due to forfeiture following non-payment of calls on partly-paid shares or because the
mortgagor fraudulently obtains a duplicate certificate and sells
them. A *bona fide* purchaser obtains a good legal title on registration.

NOTE: Such fraud is easiest in relation to National Savings Securities as
the National Savings Stock Register will not record or acknowledge any
notice of deposit or lien from a bank or other mortgagee.

(iv) There is no completely satisfactory method of protecting an
equitable mortgage of stocks and shares.

(v) Notices from a company will be sent, dividends will be paid
and rights and bonus issues will be made *to the mortgagor* (possibly without the bank's knowledge) and not to the bank.

NOTE: A *bonus issue* made to the mortgagor may seriously devalue the
securities held. A 'one-for-one' bonus issue, for example, will usually
halve the value of the shares held because each shareholder has their
holding doubled. It follows that the security held by the bank will also
be halved in value, while the mortgagor could sell the shares received
instead of depositing them to maintain the value of the security.

A *rights issue* will also reduce the value of each individual share and,
hence, its value as security. A shareholder could, similarly, sell the rights
issue. Alternatively, they could lose their rights – and thereby prejudice
the bank – by failing to take up the issue in the prescribed time. In
addition, a rights issue is often made payable by instalment. After
payment of the first instalment, the shares become partly-paid securities
and can be forfeited by failure to pay the outstanding balance.

(vi) There may be difficulty in realising the security if the mortgagor refuses to cooperate and a blank transfer form is not held: if
one *is held* it is unenforceable if the mortgagor dies.

(b) *Advantages.*

(*i*) The customer's title to the securities can easily be established.

(*ii*) The current value of quoted stocks and shares can be ascertained easily and fairly precisely.

(*iii*) The security can be taken with little difficulty, formality or expense.

(*iv*) A legal mortgage can easily and effectively be protected by registering the mortgagee as holder of the shares in the books of the company or other organisation.

(*v*) Long-term stability in value, despite periodical setbacks. (A mixed portfolio of shares as security enhances this advantage.)

(*vi*) The security can be realised easily by selling on a stock exchange if a *legal* mortgage is held or a blank transfer for an *equitable* mortgage.

(*vii*) Release of the security is simple.

(*viii*) *Bearer securities* have additional advantages.

(1) As negotiable instruments, title to them passes by mere delivery and a pledgee acquires a perfect title despite any defect in or even the non-existence of the pledgor's title.

(2) Neither a pledge nor a transfer by sale incurs stamp duty.

(3) The pledge requires no formalities.

(4) The pledgee can always sell the shares without reference to the pledgor or to the court.

(c) *Disadvantages.* Certain disadvantages attach to certain types of stocks and shares and there is one general disadvantage.

(*i*) *Fluctuation in market value.* At best, a forced sale in a depressed market would disadvantage the bank's customer; at worst, it could realise insufficient monies to repay the advance.

NOTE: National Savings and building society securities do *not* fluctuate in value and the problem can be largely avoided with commercial securities by insisting on a suitable margin of cover and periodically revaluing the securities held.

(*ii*) *Partly-paid shares.* These may be forfeited for non-payment of calls. If held as security, the bank may have to pay the call for its customer in order to retain its security and a *legal* mortgage renders the bank directly liable to pay and this liability remains for 12 months after the shares are transferred out of the bank's name *if* the transferee of the shares fails to pay any calls. Such shares are, in addition, less marketable than paid-up shares.

(*iii*) *Unquoted shares.* These are normally associated with private companies, but unquoted shares in public companies may sometimes be offered as security, they are difficult both to value and to realise. They may first have to be offered to existing company members who can, to some extent, therefore, fix the selling price. Thus, the true value of the shares may not be realised and a mortgage of such shares is often considered as little more than evidence of a customer's means.

(iv) Shares in private companies. In addition to being difficult to value (they are unquoted) – the company's Articles of Association will often affect their value as security. They may prevent their use as security altogether, prevent another registered company (that is the bank's nominee company) holding the shares (only an equitable mortgage is possible in such a case) and/or restrict their transfer, thereby affecting their realisability.

Progress test 14

1. Distinguish between registered and bearer securities. (8–9)

2. How is title to registered securities transferred? (8)

3. Give an example of a transfer of registered securities in which the stock transfer form cannot be used. (8)

4. What initial rate of stamp duty do bearer securities attract? (9)

5. How is title to bearer securities transferred? Why? (9)

6. What are scrip certificates and letters of allotment? (9)

7. How do American-type share certificates differ from other bearer securities? (9)

8. List the clauses usually found in a banker's memorandum of deposit for registered securities. (10)

9. What is the purpose of the 'continuing security' clause? (10)

10. How are a legal mortgage and an equitable mortgage of registered securities effected? (10)

11. What is a blank transfer? Why is one often taken with an equitable mortgage of registered securities? (10)

12. Why cannot a blank transfer be used when title to the securities must be transferred by deed? **(10)**

13. What advantages are gained by an equitable mortgagee of company securities who gives notice of lien to the company? **(10)**

14. By what methods can a bank as equitable mortgagee improve its position should it wish to realise the securities? **(11)**

15. How is a mortgage of registered securities discharged? **(10)**

16. Explain the doctrine of constructive notice as it applies to a pledge of bearer securities. **(11)**

17. Explain what kind of mortgage is possible of National Savings securities, unit trusts and building society shares. **(12–14)**

18. State the advantages of a legal mortgage and the disadvantages of an equitable mortgage of stocks and shares. **(15)**

19. Explain fully why a rights or bonus issue on shares deposited with a bank under an equitable mortgage can seriously prejudice its position. **(15)**

20. State the advantages and the disadvantages of a mortgage of stocks and shares as security. **(15)**

15

Guarantees

The general law

1. Definition

A guarantee is a promise to answer, 'for the debt, default or miscarriage of another' if that person fails to meet their obligation: Statute of Frauds 1677 s.4.

2. Main features of a guarantee

There are five main features of a guarantee.

(a) *Three parties* are involved: the creditor, the principal debtor and the guarantor (or surety) and *two separate contracts.*
(b) *A valid debt must exist* between the creditor and the principal debtor.
(c) Primary liability for the debt is incurred by the principal debtor, the *guarantor incurs only secondary liability*, that is the guarantor becomes liable only if the principal debtor fails to pay.
(d) The guarantor has *no direct interest* in the contract entered into by the creditor and the principal debtor.
(e) A guarantee must be *evidenced by a written note or memorandum* signed by the guarantor or his agent: Statute of Frauds 1677 s.4. Without such written evidence, a guarantee is unenforceable.

> NOTE: An exception to (b) above is found in the Minors' Contracts Act 1987 s.2. This provides that a guarantee of a loan to a minor is enforceable even though the loan itself is not. A minor can, however, ratify a loan after becoming 18.

3. Consideration

A contract of guarantee must be supported by consideration, but the written note or memorandum need not record the consideration given. Bank guarantee forms always include a statement of the consideration.

> NOTE: An existing overdraft is no consideration for a guarantee, i.e. past consideration is no consideration. However, a further advance, an exten-

sion of the repayment period or a forbearance to enforce repayment already demanded would all be sufficient consideration.

4. Guarantees and indemnities

Under a guarantee, the guarantor incurs only secondary liability. Under an *indemnity* the indemnifier incurs *primary liability*.

Example

If, when Mr Smith asks his bank for a loan, Mr Brown says, 'Lend him the money he wants. If he doesn't pay you back, I will', Mr Brown is offering to *guarantee* the loan and would incur only *secondary* liability. If, however, Mr Brown says, 'Lend him the money; I will see that you are repaid', he has offered to *indemnify* the bank and would incur *primary* liability.

The distinction is of practical importance in that, if the principal debtor cannot be held liable for the debt, nor can the guarantor.

NOTE: A guarantee of a loan to a minor is enforceable: Minors' Contracts Act 1987 s.2 (*see* 15:2).

A second distinction is that, under the Statute of Frauds 1677, a guarantee must be evidenced in writing to be enforceable while an indemnity does not. As you may imagine, this distinction is of no practical significance to banks because, quite apart from this legal rule, a bank would never lend against a *verbal* assurance of repayments from a third party.

In fact, a *bank guarantee* combines a *guarantee* with an *indemnity*. The guarantor accepts liability for the customer's debts *if* the latter defaults (a guarantee) but, by including an *ultra vires* clause (*see* 15:9), also accepts *primary liability* (an indemnity) should the debt prove unenforceable against the customer.

5. Legal capacity

(a) *Principal debtor*. The principal debtor must be legally capable of incurring the debt or other obligation guaranteed. A legal nullity cannot be guaranteed.

Hence, unless the guarantee contains a specific and adequate provision to the contrary, i.e. an *ultra vires* clause (*see* 15:9), no action can be taken against either the principal debtor or the guarantor if the debt is void.

A guarantee to a minor is enforceable even though the loan itself is not: Minors' contracts Act 1987 s.2 (*see* 15:2).

(b) *Guarantor*. The guarantor must have the legal capacity to enter into the guarantee, e.g. neither a minor nor a mentally disordered person can give a valid guarantee.

Special rules cover the following cases.

(i) Co-guarantors. A bank guarantee form will impose *joint and several liability* on two or more co-guarantors.

Joint liability enables the bank to claim against any one, or any combination of the co-guarantors (usually the one(s) in the best financial position), as each is liable for the *full* amount. It is then up to the guarantor(s) from whom the bank obtained payment to seek the appropriate contribution from the other(s). Should the bank not be repaid in full, it can still claim against the other(s) for the balance under the Civil Liability (Contribution) Act 1978.

Several liability ensures that on the death or bankruptcy of a co-guarantor, their estate remains liable on the guarantee. If liability was only joint, only the other co-guarantors would be liable for existing and future debts.

A joint guarantee must be signed by *all* the co-guarantors. If it is not, it will be void.

Example

In *National Provincial Bank* v *Brackenbury* (1906), three out of four guarantors signed the guarantee and the bank advanced money in anticipation of the remaining signature. The fourth guarantor died without signing.

In an action to enforce the guarantee, the failure to obtain the fourth guarantor's signature was held to be sufficient to discharge the other three guarantors.

NOTE: A joint guarantor is *not* liable on a guarantee if the signature of another joint guarantor is *forged*: *James Graham & Co (Timber) Ltd* v *Southgate-Sands* (1985).

Should one co-guarantor repay the whole debt, that co-guarantor has a right of contribution from the co-guarantors in proportion to their respective liabilities under the guarantee. This right is the reason for the strict approach to guarantors signing a guarantee.

(ii) Partners. A partner has no implied authority to give a guarantee in the firm name unless giving guarantees is part of the firm's usual course of business (*see* 4:6). A bank should, therefore, ensure that any guarantee given by a partnership is signed by *all* the partners in the firm. If it is not, the partners *signing* will incur personal liability, but the others will not.

(iii) Companies. Despite the abolition of the *ultra vires* rule by the Companies Act 1989, banks are likely to continue to want to see that authority to give guarantees is included in a company's objects or that it states that the company is a 'general commercial company'. Banking practice is likely to differ from the strict legal

position for some time. The 'commercial justification' principle behind the decision in *Charterbridge Corporation Ltd* v *Lloyds Bank Ltd* (1969) (*see* 5:**6**) is also likely to affect banking practice, although it is thought that, as a matter of law, the abolition of the *ultra vires* rule probably negates it.

Similarly, although the powers of a company's directors are *not* limited by anything that might be stated in the Memorandum and Articles of Association provided the other party deals in good faith, it is likely that a guarantee by a company will continue to have to be accompanied by a certified copy of the board's resolution authorising it. Banks provide draft resolutions for this purpose.

A problem can arise with *group guarantees* (guarantees under which companies in a group guarantee the borrowing of the others) if a new member joins the group and the guarantee is to be extended to cover it. If the guarantee is to be valid, either the original guarantee must allow for further parties to join in the guarantee or all the original members of the group must specifically agree to the addition of the new member. In both cases, the new member must receive consideration for its promise. Alternatively, the new member must execute a separate guarantee.

Example

In *Ford & Carter Ltd* v *Midland Bank Ltd* (1979) (HL), five companies in a group executed a group guarantee in favour of the bank. F&C, another company in the group, subsequently joined in the guarantee, but no new authority was obtained from the original five members. All six companies were eventually asked to pay under the guarantee and the liquidator of F&C challenged its liability to pay.

It was held that, on the facts, the terms of the guarantee did not cover the addition of further members of the group to the guarantee and, therefore, the guarantee did not bind F&C.

Where one or more directors has a personal interest in the giving of the guarantee, e.g. an intercompany guarantee, the resolution must be passed by a quorum of independent directors or by a general meeting of the company if this is not possible, unless the company's Articles of Association allow the interested directors to vote *see Victors Ltd* v *Lingard* (1927).

Various specific statutory restrictions are, however, still imposed on a company's powers to give a guarantee. For example, the Companies Act 1985 s.151 prohibits, with exceptions, a company from giving a guarantee which enables a person to purchase or subscribe for its own shares or those of its holding company; and the Companies

Act 1985 s.330 prohibits, with exceptions, a company guaranteeing a loan by a third person to one of its directors or a director of its holding company.

6. Reality of consent

(a) *Misrepresentation.* A misrepresentation of fact by the creditor that misleads the guarantor will entitle the guarantor to avoid liability under the guarantee.

(b) *Undue influence.* If the guarantor was unable to exercise a free and independent judgment when they entered into the agreement, the guarantor may subsequently be able to avoid the contract on the grounds of undue influence.

A bank should insist that a prospective guarantor receives independent legal advice before signing the guarantee form whenever the principal debtor may be in a position to influence their judgment. Proof of undue influence could render the guarantee voidable (*see* 11:**20**).

A *free will* clause is, therefore, often included in the guarantee form to the effect that the guarantor understands the nature of the document and the liability incurred under it. Such a clause should be witnessed by the guarantor's own solicitor, who should sign the accompanying *attestation clause*. This states that they have explained to the guarantor the nature of the guarantee and the obligations incurred under it.

No presumption of undue influence arises between husband and wife, although experience has shown that most problems concerning undue influence and guarantees occur when wives guarantee the accounts of their husbands.

NOTE: Since the passing of the Sex Discrimination Act 1975, any special treatment of a woman guarantor, e.g. including a free will clause in her guarantee, must be based on inability to understand or appreciate the arrangement and not on the grounds of sex.

(c) *Mistake as to the nature of the document signed.* As a consequence of the decision in *Saunders* v *Anglia Building Society* (1970), it is highly unlikely that a guarantor will ever be able to avoid liability by a plea of *non est factum*, that is that the guarantee was signed in the mistaken belief that it was an entirely different type of document (*see* 11:**23**).

7. Disclosure of information

A guarantee is not a contract *uberrimae fidei* (of the utmost good faith). A bank is, therefore, under no duty to disclose to the guarantor all the facts known to it that may be relevant. A guarantor must obtain or ask for all the information they require.

Example

In *Cooper* v *National Provincial Bank* (1945), the bank was held to be under no obligation to disclose to the guarantor of a wife's account that her husband was an undischarged bankrupt, that he had authority to draw on her account and that the account had previously been operated in an improper and irregular fashion.

The common law does, however, favour a guarantor. In *Royal Bank of Scotland* v *Greenshields* (1914), it was held that, in order to prevent a guarantor from being misled, and, therefore, from being able to avoid the contract:

(a) Any information volunteered by the creditor must be complete and true.
(b) An entire misapprehension of the facts of the case on the guarantor's part must be corrected by the creditor.

NOTE: To avoid breaching its duty of secrecy in this context, a bank should either obtain its customer's authority to disclose information or arrange a meeting with its customer and the prospective guarantor.

A guarantor is not entitled to inspect the debtor's account but is entitled to know the extent of their liability. The accepted practice is that, where the debt does not exceed the guarantee, the guarantor can be told the actual amount of the debt; where it does exceed the guarantee, merely that the guarantee is being fully relied on. However, where the guarantee is of a loan regulated by the Consumer Credit Act 1974, the guarantor has a statutory right (on payment of a small fee) to a statement of the principal debtor's account, as well as to a copy of the security document and the loan agreement.

A bank owes no legal duty to advise a guarantor of any material change in the circumstances of the principal debtor.

Example

In *National Provincial Bank* v *Glanusk* (1913), a guarantor was unsuccessful in seeking to avoid liability on the grounds that the bank had not informed him when it knew that the overdraft guaranteed was being used for a purpose that he had not approved.

Should such a situation arise, a meeting with the customer and guarantor can, again, be arranged. If need be, pressure can be exerted on the customer by a threat to demand repayment if the customer does not cooperate.

Bank guarantees

8.   Introduction
Bank guarantees do four main things:

(a) Precisely state the liability of the guarantor.
(b) Prevent the *Rule* in *Clayton's Case* (1816) operating to the bank's detriment.
(c) Specify the circumstances under which the guarantee can be determined.
(d) Exclude all the guarantor's important common law rights and remedies against both the principal debtor and the bank. (These extensive exclusions are necessary because the common law favours the guarantor.)

9.   Usual clauses in a bank guarantee form

(a) The *whole* of the customer's indebtedness is guaranteed but, often, with a limit on the guarantor's liability. (This is a version of the usual all monies clause.)

Example
_____
If an advance of £20 000 is to be guaranteed, the guarantor will guarantee all liabilities of the customer with a *limit* of £20 000 on the actual liability. The guarantee will not be drawn specifically to cover the £20 000 advanced.
_____

There are two reasons for drafting the guarantee in this way.
(i) Where the guarantee covers only part of the customer's debt, payment of that part entitles the guarantor to a proportionate share of any securities held by the bank under the principle of subrogation. A guarantor of the customer's total indebtedness cannot claim a part of any security held by the bank unless all of the customer's indebtedness is repaid.
(ii) If the customer is made bankrupt, a guarantee covering the whole indebtedness prevents the guarantor proving against the customer's estate in competition with the bank: *Re Sass* (1896).
The bank is able to put a guarantor's payment in discharge of their liability into a suspense account and enter a proof against its customer's estate for the entire amount owing. This means that the bank is able to recover more, perhaps all, of the debt, although the guarantor loses their right of proof. Most bank guarantees expressly prevent the guarantor from entering a proof in competition with the bank.

Example

Continuing the previous example, if the customer is made bankrupt owing £40 000 to the bank and a dividend of 50p in the £ is paid, a bank proving for the whole debt of £40 000 would receive £20 000. Adding this to the £20 000 held in a suspense account paid under the guarantee would mean that the bank would be repaid in full, while the guarantor would lose the £20 000 paid by them. Conversely, if the guarantor had guaranteed £20 000 and not the whole debt, payment of £20 000 would have to be credited to the customer's account and both the bank and the guarantor would prove against the customer's estate for £20 000. Again, assuming a dividend of 50p in the £, each would lose £10 000 on the transaction.

NOTE: Any surplus funds held in the suspense account after full repayment has been made *must* be refunded to the guarantor.

It is usual for the guarantor to bind their personal representatives for the whole debt. The guarantee then automatically remains in force should the guarantor die and it removes the need to break the customer's account to prevent the *Rule* in *Clayton's Case* (1816) acting to the bank's detriment.

(b) The guarantee is expressed as being a *continuing security* covering any amount owing on the debtor's account at any time, subject to the specified limit on the guarantor's actual liability.

This provision again excludes the *Rule* in *Clayton's Case* (1816). If not excluded, every payment into the customer's account would reduce the guarantor's liability and every payment out would be a fresh advance that would not be covered by the guarantee.

(c) The guarantor's liability arises on a *written demand for repayment* being made. By virtue of this provision, the six-year limitation period under the Limitation Act 1980 does not commence running until a proper demand has been made.

If security is held in support of the guarantee, this cannot be realised unless the guarantor is in default, which requires that a demand for payment is made and not met. It is possible that the guarantor may 'disappear', especially if the guarantee is held for some time, and to avoid this problem the clause provides that a demand is effective if it is sent to the guarantor's last known address.

(d) The guarantee is expressed to be *additional* to any other guarantee of the customer's indebtedness given by the guarantor to the bank. This prevents a claim that a subsequent additional guarantee was given in substitution for the original guarantee.

(e) The *consideration* is always expressed in such terms as 'opening or continuing an account with (the principal) or giving accommodation or granting time to (the principal)'. It is never stated to be the advance of a specific sum because this precise sum would have to be advanced in order for the guarantee to be valid.

(f) *Co-guarantors* undertake joint and several liability (*see* 15:5). It is also provided that the bank can release any one of the co-guarantors without affecting its rights against the other(s). Without this clause, the guarantee would be discharged by the release of a co-guarantor because it would deprive the remaining guarantor(s) of their right of contribution from the guarantor released.

(g) The guarantee will remain in force despite any change in the constitution of the parties, e.g. a change in the membership of a partnership, a reconstruction of a company or even the lending bank's merger with or takeover by another bank.

> NOTE: A guarantee does not bind a new partner in a firm and a bank may therefore require a new guarantee in substitution for the old when a new partner joins.

(h) The bank is given complete freedom to vary arrangements with the principal debtor. For example, securities deposited by the principal debtor may be released, time to pay may be granted and a voluntary composition outside the bankruptcy rules may be made with the principal debtor.

Without such express provisions, at common law, the guarantor would be released from their obligations by any material variation of the arrangement.

(i) The guarantor is required to give a specified period of notice, usually three months, before they can determine the guarantee. This allows the bank to make arrangements with its customer and the guarantor for repayment or the provision of alternative security. Without such a clause, the guarantor could choose to determine the guarantee when the debt is low or the account is temporarily in credit.

(j) The guarantor agrees to accept the bank's statement of its customer's account as conclusive evidence of the amount owing to the bank. This clause is necessary to avoid possible problems in producing the necessary evidence to obtain judgment against the guarantor.

(k) The bank is given the right to continue the account after notice of determination by the guarantor without subsequent credits reducing the guarantor's liability under the *Rule* in *Clayton's Case* (1816). Such a clause – held to be effective in *Westminster Bank* v *Cond* (1946) –

makes it unnecessary, as a matter of law, to break the debtor's account when notice of determination is received from the guarantor.

Despite the clause, however, it is usual to break the account.

(l) On determination of the guarantee, the bank is given the right to open a new account with its customer. Any credit balance or transaction on this account does not reduce the liability of the guarantor.

(m) The guarantor undertakes not to sue the debtor until the bank has been paid in full, nor to take security from the debtor. Should such security be taken, it will be valid, but the guarantor is deemed to hold it as trustee for the bank.

(n) The bank is given the right to keep the guarantee form uncancelled for (usually) 25 months after all the monies that it secures have been repaid. Such a clause is included in case the customer's repayment is held to be a preference (*see* 6:**34**) and the bank has to refund the money to its customer's trustee in bankruptcy. (Twenty four months is the minimum period it will be held uncancelled after repayment.)

> NOTE: Under the Insolvency Act 1986 s.342, the court has the power to revive a guarantee or other obligation in such circumstances (*see* 6:**31**).

(o) The guarantor undertakes not to withdraw any cash deposit made in support of the guarantee while liability exists on it. On determination of the guarantee, immediate recourse can be made against the deposit without reference to the guarantor.

(p) An *ultra vires* clause is included in case the debt guaranteed proves to be unenforceable against the customer due to any legal limitation or lack of contractual capacity. This could happen, e.g. where the loan is made to an unincorporated club or association or, conceivably, to an undischarged bankrupt. Under such a clause, the guarantor accepts *primary liability* as *principal debtor* for any sums that cannot be recovered from the customer. The contract is thereby enforceable as an *indemnity*.

(q) A clause preventing the guarantor raising any set-off against the bank that would have been available to the principal debtor: *Continental Illinois Bank and Trust Co of Chicago* v *Papanicolaou (The Fedora)* (1986).

(r) A free will clause will be included where there is a possibility that the guarantor may seek to avoid liability on the grounds of undue influence (*see* 15:**6**). An attestation clause, witnessing the guarantor's signature, may also be added.

(s) A guarantee taken to secure an agreement regulated by the Consumer Credit Act 1974 must conform to the statutory requirements of the Act in content and form. For example:

(i) It must be headed 'Guarantee and Indemnity subject to the Consumer Credit Act 1974' on its first page.

(ii) It must contain a statement of the guarantor's rights in the form specified in Part III of the Schedule of the Regulations, including the statement 'Under this guarantee and indemnity, you may have to pay instead of the debtor and fulfil any other obligations under the guarantee and indemnity'.

(iii) It must have a box for the guarantor's signature, which contains a statement very similar to that in (ii).

(iv) The lettering used for the terms of the guarantee must be easily legible and in a colour that is easily distinguishable from the colour of the paper.

10. Determination of a bank guarantee

(a) *Notice by the guarantor.* This must be given in accordance with the terms of the guarantee. After it has been given, the guarantor may discharge the liability by paying the amount due under the guarantee.

Once the guarantor has given notice to determine the guarantee, the guarantee can call on the principal debtor to pay even though no formal demand for repayment has been made by the bank: *Thomas* v *Nottingham Incorporated Football Club Ltd* (1972). This is an example of the equitable right of *exoneration*.

> NOTE: A bank is probably entitled to make further advances to its customer during this period of notice. However, in order not to unfairly prejudice either the guarantor – by allowing its customer to take advantage of the situation – or its customer – who may have entered into obligations relying on the guarantee – a meeting with the guarantor and its customer to discuss the situation is often arranged. If its customer proves uncooperative, the bank can fix the guarantor's liability by demanding immediate repayment from its customer.

It is usual to break the customer's account when the guarantor gives notice of determination, although the *Rule* in *Clayton's Case* (1816) is usually excluded by the guarantee form (*see* 15:9).

Where one (or some) of a number of co-guarantors gives notice of determination or withdrawal, the remaining co-guarantors should sign a fresh guarantee, even though a bank guarantee allows the bank to release a co-guarantor without affecting the liability of the other(s).

Any payment made by the guarantor under the guarantee should be placed in a suspense account. This is possible under the usual terms of a bank guarantee. The same procedure should be adopted with part payment by co-guarantors.

Once the *whole* debt has been repaid (*see* 15:9), the guarantor is subrogated ('steps into the shoes of') both the principal debtor and the bank. In the former case, the guarantor is entitled to any security deposited by the principal debtor and a proportionate share of any security that the bank holds from other guarantors of the debt. In the latter case, the guarantor is able to *sue* the principal debtor in the name of the bank for the amount of the guarantee paid, *providing* the debt was due for repayment, e.g. a formal demand had been made on the principal debtor following a default in repayment.

(b) *Notice by the bank.* A bank's guarantee form gives it the right to make an immediate demand for repayment from the guarantor. This determines the guarantee.

While the terms of the guarantee usually make this unnecessary, the normal practice is to break the customer's account.

It is up to the guarantor and not to the bank to ensure that the principal debtor makes repayment. Hence, a bank need not first seek repayment from its customer before seeking repayment from the guarantor.

(c) *Death.* Notice of the death of the principal debtor determines the guarantee and fixes the extent of the guarantor's liability.

In the event of the guarantor's death, a bank guarantee binds the personal representatives to continue it. If it did not, notice of the guarantor's death would determine the guarantee and the customer's account would have to be broken to avoid the *Rule* in *Clayton's Case* (1816) operating to the bank's detriment. A new account would have to be kept in credit or suitable alternative security for any debit balance provided.

The personal representatives can themselves determine the guarantee in accordance with its terms.

NOTE: The death of one co-surety does not end the continuing liability of the other(s) if they undertook joint and several liability. (This also applies to the mental disorder or bankruptcy of one co-surety.) The commencement of the winding up of a company that is either the principal debtor or the guarantor will determine the guarantee.

(d) *Mental disorder.* Reliable notice of the mental disorder of the principal debtor or guarantor determines the guarantee. The customer's account should be broken.

(e) *Bankruptcy.* Notice of a bankruptcy petition or the making of a bankruptcy order against the guarantor determines the guarantee.

The customer's account must be stopped and a demand for repayment made. If the customer fails to repay, the bank must pursue its claim against the guarantor in any voluntary arrangement or bankruptcy process that follows. Any part payment already made must be deducted from the bank's claim. Remember, however, that the guarantor's undertaking to guarantee the customer's whole indebtedness enables a bank to place into a suspense account any part payment by the guarantor and prove for the whole debt in its customer's bankruptcy.

> NOTE: At common law, a guarantee would also be determined in a number of other situations. For example a variation of the arrangements with the principal debtor, a change in the parties to the agreement or a release of securities held from the principal debtor. Bank guarantee forms exclude the common law in these respects – only misrepresentation entitles the guarantor to set aside the contract at common law.

11. Letters of comfort

A *letter of comfort* is difficult to define, but can be described as a type of guarantee that may be accepted by a bank instead of a formal guarantee, even though it amounts to no more than a 'gentleman's agreement', i.e. it is not intended to be legally binding.

A letter of comfort may be given by a parent company to 'secure' a loan to a subsidiary company. In it, the parent company (typically) undertakes to maintain its holding in the subsidiary and declares that its policy is to ensure that the subsidiary will always be in a position to meet its liabilities to the bank.

Such undertakings and declarations were held by the Court of Appeal in *Kleinwort Benson Ltd* v *Malaysia Mining Corporation Berhad* (1989) to amount merely to statements of fact and not to a contractual promise to *meet* the debts of the subsidiary company. From a commercial point of view, therefore, the value of such a letter depends on the standing of the parent company in the commercial world.

> NOTE: It does not follow that what appears to be a letter of comfort will never be legally enforceable. It depends whether consideration is present between the parties and, more importantly, whether, on the true construction of the terms of the letter, the parties intended the agreement to be legally binding. If this is the case, it would *not* be a letter of comfort but, instead, a *guarantee*.

12. The guarantor's rights

Most of the guarantor's common law rights are removed by the clauses in the guarantee. With the exception of (a) (v) below, those that remain under a bank guarantee have been discussed in context above. Here they are summarised.

(a) *Rights against the bank (the creditor).*

(i) To be informed of their liability under the guarantee.

(ii) If creditor repays the whole debt after payment is due, to be subrogated to the bank's rights against the principal debtor and to any securities held by the bank from the principal debtor or third parties in support of the guarantee. In the latter case, the right of subrogation is pro rata (rateable) to the guarantor's payment.

(iii) If sued by the bank, to raise any set-off against the bank that the principal debtor could have raised.

(iv) To expect the bank to exercise any rights of set-off that it has against the principal debtor and only seek the net indebtedness from the guarantor.

(v) To expect the bank to realise the best market price for a security it holds from the principal debtor: *Standard Chartered Bank* v *Walker and Another* (1982) (CA), which extended the duty owed by a mortgagee to the mortgagor in this respect established in *Cuckmere Brick Co Ltd* v *Mutual Finance Ltd* (1971) to a guarantor of the mortgagee's indebtedness. The receiver appointed by the bank is under the same duty.

However, in *China and South Sea Bank* v *Tan Soon Gin* (1990) (PC), it was held that a bank owes *no* duty to a guarantor in deciding when to exercise its power of sale over security it holds from the principal debtor and can decide this on the basis of its own interests. In other words it has complete discretion as to *when* it exercises its power. This means that the bank is not liable to the guarantor for a decline in the value of the security – which will mean an increase in the guarantor's actual liability – unless it is personally responsible for the decline.

In *China and South Sea Bank* v *Tan Soon Gin* (1990), the bank took a guarantee supported by a charge over shares. In the period between the principal debtor defaulting and the bank enforcing its security, the value of the shares fell, thereby increasing the guarantor's liability. The guarantor argued, unsuccessfully, that his liability was extinguished, or at least reduced, by the bank's failure to sell the shares sooner and at a time when they covered the amount of the debt.

NOTE: Should a bank attempt to exclude its duty under the *Standard Chartered Case*, the clause purporting to do so would be subject to the Unfair Contract Terms Act 1977 and, quite probably, would be held to be *void*.

(vi) To an action against the bank for a receiver's conduct to the extent that the bank directs or interferes with the receiver's activities: *Standard Chartered Bank* v *Walker and Another* (1982). In the absence of such interference or direction, the receiver is the agent of the mortgagor/guarantor and not the mortgagee/bank (*see* 16:**15**).

(vii) To avoid the contract for misrepresentation.

(b) *Rights against the principal debtor.*

(i) To an indemnity (compensation) for any payments made under the guarantee, although this right can *only* be exercised *after* payment becomes legally due and the *whole* debt has been repaid.

(ii) After the guarantor has given notice of determination, to call on the debtor to make repayment, even though no formal demand to do so has been made by the bank and the guarantor has paid nothing under the guarantee.

(c) *Rights against co-guarantors.*

(i) A co-guarantor who pays more than their proportion of the guarantee, for example where the bank enforces the guarantee against only one or some of the guarantors, is entitled to seek a contribution in proportion to their liability (rateably) from the other(s). If the principal debtor is solvent, they must be joined in any action to enforce the right of contribution.

(ii) Where one co-guarantor pays the guarantee, they are subrogated to the bank's rights against any security deposited by the other co-guarantors.

(iii) Where a co-guarantor becomes insolvent and another co-guarantor pays more than their share under the guarantee, that co-guarantor is subrogated to the bank's right of proof in the insolvency of the co-guarantor to the extent of their right of contribution, *providing* the bank has been repaid in full.

13. Advantages and disadvantages as security

(a) *Advantages.*

(i) A guarantee is a very *simple* security to take – no registration is involved and no complications concerning proof of title arise. (Compare mortgages.)

(ii) A guarantee can easily and immediately be enforced by court action.

(iii) As with any other security given by a third party (*collateral security*), it can be ignored when claiming against the principal debtor.

(iv) As several parties can guarantee a loan, it is useful security

where the principal debtor is unable to provide security but offers a viable business loan proposition.

(b) *Disadvantages*:

(i) Unless supported by a cash deposit or other security, a guarantee is always of an uncertain value as a security – a guarantor's financial position can change very quickly. A bank should only accept an unsupported guarantee after careful investigation into the proposed guarantor's financial circumstances.

(ii) Court action may be necessary to realise the security and a technicality may possibly defeat the bank's claim. For example, special rules apply to guarantees taken from partnerships and companies, although a defeat of the bank's claim would almost certainly be the result of carelessness when taking the security.

(iii) Enforcing a guarantee may cause bad feeling, particularly if the guarantor is a valued customer. However, should this happen, it would probably be the result of poor banking practice and failure to explain, or have explained by an independent solicitor, to the guarantor the obligations involved.

(iv) Litigation may be necessary to enforce payment where the guarantee was not supported by other (realisable) security.

Progress test 15

1. Define a guarantee. **(1)**

2. List the main features of a guarantee. **(2)**

3. Distinguish between a guarantee and an indemnity. **(4)**

4. State the reasons why co-guarantors should always undertake joint and several liability on the guarantee. **(5)**

5. Why must every co-guarantor sign the memorandum? **(5)**

6. Give reasons why care must be taken when a prospective guarantor is a partnership. **(5)**

7. What is the purpose of the free will clause in a bank guarantee form? **(6)**

8. To what extent must a bank disclose to the guarantor information about the circumstances surrounding the guarantee? **(7)**

9. List the four main things done by a bank's guarantee form. **(8)**

10. Explain why the whole of the customer's indebtedness is guaranteed by the surety. **(9)**

11. What is the purpose of the guarantor binding their personal representatives to the guarantee? **(9)**

12. Explain the effect of the *Rule* in *Clayton's Case* (1816) in the context of a bank guarantee. **(9)**

13. What is the purpose of providing that the guarantor's liability arises on a written demand for repayment being made? **(9)**

14. Explain the purpose of a bank guarantee form giving the bank the right to retain the guarantee form uncancelled for a minimum period of 24 months. **(9)**

15. What is the purpose of putting any sum received from the guarantor into a suspense account? **(9)**

16. What is the effect of an *ultra vires* clause in a bank guarantee form? **(9)**

17. Explain the effect of death, mental disorder and bankruptcy of the principal debtor or guarantor on a guarantee. **(10)**

18. Explain the difference between a guarantee and a letter of comfort. **(11)**

19. List a guarantor's rights under a bank guarantee. **(12)**

20. State the advantages and disadvantages of a guarantee as a security for a banker's advance. **(13)**

16

Securities given by companies

Charges and their registration

1. Registrable charges

The Companies Act 1985 s.395 requires that certain types of charges created by companies must be registered with the Registrar of Companies. (All following references in this chapter are to the Companies Act 1985 unless otherwise stated). Under s.396 these are:

(a) A charge on land or any interest in land;
(b) A charge on goods or any interest in goods, unless the chargee is entitled to possession of the goods or documents of title to them;
(c) A charge on goodwill, intellectual property (patents, trademarks, registered designs, and copyright or any licence in respect of them), book debts, or uncalled share capital;
(d) A charge for securing an issue of debentures;
(e) A floating charge.

> NOTE: The registration requirements do not apply to charges given by third parties, such as directors, to secure a company's borrowing.

2. Registration of charges

(a) *Registration.* Registration is effected by delivering the prescribed particulars of the charge (not the charge itself) to the Registrar of Companies within 21 days of its creation, i.e. the date it was actually *executed* by the company, not necessarily the date it bears: s.395. If the execution was conditional, the 21-day period runs from the date of the condition being fulfilled. Under s.398, the Registrar must send a copy of the registered particulars and a note of their date of delivery to both the company and the chargeholder.

A certificate stating the date the particulars were registered will be provided by the Registrar to the chargeholder on request. This is *conclusive evidence* that the particulars were delivered by the date stated (s.397), but the certificate is *not* conclusive evidence that *registration requirements* have been satisfied. Thus, a liquidator can dispute the validity of the charge *despite* the certificate, e.g. on the grounds that the particulars delivered were incomplete.

It is the company's duty to deliver the prescribed particulars of a registrable charge, but any person interested in the charge can deliver them on the company's behalf. Thus, it is usual for the bank taking the charge to deliver the particulars and to claim back from the company the expenses involved.

A company must keep a copy of every charge at its registered office and maintain a register of charges, both of which must be open to inspection.

NOTE: Under s.409, the registration requirements of s.395 are extended to companies registered overseas that have established a place of business in the UK. If charges by such companies over UK assets are not registered, they will be *void* against a liquidator. A foreign company that is not a registered overseas company is not obliged to register its charges, and, therefore, will not be void against a liquidator for lack of registration, even though it may have established a place of business in the UK and so be in breach of its obligation to register as an overseas company.

(b) *Particulars of the charge*:

(i) Negative pledge clauses. An undertaking not to create other charges that rank in priority to or *pari passu* with the charge (a *negative pledge clause*), must be included in the particulars filed. As s.416 provides that a person taking a charge over a company's property is deemed to have notice of any matter requiring registration and disclosed on the Register at the time the charge is created, delivery of particulars of a negative pledge clause prevents a subsequent *fixed charge* taking priority over an existing *floating charge* (*see* 16:**10**).

(ii) Incomplete or inaccurate particulars. Where the particulars of the charge are incomplete and inaccurate the charge is void, unless the court orders otherwise, to the extent that rights are not disclosed because of the incomplete or inaccurate particulars: s.402. Thus, the charge is void to the extent of the inaccuracy against an administrator or liquidator of the company if insolvency proceedings begin at a time when the particulars were incomplete or inaccurate. However, the court may exercise its power to validate the charge provided it is satisfied that, during the time the registered particulars were incomplete or inaccurate, no existing unsecured creditor was materially misled to their prejudice or that no person became an unsecured creditor during that time.

The charge is similarly void against a person who, for value, acquires an interest in or rights over the property subject to the charge. Again, the court can validate the charge against such a person if it is satisfied that they did not rely on the incomplete or inaccurate particulars when acquiring the interest or right.

NOTE: The charge is not void against a subsequent unregistered charge (s.404) or against a person acquiring an interest in or right over property where the acquisition is expressly subject to the charge.

The whole of the sum secured by a charge that becomes partially void because incomplete or inaccurate particulars have been delivered, becomes immediately payable on demand.

(iii) Further particulars. Further particulars of a charge in the prescribed form may be delivered for registration at any time (s.401), for example to correct mistakes in the original particulars or as a result of changes in the terms of a charge. It is important to register further particulars immediately the need to do so becomes apparent in order to avoid the charge becoming void to the extent of the inaccuracy or incompleteness against a liquidator or administrator or a person who, for value, acquires an interest in or rights over the property.

NOTE: Banks must check very carefully that the particulars delivered are complete and accurate. If they are not, the validity of the charge may be challenged (considerably later perhaps) by, say, a liquidator and the position of an administrative receiver appointed by the bank would be undermined. For example, the appointment of an administrative receiver in such circumstances does not necessarily mean that a court will dismiss a petition for an administration order (*see* 6:**28–33**).

(c) *Failure to register.* Under s.399, failure to deliver particulars for registration within 21 days results in the charge being void against:
   (i) An administrator or liquidator of the company; and
   (ii) Any person who, for value, acquires an interest in or right over property subject to the charge. Usual examples of such a person include a purchaser or second mortgagee of the property charged. The loan itself, however, is not affected if the charge becomes void to any extent and the whole of the secured sum plus interest becomes payable immediately on demand. If the company goes into liquidation, a bank holding an unregistered charge becomes an unsecured creditor.

NOTE: The invalidity of the charge arises where the relevant event occurs before or after the end of the 21-day period following the creation of the charge.

The company and its officers responsible for the default commit an offence if particulars of the charge are not delivered as required.

(d) *Late delivery of particulars.* A charge *can* be registered *after* the statutory 21-day period but:

(i) The rights of creditors who have registered charges in the meantime are protected; and

(ii) It will be void against a liquidator or administrator if the company was unable to pay its debts at the date the particulars were delivered, or subsequently became so as a result of the transaction under which the charge was created, and insolvency proceedings began against the company within (1) two years of the date of delivery of the particulars in the case of a floating charge in favour of a connected person (*see* 6:**34**) or (2) one year in the case of a floating charge in favour of any other person, e.g. a bank, or (3) six months in any other case.

NOTE: Late registration does not avoid the charge against a person who, for value, acquires an interest in or right over property *after* the particulars are delivered.

(e) *Release of registered charges.* A memorandum of discharge in the prescribed form signed by or on behalf of the company and the bank may be filed with the Registrar who is required to file it and note the date of its delivery in the Register of Charges: s.403.

Debentures

3. Definition

Debentures are documents issued by a company acknowledging a loan and any charge securing it. It is by the issue of debentures that companies usually borrow money.

4. Types of debentures

(a) *Secured and unsecured.* An *unsecured debenture* is, as its name suggests, given *without* security; it merely acknowledges the debt. A *secured debenture* grants a mortgage or charge over property of the company.

(b) *Single or series.* A *single debenture* is issued to cover a *single debt*, for example to a bank to secure an overdraft. More usually, however, debentures are issued in *series*, to several holders. These debentures will rank *pari passu* (equally) among themselves.

(c) *Registered or bearer.* Most debentures are *registered* in the names of the various holders in the same way as shares; their transfer is similarly registered (*see* 9:8). However, *bearer debentures* may be issued. These are *negotiable instruments*, transferable by delivery. They are not registered and Treasury consent is required for their issue.

(d) *Perpetual or redeemable*. The former are only repaid when the company is wound up; the latter are repayable on or before a specified date.

5. Debentures issued to the public

These are usually *fixed-sum debentures*. They provide for repayment at or before a specific date and they are issued in series ranking *pari passu* with each other. Interest is paid on them at a specified rate. They are normally registered and frequently quoted on a stock exchange.

Large companies now frequently issue *debenture stock* to the public. This takes the form of a single loan in which each lender has a specified holding.

A large public issue of debentures or debenture stock often involves the execution of a *trust deed*, under which the assets charged are transferred by the company to *trustees* to hold on behalf of the debenture or debenture stock holders.

6. Debentures issued to a bank

A bank will almost invariably take an *all monies debenture* on its standard terms. This is because such a debenture will secure all monies owing on any account at any time and it will always keep pace with the overdrawn balance(s).

Should a *fixed-sum debenture* be accepted, a special *memorandum of deposit* (a 'Buckley agreement') must be taken in order to link the debenture with the advance and to secure a fluctuating debit balance.

The following provisions are found in a bank's standard debenture form.

(a) An all monies clause.

(b) An undertaking to repay on demand.

(c) A clause making the debenture a continuing security.

(d) A clause dealing with the payment of interest.

(e) Conditions on which the monies secured by the debenture become payable (to avoid the *Rule* in *Clayton's Case* (1816), working to the bank's detriment).

(f) A combination of fixed and floating charges over the company's assets.

(g) Restrictions on the company's power to grant any charge that ranks in priority to, or equally with, the debenture – a *negative pledge* clause.

(h) An undertaking not to dispose of the assets covered by the charge except in the ordinary course of business.

(i) An undertaking not to assign its book debts to a third party and to pay them into its account with the bank when they are received.

(j) A clause specifying the events that crystalise the bank's floating charge.

(k) A clause enabling the bank to appoint a receiver and manager who is declared to be the agent of the company not the bank (*see* 16:**15**).

(l) A clause giving a receiver a right to remuneration from the proceeds of the realisation of the company's assets.

(m) A clause referring to an administrative receiver's statutory powers under the Insolvency Act 1986.

(n) An undertaking to supply the bank with regular copies of the company's balance sheet, profit and loss and trading account duly certified by the company's auditors.

(o) An undertaking to keep its property and assets repaired and insured.

(p) An undertaking to deposit with the bank all deeds and documents of title to the company's freehold and leasehold property while the debenture is being relied on.

(q) An undertaking to grant a legal mortgage to the bank of any land it may acquire in the future.

(r) Exclusion of the Law of Property Act 1925, ss.93 and 103 (*see* 12:**27**).

(s) A clause providing that a notice of demand for repayment under the debenture will be deemed to have been served if made to the registered address of the company, whether or not it is received by the company.

The normal form of a bank debenture involves a fixed charge on the goodwill of the business, present and future book debts, and any uncalled capital; a fixed charge by way of legal mortgage on any freehold or leasehold properties, including all fixtures and fixed plant and machinery from time to time therein; and a first floating charge on all the other assets of the company.

NOTE: A fixed charge over present and future book debts can be created in a bank debenture provided the debenture requires the company to pay into its account with the bank all monies received in respect of book debts and prohibits the company from assigning such debts elsewhere without the bank's consent: *Siebe Gorman & Co Ltd* v *Barclays Bank Ltd* (1979). Details of the obligation and the prohibition on assignments must be included in the particulars delivered to the Registrar of Companies: s.39. A credit balance in a bank account is not a book debt.

7. Transfer and discharge of debentures

Fixed-sum debentures quoted on a stock exchange are readily transferable by an ordinary instrument of transfer. A *bearer* debenture can be transferred by mere delivery.

Banks' debentures are usually transferable, but one bank that accepts a transfer of a debenture from another or from a non-bank will seldom rely on the wording of the original debenture. This is because each bank drafts its own standard debenture to cover all foreseeable contingencies in conformity with its own practices and procedures. It will normally insist, therefore, on taking its own debenture and having the original discharged.

A bank's debenture form usually includes a form of receipt. When the bank is repaid, it will impress its seal on the receipt as evidence of the discharge.

A *memorandum of satisfaction* should then be filed by the company with the Registrar of Companies.

Fixed and floating charges

8. Fixed charge

This is a legal or equitable mortgage of specific property.

A fixed charge is to a bank's *advantage* in that specific property is always available as security for the advance, but to its *disadvantage* in that the property charged may depreciate in value as, for example, does plant and machinery.

To a company, the *disadvantage* of a fixed charge is that it cannot dispose of the property charged without the consent of the holder of the charge.

NOTE: The making of an administration order (*see* 6:**28**) prevents any chargeholder realising their security, i.e. a fixed chargeholder cannot sell the assets charged and a floating chargeholder cannot appoint an administrative receiver, although the security remains valid. While a floating chargeholder can prevent an administration order being made by appointing an administrative receiver (*see* below), a fixed chargeholder has no way of preventing the making of the order. Once an order is made, assets subject to a fixed charge can only be sold by agreement with the administrator or by order of the court.

9. Floating charge

This is an equitable charge that floats over the fluctuating assets of a company, for example its stock, without attaching to specific assets until *crystallisation*. Only a company can create a floating charge over its assets.

Crystallisation means that the *floating charge* becomes *fixed*, that is that the bank obtains a fixed charge on all the property owned by the company at the time of crystallisation. Crystallisation thereby prevents the company dealing with the property. It occurs automatically at law:

(i) If *winding up* – compulsory or voluntary – commences;

(ii) If the company *ceases business* or disposes of its assets for this purpose;

(iii) If a *receiver* is appointed by the bank under the terms of its debenture.

Crystallisation can also take place:

(iv) Contractually under *specific terms of the debenture*, for example, by the bank giving notice to the company or by the company committing a breach of the debenture, such as failing to make repayment on demand or attempting to create another charge over the assets charged: *Re Brightlife Ltd* (1987). (This is sometimes known as *pre-crystallisation*.)

Until crystallisation, a company can freely dispose of assets covered by a floating charge. This is an important *advantage* to a company.

A bank obtains the benefit of a range of assets as security and all assets acquired in the future are automatically covered.

An additional, and considerable, *advantage* of a floating charge is that its holder is able to appoint an administrative receiver and, therefore, take control of the situation if the company gets into serious financial difficulties'. Appointing an administrative receiver also prevents the making of an administration order: Insolvency Act 1986 s.9 (*see* 6:**28**). For this reason alone, a bank will always take a floating charge when it takes security from a company.

However, the *disadvantages* (*see* 16:**10**) of a floating charge are such that a bank will not wish to take such a charge *by itself*, unless no other security can be offered.

10. Defects of a floating charge

(a) *Running down of assets.* The value of a floating charge depends on the value of the assets when it crystallises. As a company can freely dispose of the assets charged, a bank's position depends to some extent on the conduct of the company. It could, for example, realise the assets to repay other creditors. Although such action may be a breach of the company's undertaking not to dispose of assets covered by the charge (*see* 16:6), this will offer no assistance to the bank if the company is solvent.

A bank will wish to see, therefore, that the assets charged are maintained at a satisfactory level, but this is still no protection against a sudden depletion of the assets or a sudden fall in their value.

(b) *Fixed charges have priority.* A subsequent *fixed charge* on a company's assets will take priority over existing floating charges, *provided* the fixed charge was taken for value and without notice of any prohibition or restriction in the original debenture on the company's power to create such a charge.

In practice, the inclusion of a *negative pledge clause* in the debenture, i.e. an undertaking not to create other charges ranking in priority to or *pari passu* with the charge and delivering particulars of this to the Registrar, will prevent a subsequent fixed charge taking priority. Existing registered fixed or floating charges do, of course, have priority.

(c) *Other postponements.* The rights of a holder of a floating charge are also postponed to:

(*i*) A landlord's right to distress for rent before crystallisation.

(*ii*) A judgment creditor if, before crystallisation, the goods are seized and sold by the sheriff or if the judgment creditor obtains a garnishee order absolute.

(*iii*) The rights of preferential creditors after crystallisation (*see* 6:**46**).

NOTE: Under the Insolvency Act 1986 s.251, a floating charge 'means a charge which, as created, was a floating charge'. Thus, it is not possible to gain priority over preferential creditors by *converting* a floating charge to a fixed charge before crystallisation. This would include pre-crystallisation of a floating charge under the terms of the debenture (*see* 16:**9**).

(*iv*) The administrator's fees and expenses under an administration order: Insolvency Act 1986 s.19(4).

(*v*) The rights of a third party who has retained ownership of the goods covered by the charge through the inclusion of a *retention of title clause* (a *Romalpa* clause) in the contract of sale under which the goods were supplied (*see* 16:**11**).

(d) *Invalidation by the Insolvency Act 1986 s.245.* Except to the extent that consideration is received by the company at the same time as or after the charge is created, a floating charge is invalidated on the application of the liquidator or administrator if it was created within the following periods before the commencement of a liquidation or the application for an administration order:

(*i*) *Two* years – in favour of a connected person;

(*ii*) *One* year – in favour of any other person, *provided*, in this latter case only, at the time the charge was created the company was unable to pay its debts or became unable to pay its debts as a result of the transaction under which the charge was created.

Section 245 prevents insolvent companies from creating floating charges to secure past debts to the prejudice of their other unsecured creditors.

A charge is also invalidated if it is made in the period between the petition for and the making of an administration order.

Consideration under s.245 would not be received by the company when a loan is granted after a floating charge was created if it is granted on condition that it be used to repay an existing debt: *Re G T Whyte & Co Ltd* (1982).

> NOTE: The charge is merely invalidated; the creditor remains an unsecured creditor. Thus, the liquidator cannot recover repayments to the creditors made before liquidation commences merely because their floating charge is invalidated by s.245.

The *Rule* in *Clayton's Case* (1816) (*see* 1:**15**) may assist a bank in this situation because subsequent payments in will reduce, and perhaps eventually extinguish, the past (unsecured) advances made by it, and any fresh advance will be covered by the floating charge in accordance with s.245.

Example

In *Re Yeovil Glove Co Ltd* (1965) (CA), all the company's accounts were overdrawn and the bank, which held a floating charge from the company, had been making drawings from the No. 1 account and crediting these to two others for the payment of wages and salaries, thereby allowing the bank to monitor its preferential claim (*see* 5:**21**).

It was held that the drawings made after the charge was taken were advances made in consideration of it and subsequent payments into the No. 1 account were set against drawings made before the charge was taken. It made no difference that payments in and payments out were more or less equal.

> NOTE: In order for the *Rule* in *Clayton's Case* to assist a bank in these circumstances, the transactions on the account must be genuine and not payments made merely to enable the floating chargeholder to take advantage of the *Rule*. This is a question of fact in each case.

(e) *Invalidation by the Insolvency Act 1986 s.239.* If created within six months, or two years in the case of a connected person, of a company going into liquidation or an administration order being made against it, a floating charge may be invalidated as a *preference* under s.239 (*see* 6:**34**).

11. Transfer of title (*Romalpa*) clauses

Where such a clause is included in a supplier's contract of sale, the company does not acquire ownership of the goods until the purchaser has paid for them. As the goods do not form part of the company's assets, they are not subject to a bank's floating charge. In practice, such a clause is a greater problem to a bank than a previous fixed charge (*see* below).

The name given to such a clause is taken from the Court of Appeal's decision in *Aluminium Industrie Vassen BV* v *Romalpa Aluminium Ltd* (1976), where the plaintiff company successfully claimed from the receiver appointed by the defendant company's bank under its debenture:

(a) Redelivery of aluminium foil that it had supplied to the defendant company (a claim admitted by the receiver); and
(b) The proceeds of the resale of the foil by the defendant company.

The essence of the decision was that the plaintiff company (the suppliers), in their contract with the defendants, had expressly reserved title to the foil supplied (ownership under the Sale of Goods Act 1979) to itself until it had been paid in full. This entitled it to trace the proceeds of the resale of the goods in priority to the bank secured by its floating charge.

The *Romalpa* decision is of great importance in the general law on the sale of goods and it has considerable significance to banks because the security created by the decision, a security that is neither registered nor open to public inspection, undermines the value of a floating charge. Even preferential claims, e.g. to cover wages, are postponed to a supplier protected by a *Romalpa* clause. A bank must bear this in mind before accepting a floating charge as security for an advance.

The present law can be summarised as follows.

(a) Provided the goods remain *identifiable in their original state*, the seller can reserve title in them *see Romalpa* case (1976).

NOTE: A retention of title clause does not create a security right in favour of the supplier capable of registration under the Companies Act 1985 s.395: *Armour* v *Thyssen Edelstahlwerke* (1990) (HL).

(b) If the goods are *changed into* or *become part of another object*, or *become mixed* with other such goods, such as liquids, hence losing their separate identity, the seller cannot retain title to them: *Borden (UK) Ltd v Scottish Timber Products Ltd and another* (1979).

(c) Where separate identity has been lost, a *Romalpa* clause giving the seller equitable and beneficial ownership of the new product creates a *floating charge* over that product in favour of the seller and this charge requires registration under the Companies Act 1985, s.395: *Re Bond Worth Ltd* (1979).

(d) If the seller knew that the goods were to be *on-sold* by the buyer, the seller's rights pass to the proceeds of the sale: *Romalpa* case (1976).

> NOTE: A fixed charge over present and future book debts (invariably found in a bank's debenture) will cover such proceeds of sale and take precedence over the retention of title clause.

Remedies of debenture holders

12. Introduction

A bank's debenture will specify in detail the circumstances in which it can intervene to enforce its security. (In a quoted public issue of debentures, the associated trust deed will also provide for intervention.)

The intervention crystallises any floating charge contained in the debenture.

13. Unsecured debenture holders

Unsecured debenture holders may:

(a) Sue for the principal and interest due;

(b) Petition for the winding up of the company on the ground that it is unable to pay its debts.

14. Secured debenture holders

Secured debenture holders may in addition:

(a) Exercise any of the powers conferred by the debenture (or the trust deed), for example appoint a receiver or an administrative receiver (*see* 16:**15**); sell the assets charged; or take possession of the assets and carry on the business (a bank's debenture will confer such powers);

(b) If such powers are not conferred by the debenture (or trust deed), apply to the court for the appointment of a receiver or a receiver and manager or an order for sale or for foreclosure.

15. Receivers

(a) *Introduction.* A *receiver* is distinct from a *liquidator*. The former is appointed when the creditors believe that they can recover their money without necessarily closing down the company. The latter is appointed to wind up the company. Liquidation does, however, often eventually follow the appointment of a receiver. A *manager* is appointed (usually the same person is appointed to be both receiver and manager) when it appears possible to sell the company as a going concern. With the court's permission, a manager may borrow money in order to do so and charge the company's property as security, the charge taking priority over the rights of the debenture holders.

(b) *The role of the receiver.* The receiver's task is to take possession of the assets charged by the debenture and to realise them for the benefit of the debenture holder(s).

Payments from the proceeds of the realisation must be made by the receiver in the following order.

(i) To meet the costs of the receivership.

(ii) To preferential creditors.

(iii) In full or partial discharge of the debts owed to debenture holders secured by floating charges.

(iv) To the company where there are any assets left.

NOTE: Holders of fixed charges are unaffected by these payments. Furthermore a bank can appropriate the proceeds of the sale of security subject to a fixed charge to non-preferential debts in an account containing both preferential and non-preferential debts, leaving the bank to claim as a preferential creditor for the balance: *Re William Hall (Contractors) Ltd* (1967) (*see* 1:**16**).

Once the receiver has repaid the creditors, the company can recommence normal business if it is financially viable. Usually, however, this is not so and a creditor will present a winding-up petition. The receiver may petition where it is necessary to protect the company's assets: *Re Emmadart* (1979). The liquidator appointed takes over any surplus from the receiver.

NOTE: In the case of a compulsory winding up, a receiver appointed *before* the liquidator can continue to sell assets, but not one appointed after. In a voluntary winding up, a receiver may sell assets *even if* appointed after the liquidator.

Where an *administration order* has been made, any receiver of part of the company's property, i.e. a receiver appointed under a fixed charge, must vacate the office if asked to do so by the administrator: Insolvency Act 1986 s.11 (*see* 16:**28–33**).

(c) *The administrative receiver.* The administrative receiver is a receiver or manager of *the whole or substantially the whole* of the company's property appointed by the holder of any debenture secured either by a *floating charge* or by such a charge and one or more other securities: s.29. The term reflects the wider functions that an administrative receiver has compared to those of a receiver appointed under the Law of Property Act 1925 (by the holder of a fixed charge) or by the court. An administrative receiver must be an authorised insolvency practitioner.

Bank debentures secured by floating (and other) charges always contain the right to appoint an administrative receiver.

Any right in a floating charge to appoint an administrative receiver cannot be exercised after an *administration order* has been made, but the prior appointment of an administrative receiver prevents the order being made. An application for an order does not prevent an appointment, however. Once appointed, an administrative receiver can *only be removed by the court.*

The administrative receiver must advertise their appointment in the *London Gazette* and in a local newspaper. Within 28 days the receiver must inform all creditors of the appointment. Within a further 21 days, a statement of affairs of the company must be submitted to him or her. The administrative receiver must then submit a report to the Registrar of Companies and send it to all creditors, usually within three months, and present it to a meeting of the company's creditors. The meeting may appoint a *committee of creditors* that can request information from the administrative receiver. It has, however, no power to supervise or direct the receiver. Notice of the appointment must appear on company stationery.

The bank must give notice of the appointment to the Registrar of Companies within seven days and it will then appear on the company's charges register.

An administrative receiver has the *powers* given by the floating charge under which they were appointed. These are deemed to include those set out in Schedule 1 of the Insolvency Act 1986 unless they are inconsistent with the charge. The administrative receiver has, therefore, powers similar to an *administrator* and, as with an administrator, a person dealing with them in good faith and for value need not enquire whether they are acting within those powers. The powers include:

(*i*) Carrying on the business of the company as its agent;

(ii) Selling the business;

(iii) Borrowing money and granting security for it over the company's property;

(iv) Making an arrangement or compromise with creditors;

(v) Taking possession of and getting in the property charged.

With the consent of the court, the administrative receiver also has the power to dispose of property charged to creditors other than the debenture holder. The net proceeds of the sale must be applied in discharge of the sums secured by the charge. If the proceeds are, in the court's opinion, less than the market value of the assets concerned, the administrative receiver must make up the difference.

(d) *A receiver's legal position.* A bank's debenture will provide that the receiver is the agent of the company, despite the fact that the receiver does not take instructions from the company and, under the Insolvency Act 1986 s.44, this is deemed to be the case unless the company is in liquidation. Thus, the company and not the bank is primafacie liable for the receiver's acts and obliged to indemnify the receiver for liabilities properly incurred. Unless the contrary is stated in each contract, the receiver is also personally liable on contracts they make while carrying out their functions and on any existing contract of employment adopted. Because of this personal liability, it is usual for a receiver to demand an indemnity from the bank before agreeing to act.

Despite the wording of the debenture, it is possible that the bank will be liable for the receiver's action, not the company, where the bank gives the receiver specific instructions.

Example

In *Standard Chartered Bank Ltd v Walker and Another* (1982) (CA), the bank made a loan to a company secured by a debenture that gave the bank a floating charge on the company's assets and power to appoint a receiver. Subsequently, the directors of the company guaranteed the loan. The company's business declined and the bank eventually appointed a receiver, instructing him to realise the assets as soon as possible. He, in turn, instructed auctioneers to sell the company's machinery. The auction realised less than half the amount expected because it was held at the wrong time of year and was poorly advertised. This amount only just covered the costs of the realisation and, after payment of preferential creditors, nothing remained to pay off the bank's overdraft. The bank therefore sought to enforce its guarantee.

The bank's action failed. It was liable for the incompetent conduct of the auction sale because it had authorised it by virtue of its instruction to the receiver.

NOTE: The case also established that a receiver acting under a debenture owes a duty to obtain the *best possible price for the assets*, not only to the company, but also to a guarantor of the company's liability under the debenture. This is because the guarantor is liable to the same extent as the company.

Receivers appointed by the court incur personal liability for their acts although they are entitled to an indemnity paid from the company's assets in priority to the debenture holders.

Progress test 16

1. List the charges that must be registered under the Act. **(1)**

2. How is registration effected? **(2)**

3. Can a liquidator challenge the validity of a charge if the Registrar has issued a certificate confirming that the particulars of the charge have been registered? **(2)**

4. When must a company incorporated overseas register a charge over any of its UK property? **(2)**

5. What is meant by a 'negative pledge clause'? **(2)**

6. Explain the main consequence of registering incomplete or inaccurate particulars of a charge. **(2)**

7. Is it possible to register further particulars of a charge after the 21-day registration period has expired? **(2)**

8. Explain the consequences of failure to register particulars of a charge. **(2)**

9. Explain the consequences of delivering particulars of the charge *after* the 21-day registration period. **(2)**

10. Define a debenture. **(3)**

11. List the clauses in a bank's standard debenture. **(6)**

12. What is the effect of the making of an administration order on a chargeholder? **(6)**

13. Define and distinguish between a fixed charge and a floating charge. **(8 and 9)**

14. What is meant by crystallisation and when does it take place? (9)

15. What are the two main advantages of a floating charge to a bank? (9)

16. List the main disadvantages of a floating charge to a bank. (10)

17. How can a bank prevent a company granting a subsequent fixed charge that will take priority over its floating charge? (10)

18. Explain how a floating charge can be invalidated under the Insolvency Act 1986 s.245. (10)

19. How may *Clayton's Case* (1816) assist a bank in relation to invalidation under s.245? (10)

20. Explain how a floating charge can be invalidated under the insolvency Act 1986 s.239. (10)

21. Explain how when a *Romalpa* clause can affect a bank's security. (11)

22. A supplies B & Co with 10 000 gallons of heating oil, which is transferred into a 20 000 gallon storage tank that is already 25 per cent full with oil supplied by C & Co B & Co's standard terms of business include a clause stating that 'all oil supplied under this contract shall only become the property of the purchaser when all sums due to B & Co from the purchaser have been paid'. Midtown Bank hold a debenture from B & Co containing the usual combination of fixed and floating charges. B & Co cease trading before the heating oil has been paid for. Is Midtown Bank legally entitled under its floating charge to sell the heating oil for its own benefit? (11)

23. List the remedies of an unsecured debenture holder. (13)

24. List the remedies of a secured debenture holder. (14)

25. Distinguish between a receiver and a liquidator. (15)

26. Outline the role of a receiver. (15)

27. Who can appoint an administrative receiver? (15)

28. Explain the relationship between a petition for an administration order and the ability to appoint an administrative receiver. (15)

29. List the main powers possessed by an administrative receiver. (15)

30. Who is liable for the actions of an administrative receiver? (15)

Appendix:
Excerpts from statutes

Bills of Exchange Act 1882

2. In this Act, unless the context otherwise requires:
"Banker" includes a body of persons whether incorporated or not who carry on the business of banking.
"Bearer" means the person in possession of a bill or note which is payable to bearer.
"Delivery" means transfer of possession, actual or constructive, from one person to another.
"Holder" means the payee or indorsee of a bill or note who is in possession of it, or the bearer thereof.
"Value" means valuable consideration.

3. (1) A bill of exchange is an unconditional order in writing, addressed by one person to another, signed by the person giving it, requiring the person to whom it is addressed to pay on demand or at a fixed or determinable future time a sum certain in money to or to the order of a specified person, or to bearer.

7. (1) Where a bill is not payable to bearer, the payee must be named or otherwise indicated therein with reasonable certainty.

(2) A bill may be payable to two or more payees jointly, or it may be made payable in the alternative to one of two, or one or some of several payees. A bill may also be made payable to the holder of an office for the time being.

(3) Where the payee is a fictitious or non-existing person the bill may be treated as payable to bearer.

8. (1) When a bill contains words prohibiting transfer, or indicating an intention that it should not be transferable, it is valid as between the parties thereto, but is not negotiable.

(2) A negotiable bill may be payable either to order or to bearer.

(3) A bill is payable to bearer which is expressed to be so payable, or on which the only or last indorsement is an indorsement in blank.

(4) A bill is payable to order which is expressed to be so payable, or which is expressed to be payable to a particular person, and does not contain words prohibiting transfer or indicating an intention that it should not be transferable.

20. (1) Where a simple signature on a blank ... paper is delivered by the signer in order that it may be converted into a bill, it operates as a prima facie authority to fill it up as a complete bill for any amount ... using the signature

for that of the drawer, or the acceptor, or an indorser; and, in like manner, when a bill is wanting in any material particular, the person in possession of it has a prima facie authority to fill up the omission in any way he thinks fit.

(2) In order that any such instrument when completed may be enforceable against any person who became a party thereto prior to its completion, it must be filled up within a reasonable time, and strictly in accordance with the authority given. Reasonable time for this purpose is a question of fact.

Provided that if any such instrument after completion is negotiated to a holder in due course it shall be valid and effectual for all purposes in his hands, and he may enforce it as if it had been filled up within a reasonable time and strictly in accordance with the authority given.

23. No person is liable as drawer, indorser, or acceptor of a bill who has not signed it as such; provided that:

(1) Where a person signs a bill in a trade or assumed name, he is liable thereon as if he had signed it in his own name;

(2) The signature of the name of a firm is equivalent to the signature by the person so signing of the names of all persons liable as partners in that firm.

24. Subject to the provisions of this Act, where a signature on a bill is forged or placed thereon without the authority of the person whose signature it purports to be, the forged or unauthorised signature is wholly inoperative, and no right to retain the bill or to give a discharge therefore or to enforce payment thereof against any party thereto can be acquired through or under that signature, unless the party against whom it is sought to retain or enforce payment of the bill is precluded from setting up the forgery or want of authority.

Provided that nothing in this section shall affect the ratification of an unauthorised signature not amounting to a forgery.

25. A signature by procuration operates as notice that the agent has but a limited authority to sign, and the principal is only bound by such signature if the agent in so signing was acting within the actual limits of his authority.

27. (1) Valuable consideration for a bill may be constituted by:

(*a*) Any consideration sufficient to support a simple contract;

(*b*) An antecedent debt or liability. Such a debt or liability is deemed valuable consideration whether the bill is payable on demand or at a future time.

(2) Where value has at any time been given for a bill the holder is deemed to be a holder for value as regards the acceptor and all parties to the bill who became parties prior to such time.

(3) Where the holder of a bill has a lien on it, arising either from contract or by implication of law, he is deemed to be a holder for value to the extent of the sum for which he has a lien.

29. (1) A holder in due course is a holder who has taken a bill, complete and regular on the face of it, under the following conditions; namely:

(*a*) That he became the holder of it before it was overdue, and without notice that it had been previously dishonoured, if such was the fact;

(*b*) That he took the bill in good faith and for value, and that at the time the bill was negotiated to him he had no notice of any defect in the title of the person who negotiated it.

(2) In particular the title of a person who negotiates a bill is defective within the meaning of this Act when he obtained the bill, or the acceptance thereof, by fraud, duress, or force and fear, or other unlawful means, or for an illegal consideration, or when he negotiates it in breach of faith, or under such circumstances as amount to a fraud.

(3) A holder (whether for value or not), who derives his title to a bill through a holder in due course, and who is not himself a party to any fraud or illegality affecting it, has all the rights of that holder in due course as regards the acceptor and all parties to the bill prior to that holder.

30. (1) Every party whose signature appears on a bill is prima facie deemed to have become a party thereto for value.

(2) Every holder of a bill is prima facie deemed to be a holder in due course; but if in an action on a bill it is admitted or proved that the acceptance, issue, or subsequent negotiation of the bill is affected with fraud, duress, or force and fear, or illegality, the burden of proof is shifted, unless and until the holder proves that, subsequent to the alleged fraud or illegality, value has in good faith been given for the bill.

31. (1) A bill is negotiated when it is transferred from one person to another in such a manner as to constitute the transferee the holder of the bill.

(2) A bill payable to bearer is negotiated by delivery.

(3) A bill payable to order is negotiated by the indorsement of the holder and completed by delivery.

(4) Where the holder of a bill payable to his order transfers it for value without indorsing it, the transfer gives the transferee such title as the transferor had in the bill, and the transferee in addition acquires the right to have the indorsement of the transferor.

(5) Where any person is under obligation to indorse a bill in a representative capacity, he may indorse the bill in such terms as to negate personal liability.

32. An indorsement in order to operate as a negotiation must comply with the following conditions namely:

(1) It must be written on the bill itself and be signed by the indorser. The simple signature of the indorser on the bill, without additional words, is sufficient.

(2) It must be an indorsement of the entire bill. A partial indorsement, that is to say, an indorsement which purports to transfer to the indorsee a part only of the amount payable, or which purports to transfer the bill to two or more indorsees severally, does not operate as a negotiation of the bill.

(3) Where a bill is payable to the order of two or more payees or indorsees who are not partners all must indorse, unless the one indorsing has authority to indorse for the others.

(4) Where, in a bill payable to order, the payee or indorsee is wrongly designated, or his name is mis-spelt, he may indorse the bill as therein described, adding, if he think fit, his proper signature.

(5) Where there are two or more indorsements on a bill, each indorsement is deemed to have been made in the order in which it appears on the bill, until the contrary is proved.

(6) An indorsement may be made in blank or special. It may also contain terms making it restrictive.

33. Where a bill purports to be indorsed conditionally the condition may be disregarded by the payer, and payment to the indorsee is valid whether the condition has been fulfilled or not.

34. (1) An indorsement in blank specifies no indorsee, and a bill so indorsed becomes payable to bearer.

(2) A special indorsement specifies the person to whom, or to whose order, the bill is to be payable.

(4) When a bill has been indorsed in blank, any holder may convert the blank indorsement into a special indorsement by writing above the indorser's signature a direction to pay the bill to or to the order of himself or some other person.

35. (1) An indorsement is restrictive which prohibits the further negotiation of the bill or which expresses that it is a mere authority to deal with the bill as thereby directed and not a transfer of the ownership thereof, as, for example, if a bill be indorsed "Pay D only," or "Pay D for the account of X," or "Pay D or order for collection."

(2) A restrictive indorsement gives the indorsee the right to receive payment of the bill and to sue any party thereto that his indorser could have sued, but gives him no power to transfer his rights as indorsee unless it expressly authorises him to do so.

(3) Where a restrictive indorsement authorises further transfer, all subsequent indorsees take the bill with the same rights and subject to the same liabilities as the first indorsee under the restrictive indorsement.

38. The rights and powers of the holder of a bill are as follows:

(1) He may sue on the bill in his own name:

(2) Where he is a holder in due course, he holds the bill free from any defect of title of prior parties, as well as from mere personal defences available to prior parties among themselves, and may enforce payment against all parties liable on the bill:

(3) Where his title is defective (a) if he negotiates the bill to a holder in due course, that holder obtains a good and complete title to the bill, and (b) if he obtains payment of the bill the person who pays him in due course gets a valid discharge for the bill.

55. (1) The drawer of a bill by drawing it:

(a) Engages that on due presentment it shall be accepted and paid according to its tenor, and that if it be dishonoured he will compensate the holder or any indorser who is compelled to pay it, provided that the requisite proceedings on dishonour be duly taken;

(*b*) Is precluded from denying to a holder in due course the existence of the payee and his then capacity to indorse.

(2) The indorser of a bill by indorsing it:

(*a*) Engages that on due presentment it shall be accepted and paid according to its tenor, and that if it be dishonoured he will compensate the holder or a subsequent indorser who is compelled to pay it, provided that the requisite proceedings on dishonour be duly taken;

(*b*) Is precluded from denying to a holder in due course the genuineness and regularity in all respects of the drawer's signature and all previous indorsements;

(*c*) Is precluded from denying to his immediate or a subsequent indorsee that the bill was at the time of his indorsement a valid and subsisting bill, and that he had then a good title thereto.

58. (1) Where the holder of a bill payable to bearer negotiates it by delivery without indorsing it, he is called a "transferor by delivery."

(2) A transferor by delivery is not liable on the instrument.

(3) A transferor by delivery who negotiates a bill thereby warrants to his immediate transferee being a holder for value that the bill is what it purports to be, that he has a right to transfer it, and that at the time of transfer he is not aware of any fact which renders it valueless.

59. (1) A bill is discharged by payment in due course by or on behalf of the drawee or acceptor.

"Payment in due course" means payment made at or after the maturity of the bill to the holder thereof in good faith and without notice that his title to the bill is defective.

60. When a bill payable to order on demand is drawn on a banker, and the banker on whom it is drawn pays the bill in good faith and in the ordinary course of business, it is not incumbent on the banker to show that the indorsement of the payee or any subsequent indorsement was made by or under the authority of the person whose indorsement it purports to be, and the banker is deemed to have paid the bill in due course, although such indorsement has been forged or made without authority.

64. (1) Where a bill or acceptance is materially altered without the assent of all parties liable on the bill, the bill is avoided except as against a party who has himself made, authorised, or assented to the alteration, and subsequent indorsers.

Provided that, where a bill has been materially altered, but the alteration is not apparent, and the bill is in the hands of a holder in due course, such holder may avail himself of the bill as if it has not been altered, and may enforce payment of it according to its original tenor.

(2) In particular the following alterations are material, namely, any alter-

ation of the date, the sum payable, the time of payment, the place of payment, and, where a bill has been accepted generally, the addition of a place of payment without the acceptor's assent.

73. A cheque is a bill of exchange drawn on a banker payable on demand.

Except as otherwise provided in this Part, the provisions of this Act applicable to a bill of exchange payable on demand apply to a cheque.

75. The duty and authority of a banker to pay a cheque drawn on him by his customer are determined by:

(1) Countermand of payment;

(2) Notice of the customer's death.

76. (1) Where a cheque bears across its face an addition of:

(*a*) The words "and company" or any abbreviation thereof between two parallel transverse lines, either with or without the words "not negotiable"; or

(*b*) Two parallel transverse lines simply, either with or without the words "not negotiable";

that addition constitutes a crossing, and the cheque is crossed generally.

(2) Where a cheque bears across its face an addition of the name of a banker, either with or without the words "not negotiable," that addition constitutes a crossing, and the cheque is crossed specially and to that banker.

78. A crossing authorised by this Act is a material part of the cheque; it shall not be lawful for any person to obliterate or, except as authorised by this Act, to add to or alter the crossing.

79. (1) Where a cheque is crossed specially to more than one banker except when crossed to an agent for collection being a banker, the banker on whom it is drawn shall refuse payment thereof.

(2) Where the banker on whom a cheque is drawn which is so crossed nevertheless pays the same, or pays a cheque crossed generally otherwise than to a banker, or if crossed specially otherwise than to the banker to whom it is crossed, or his agent for collection being a banker, he is liable to the true owner of the cheque for any loss he may sustain owing to the cheque having been so paid.

Provided that where a cheque is presented for payment which does not at the time of presentment appear to be crossed, or to have had a crossing which has been obliterated, or to have been added to or altered otherwise than as authorised by this Act, the banker paying the cheque in good faith and without negligence shall not be responsible or incur any liability, nor shall the payment be questioned by reason of the cheque having being crossed, or of the crossing having been obliterated or having been added to or altered otherwise than as authorised by this Act, and of payment having been made otherwise than to a banker or to the banker to whom the cheque is or was crossed, or to his agent for collection being a banker, as the case may be.

80. Where the banker, on whom a crossed cheque is drawn, in good faith and without negligence pays it, if crossed generally, to a banker, and if crossed specially, to the banker to whom it is crossed, or his agent for collection being a banker, the banker paying the cheque, and, if the cheque has come into the hands of the payee, the drawer, shall respectively be entitled to the same rights and be placed in the same position as if payment of the cheque had been made to the true owner thereof.

81. Where a person takes a crossed cheque which bears on it the words "not negotiable," he shall not have and shall not be capable of giving a better title to the cheque than that which the person from whom he took it had.

Cheques Act 1957

1. (1) Where a banker in good faith and in the ordinary course of business pays a cheque drawn on him which is not indorsed or is irregularly indorsed, he does not, in doing so, incur any liability by reason only of the absence of, or irregularity in, indorsement, and he is deemed to have paid it in due course.

(2) Where a banker in good faith and in the ordinary course of business pays any such instrument as the following, namely:

(*a*) A document issued by a customer of his which, though not a bill of exchange, is intended to enable a person to obtain payment from him of the sum mentioned in the document;

(*b*) A draft payable on demand drawn by him upon himself, whether payable at the head office or some other office of his bank;

he does not, in doing so, incur any liability by reason only of the absence of, or irregularity in, indorsement, and the payment discharges the instrument.

2. A banker who gives value for, or has a lien on, a cheque payable to order which the holder delivers to him for collection without indorsing it, has such (if any) rights as he would have had if, upon delivery, the holder had indorsed it in blank.

4. (1) Where a banker, in good faith and without negligence:

(*a*) Receives payment for a customer of an instrument to which this section applies; or

(*b*) Having credited a customer's account with the amount of such an instrument, receives payment thereof for himself;

and the customer has no title, or a defective title, to the instrument, the banker does not incur any liability to the true owner of the instrument by reason only of having received payment thereof.

(2) This section applies to the following instruments, namely:

(*a*) Cheques;

(*b*) Any document issued by a customer of a banker which, though not a bill of exchange, is intended to enable a person to obtain payment from that banker of the sum mentioned in the document;

(*c*) Any document issued by a public officer which is intended to enable a person to obtain payment from the Paymaster General or the Queen's and Lord Treasurer's Remembrancer of the sum mentioned in the document but is not a bill of exchange;

(*d*) Any draft payable on demand drawn by a banker upon himself, whether payable at the head office or some other office of his bank.

(3) A banker is not to be treated for the purposes of this section as having been negligent by reason only of his failure to concern himself with absence of, or irregularity in, indorsement of an instrument.

Cheques Act 1992

1. After section 81 of the Bills of Exchange Act 1882 there shall be inserted the following section—

81A.—(1) Where a cheque is crossed and bears across its face the words "account payee" or "a/c payee", either with or without the word "only", the cheque shall not be transferable, but shall only be valid as between the parties thereto.

(2) A banker is not to be treated for the purposes of section 80 above as having been negligent by reason only of his failure to concern himself with any purported indorsement of a cheque which under subsection (1) above or otherwise is not transferable."

2. In section 80 of the Bills of Exchange Act 1882 (protection to banker and drawer where cheque is crossed) after "crossed cheque" there shall be inserted "(including a cheque which under section 81A below or otherwise is not transferable)".

3. In section 4(2)(a) of the Cheques Act 1957 (protection of bankers collecting payment of cheques, etc) there shall be inserted after the word "cheques" the words "(including cheques which under section 81A(1) of the Bills of Exchange Act 1882 or otherwise are not transferable)".

Companies Act 1989

108. (1) In Chapter III of Part I of the Companies Act 1985 (a company's capacity; formalities of carrying on business), for section 35 substitute—

35. (1) The validity of an act done by a company shall not be called into question on the ground of lack of capacity by reason of anything in the company's memorandum.

(2) A member of a company may bring proceedings to restrain the doing of an act which but for subsection (1) would be beyond the company's capacity; but no such proceedings shall lie in respect of an act to be done in fulfilment of a legal obligation arising from a previous act of the company.

(3) It remains the duty of the directors to observe any limitations on their powers flowing from the company's memorandum; and action by the directors which but for subsection (1) would be beyond the company's capacity may only be ratified by the company by special resolution.

A resolution ratifying such action shall not affect any liability incurred by the directors or any other person; relief from any such liability must be agreed to separately by special resolution.

35A. (1) In favour of a person dealing with a company in good faith, the power of the board of directors to bind the company, or authorise others to do so, shall be deemed to be free of any limitation under the company's constitution.

(2) For this purpose—

(*a*) a person 'deals with' a company if he is a party to any transaction or other act to which the company is a party;

(*b*) a person shall not be regarded as acting in bad faith by reason only of his knowing that an act is beyond the powers of the directors under the company's constitution; and

(*c*) a person shall be presumed to have acted in good faith unless the contrary is proved.

(3) The references above to limitations on the directors' powers under the company's constitution include limitations deriving—

(*a*) from a resolution of the company in general meeting or a meeting of any class of shareholders, or

(*b*) from any agreement between the members of the company or of any class of shareholders.

(4) Subsection (1) does not affect any right of a member of the company to bring proceedings to restrain the doing of an act which is beyond the powers of the directors; but no such proceedings shall lie in respect of an act to be done in fulfilment of a legal obligation arising from a previous act of the company.

(5) Nor does that subsection affect any liability incurred by the directors, or any other person, by reason of the directors' exceeding their powers.

35B. A party to a transaction with a company is not bound to enquire as to whether it is permitted by the company's memorandum or as to any limitation on the powers of the board of directors to bind the company or authorise others to do so.

130. (1) In Chapter III of Part I of the Companies Act 1985 (a company's capacity; the formalities of carrying on business) , for section 36 (form of company contracts) substitute—

36C. (1) A contract which purports to be made by or on behalf of a company at a time when the company has not been formed has effect, subject to any agreement to the contrary, as one made with the person purporting to act for the company or as agent for it, and he is personally liable on the contract accordingly.

142. (1) In Part XXIV of the Companies Act 1985 (the registrar of companies, his functions and offices), after section 711 insert—

711A. (1) A person shall not be taken to have notice of any matter merely because of its being disclosed in any document kept by the registrar of companies (and thus available for inspection) or made available by the company for inspection.

(2) This does not affect the question whether a person is affected by notice of any matter by reason of a failure to make such inquiries as ought reasonably to be made.

(3) In this section 'document' includes any material which contains information.

(4) Nothing in this section affects the operation of section 416 of this Act (under which a person taking a charge over a company's property is deemed to have notice of matters disclosed on the companies charges register).

Consumer Credit Act 1974

11. (1) A restricted-use credit agreement is a regulated consumer credit agreement—

(a) to finance a transaction between the debtor and the creditor, whether forming part of that agreement or not, or

(b) to finance a transaction between the debtor and a person (the 'supplier') other than the creditor, or

(c) to refinance any existing indebtedness of the debtor's, whether to the creditor or another person,

and 'restricted-use credit' shall be construed accordingly.

(2) An unrestricted-use credit agreement is a regulated consumer credit agreement not falling within subsection (1), and 'unrestricted-use credit' shall be construed accordingly.

(3) An agreement does not fall within subsection (1) if the credit is in fact provided in such a way as to leave the debtor free to use it as he chooses, even though certain uses would contravene that or any other agreement.

(4) An agreement may fall within subsection (1)(b) although the identity of the supplier is unknown at the time the agreement is made.

12. A debtor-creditor-supplier agreement is a regulated consumer credit agreement being—

(a) a restricted-use credit agreement which falls within section 11(1)(a), or

(b) a restricted-use credit agreement which falls within section 11(1)(b) and is made by the creditor under pre-existing arrangements, or in contemplation of future arrangements, between himself and the supplier, or

(c) an unrestricted-use credit agreement which is made by the creditor under pre-existing arrangements between himself and a person (the 'supplier') other than the debtor in the knowledge that the credit is to be used to finance a transaction between the debtor and the supplier.

13. A debtor-creditor agreement is a regulated consumer credit agreement being—

(a) a restricted-use credit agreement which falls within section 11(1)(b) but is not made by the creditor under pre-existing arrangements, or in contemplation of future arrangements, between himself and the supplier, or (*b*)   a restricted-use credit agreement which falls within section 11(1)(c), or

(*c*)   an unrestricted-use credit agreement which is not made by the creditor under pre-existing arrangements between himself and a person (the 'supplier') other than the debtor in the knowledge that the credit is to be used to finance a transaction between the debtor and the supplier.

14. (1) A credit-token is a card, check, voucher, coupon, stamp, form, booklet or other document or thing given to an individual by a person carrying on a consumer credit business, who undertakes —

(*a*)   that on the production of it (whether or not some other action is also required) he will supply cash, goods and services (or any of them) on credit, or

(*b*)   that where, on the production of it to a third party (whether or not any other action is also required), the third party supplies cash, goods and services (or any of them), he will pay the third party for them (whether or not deducting any discount or commission), in return for payment to him by the individual.

(2)   A credit-token agreement is a regulated agreement for the provision of credit in connection with the use of a credit-token.

(3)   Without prejudice to the generality of section 9(1), the person who gives to an individual an undertaking falling within subsection (1)(b) shall be taken to provide him with credit drawn on whenever a third party supplies him with cash, goods or services.

(4)   For the purposes of subsection (1), use of an object to operate a machine provided by the person giving the object or a third party shall be treated as the production of the object to him.

16. (1) This Act does not regulate a consumer credit agreement where the creditor is a local authority ..., or a body specified, or of a description specified, in an order made by the Secretary of State, being —

(*a*)   an insurance company,

(*b*)   a friendly society,

(*c*)   an organisation of employers or organisation of workers,

(*d*)   a charity,

(*e*)   a land improvement company, or

(*f*)   a body corporate named or specifically referred to in any public general Act.

(2)   Subsection (1) applies only where the agreement is —

(*a*)   a debtor-creditor-supplier agreement financing —

 (i)   the purchase of land, or

 (ii)   the provision of dwellings on any land,

and secured by a land mortgage on that land; or

(*b*)   a debtor-creditor agreement secured by any land mortgage; or

(*c*)   a debtor-creditor-supplier agreement financing a transaction which is a linked transaction in relation to —

 (i)   an agreement falling within paragraph (a), or

 (ii)   an agreement falling within paragraph (b) financing —

  (aa)   the purchase of any land, or

(bb)   the provision of dwellings on any land,
and secured by a land mortgage on the land referred to in paragraph (a) or, as the case may be, the land referred to in sub-paragraph (ii).

48. (1) An individual (the 'canvasser') canvasses a regulated agreement off trade premises if he solicits the entry (as debtor or hirer) of another individual (the 'consumer') into the agreement by making oral representations to the consumer, or any other individual, during a visit by the canvasser to any place (not excluded by subsection (2)) where the consumer, or that other individual, as the case may be, is, being a visit—

(*a*)   carried out for the purpose of making such oral representations to individuals who are at that place, but

(*b*)   not carried out in response to a request made on a previous occasion.

(2) A place is excluded from subsection (1) if it is a place where a business is carried on (whether on a permanent or temporary basis) by—

(*a*)   the creditor or owner, or

(*b*)   a supplier, or

(*c*)   the canvasser, or the person whose employee or agent the canvasser is, or

(*d*)   the consumer.

49. (1) It is an offence to canvass debtor-creditor agreement off trade premises.

(2) It is also an offence to solicit the entry of an individual (as debtor) into a debtor-creditor agreement during a visit carried out in response to a request made on a previous occasion, where—

(*a*)   the request was not in writing signed by or on behalf of the person making it, and

(*b*)   if no request for the visit had been made, the soliciting would have constituted the canvassing of a debtor-creditor agreement off trade premises.

(3) Subsections (1) and (2) do not apply to any soliciting for an agreement enabling the debtor to overdraw on a current account of any description kept with the creditor, where—

(*a*)   the Director has determined that current accounts of that description kept with the creditor are excluded from subsections (1) and (2), and

(*b*)   the debtor already keeps an account with the creditor (whether a current account or not).

(4) A determination under subsection (3)(a)—

(*a*)   may be made subject to such conditions as the Director thinks fit, and

(*b*)   shall be made only where the Director is of opinion that it is not against the interests of debtors.

61. (1) A regulated agreement is not properly executed unless—

(*a*)   a document in the prescribed form itself containing all the prescribed terms and conforming to regulations under section 60(1) is signed in the prescribed manner both by the debtor or hirer and by or on behalf of the creditor or owner, and

(*b*)   the document embodies all the terms of the agreement, other than implied terms, and

(c) the document is, when presented or sent to the debtor or hirer for signature, in such a state that all its terms are readily legible.

(2) In addition, where the agreement is one to which section 58(1) applies, it is not properly executed unless —

(a) the requirements of section 58(1) were complied with, and

(b) the unexecuted agreement was sent, for his signature, to the debtor or hirer by post not less than seven days after a copy of it was given to him under section 58(1), and

(c) during the consideration period, the creditor or owner refrained from approaching the debtor or hirer (whether in person, by telephone or letter, or in any other way) except in response to a specific request made by the debtor or hirer after the beginning of the consideration period, and

(d) no notice of withdrawal by the debtor or hirer was received by the creditor or owner before the sending of the unexecuted agreement.

(3) In subsection (2)(c), 'the consideration period' means the period beginning with the giving of the copy under section 58(1) and ending —

(a) at the expiry of seven days after the day on which the unexecuted agreement is sent, for his signature, to the debtor or hirer, or

(b) on its return by the debtor or hirer after signature by him, whichever first occurs.

75. (1) If the debtor under a debtor-creditor-supplier agreement falling within section 12(b) or (c) has, in relation to a transaction financed by the agreement, any claim against the supplier in respect of a misrepresentation or breach of contract, he shall have a like claim against the creditor, who, with the supplier, shall accordingly be jointly and severally liable to the debtor.

(2) Subject to any agreement between them, the creditor shall be entitled to be indemnified by the supplier for loss suffered by the creditor in satisfying his liability under subsection (1), including costs reasonably incurred by him in defending proceedings instituted by the debtor.

(3) Subsection (1) does not apply to a claim —

(a) under a non-commercial agreement, or

(b) so far as the claim relates to any single item to which the supplier has attached a cash price not exceeding [£100] or more than [£30,000].

84. (1) Section 83 does not prevent the debtor under a credit-token agreement from being made liable to the extent of [£50] (or the credit limit if lower) for loss to the creditor arising from use of the credit-token by other persons during a period beginning when the credit-token ceases to be in the possession of any authorised person and ending when the credit-token is once more in the possession of an authorised person.

(2) Section 83 does not prevent the debtor under a credit-token agreement from being made liable to any extent for loss to the creditor from use of the credit-token by a person who acquired possession of it with the debtor's consent.

(3) Subsections (1) and (2) shall not apply to any use of the credit-token

after the creditor has been given oral or written notice that it is lost or stolen, or is for any other reason liable to misuse.

(4) Subsections (1) and (2) shall not apply unless there are contained in the credit-token agreement in the prescribed manner particulars of the name, address and telephone number of a person stated to be the person to whom notice is to be given under subsection (3).

Insolvency Act 1986

84. (1) A company may be wound up voluntarily —

(*a*) when the period (if any) fixed for the duration of the company by the articles expires, or the event (if any) occurs, on the occurrence of which the articles provide that the company is to be dissolved, and the company in general meeting has passed a resolution requiring it to be wound up voluntarily;

(*b*) if the company resolves by special resolution that it be wound up voluntarily;

(*c*) if the company resolves by extraordinary resolution to the effect that it cannot by reason of its liabilities continue its business, and that it is advisable to wind up.

122. (1) A company may be wound up by the court if —

(*a*) the company has by special resolution resolved that the company be wound up by the court,

(*b*) being a public company which was registered as such on its original incorporation, the company has not been issued with a certificate under section 117 of the Companies Act (public company share capital requirements) and more than a year has expired since it was so registered,

(*c*) it is an old public company, within the meaning of the Consequential Provisions Act,

(*d*) the company does not commence its business within a year from its incorporation or suspends its business for a whole year,

(*e*) the number of members is reduced below 2,

(*f*) the company is unable to pay its debts,

(*g*) the court is of the opinion that it is just and equitable that the company should be wound up.

123. (1) A company is deemed unable to pay its debts —

(*a*) if a creditor (by assignment or otherwise) to whom the company is indebted in a sum exceeding £750 then due has served on the company, by leaving it at the company's registered office, a written demand (in the prescribed form) requiring the company to pay the sum so due and the company has for 3 weeks thereafter neglected to pay the sum or to secure or compound for it to the reasonable satisfaction of the creditor, or

(*b*) if, in England and Wales, execution or other process issued on a judgment, decree or order of any court in favour of a creditor of the company is returned unsatisfied in whole or in part, or

(e) if it is proved to the satisfaction of the court that the company is unable to pay its debts as they fall due.

(2) A company is also deemed unable to pay its debts if it is proved to the satisfaction of the court that the value of the company's assets is less than the amount of its liabilities, taking into account its contingent and prospective liabilities.

175. (1) In a winding up the company's preferential debts shall be paid in priority to all other debts.

(2) Preferential debts —

(*a*) rank equally among themselves after the expenses of the winding up and shall be paid in full, unless the assets are insufficient to meet them, in which case they abate in equal proportions; and

(*b*) so far as the assets of the company available for payment of general creditors are insufficient to meet them, have priority over the claims of holders of debentures secured by, or holders of, any floating charge created by the company, and shall be paid accordingly out of any property comprised in or subject to that charge.

213. (1) If in the course of the winding up of a company it appears that any business of the company has been carried on with intent to defraud creditors of the company or creditors of any other person, or for any fraudulent purpose, the following has effect.

(2) The court, on the application of the liquidator may declare that any persons who were knowingly parties to the carrying on of the business in the manner above-mentioned are to be liable to make such contributions (if any) to the company's assets as the court thinks proper.

214. (1) Subject to subsection (3) below, if in the course of the winding up of a company it appears that subsection (2) of this section applies in relation to a person who is or has been a director of the company, the court, on the application of the liquidator, may declare that that person is to be liable to make such contribution (if any) to the company's assets as the court thinks proper.

(2) This subsection applies in relation to a person if —

(*a*) the company has gone into insolvent liquidation,

(*b*) at some time before the commencement of the winding up of the company, that person knew or ought to have concluded that there was no reasonable prospect that the company would avoid going into insolvent liquidation, and

(*c*) that person was a director of the company at that time.

(7) In this section 'director' includes a shadow director.

238. (4) For the purposes of this section and section 241, a company enters into a transaction with a person at an undervalue if —

(*a*) the company makes a gift to that person or otherwise enters into a transaction with that person on terms that provide for the company to receive no consideration, or (*b*) the company enters into a transaction with that person for a consideration the value of which, in money or money's worth is significantly less than the value, in money or money's worth, of the consideration provided by the company.

(5) The court shall not make an order under this section in respect of a transaction at an undervalue if it is satisfied—

(*a*) that the company which entered into the transaction did so in good faith and for the purpose of carrying on its business, and

(*b*) that at the time it did so there were reasonable grounds for believing that the transaction would benefit the company.

239. (4) For the purposes of this section and section 241, a company gives a preference to a person if—

(*a*) that person is one of the company's creditors or a surety or guarantor for any of the company's debts or other liabilities, and

(*b*) the company does anything or suffers anything to be done which (in either case) has the effect of putting that person into a position which, in the event of the company going into insolvent liquidation, will be better than the position he would have been in if that thing had not been done.

(5) The court shall not make an order under this section in respect of a preference given to any person unless the company which gave the preference was influenced in deciding to give it by a desire to produce in relation to that person the effect mentioned in subsection (4)(b).

(6) A company which has given a preference to a person connected with the company (otherwise than by reason only of being its employee) at the time the preference was given is presumed, unless the contrary is shown, to have been influenced in deciding to give it by such a desire as is mentioned in subsection (5).

(7) The fact that something has been done in pursuance of the order of a court does not, without more, prevent the doing or suffering of that thing from constituting the giving of a preference.

240. (1) Subject to the next subsection, the time at which a company enters into a transaction at an undervalue or gives a preference is a relevant time if the transaction is entered into, or the preference given—

(*a*) in the case of a transaction at an undervalue or of a preference which is given to a person who is connected with the company (otherwise than by reason only of being its employee), at a time in the period of 2 years ending with the onset of insolvency (which expression is defined below),

(*b*) in the case of a preference which is not such a transaction and is not so given, at a time in the period of 6 months ending with the onset of insolvency, and

(*c*) in either case, at a time between the presentation of a petition for the making of an administration order in relation to the company and the making of such an order on that petition.

(2) Where a company enters into a transaction at an undervalue or gives a preference at a time mentioned in subsection (1)(a) or (b), that time is not a

relevant time for the purposes of section 238 or 239 unless the company —

(*a*) is at that time unable to pay its debts within the meaning of section 123, or

(*b*) becomes unable to pay its debts within the meaning of that section in consequence of that transaction or preference;

but the requirements of this subsection are presumed to be satisfied, unless the contrary is shown, in relation to any transaction at an undervalue which is entered into by a company with a person who is connected with the company.

(3) For the purposes of subsection (1), the onset of insolvency is —

(*a*) in a case where section 238 or 239 applies by reason of the making of an administration order or of a company going into liquidation immediately upon the discharge of an administration order, the date of the presentation of the petition on which the administration order was made, and

(*b*) in a case where the section applies by reason of a company going into liquidation at any other time, the date of the commencement of the winding up.

241. (1) Without prejudice to the generality of sections 238(3) and 239(3), an order under either of those sections with respect to a transaction or preference entered into or given by a company may (subject to the next subsection) —

(*a*) require any property transferred as part of the transaction, or in connection with the giving of the preference, to be vested in the company,

(*b*) require any property to be so vested if it represents in any person's hands the application either of the proceeds of sale of property so transferred or of money so transferred,

(*c*) release or discharge (in whole or in part) any security given by the company,

(*d*) require any person to pay, in respect of benefits received by him from the company, such sums to the office-holder as the court may direct,

(*e*) provide for any surety or guarantor whose obligations to any person were released or discharged (in whole or in part) under the transaction, or by the giving of the preference, to be under such new or revived obligations to that person as the court thinks appropriate,

(*f*) provide for security to be provided for the discharge of any obligation imposed by or arising under the order, for such an obligation to be charged on any property and for the security or charge to have the same priority as a security or charge released or discharged (in whole or in part) under the transaction or by the giving of the preference, and

(*g*) provide for the extent to which any person whose property is vested by the order in the company, or on whom obligations are imposed by the order, is to be able to prove in the winding up of the company for debts or other liabilities which arose from, or were released or discharged (in whole or in part) under or by, the transaction or the giving of the preference.

(2) An order under section 238 or 239 may affect the property of, or impose any obligation on, any person whether or not he is the person with whom the company in question entered into the transaction or (as the case may be) the

person to whom the preference was given; but such an order—

(*a*) shall not prejudice any interest in property which was acquired from a person other than the company and was acquired in good faith, for value and without notice of the relevant circumstances, or prejudice any interest deriving from such an interest, and

(*b*) shall not require a person who received a benefit from the transaction or preference in good faith, for value and without notice of the relevant circumstances to pay a sum to the office-holder, except where that person was a party to the transaction or the payment is to be in respect of a preference given to that person at a time when he was a creditor of the company.

245. (2) Subject as follows, a floating charge on the company's undertaking or property created at a relevant time is invalid except to the extent of the aggregate of—

(*a*) the value of so much of the consideration for the creation of the charge as consists of money paid, or goods or services supplied, to the company at the same time as, or after, the creation of the charge,

(*b*) the value of so much of that consideration as consists of the discharge or reduction, at the same time as, or after, the creation of the charge, of any debt of the company, and

(*c*) the amount of such interest (if any) as is payable on the amount falling within paragraph (a) or (b) in pursuance of any agreement under which the money was so paid, the goods or services were so supplied or the debt was so discharged or reduced.

(3) Subject to the next subsection, the time at which a floating charge is created by a company is a relevant time for the purposes of this section if the charge is created—

(*a*) in the case of a charge which is created in favour of a person who is connected with the company, at a time in the period of 2 years ending with the onset of insolvency,

(*b*) in the case of a charge which is created in favour of any other person, at a time in the period of 12 months ending with the onset of insolvency, or

(*c*) in either case, at a time between the presentation of a petition for the making of an administration order in relation to the company and the making of such an order on that petition.

(4) Where a company creates a floating charge at a time mentioned in subsection (3)(b) and the person in favour of whom the charge is created is not connected with the company, that time is not a relevant time for the purposes of this section unless the company—

(*a*) is at that time unable to pay its debts within the meaning of section 123, or

(*b*) becomes unable to pay its debts within the meaning of that section in consequence of the transaction under which the charge is created.

(5) For the purposes of subsection (3), the onset of insolvency is—

(*a*) in a case where this section applies by reason of the making of an administration order, the date of the presentation of the petition on which the order was made, and (*b*) in a case where this section applies by reason of a company going into liquidation, the date of the commencement of the winding up.

249. For the purposes of any provision in this Group of Parts, a person is connected with a company if—

(*a*) he is a director or shadow director of the company or an associate of such a director or shadow director, or

(*b*) he is an associate of the company;

and 'associate' has the meaning given by section 435 of this Act.

284. (1) Where a person is adjudged bankrupt, any disposition of property made by that person in the period to which this section applies is void except to the extent that it is or was made with the consent of the court, or is or was subsequently ratified by the court.

(2) Subsection (1) applies to a payment (whether in cash or otherwise) as it applies to a disposition of property and, accordingly, where any payment is void by virtue of that subsection, the person paid shall hold the sum paid for the bankrupt as part of his estate.

(3) This section applies to the period beginning with the day of the presentation of the petition for the bankruptcy order and ending with the vesting of the bankrupt's estate in a trustee.

(4) The preceding provisions of this section do not give a remedy against any person—

(*a*) in respect of any property or payment which he received before the commencement of the bankruptcy in good faith, for value and without notice that the petition had been presented, or

(*b*) in respect of any interest in property which derives from an interest in respect of which there is, by virtue of this subsection, no remedy.

(5) Where after the commencement of his bankruptcy the bankrupt has incurred a debt to a banker or other person by reason of the making of a payment which is void under this section, that debt is deemed to have been incurred before the commencement of the bankruptcy unless—

(*a*) that banker or person had notice of the bankruptcy before the debt was incurred, or

(*b*) it is not reasonably practicable for the amount of the payment to be recovered from the person to whom it was made.

Index